"*Confronting Violence* is an invaluable resource for citizens seeking to address and prevent violence in America. The straightforward, factual approach gives the reader a sense of empowerment and hope without generating fear."

—John A. Calhoun
Former Executive Director, National Crime Prevention Council

"George Gellert has produced a most useful book for professionals and laypeople alike. Professionals will find it a fact-filled orientation and invaluable resource for an important public health issue. Average Americans, who most need to read the book, will find the language approachable and won't be disappointed."

—Alfred Sommer
Dean Emeritus and Professor, Johns Hopkins Bloomberg School of Public Health

"This is an exceptionally well-done handbook for professionals in any field interested in actually doing something about the prevention of violence rather than just talking about it—or worse, ignoring it."

—Richard D. Krugman
Dean, University of Colorado School of Medicine;
Former Director, The Kempe Center
for the Prevention of Child Abuse and Neglect

"*Confronting Violence* is an excellent and long-needed resource for families and professionals who must respond to and manage violence. George Gellert has done a remarkable job of reducing the vast amount of research on violence in America into a meaningful, usable, and timely volume. This is the one-stop source of information for victims and those seeking answers and understanding about the violence in their lives."

—Michael B. Libby
Former Executive Director, Police Association of the District of Columbia

"This book presents the complex problem of violence in America using a question-and-answer format . . . The questions are straightforward . . . The answers are direct, easily understood, and aimed at the general public. The book is also intended for professionals and can be a resource for doctors, nurses, and emergency room personnel to refer to or provide to patients, clients, or relatives . . . The book provides easy-to-understand, no-nonsense statistics, demographics, and epidemiologic information, simple and accurate definitions of terms and concepts, and a lay explanation of the psychological dynamics of victims and perpetrators . . . Dr. Gellert's book appears free of ideology . . . *Confronting Violenc*

—Reviewed in the *Journal of the A*   *MA)*

D1378263

"*Confronting Violence* is the most comprehensive guide to violence in our society. The interrelationship of all aspects of violence is clearly laid out in a logical and readable format, punctuated by questions that are at the very core of the issues. This book is useful for victims of violence and their families as well as the professionals who care for them."

—Carol D. Berkowitz
Executive Vice Chair, General and Emergency Pediatrics,
David Geffen School of Medicine at UCLA;
Editor of Pediatrics: A Primary Care Approach

"This comprehensive manual is a superb starting place to learn about violence against children and adults. George Gellert provides straightforward answers to common questions, refutes widespread myths, and offers sensible advice for victims, perpetrators, and concerned citizens. To prevent violence we must know the facts; everyone should read *Confronting Violence*."

—David S. Liederman
Former Executive Director,
Child Welfare League of America

"*Confronting Violence* is an excellent source of factual information about many types of violence affecting American families. I believe it is a must-read for professionals and everyone concerned about violence in our society."

— Toshio Tatara
Former Director, National Center on Elder Abuse

"This book is written in everyday English that Americans from every walk of life will understand. It will answer the questions of virtually every reader about every kind of violence. *Confronting Violence* is a long-overdue resource that no American family should be without."

—Ellen Bernstein
Former Editor of *The Encyclopedia Britannica
Medical and Health Annual*

"I found a great deal of valuable information in *Confronting Violence*, a splendid reference on this extremely important subject. The lists of referral agencies and organizations, and the practical advice on how to minimize the risk of becoming a victim of violence and how to detect if individuals have experienced violence, make this book worth having. I do not know of anything comparable."

—the late John M. Last
Former Editor-in-Chief of *Public Health and Preventive Medicine;*
Former Scientific Editor of *Canadian Journal of Public Health*

"This comprehensive, straightforward, and easy-to-read book would be a valuable addition to every ER and violence shelter in the country, equipping staff members with the facts and wise counsel needed to better serve those traumatized by our nation's worst epidemic. For families, whether victims of violence or the fearful well, *Confronting Violence* is essential reading."

—Jean A. Wright
Professor of Pediatrics, Mercer University School of Medicine

"George Gellert presents a compelling blend of science and common sense in this invaluable resource book. Violence is a tragedy, and the dimensions of the problem are conveyed in *Confronting Violence* with complete honesty."

—Mimi L. Fields
Former Deputy Secretary of Health and State Health Officer,
State of Washington Department of Health

"George Gellert, with a calm and reserved voice, takes the reader through the harrowing facts of violence in its many forms. For scholars, *Confronting Violence* is a treasure of documented insights; for public health and other professionals, it is a clear call to sensible action; and for the public at large, it points the way to resources that can empower and support individuals and communities in trying to survive in these violent times."

—Lowell S. Levin
Professor Emeritus of Public Health, Yale School of Public Health

"*Confronting Violence* is uniquely comprehensive and readable, with practical interventions for us all. A most valuable book for the involved citizen, whether a victim of violence or not, and for the pragmatic professional who must respond to the fallout from violence."

—Michael Durfee
Former Coordinator of Child Abuse Prevention, Los Angeles County Department of Health Services; Former Co-Chair, California Child Death Review Board

"An excellent sourcebook on the subject of violence. As a physician, I believe that destructive behavior, whether against oneself or others, is our leading health problem. *Confronting Violence* contains the information necessary for transformation. Hopefully, it will help lead us away from violence toward ourselves and others."

—Bernie Siegel
Author of *Love, Medicine and Miracles* and *Faith, Hope and Healing*

APHA Mission Statement

The American Public Health Association is an association of individuals and organizations working to improve the public's health. It promotes the scientific and professional foundation of public health practice and policy, advocates the conditions for a healthy global society, emphasizes prevention, and enhances the ability of members to promote and protect environmental and community health.

Confronting Violence

Answering Questions About the Epidemic Destroying America's Homes and Communities

Third Edition

George A. Gellert, M.D., M.P.H., M.P.A., F.A.B.P.M.

Forewords By
Kathleen Kennedy Townsend
Former Lt. Governor of Maryland

Frank Keating
Former Governor of Oklahoma

American Public Health Association
Washington, DC

American Public Health Association
800 I Street, NW
Washington, DC 20001-3710
www.apha.org

© 2010 by the American Public Health Association

All rights reserved. No part of this publication may be reproduced, stored in a retrieval system, or transmitted in any form or by any means, electronic, mechanical, photocopying, recording, scanning, or otherwise, except as permitted under Sections 107 and 108 of the 1976 United States Copyright Act, without either the prior written permission of the Publisher or authorization through payment of the appropriate per-copy fee to the Copyright Clearance Center [222 Rosewood Drive, Danvers, MA 01923, (978) 750-8400, fax (978) 646-8600, www.copyright.com]. Requests to the Publisher for permission should be addressed to the Permissions Department, American Public Health Association, 800 I Street, NW, Washington, DC 20001-3710; fax (202) 777-2531.

DISCLAIMER: Any discussion of medical or legal issues in this publication is being provided for informational purposes only. Nothing in this publication is intended to constitute medical or legal advice, and it should not be construed as such. This book is not intended to be and should not be used as a substitute for specific medical or legal advice, since medical and legal opinions may only be given in response to inquiries regarding specific factual situations. If medical or legal advice is desired by the reader of this book, a medical doctor or attorney should be consulted.

The use of trade names and commercial sources in this book does not imply endorsement by either the APHA or the editorial board of this volume.

While the publisher and author have used their best efforts in preparing this book, they make no representations with respect to the accuracy or completeness of the content.

Georges C. Benjamin, M.D., F.A.C.P., F.A.C.E.P., (E) *Executive Director*
Carlos Castillo–Salgado, M.D., J.D., M.P.H., Dr.P.H., *Publications Board Liaison*

Printed and bound in the United States of America
Interior Design and Typesetting: Vanessa Sifford and The Manila Typesetting Company
Cover Design: Jennifer Strass
Printing and Binding: Victor Graphics, Inc.

Library of Congress Cataloging-in-Publication Data

Gellert, George A., 1958-
  Confronting violence : answering questions about the epidemic destroying america's homes and communities / George A. Gellert ; forewords by Kathleen Kennedy Townsend, Frank Keating. — 3rd ed.
    p. cm.
  ISBN-13: 978-0-87553-196-0
  ISBN-10: 0-87553-196-2
  1. Violence—United States. 2. Violence—United States—Prevention. 3. Violent crimes—United States.
  4. Violent crimes—United States—Prevention. I. Title.
  HN90.V5G44 2010
  303.6--dc22

                              2010001863

ISBN 13: 978-0-87553-196-0
ISBN 10: 0-87553-196-2
1500/5/2010

CONTENTS

CONTENTS

CONTENTS

CONTENTS

CONTENTS

CONTENTS

Foreword to the Third Edition

I was 12 years old when my uncle, President John F. Kennedy, was killed and 16 years old when my father was murdered. A long time ago, one could argue. Time has passed, and yet the wounds have not healed. I still suffer these losses to our country and to my family. Our nation and the world would be a better place had they lived. We would have made greater strides in reducing poverty, extending health care to all, and dealing with the scourge of violence, which is our nation's curse. I make the same claim about Abraham Lincoln and Martin Luther King, Jr. Had they lived longer, the healing this country needed might have come much sooner.

And it is not only our nation that is worse off, so is my family. My father's 11 children, of whom I am the eldest, grew up missing him—his steadiness, his guidance, and his love and support. Although my mother's life has been well occupied with her children, her more than 33 grandchildren, and her work for the Robert Kennedy Memorial, it has not been nearly as joyful as it could have been had he lived. The effects of violence stay with us, diminish us, and harm us. Every family that has been scarred by violence suffers wounds that never fully heal.

In referring to "violence," I do not limit myself to murder. Children who are bullied seldom recover their happy resilience. Worse, they may become bullies themselves, widening the circles of pain through generations. The effects of spousal abuse are also horrendous, ranging from a shrunken sense of self to sickness and even death. Children who would have enjoyed the blessings of a mother's attention, care, and love must go without.

The violent death of a public figure infects our public consciousness, making us distrustful, wary, and worried. The less publicized but far more numerous acts of everyday violence cast a shadow over millions of our fellow Americans and, yes, our country itself. America is one of the most violent nations on earth. Millions of men and women are broken by loss. While they still may have the right to "pursue happiness," they don't have the same grand capacity to embrace joy. Too many of our fellows—our coworkers, parents, children, cousins, and friends—have been crushed.

On April 5, 1968, the day after Martin Luther King, Jr., was killed, my father, Robert F. Kennedy, spoke at The City Club of Cleveland and delivered one of the best indictments against this culture of violence:

"This is a time of shame and sorrow. It is not a day for politics. I have saved this one opportunity to speak briefly to you about this mindless menace of violence in America which again stains our land and every one of our lives.

It is not the concern of any one race. The victims of the violence are black and white, rich and poor, young and old, famous and unknown. They are, most important of all, human beings whom other human beings loved and needed. No one—no matter where he lives or what he does—can be certain who will suffer from some senseless act of bloodshed. And yet it goes on and on.

Why? What has violence ever accomplished? What has it ever created?. . . .

Whenever any American's life is taken by another American unnecessarily— whether it is done in the name of the law or in the defiance of law, by one man or a gang, in cold blood or in passion, in an attack of violence or in response to violence—whenever we tear at the fabric of life which another man has painfully and clumsily woven for himself and his children, the whole nation is degraded. . . .

Yet we seemingly tolerate a rising level of violence that ignores our common humanity and our claims to civilization alike. We calmly accept newspaper reports of civilian slaughter in far off lands. We glorify killing on movie and television screens and call it entertainment. We make it easy for men of all shades of sanity to acquire weapons and ammunition they desire.

Too often we honor swagger and bluster and the wielders of force; too often we excuse those who are willing to build their own lives on the shattered dreams of others. . . .

Some look for scapegoats, others look for conspiracies, but this much is clear; violence breeds violence, repression brings retaliation, and only a cleaning of our whole society can remove this sickness from our soul.

For there is another kind of violence, slower but just as deadly, destructive as the shot or the bomb in the night. This is the violence of institutions; indifference and inaction and slow decay. This is the violence that afflicts the poor, that poisons relations between men because their skin has different colors. This is a slow destruction of a child by hunger, and schools without books and homes without heat in the winter.

This is the breaking of a man's spirit by denying him the chance to stand as a father and as a man among other men. And this too afflicts us all. . . . When you teach a man to hate and fear his brother, when you teach that he is a lesser man because of his color or his beliefs or the policies he pursues, when you teach that those who differ from you threaten your freedom or your job or your family, then you also learn to confront others not as fellow citizens but as enemies—to be met not with cooperation but with conquest, to be subjugated and mastered.

We learn, at the last, to look at our brothers as aliens, men with whom we share a city, but not a community, men bound to us in common dwelling, but not in common effort. We learn to share only a common fear—only a common desire to retreat from each other—only a common impulse to meet disagreement with force. For all this there are no final answers.

Yet we know what we must do. It is to achieve true justice among our fellow citizens. . . . The question is whether we can find in our own midst and in our own hearts that leadership of human purpose that will recognize the terrible truths of our existence.

We must admit the vanity of our false distinctions among men and learn to find our own advancement in the search for the advancement of all. . . . We must recognize that this short life can neither be ennobled or enriched by hatred or revenge.

Our lives on this planet are too short and the work to be done too great to let this spirit flourish any longer in our land. Of course we cannot vanish it with a program, nor with a resolution.

But we can perhaps remember—even if only for a time—that those who live with us are our brothers, that they share with us the same short movement of life, that they seek—as we do—nothing but the chance to live out their lives in purpose and happiness, winning what satisfaction and fulfillment they can.

Surely this bond of common faith, this bond of common goal, can begin to teach us something. Surely we can learn, at least, to look at those around us as fellow men and surely we can begin to work a little harder to bind up the wounds among us and to become in our hearts brothers and countrymen once again."

So in the midst of horrendous pain, my father asked us to reach out to our fellow human beings with love and compassion. He quoted Aeschylus: "Let us tame the savageness of man and make gentle the life of the world."

I write this introduction at St. Mary's College, located near Oakland, California, where I have been serving as a Woodrow Wilson Fellow. One of the Christian Brothers at the college told a story about one of his students. The student had asked permission to travel to New York for the January term service project. Brother Michael Avila called his colleague in New York, but was told there was no room. A few days later, another student approached Brother Avila and explained that the first student needed to go to New York because a member of his family had been killed in the Twin Towers on 9/11. On hearing this, the priest in New

York found it in his heart to welcome him and let him stay in the priest's own room.

The student played the clarinet, and one night he went out on the street to play. A passerby stopped to listen. At the end of the recital, the passerby said that he had been on his way to murder someone, but now had changed his mind. The beauty of the music had moved him.

Just as violence is catching, so too are peace and beauty and love.

This book is filled with haunting statistics, each number marking a story of pain and loss. But the book is also filled with the names of hundreds of groups that are determined to reverse the tide, to stop the terrible pandemic of violence, and to show us another way. The stories of these countless courageous people, such as the priest who opens up his apartment to a stranger or the student whose beautiful music can change a murderous heart, embody the hopes of our nation to bind our wounds and find a common faith.

Kathleen Kennedy Townsend
Former Lt. Governor of Maryland

Foreword to the First and Second Editions

On the morning of April 19, 1995, I was sitting in my office on the second floor of Oklahoma's State Capitol, less than two miles northeast of Oklahoma City's central business district. The sudden shock of an explosion rattled the windows, and within seconds a dark and ominous cloud of oily, black smoke rolled up from the southwest. By noon we knew two ugly facts: a truck bomb packed with nearly 5,000 pounds of volatile explosives had detonated in front of the Alfred P. Murrah Federal Building, and the loss of life would be severe.

For the next two weeks, Oklahomans toiled to comfort the families of those who had died and to assist the huge numbers of wounded. The ultimate death toll of 169 included 19 children. More than 500 were injured badly enough to require hospital treatment. The search and recovery effort, which went on for 16 grueling days and nights, was perhaps the most agonizing period in our state's history. I am immensely proud of the way Oklahoma responded to this crime, of the valiant work of the rescuers and helpers, and of the outpouring of love and support we received from across America and around the world. In the wake of a barbaric act, Americans showed that we are not barbarians.

In the months that followed, we analyzed and dissected the Murrah Federal Building bombing. Was it a "next step" in domestic terrorism? A warped symbol of dissent and rage? The supposed American tendency toward violence, writ large?

The bombing was ultimately a mass murder. Had the bombers wished to make a political statement against the government, they could have destroyed the building at night, with less risk of detection or capture. There is ample evidence that this act was planned to take a maximum human toll; just across the street from the spot where the truck was parked was a playground for the neighboring Young Men's Christian Association (YMCA) day-care center. Had the timing been slightly different, up to 60 children would have been on that playground, instead of inside the YMCA building, where many of them nevertheless suffered serious injuries. These killers came within moments of murdering not 19 but more than

70 small children, in addition to the 150 adult victims. All murder is cruel, but our society rightly condemns as especially heinous the murder of a child.

This book's central goal is not so much to explain violence, but to measure its reach and impact, and to provide resources for its victims and those who would oppose barbarism. It has become a modern axiom that America is uniquely violent, and in many ways that is true. But it is important to measure that violence against the counterbalancing forces of good. One truck bomb was delivered to Oklahoma City on April 19, 1995. On one day alone in the weeks that followed, my office received 10,000 pieces of mail containing messages of hope for the victims and contributions to help them endure. If America is a violent society, we are also a fundamentally compassionate one.

Dr. Gellert avoids the simplistic liberal trap that views an individual's violent act and promptly indicts society, or poverty, or some other social force, as if individuals with free will were somehow inevitably programmed to bad action. Social problems—especially drug and alcohol abuse—certainly play a role in violence. But violence is at its core the behavior of individuals, and to excuse or explain a violent act in other terms is to send a most destructive message.

The author also shuns the disturbing belief that has arisen in some sectors of odd-think that traditional deterrents to crime, including jail, are ineffective. They are not perfect, but, as Dr. Gellert notes, a prison that incarcerates a predator keeps that predator out of your living room, at least for the duration of his sentence. Dr. Gellert rightly seeks a balance among such strategies as prevention and education, drug and alcohol treatment, and a tough, fair criminal justice system with adequate penalties.

His exhaustive lists of resources are especially compelling. Even the casual reader will find someone to write or call with concerns or questions about a troublesome aspect of violence. There are resources for victims, for molders of public policy, and for citizens who have simply "had enough." Researchers, students in the helping professions, and parents alike will appreciate his useful question-and-answer format of the text; librarians will wonder whether to shelve this book in the crime section or on the reference rack, so complete is its extensive bibliography.

Confronting Violence is a definitive reference work and a call to action, written with a public health physician's eye for public safety and a scientist's evenhanded respect for evidence. Before I was elected governor of Oklahoma, I spent most of my career in law enforcement as a special agent of the Federal Bureau of Investigation, as a federal prosecutor, and as a subcabinet officer overseeing our federal law enforcement and penal agencies. Throughout those years I relied on a myriad of sources and many different interpretations of violence. Now,

Dr. Gellert has brought it all together in a single volume. He has made a significant contribution to the literature, and he has given us a single-source tool of great value.

I am not a pessimist by nature. In the darkest days of 1995, when Oklahoma suffered a collective emotional agony without precedent, I saw thousands of acts of courage and kindness and an immense nobility of spirit. As we coped with one of the most vicious acts of violence in American history, we also discovered a million reasons for hope. *Confronting Violence* will arm you with information. Let it also arm you with hope and a strong faith in America's goodness. There is nothing inevitable about the bleak and sometimes discouraging picture that Dr. Gellert presents; there is everything to build on in his call for individual and collective action. As the Oklahoma City bombing becomes a tragic chapter in our history, so, too, can the violence epidemic.

Frank Keating
Former Governor of Oklahoma

Preface to the Third Edition

I have a vivid childhood memory of a liquor store holdup in my Chicago neighborhood. As the perpetrator tried to leave the scene of the crime, holding a gun to the store clerk, all of my neighbors were on their front porches, shouting, "Don't shoot him! Let him go!" How likely would that scene be in any community today?

Now, it is far too common that people do not want to get involved when faced with a violent situation. By not getting involved, we are allowing more and more violent episodes to happen. After engaging in violent arguments with his family and the Internal Revenue Service (IRS), a 53-year-old man from Austin, Texas, burned his house to the ground and then flew a single-engine plane into a government office building, killing himself and an IRS worker: What was missed before he committed such a desperate act? A 45-year-old University of Alabama biology professor opened fire on her colleagues at a staff meeting, killing three of them. Investigations into her past found a history of violence that went back to her shooting her brother 20 years earlier: How did the dots not get connected? Then there was the beating of a 15-year-old girl by another girl in a downtown Seattle bus tunnel. The beating was observed by three adult security guards who stood nearby but did not intervene. Their standing orders were to observe events and call police but not get involved. The guards followed their orders despite the obvious brutality of the crime and their capacity to stop it. Tragically, although violence is a presence in our society, complacency and missed opportunities to prevent it are all too often factors in its propagation.

There are many other factors that contribute to violence as a societal problem. They include a well-known but complex series of negative human behaviors and environmental influences. We also now have a new set of emerging technologies that enhance these factors, including the media, interactive video games, the internet, social networking tools, and advanced firearm designs.

Media coverage is becoming increasingly more graphic and unrestrained. Interactive video games may desensitize children to the reality of gore and death through violent acts, and internet and social networking sites allow for mass dissemination of violent concepts and fear in an impersonal way. By enabling depersonalized forms of communication, these new technologies, in effect, help people avoid the kind of person-to-person interaction that can often serve as a mitigating or prohibitive barrier to verbal violence.

The public health impact of firearm injuries, one of the many important measures defined in this book, is an extremely important concern. Firearms have caused more than 32,000 deaths on average over the past 30 years, and the death rate is more than twice the goal set by the Healthy People 2010 initiative. Firearms are the second leading cause of injury behind motor vehicle crashes, with a fatality rate of 10.2 per 100,000 and a nonfatal rate of 23 per 100,000 (as of 2006). With today's sophisticated, semiautomatic weapons, a shooter can release a spray of bullets with the squeeze of a trigger, killing more people in an indiscriminate manner than would have been possible with older weapons. Although it is true that people kill people and that firearms do not cause injuries or deaths by themselves, guns remain an important vector in their propagation. Study after study has linked the easy availability of firearms to a higher likelihood of injury or death. Therefore, it is no surprise that the important data included in this book's chapter on youth violence support the fact that the United States has the highest rate of youth firearm-related violence in the industrialized world. The book's chapter on firearms also seeks to answer the question of whether having a firearm increases or decreases the risk of firearm-related violence. The facts in these two chapters are compelling and make a strong case that anyone who works in violence prevention must address the role that firearms play in any injury-control strategy.

This book points out that violence is not limited to any one risk factor or demographic group. Victims can be any age, and strangers as well as intimate partners and family members can be the perpetrators. Consequently, our young, our old, our close household members, and, tragically, even pregnant women are all at risk. This is a public health problem of immense proportions that requires a solid public health approach. As we look at violence through a public health lens, it is critical not only to define the problem as clearly as possible—through epidemiological studies and surveillance—but also to offer evidence-based solutions and strategies. We can educate ourselves about the problem by learning the warning signs of suicide and other mental and psychological risk factors; the different types of bullying, abuse, and aggressive experiences that can traumatize our youth and lead to violent patterns later in life; the parenting patterns that promote or diminish violent behaviors; and the role of technology and the media as influencers of sociological and individual behavior. We must also get involved individually and as a society if we are going to be successful in reducing violent behavior. We need not wait until we have all the answers, but we do need to act on what we know as soon as we know it.

Every year we learn more and more about how to address these problems. Unfortunately, violence is a problem that continues. This third edition of *Confronting Violence* is an important update of our current understanding of what we can do as a society, and as individuals, to address this ongoing public health dilemma.

There is a lot we can do, and it is all about getting our hands around the problems early. It is about identifying people at risk and putting systems in place to respond and act quickly. This must occur in all aspects of our society: at home, in schools, on our streets, and at work. Finally, as a community, we must stand up together against the real villain here—complacency—and say with one voice as loudly as we can, "Don't shoot!"

Georges C. Benjamin, M.D., F.A.C.P., F.A.C.E.P., (E)
Executive Director
American Public Health Association

Acknowledgments

I am indebted to a number of individuals and organizations for their inspiration and contributions to the writing of this book. The content of the book represents a distillation of thousands upon thousands of hours of research, practice, work, and dedication on the part of many unacknowledged individuals in the public health, medical, social services, mental health, law enforcement, and criminal justice fields. The value of the book derives directly from the efforts of these professionals who struggle to prevent violence, treat violence victims and perpetrators, apprehend and prosecute perpetrators, collect and analyze data on violence, and conduct research on the dimensions and underlying nature of violence in America. Although there are too many specific institutions to applaud for their work in this field, I would be remiss if I did not cite the enormous contributions of the U.S. Department of Justice and the U.S. Centers for Disease Control and Prevention.

I owe my first opportunity to work professionally on the problem of violence to Michael Durfee, M.D., and Carol Berkowitz, M.D., and I thank them for their inspiration, warm collaboration, and provocative dialogue. Eric Kom, Dale Nordenberg, M.D., Bob Gordon, M.D., Scott Klesmer, and Lucy Reckseit have consistently inspired me to write with their unwavering belief in my ability. I hope that I am as supportive of their journeys as they have been of mine. Three colleagues cultivated a desire to write as much by their actions as their words: Roberta Maxwell, Ph.D., Kathleen Higgins, and Rosanne Lowery. I will always miss working with such elegant and joyous dynamos. Jean McGowan has been a kind friend. The guidance and support offered by several educators at key junctures in my life cannot be overstated: Herbert Ladd, Ph.D., Morris Shames, Ph.D., Bernie Siegel, M.D., Lowell Levin, Ed.D., Eliot Nelson, M.D., Alfred Neumann, M.D., and Ellen Alkon, M.D. Their genuine mentorship and enormous generosity of spirit will never be forgotten.

Michael Gellert, my brother and cherished friend, provided significant insight into the writing and publication of a book, and as always, showed that it could be done. His loving support is one of life's great immaterial treasures. My dear parents gave me everything, including the desire to contribute something of meaning. If all parents were as loving as they, much of this book would not need to be written. My wife, Noelle, permeates my life with a remarkable depth of love and capacity for caring, and was always there to cheer me on along the long road to finishing the first edition of the book. Her thoughtful review of each chapter has been invaluable. My children, Tess and Gabriel, were most supportive and patient, especially in tolerating my being missing in action throughout the preparation of this third edition. Thank you all.

George A. Gellert

Introduction: How Should This Book Be Used?

This book is intended for readers from two broad audiences. The first is the general public. The information contained here may be of use to individuals concerned about how violence can affect their lives, and if violence affects their lives currently, what they can do about it. My objective was to create a quick and easy-to-use reference handbook, written in everyday nontechnical English, that will provide families and individuals at risk for violence (or who perceive themselves as being at risk) with an overview of violence problems. Each chapter focuses on a specific kind of violence and walks through a standard set of questions, such as how common a problem is, who is involved, in what settings, what to do if one is a victim, and how to prevent becoming a victim. Chapters conclude with national and state-by-state lists of telephone contacts and websites where the reader can obtain more information and assistance in dealing with violence.

The second audience consists of professionals who, in the course of their everyday work, interact with or provide services to people affected by violence. The book's general overview of violence is not intended for the specialist in violence treatment or prevention. It is instead oriented toward professionals without specific or extensive training in responding to violence problems, but who nonetheless encounter them on the front line in our frequently violent social environment. This includes health professionals, such as physicians, nurses, and public health workers; social service professionals, such as social workers, counselors, and psychologists; and those working in law enforcement and the judicial system. For these professionals, the book can serve as a rapid source of factual information on specific violence problems and a summary of the violence epidemic. My hope is that professionals will use the volume not only to answer their own questions about violence problems but also as a tool to educate, counsel, and assist their patients and clients, perhaps copying and providing select pages to them as part of their care and management.

Writing a brief volume on a vast problem like violence, with its many subtleties and complexities, is a challenge in the best of circumstances. In attempting to address overlapping audiences, there is a risk of compromising the technical depth and level of detail desired by the professional to make the information readable and useful for the layperson. Despite this challenge, and the obvious flaws that may result, I hope that the end result is of value to both types of readers.

By its very nature, a book on the violence epidemic must be a static picture of a single point in time. Any description of the epidemic must be based on prior research and published data. Therefore, some of the statistics and trends outlined in this book will be dated even as the book is published. Many databases on violence have a lengthy multi-year lag period between when information is collected and analyzed, and when it is reported to the public. More current information can always be found in the professional and research literature, although even these are dated by the time they appear. Up-to-date and online information may also be found in the departments and bureaus of governmental agencies and non-governmental organizations whose mission it is to track the epidemic, such as the Federal Bureau of Investigation, the U.S. Department of Justice, and the U.S. Public Health Service. While for readability I have not provided reference citations for each and every fact in the text, the large majority of statistics were obtained from studies conducted by one of these agencies. All cited references, data, and many other key sources of information are listed alphabetically by author and chapter by chapter in Appendix 2 at the end of the book (References and Suggestions for Further Reading). Additional online information resources are provided as website URLs at the conclusion of each chapter.

With respect to the views expressed in this book about the origins, occurrence, and prevention of various forms of violence, I have attempted to present those data, insights, and perspectives that have withstood the test of time and that appear to be shaping views about violence. Where opposing viewpoints on an issue, such as the impact of firearms on the incidence of intentional injuries, cannot be easily reconciled, I have attempted to portray all of the major perspectives on a specific issue or policy. Controversial positions are supported by the data and evidence provided, but as the ongoing debate on a number of issues indicates, contradictory research and findings on violence are a discomfiting and frequent reality.

My greatest hope for the book is that it can help individuals to help themselves. If it is of use to both kinds of reader—serving as an educational reference book for families *and* as an introduction and resource guide on violence for professionals—it will have exceeded expectations.

George A. Gellert

CHAPTER 1

Determinants of Violence — Is America More Violent Than Other Societies?

A merican life is inundated with violence. Violence has become common in our culture, media, and entertainment. We witness, hear about, or experience real or dramatized violence in some way almost every day. Who among us can recall a day that was completely violence-free? The United States is one of the most violent industrialized nations not engaged in civil war. The U.S. homicide rate is 3–8 times greater than that in any other Western democracy. Every year violence causes an estimated 2.2 million injuries and more than 40,000 deaths in the United States (more than two-thirds of the fatalities of the Vietnam War). According to the Federal Bureau of Investigation (FBI), in 2008 a violent crime occurred in the United States every 23 seconds, a murder every 33 minutes, and a rape every 6 minutes. An incident of child abuse or neglect is reported every 13–35 seconds; an elderly person is victimized every 3 minutes. An American woman is victimized by an intimate partner every 1.3 minutes; a man is victimized every 6.7 minutes. An American commits suicide every 16 minutes and attempts suicide every 39 seconds.

SCOPE OF THE U.S. VIOLENCE PROBLEM

At least 23 million Americans are victims of crime each year, and 5.2 million are victims of violent crimes. Available statistics underestimate the true extent of violence in the United States. Reported crimes represent only a fraction of all crimes. The Department of Justice has estimated that only 37% of all crimes are reported to police. Perhaps half of all violent crimes are reported. Let us briefly highlight what we know about the scope and extent of different forms of violence in the United States.

Over three million reports of child abuse are made every year in the United States. In 2007, approximately 5.8 million children were involved in an estimated

3.2 million child abuse reports and allegations. An estimated 794,000 children were victims of maltreatment during 2007. Furthermore, 1,760 children died of abuse and neglect in the United States in 2007. Every day more than 2,000 children become victims of abuse or neglect. Between 2% and 3% of the total population under the age of 18 years may be abused. One study using self and parental reports estimated that approximately 8,755,000 children are victims of child maltreatment each year. This means that more than one-seventh of children between the ages of 2 and 17 years experience some form of maltreatment, including physical abuse, sexual abuse, psychological or emotional abuse, neglect, and custodial interference or family abduction. Child homicide is among the top 5 causes of death in childhood and accounts for approximately 5% of all deaths among individuals aged less than 18 years. Approximately five children die every day as a result of child abuse.

In 2007, 7.6% of all abuse, or more than 60,000 incidents, involved sexual abuse. Estimates are that 1 in every 3–4 females is sexually abused before age 18 years; others range from 5% to 15% of all males and 15% to 30% of all females reporting some form of child sexual abuse. A 2008 national youth survey found that 6.1% of all children responding had been sexually victimized in the past year and that approximately 1 in 10 had been victimized over their lifetimes. It is estimated that there are 39–60 million survivors of childhood sexual abuse in America today. Approximately 31% of women in U.S. prisons state that they had been abused as children. Some experts estimate that perhaps 1 man in every 100 is a child sexual abuser. This would mean that there are more than one million child molesters in the United States.

Youth violence is widespread in America. Young people are more likely than any other group to be victims of violent crime. In 2005–2006, 86% of public schools in the United States reported 1 or more violent incidents and thefts, amounting to 2.2 million crimes. In 2005, 5,686 young people aged 10–24 years were murdered, or an average of 16 each day. Homicide was the second leading cause of death for this age group. More than 720,000 violence-related injuries in young people aged 10–24 years were treated in U.S. emergency departments in 2006. A 2008 national youth survey found that 61% of children and adolescents (birth to age 17 years) were exposed to violence, abuse, or a criminal victimization in the previous year. More than one-fourth (25.3%) witnessed a violent act and more than one-third experienced two or more different kinds of violence exposures in the past year (11% had five or more exposures). More than one-third (38.7%) experienced two or more direct victimizations in the previous year, and 10.9% experienced five or more. A national survey in 2007 found that 35.5% of high school students reported being in a physical fight during the prior year and that 18% reported carrying a gun, knife, or club to school in the prior 30 days. Approximately 8% reported being threatened or injured with a weapon on school property 1 or more times in the 12 months preceding the survey. A 2008 survey reported that 13.2% of young people had been bullied physically within the past year and that 21.6% had been bullied during their lifetimes. In 2005–2006, 24% of U.S. public schools reported that student bullying was a daily or weekly problem.

Violence against women in the United States is primarily intimate partner violence: 64% of the women who reported being raped, physically assaulted, or stalked since age 18 years were victimized by a current or former husband, cohabiting partner, boyfriend, or date. The National Crime Victimization Survey in 2008 reported 504,980 incidents of intimate partner violence against females (a rate of 3.9 per 1,000) and 88,120 incidents against males (a rate of 0.7 per 1,000). Approximately 1.3 million women and 835,000 men are physically assaulted by an intimate partner annually in the United States. Four to eight percent of pregnant women are physically assaulted. These figures do not consider the many victims who are victimized more than once, which could increase the number of victimizations to as high as 4.8 million annual intimate partner physical assaults and rapes against U.S. women and up to 2.9 million assaults against U.S. men. The Department of Justice reported that approximately 25% of surveyed women and 7.6% of surveyed men said they had been physically assaulted or raped by a current or former spouse, cohabiting partner, or date at some point in their lifetimes; 1.5% of women and 0.9% of men said that such an assault by an intimate partner had occurred in the previous 12 months.

In the United States, 1 in 6–10 women and 1 in 33–50 men have experienced an attempted or completed rape at some time in their lives. Estimates run as high as 17.7 million U.S. women having been the victims of an attempted or completed rape and 2.78 million men the victims of sexual assault or rape. A national survey published in 2007 found that 10.6% of women and 2.1% of men reported experiencing forced sex at some point, and that 2.5% of women and 0.9% of men reported experiencing some form of unwanted sexual activity in the prior 12 months. The Department of Justice states that 20%–25% of women in college have reported experiencing an attempted or a completed rape while in college. The National Crime Victim Survey estimates that in 2008 there were 203,830 rapes and sexual assaults in the United States (including crimes both reported and unreported to police). The National Violence Against Women Survey estimated in 2006 that more than 300,000 women and approximately 93,000 men are raped annually in the United States. Other studies suggest that at least 20% of adult women, 15% of college women, and 12% of adolescent girls have experienced sexual abuse or assault during their lifetimes. The Department of Justice reports that more than 1 million women and approximately 400,000 men are stalked each year in the United States.

Estimates range from 2% to 10% of the nation's elderly having been abused at some point in their lives. In 2004, between one and two million elders in the United States were estimated to have been injured, exploited, or otherwise mistreated by a caregiver. There may be as many as two million cases of elder abuse each year. In studies of abuse in residential institutions for the elderly, more than one-third of nurses and nursing aides reported witnessing physical abuse of an elderly resident during the prior year. Psychological abuse was observed by more than 80% of the staff, including yelling, insulting, or swearing at a resident. Approximately one-quarter witnessed a patient being socially isolated.

In 2008 there were 16,272 murders in the United States. For the 5-year period between 2003 and 2007, the number of murder victims per year in the United States hovered between a low of 14,210 and a peak of 15,087. Murder across the country has become more of a random event than in the past, with less murder occurring between individuals who are related or acquainted with each other and more occurring between strangers. As a result, the FBI states that "every American now has a realistic chance of murder victimization in view of the random nature the crime has assumed."

Firearm injury in the United States caused an average of 32,300 deaths annually between 1980 and 2006. It is the second leading cause of death from injury, exceeded only by motor vehicle crashes. An estimated 4–6 nonfatal injuries occur for every firearm death. Firearm injury has an enormous public health impact, accounting for 6.6% of premature death in this country (years of potential life lost before age 65 years). In 2004 alone, 29,569 Americans died by gunfire: 16,750 in firearm suicides, 11,935 in firearm homicides, 649 in unintentional shootings, and 235 in firearm deaths of unknown intent. In 2008, there were 343,550 firearm victims in the United States (including robberies), accounting for 7% of all violent incidents. Offenders used firearms in more than two-thirds of U.S. murders, 43.5% of robberies, and 21.4% of aggravated assaults. Firearms are involved in 52% of suicides. Among industrialized nations, the U.S. firearm-related death rate is more than twice that of the next highest country and eight times the average rate of its economic counterparts. Guns kept at home for protection against crime are 22–43 times more likely to kill a family member, friend, or acquaintance than to kill an intruder in self-defense.

In 2005 there were 32,637 suicides, which accounted for 1.3% of all deaths in the United States, ranking it as the 11th leading cause of death. If we consider the number of people who kill themselves and the years by which their lives are reduced, a total of approximately one million years of life are lost annually because of suicide in America. Since 1950, the suicide rate among children and adolescents has nearly tripled. In 2006, 162,359 people were hospitalized for self-inflicted injury. In 2008, more than 395,000 people with self-inflicted injuries were treated in U.S. emergency departments. For every completed suicide in the United States, it is believed that there are between 8 and 25 suicide attempts. Thus, every year between 261,000 and 816,000 suicide attempts are made in the United States. An estimated 5–7 million living Americans have tried to kill themselves at some time.

Although these statistics are alarming, in actuality, the news is far from all bad. Violence has been trending downward quite substantially in the United States over the past several decades. Violent crime rates have been generally stable at their lowest levels since 2004 after declining from 1984 to 2002. The overall violent crime rate decreased 44% from 50 to 28 victimizations per 1,000 persons between 1993 and 2000. Since 1994, violent crime rates have steadily declined, reaching the lowest level ever in 2005. Serious violent crime rates declined in recent years for both Blacks and Whites. Firearm-related crime has plummeted since 1993, slightly increasing in 2005. Homicide rates recently declined to levels last seen in the mid-1960s. Rape rates have been stable in recent years. Assault rates declined since 1994. The proportion of serious violent crimes committed by juveniles has generally declined since 1993. According to the FBI, violent crime in the nation decreased 3.5% during the first 6 months of 2008 compared with the same period in 2007.

Nonetheless, Americans remain appropriately concerned about violent crime. The rash of school and youth shootings, the abductions and sexual assault of young girls, and the murderous rampages by individuals at their places of work have drawn public attention across the nation and heightened concerns about violence. The fact remains that there were an estimated 1.4 million violent crimes in 2007, approximately 467 for every 100,000 people. The United States remains by far the most "criminal" country in the world, with 5% of the world's population and 25% of its prisoners. We spend $68 billion per year on corrections, and one-third of those incarcerated are serving time for nonviolent drug crimes. America spends more than $150 billion per year on policing and courts. Since 1982, expenditures for operating the criminal justice system increased 418%, not accounting for inflation.

A RISK FACTOR FRAMEWORK FOR UNDERSTANDING VIOLENCE

A National Academy of Sciences Panel on the Understanding and Control of Violent Behavior was established to provide an overview of what is known about violence in the United States and to develop recommendations toward its control. The Panel identified various contributing or risk factors for violence and classified these along broad dimensions. First the Panel considered how close in time risk factors occur relative to particular violent events. The proximity in time of a risk factor to a violent incident can range widely, from those that are far removed from an act but still contribute to its occurrence years later to those that precipitate violence almost immediately. For instance, an abused child may develop a potentially violent personality by the time he or she reaches adulthood. Activating events are those that can produce an act of violence immediately.

The Panel considered four levels at which risk factors can influence behavior, including the macrosocial, microsocial, psychosocial, and biological. The macrosocial level involves the characteristics of society, communities, or the nation that either promote or decrease violence. Social values are an example of a risk factor at the macrosocial level. This level also can include events that catalyze violence, such as the outcome of a trial. Other predisposing macrosocial factors are poverty, lack of economic opportunity, and the nature of gender roles in a culture. With respect to situational factors, macrosocial considerations include the way the community is laid out or how readily an individual can access weapons.

The microsocial level concerns encounters and relationships between people. It pertains to considerations such as the strength of community organizations, the breakdown of families, and the presence of gangs. Whether weapons are carried or displayed, and whether bystanders get involved and try to prevent the escalation of a conflict or argument also occur at the microsocial level. An activating factor at the microsocial level would be how individuals communicate and such things as whether insults are exchanged.

The next level focuses on the individual and considers the psychosocial environment. Here predisposing risk factors for violence include the temperament of individuals, how they have learned to respond to each other socially, their understanding of the rewards and penalties for committing violent acts, their social skills, whether they use alcohol and drugs, whether they are under stress, and how they typically express anger. Situational individual risk factors for violence would include the consumption of alcohol or drugs, the accumulation of negative emotions, or whether an individual is sexually aroused. Activating factors at the individual level include a sudden impulse or urge within a person who is predisposed to violence in a situation that promotes aggression, along with the opportunity to act violently given this combination of setting and individual characteristics.

The final level for risk factors is the biological, which includes various hormonal and chemical influences on the brain and which affects all behaviors.

All behaviors, including violent and aggressive acts, are the results of biological and chemical processes in the brain. Biologically determined behavioral traits are considered at this level, such as characteristics or conditions created by birth or a history of trauma. Genetic characteristics, as well as the use of drugs that influence mental states, may predispose to violence at a biological level. Studies have suggested that violence may be associated with several permanent and temporary conditions of the nervous system. Hormones and neurotransmitters in the brain and physical abnormalities in brain structure at birth or from injury can influence mental states and predispose to violence. Abnormal functioning of the brain that interferes with thinking processes or communication can produce poor school performance and other problems in childhood, which, in turn, increase the risk of violent behavior.

Our understanding of behavioral processes and their relationship to violence remains too rudimentary at present to say whether there is a definite neurological or other biological marker for violence. Scientists have long been interested in whether violence could be predicted on biological grounds so that perhaps individuals who screen positively for a "violence marker" could be provided with special attention to reduce their propensity or opportunity for violence. Statistical studies of twins and adopted children have produced evidence that genetic and social processes can interact and increase the likelihood that an individual may become antisocial, engage in juvenile delinquency, or become an alcoholic. The little data that look specifically at violence have suggested only a weak influence of individual genetic makeup on the risk of acting violently. Even if a genetic influence on risk of violence is identified by research, it would most probably involve many genes rather than a single "violence gene." Genetics most likely interact in a subtle, complex manner with a wide array of social, situational, and cultural factors and life events. In sum, any violent act is the outcome of a long and diverse chain of preceding influences and events. Many violence prevention efforts seek to interrupt this progression and break the chain of events that result in a violent outcome.

One approach to understanding criminal behavior suggests that a subculture of violence exists in America, including people living in poverty, young people, and members of lower socioeconomic classes and racial minorities who are disenfranchised politically from mainstream society. In this view, individuals within this subculture do not share the values and beliefs of greater society and because they are angry and frustrated at being left out of social and economic opportunities, violence is used as a means of getting what they want. This characteristic is most notable among young, unemployed, and often unskilled men within the subculture. Much violence, particularly stranger and economically motivated violence, is committed by persons in this disenfranchised segment of society, which often coincides with inner-city populations. A large number of victims of violence are found in these same communities.

CONTRIBUTORS TO AMERICAN VIOLENCE AND ITS RECENT DECLINE

Explanations for the decline in violent crime rates since the 1990s are as diverse as they are incomplete and ultimately unsatisfactory. Changes in demographics that decreased the number of individuals in more highly violent age groups have been cited as responsible for the violence decline, as have increased incarceration of violent perpetrators, increased police deployment, improved police work, stricter enforcement of existing laws, a robust and growing economy (until recently), and so on. Intelligent new strategies to reduce the use of guns by—and thus the lethality of—violent perpetrators may have contributed to the decline in violence. Rigorous law enforcement tracing of guns used in crimes, heightened oversight of gun dealers who provide guns to the perpetrators of violent crimes, and mandatory sentencing and out-of-state prison time for crimes committed with a firearm may all have had a significant impact in recent years by reducing the lethality of crimes committed, particularly by career criminals, youthful offenders, and gangs. Let us consider some of these determinants of violence and violent crime in greater depth.

A growing and strong economy and job market would have only likely affected the rate of crimes with a financial motivation, such as burglary, robbery, and auto theft. Economic improvements are not known or thought to reduce the level of violent crimes, including homicide, assault, and rape. Most studies show that a decline in unemployment of 1% is associated with a similar decline in nonviolent crime. During the 1990s unemployment decreased 2% and nonviolent crime decreased by 40%. Most studies have shown the absence of an association between the state of the economy and violent crime (e.g., in the 1960s the economy grew aggressively at the same time as violent crime did).

Another explanation for the decline in violence argues that the U.S. population aged significantly during recent decades and rates of violence decreased because older people do not tend to perpetrate violence or violent crime. However, most experts suggest that because such demographic change is a rather slow process, taking many decades and not years to affect crime rates, its impact on the recent crime drop is likely small.

A more incarceration-oriented and less lenient justice system is frequently cited as a primary cause of the recent decline in violent crimes. In the 1960s conviction rates declined and criminals who were convicted served shorter prison terms under a movement that sought to expand the rights of people accused of crimes. Eventually these practices were understood to have fostered crime and were reversed, with more criminals being locked up. Between 1980 and 2000 there was a 15-fold increase in the number of people sent to prison on drug charges, for example, and sentences, especially for violent crime, were lengthened. By 2000, more than two million people were in U.S. prisons, four times the number in 1972, with half of the increase occurring during the 1990s. Imprisonment seems to have contributed significantly, some argue for up to one-third, to the reduction in crime in recent decades. Increased use of capital punishment, however, is not likely to have meaningfully contributed to the decline because it is rarely applied for crimes other than homicide, and thus, could not affect the large decreases observed in other violent crimes. Furthermore, given the impulsive, psychopathological, and often unpremeditated nature of many violent crimes (e.g., child sexual abuse and murder among intimates), it would seem reasonable to conclude that there is some natural limit to the impact that a less lenient justice system could have on deterring certain forms of violence.

Increased numbers of police hired and deployed across the United States is often cited as having contributed to the decline in violent crime. Between 1960 and 1985 the number of police officers in the United States decreased by more than 50% relative to the number of crimes. By the 1990s this trend was reversed with extensive hiring of new police in cities across the nation. The added police seem to have acted as a crime deterrent and provided the resources needed to imprison criminals who otherwise might have escaped capture. Some have argued that the hiring of additional police accounted for up to 10% of the crime drop during the 1990s.

It is well documented that much crime is drug-related. Two-thirds of homicide and attempted homicide offenders use alcohol, drugs, or both during commission of the crime. In 2002, more than two-thirds of jail inmates who committed violent or public order offenses met the criteria for substance dependence or abuse. Approximately half (47%) of all jail inmates convicted of violent offenses were under the influence of alcohol or other drugs at the time of the offense; 42% of homicide offenders, 40% of assault offenders, 38% of robbery offenders, and 37% of sexual assault offenders were under the influence of alcohol at the time of the offense. Twenty-two percent of inmates convicted of violent offenses were under the influence of drugs at the time of the offense: 20% of homicide offenders, 18% of assault offenders, 40% of robbery offenders, and 14% of sexual assault offenders. Girls who have been sexually or physically abused are twice as likely to use drugs (30% vs. 13%) or drink (22% vs. 12%) than girls who have not been abused.

The crack cocaine epidemic has been widely seen as contributing to increasing levels of violent crime. One study found that more than 25% of homicides in New York City in 1988 were related to crack cocaine. Although crack use has not declined significantly over the past decades, profits from selling crack have plummeted. These smaller profits are thought by some to have greatly reduced the incentives for younger dealers to accept the risk associated with these narcotic sales. Support for this view comes from data showing that from 1991 to 2001 homicide rates among young Black men (who are disproportionately represented among crack dealers) decreased 48% in comparison with 30% for older Black and older White men. It has been suggested that this crash of the crack market could account for as much as 15% of the decline in crime in the 1990s.

Tougher gun laws established during the early 1990s also are cited often to explain the decrease in U.S. crime. There are enough guns in the United States such that if a gun was given to every American adult, one would likely burn through the adult population before exhausting the existing supply of guns. Approximately two-thirds of American homicides involve a gun, a level much greater than in most other industrialized nations. Because the U.S. homicide rate is much higher than in these other countries, it would seem that the easy availability of guns contributes to the high rate, which has been confirmed by prior research. But guns are not fully explanatory. In Switzerland, for example, every adult male is issued an assault rifle for militia duty and allowed to keep it at home. The result is that Switzerland has more firearms per capita than almost any nation in the world. Yet its rates of violent crime and homicide are a fraction of that of the United States. Thus, there is an element of truth in the claim of opponents of gun control that guns do not kill or cause crime, per se (these issues are discussed in greater depth in Chapter 11).

A critical difference seems to be in the effectiveness of measures used by nations to keep guns away from individuals who engage in violence. The most prominent U.S. gun control legislation in recent decades was the Brady Act of 1993, which requires a criminal check and waiting period before someone can purchase a handgun. However, economists have pointed out a fundamental conceptual flaw in the strategy underlying the law: Regulation of a legal market is virtually destined to fail when a healthy black market exists for the same product. With guns so cheap and readily available, criminals have no need to complete a firearms application and wait for approval. Studies of imprisoned felons have shown that, even before the Brady Act, only one-fifth of criminals had purchased firearms through a licensed dealer. Thus, the real-world impact of the Brady Act on criminal access to handguns and associated violence has been questioned.

Gun buy-backs, in which gun owners are invited to sell their guns to the police department for $50 or $100, are much celebrated by local media. The probability that a particular gun among the millions in the hands of the U.S. population will commit a homicide in a particular year is approximately 1 in 10,000. A typical gun buy-back program yields approximately 1,000 guns, which means that less than one-tenth of a single homicide might be prevented by a single buy-back effort, not enough to have affected the decline of U.S. violent crime in recent years. Another strategy advocated by firearm proponents is to distribute more guns but ensure that they are placed into the hands of the right people, that is, law-abiding citizens who are defending themselves from criminals. Advocates of this view further argue that concealed weapons carried by citizens will deter criminals if they suspect that their potential victims may be armed. However, studies have failed to demonstrate that right-to-carry laws actually bring down crime rates. A deterrent that has proven to be moderately effective is increasing the prison sentences for individuals caught in possession of an illegal gun.

Economist Steven Levitt has suggested that the legalization of abortion in the United States in January 1973 had an indirect yet profound impact on crime rates that manifested two decades later in the 1990s. Levitt notes that by 1980 there were 1.6 million abortions in the nation and that following *Roe v. Wade* the large increase in demand for abortions was not from middle- and upper-class women but often from unmarried teenagers from poor families. One study has shown that the typical child who went unborn in the earliest years of legalized abortion would have been 50% more likely than average to live in poverty and 60% more likely to have grown up with a single parent. Childhood poverty and a single-parent household are strong predictors of future criminal involvement. Growing up in a single-parent home approximately doubles the chance that a child will commit a crime, as does having a teenage mother. Low maternal education has been shown to be one of the most powerful factors predicting that a child will engage in future criminality.

Levitt states that "the very factors that drove millions of American women to have an abortion also seemed to predict that their children, had they been born, would have led unhappy and possibly criminal lives." He notes that in the early 1990s, just as the first cohort of children born after *Roe v. Wade* were entering their late teenage years (and a period of high criminality), the crime rate began to fall. However, this cohort was now missing the children who were at greatest risk of becoming criminals. The crime rate continued to fall, Levitt speculates, as an entire generation came of age minus the children whose mothers had not wanted them. "Legalized abortion led to less unwantedness; unwantedness leads to high crime; legalized abortion, therefore, led to less crime."

Levitt supports his theory by analyzing crime data in the five states where abortion was made legal before the Supreme Court extended abortion rights to the rest of the United States (New York, California, Washington, Alaska, and Hawaii). These early-legalizing states, in fact, saw crime begin to fall earlier than the other 45 states and the District of Columbia. Furthermore, states having the highest abortion rates in the 1970s experienced the greatest crime drops in the 1990s, whereas states with low abortion rates experienced smaller declines. No link was observed between a state's abortion rate and its crime before the late 1980s, when the first cohort affected by legalized abortion was reaching its criminal prime, another indication that *Roe v. Wade* affected subsequent crime rates. Levitt concludes: "The crime drop was, in the language of economists, an 'unintended benefit' of legalized abortion. But one need not oppose abortion on moral or religious grounds to feel shaken by the notion of a private sadness being converted into a public good."

In recent years a new and unexpected pattern of crime has appeared in the United States. Although crime rates in most large American cities remain level, homicide rates in many mid-size cities (population between one-half and one million) have increased, in a number of instances by as much as 20% per year. National police groups that survey cities across the United States have been perplexed about the cause of this shift. According to 2008 FBI data, America's most dangerous locales are not the big cities but places such as Florence, South Carolina; Charlotte–Mecklenburg, North Carolina; Kansas City, Missouri; Reading, Pennsylvania; Orlando, Florida; and Memphis, Tennessee.

Journalist Hanna Rosin interviewed law enforcement leaders in cities most affected by growing crime across the nation, and her findings implicated an important anti-poverty program. The program involved demolishing these cities' public housing projects as part of the nationwide effort to free the poor from the destructive impact of concentrated poverty. Residents were provided "Section 8" rent subsidy vouchers and encouraged to move out to new, less impoverished neighborhoods, with tenants paying 25% of their income for rent and the government paying the rest. Public housing residents all over the United States left their inner-city project apartments for new developments beyond the city core. The provision of a healthier environment, better schools, and an opportunity to live in a safe and decent home were among the program's primary objectives. This initiative resulted in the dispersion of tens of thousands of poor people into the wider metro community of many U.S. cities.

One unanticipated consequence of this noble intent was that gang leaders, who were also freed from the housing projects, adapted their recruiting efforts and operations to their new, often suburban settings. The national effort to diffuse poverty has succeeded programmatically, with the number of Americans living in neighborhoods of concentrated poverty (defined as 40% of households with incomes below the federal poverty level) having declined by 24%. But increasing numbers of the very poor now live in locations with moderate poverty rates (20%–40%) because many relocating recipients of the Section 8 vouchers tended to cluster in moderately poor neighborhoods that were already declining. Housing experts note that this pattern is not necessarily better for poor people or for cities. Some believe the impact has been to push a greater number of total neighborhoods past a tipping point at which crime explodes and other severe social problems emerge. In 2003 the Brookings Institution published a list of the 15 American cities where the number of high poverty neighborhoods had most declined, and many of these cities have become the most violent in the United States according to the FBI.

None of the experts have claimed that vouchers or any single factor has caused the increase in crime in these cities. Crime did not rise in every city where the housing projects were demolished, and diverse factors contributed to crime increasing (including unemployment, gangs, and gentrification displacing many poor people not living in the projects). Yet Rosin reports that researchers have identified a recurring pattern of crime pushing outward from inner cities as projects were closed, destabilizing cities or their surrounding areas. This seems to have been the case in Chicago, Illinois; Atlanta, Georgia; Memphis, Tennessee; and Louisville, Kentucky. New York, where the rate of violent crime has fallen dramatically, may have pushed many of its poor to New Jersey, where crime has increased in nearby cities and suburbs. Similarly, Washington, D.C., may have exported some of its crime to neighboring counties in Virginia and Maryland.

The physical redistribution of the poor may have been desirable and even necessary, but at this point in time and in retrospect many experts believe that a poorly planned process left these individuals inadequately coached and supported. The social, human, and other services of importance to the poor remained downtown while the clients were scattered all over a city, often with no convenient transportation. Despite many flaws, it now seems that the high-rise projects may have conveyed some positives, such as a sense of belonging, easy access to social, health, and human services, and an informal economy, not to mention an address for the police. Recreating outreach centers for the poor to access in new outlying neighborhoods has now assumed some urgency. It seems, however, that the projects are gone in name only, and we still do not well understand the connected problems of poverty, crime, and violence and their solution among the most vulnerable in our society.

In summary, the fact remains that no single explanation or combination of explanations adequately explains why the overall violent crime rate has decreased across the nation over these past decades. The reality is that we simply do not know why, and that reality remains disconcerting despite the good news in the declining violence statistics. Because we lack a good understanding of why violence has decreased, we cannot be confident that the decline will continue, or that violence will not rise again as quickly as it did throughout the 1970s and early 1980s. And even as we seek reassurance in the current downward trend in violence, the fact remains that America and Americans are more violent—and far more lethally violent—than any other nation or society in the industrialized world. Modest declines from the heights of this violence are welcome, but are surely no basis for complacency.

A WORLD LEADER IN VIOLENCE

Levels of American violence remain unacceptably high. As a society we share a number of myths in our common perceptions about violence in America. It is true that for most forms of violence, higher rates can be found in urban areas and particularly in cities with more than one million residents. This has averaged around three times the rate for the nation as a whole. But as noted earlier, since 1980 serious violent crime has increased in smaller cities with less than a half-million residents. Violence in America is not, as portrayed in popular culture, limited largely to young men in large cities. It is not predominantly a behavior that occurs between strangers. Indeed, most victims of violence know the perpetrator.

Violence in America varies dramatically across racial lines and has its greatest impact on ethnic-minority males, particularly those who live in urban areas. The lifetime risk of being murdered in the United States is 5–7 times greater for Black males than for White males. The disparity in these racial statistics, and how the justice system responds to the problem, is evidenced by the stunning figure that 1 of every 4 young Black men between the ages of 18 and 30 years is in jail, is awaiting trial, or is on probation. Black males are incarcerated at a per capita rate six times that of White males. Approximately 11% of all Black men ages 30–34 years were behind bars as of July 2007.

More people are in U.S. prisons today than ever before, and violence persists. As of mid-2007, 2.3 million Americans were incarcerated in U.S. prisons and jails, an all-time high. More than five million Americans are in prison or jail, or on probation and parole. This equals 2.8% of all U.S. adults. In 1995, the United States—for the first time in its history—spent more money on building prisons than it did on building universities. At present incarceration rates, 1 of every 20 U.S. residents will be confined in a state or federal prison during his or her lifetime. This represents an incarceration rate of 762 per 100,000 U.S. residents, the highest such rate in the world. By contrast, the United Kingdom's incarceration rate is 152 per 100,000 residents; the rate is 108 in Canada and 91 in France. Incarceration rates in the United States are seven times those in most European nations. In many quarters, there is a sense that the criminal justice approach, which focuses on punishing those who break the law, cannot by itself substantially address the problem.

Imprisonment of offenders, although critical to any coherent public response to violence, does not address the cyclical nature of violence—the way that it breeds itself and self-perpetuates within communities, in families, and across generations. A majority of the men and women currently in U.S. prisons are believed to have been abused at some point during their lifetimes. It could be argued that our society tends to view violence (because it is so common) with a certain fatalism, as inevitable. Community, political, and public health leaders, however, have argued that no civilized society should be so permeated by assault, homicide, rape, and child abuse. Violence in America is a social and public health crisis that demands immediate attention and corrective action.

The United States has the highest rates of violence in the industrialized world. In fairness, when considering the epidemic of civilian violence that is affecting the United States, it is important to bear in mind the world in which Americans live. The twentieth century offered a dark history of global participation in national and international violence, often of a political or ethnic nature. It has been estimated that since 1900, nation-states have executed political and military actions directly responsible for the violent or unnatural deaths of more than 100 million people. Genocide has been conducted by at least 40 nations. Since World War II, there have been at least 155 episodes of mass violence, causing in excess of 25 million deaths, many of which involved genocide against large, vulnerable populations. When viewed from this perspective, it is clear that although America is a violent society, violence is a disease affecting people the world over. (This book focuses on "interpersonal" violence typically involving few assailants and victims per incident. Our examination of violence will not consider large-scale and population-scale violence perpetrated by nations or governments in war or genocide.)

A LOVE–HATE RELATIONSHIP

America's tragedy of violence appalls us. We condemn it individually and collectively. It upsets us as individuals, as families, as communities, and as a society. Violence represents perhaps the most frustrating problem that America has ever faced as a nation. And the impact of violence goes far beyond what statistics can convey if, for example, one considers that approximately one-half of all homeless women and children in America are runaways from domestic violence, or if we consider the synergy that exists between our nation's drug and violence epidemics.

Yet, although we are aware of violence and find it unacceptable, in some ways we condone and even promote it. In the blood-and-guts realism of our information media and entertainment, from television and newspapers to the movies, children's cartoons, and video games, we seem, at some level, to have an insatiable appetite for violence. We consume violence even as it consumes us. Constant exposure has produced a new public indifference to violence. Like an overworked muscle, we hardly respond anymore to the barbaric assault on our senses. The violence of a 1970s movie seems almost comically tame compared with today's movies. Any instinctive repulsion to violence is gradually being dulled. Are we moving beyond adapting to violence by accepting it with resignation?

Many U.S. Surgeon Generals have been outspoken about violence as a national health problem and have held the view that violence in this country constitutes a public health emergency. Public health experts ask, would we be this complacent if so many Americans were being killed and made ill by an infectious disease? Or would a major research and disease-control effort have been implemented long ago? They note that although violence is not a disease in the classic sense, its impact on individual health and the public's health is as pervasive and profound as any disease. Leaders in medicine and public health have argued for years that violence prevention programs need to be established in schools, clinics, churches, and other community settings to respond to this epidemic. These programs must involve parents, educators, law enforcement personnel, social service workers, clergy, community leaders, government personnel, and health care professionals.

Criminal justice measures often have been the focus of our efforts to protect ourselves from violence. While useful, they have not been adequate. The reason is that violence does not begin in the commission of a crime or in some vague "criminal mind," but in the relationships between individuals who know each other—acquaintances, intimates, friends, and family members. These are the associations in which most violent acts occur, sometimes over serious arguments, but often enough over trivialities. Despite considerable research and inquiry, the causes of much violence remain poorly understood.

SHOCKING BUT NOT SURPRISING

Several violent events over recent decades, unusual in the extent to which they captured public attention—and in the nature of their barbarism—have focused society on the epidemic of violence in America. These include the Virginia Tech, Columbine High, and other school, campus, and lone wolf shootings; the murders of O.J. Simpson's former wife Nicole Brown and her friend Ron Goldman; the Oklahoma City bombing; the abductions and sexual assault of young girls, such as Elizabeth Smart or Jaycee Dugard; and the murder of the youngest of our children, such as Caylee Anthony. The sexual abuse of children by priests within the Catholic Church has shocked and alarmed the American public. The homicidal attack on a federal government building in Oklahoma City, in the heartland of the nation, provoked fear, outrage, and grief among many Americans at the sudden loss of so many lives and still, 15 years later, challenges and haunts our sense of public safety.

Without diminishing the magnitude of this tragedy, Americans should appreciate that deaths by violence in Oklahoma are neither infrequent nor unusual. Americans have become the world's greatest harvesters of homegrown civilian violence. In 2008, there were 16,272 victims of homicide in the United States. This figure has declined considerably since its peak in recent decades, but the number of American homicides is still equivalent to 96 Oklahoma City bombings per year, or one every fourth day. Our nation's homicide rate is equivalent to more than five 9/11 events every year, one almost every other month, year after year. And there is little to the notion that such things should not or do not occur in peaceful places like Oklahoma City. In 2008, there were 212 homicides statewide in Oklahoma, 1.3% of the national homicide total in a state with 1.2% of the nation's population.

The fact that the motive for the Oklahoma homicides was ostensibly political makes them different only in quality from the thousands of other violent deaths and losses suffered by American families each year. Although it may be arguable the extent to which political alienation contributed to these attacks, their tragedy should not be divorced from the greater context of violence in contemporary American life. Terrorism is homicide disguised as a rational process, but homicide it is. Just like other forms of homicide, terrorism is viewed as a means to an end—a political if not interpersonal or material one.

Americans should not delude themselves into thinking of these domestic outbreaks of violence as isolated, self-limited crises with an eventual resolution. Terror and violence are happening all the time in America, further down the visibility spectrum and with far less notoriety, but with no less human suffering. Rape, school violence, child abuse, intimate violence—these are acts of terror, albeit apolitical ones. Sadly, beating wives and abusing children have become an integral, everyday part of the American social and psychological landscape. We are not much shocked by them anymore. Yet this crisis in American life is much broader, deeper, more pernicious and resistant to resolution than any single terror attack, school shooting, raped child, or double murder, however despicable were these acts.

Underlying the sensational terror at Columbine High School, Virginia Tech, or Oklahoma City; the relationship between Nicole Brown and her former husband; or the child sex abuse crisis in the Catholic Church is the mundane but profoundly damaging violence that occurs in millions of American homes and innumerable schools and communities every single day of the year. Absent the relentless violence, alienation, and anger that permeate so many dimensions of American life, these events never could have occurred. It is unlikely that the perpetrators of this bombing, various school attacks, and other infamous murders would have been impelled to such violent acts without having been exposed in some way to thousands of acts of brutality over the course of their lives.

These infamously celebrated episodes or spasms of violence emerge as just a few swells within the endless tide of American violence. We deceive ourselves by imagining that no relationship exists between the murdered individuals at Columbine High, in Virginia and Oklahoma City, and the hundreds of thousands of women who are raped, the million children who are abused or neglected, and the millions of other violent victimizations that occur every year in the United States. They are all, equally, the victims of violence, America's deadliest epidemic.

FOR FURTHER INFORMATION ABOUT VIOLENCE

Appendix 1 at the back of the book provides a state-by-state website listing of compensation and assistance programs for victims of violence and crime. You may find assistance by contacting one of your state programs. Appendix 2 is a bibliography for further reading on each of the violence topics discussed in this volume, organized chapter by chapter. The following websites present general information about many forms of violence in the United States.

USEFUL INTERNET WEBSITES

American Medical Association: www.ama-assn.org
American Psychological Association: www.apa.org
American Public Health Association: www.apha.org
Bureau of Justice Assistance: www.ojp.usdoj.gov/BJA
Bureau of Justice Statistics: www.ojp.usdoj.gov/bjs
Center for Substance Abuse Prevention: http://prevention.samhsa.gov
Center for Substance Abuse Treatment: http://csat.samhsa.gov
Centers for Disease Control and Prevention: www.cdc.gov
Centers for Disease Control Division of Violence Prevention in the National Center for Injury Prevention and Control: www.cdc.gov/ncipc/dvp/dvp.htm
Coalition for Juvenile Justice: www.juvjustice.org
Communities Against Violence Network: www.cavnet.org
Community Anti-Drug Coalition of America: www.cadca.org
Federal Bureau of Investigation: www.fbi.gov
Federal Judicial Center: www.fjc.gov

Institute on Domestic Violence in the African American Community:
www.dvinstitute.org

Institute on Violence, Abuse and Trauma: www.ivatcenters.org

Joint Center on Violence and Victim Studies: www.washburn.edu/ce/jcvvs

National Alliance for Drug Endangered Children: www.nationaldec.org

National Alliance to End Sexual Violence: www.naesv.org

National Association of Crime Victim Compensation Boards: www.nacvcb.org

National Center for Posttraumatic Stress Disorder: www.ncptsd.va.gov

National Center for Victims of Crime: www.ncvc.org

National Clearinghouse for Alcohol and Drug Information: http://ncadi.samhsa.
gov

National Coalition Against Domestic Violence: www.ncadv.org

National Consortium on Violence Research: www.ncovr.heinz.cmu.edu

National Crime Prevention Council: www.ncpc.org

National Crime Victim Law Institute: www.lclark.edu/org/ncvli

National Crime Victims Research and Treatment Center: www.musc.edu/ncvc

National Criminal Justice Reference Service: www.ncjrs.gov

National Institute on Alcohol Abuse and Alcoholism: www.niaaa.nih.gov

National Institute on Drug Abuse: www.drugabuse.gov

National Organization of Parents of Murdered Children, Inc.: www.pomc.com

National Organization for Victim Assistance: www.trynova.org

National Resource Center on Domestic Violence: www.nrcdv.org

National Victim Assistance Academy: www.ojp.usdoj.gov/ovc/assist/vaa.htm

National Women's Health Information Center: www.womenshealth.gov

Office for Victims of Crime: www.ovc.gov

Office on Violence Against Women: www.usdoj.gov/ovw

Post Trauma Resources: www.posttrauma.com

Uniform Crime Reports: www.fbi.gov/ucr/ucr.htm

U.S. Department of Justice, Office of Justice Programs, Bureau of Justice Statistics:
www.ojp.usdoj.gov/bjs

Victims' Assistance Legal Organization (VALOR): www.valor-national.org

Victim Assistance Online: www.vaonline.org

Victim Law: www.victimlaw.info

Violence Policy Center: www.vpc.org

Voices for America's Children: www.childadvocacy.org

Witness Justice: www.witnessjustice.org

Women's Justice Center: www.law.pace.edu/bwjc

CHAPTER 2

Physical and Emotional Abuse of Children

- What is child abuse?
- Are there different kinds of child abuse?
- What is emotional child abuse?
- What is shaken baby syndrome?
- When was child abuse recognized?
- How common is child abuse?
- What are the signs that a child is being abused?
- What are the long-term consequences of child abuse?
- Does abuse kill children?
- Who perpetrates child abuse?
- Which children are abused?
- Are only young children abused?
- In what situations and why do people abuse children?
- Is child abuse falsely alleged or misdiagnosed?
- How can child abuse be prevented?
- What do I do if I learn that my child is being abused?
- What do I do if my spouse is abusing my child?
- What do I do if I am abusing my child?
- What do I do if I am a victim of abuse?
- What happens after child abuse is disclosed?
- Where can I get more information and help?

WHAT IS CHILD ABUSE?

The Centers for Disease Control and Prevention defines child abuse as any act or series of acts of commission or omission by a parent or other caregiver that results in harm, potential harm, or threat of harm to a child. The physical or mental injury is typically inflicted in a non-accidental manner. Child abuse is a general term and includes four categories of violence: physical abuse; psychological or emotional abuse; sexual abuse, assault, or exploitation; and neglect.

A common element in all forms of abuse is the failure of a caretaker to provide responsible care for a child. The mandatory reporting systems for child abuse in many jurisdictions actually limit abuse to acts committed only by family household members or other caretakers. Child abuse may or may not involve the actions of strangers or acquaintances of the child. There is no standard definition of child abuse across the United States. Each state has created its own legal definition.

Child abuse can involve acts of commission or omission. Acts of commission are deliberate and intentional. However, harm to a child may or may not be the intended consequence. Intentionality only applies to the caregiver's acts and not to the consequences of those acts. For example, a caregiver may intend to hit a child as punishment (e.g., striking a child is not accidental or unintentional), but the intent was not to cause the child a broken arm. Physical abuse, sexual abuse, and psychological abuse all involve acts of commission. Acts of omission involve the failure to provide for a child's basic physical, emotional, or educational needs, or to protect a child from harm or potential harm. Similar to acts of commission, harm to a child may or may not be the intended consequence. Failure to provide for a child physically, emotionally, and educationally; to ensure medical and dental care; and to provide supervision and prevent exposure to violent environments all could result in child abuse through acts of omission.

Neglect is thought to be the most common of the four types of child abuse and can be the most life-threatening to the child. Features of neglect include the failure of a caretaker to provide basic shelter, medical and dental care, supervision, or emotional support to a child. Failure to provide adequate nutrition, hygienic care, and education may also occur with child neglect. Physical child abuse involves inflicting injury to a child through excessive force or forcing a child to engage in physically harmful activities. Child homicide or fatal child abuse may sometimes result from chronic and sustained physical assault, an intense assault, or shaken baby syndrome (discussed later).

Child sexual abuse is defined as any sexual contact between a child and an adult, or if there is a sufficient age difference, between juveniles. This definition includes many inappropriate behaviors, for example, not only a father having incestuous sexual intercourse with his daughter but also an individual exposing himself sexually in front of a child. Most forms of sexual abuse fall between these two behaviors. The major categories of child sexual abuse include incest, pedophilia (literally "love of children," often involving fondling but which may include penetration), exhibitionism, molestation, statutory rape and rape, child prostitution, and child pornography.

There is imprecision in these definitions. In many states, for example, the term "family" has been defined to include relatives who do not live regularly with the child. As in most other forms of violence, child abuse is characterized by much denial, in this case not only at the individual or family level but also more generally across society. The lack of a widely accepted definition of child abuse creates obstacles to understanding the nature of this problem and developing appropriate and effective efforts to prevent it.

ARE THERE DIFFERENT KINDS OF CHILD ABUSE?

Yes. As described earlier, there are several different forms of child abuse. Child abuse can include physical abuse and assault of a victim child. It may also include neglect or failure to provide for the essential needs and welfare of a child. Some experts have described educational neglect as a form of child maltreatment. Educational neglect includes permitting chronic school truancy or other inattention to a child's educational needs. Child sexual abuse and exploitation are common forms of child abuse and may coexist with other forms. Emotional abuse of children occurs when they are placed in severely stressful and psychologically damaging circumstances.

Child abuse is, therefore, a diverse problem in which a child victim can be the target of multiple different forms of abuse at once or, as is more usual, the target of a single form over a long period. Several forms of child maltreatment may occur with other forms of violence within a single family. Child abuse and neglect frequently occur with other forms of family violence, including spouse abuse.

WHAT IS EMOTIONAL CHILD ABUSE?

Emotional abuse involves coercive, demeaning, or very distant behavior by a parent or other caretaker that interferes with a child's normal psychological or social development. Emotional abuse involves acts, or the failure to act, on the part of parents and other caregivers that may cause serious emotional, cognitive, or behavioral problems in a child. These acts, or inattention and indifference to emotional needs, negatively affect the well-being of a child. Emotional neglect includes inadequate nurturance or affection, allowance of maladaptive behavior, and other inattention to emotional and developmental needs.

Emotional abuse can involve several different kinds of traumatic acts or attitudes on the part of parents and caregivers, including rejecting a child's worth or the legitimacy of the child's needs, isolating a child from usual social experiences, and making the child feel alone in the world. Imposing unreasonable parental demands on a child or creating unrealistically high objectives or standards of achievement can be emotionally abusive. Terrorizing the child by frightening, bullying, and verbally assaulting him/her is emotionally abusive.

In addition, ignoring a child's need for developmental and emotional stimulation can compromise that individual's growth to healthy adulthood. Compelling children to engage in destructive and antisocial behaviors has a corrupting impact that makes the child unfit for normal social experiences and is another form of emotional abuse. The frequency of emotional abuse is not well measured. Different forms of child abuse may occur together, and the child who is physically or sexually abused or neglected is, almost by definition, harmed psychologically.

WHAT IS SHAKEN BABY SYNDROME?

Shaken baby (or shaken impact) syndrome is an injury to an infant, a toddler, or a young child resulting from being shaken violently. Shaken baby syndrome can occur when a child receives as few as three rapid shakes; an impact to the head is not necessary (although frequently occurs). Injuries can include brain damage, blindness, seizures, speech and learning disorders, including mental retardation, cerebral palsy, and damage to neck vertebrae and the spinal cord resulting in severe motor dysfunction, paralysis, and death.

A baby's head is 15% of its body weight (compared with only 2%–3% in an adult) and cannot be supported independently by an infant. Furthermore, an infant's brain tissue is softer and the protective tissue that surrounds the brain only begins to form at birth. The blood vessels around the brain are more susceptible to tearing than in older children or adults. Even when caregivers, well-intentioned parents, and babysitters become angry and lose control, this serious form of child abuse can occur. Caregivers may be inadequately prepared for parenting or under stress and cannot deal with the frustrations of parenting. When enraged, these parents shake the infant and can cause such injuries.

Neurological signs and symptoms range from minor (irritability, lethargy, tremors, vomiting) to major (seizures, coma, stupor, death). These neurological changes are due to destruction of brain cells secondary to trauma, lack of oxygen to the brain cells, and swelling of the brain. Extensive retinal hemorrhages in one or both eyes are found in the majority of these cases. The classic triad of subdural hematoma (bleeding on the brain), brain swelling, and retinal hemorrhages are accompanied in some, but not all, cases by bruising of the part of the body used as a "handle" for shaking. Fractures of the long bones or the ribs may also be seen in some cases.

Approximately 20% of cases are fatal in the first few days after injury, and the majority of the survivors are left with handicaps ranging from mild (learning disorders, behavioral changes) to moderate and severe (profound mental and developmental disability, paralysis, blindness, inability to eat, or life in a permanent vegetative state). There are no firm statistics regarding the actual incidence of the syndrome because there are no central reporting registries to collect these data. However, estimates have been made on the basis of clinical experience and extrapolated from hospitals caring for children. Estimates range from annual U.S. figures as low as 600 cases per year to as high as 1,400 cases. Shaken baby syndrome accounts for an estimated 10%–12% of all deaths due to abuse or neglect. It is thought to be the most common cause of mortality and accounts for the most long-term disability caused by physical child abuse in infants and young children.

Researchers have found that the age of the victims ranges from the newborn period to four years. The majority of incidents occur before the infant's first birthday, and the average age of victims is 3–8 months. Sixty-three percent of victims are male. The average age of perpetrators is 22 years, 75% are male, 81% have no history of child abuse, and 75% have no history of substance abuse. The perpetrator was one of the natural parents of the victim in 50% of incidents, the biological father in 37% of incidents, and boyfriends of the mother in 21% of incidents. The perpetrator was the mother in 12% of instances and a female child care provider in 17% of instances.

WHEN WAS CHILD ABUSE RECOGNIZED?

Child abuse was first recognized more than 100 years ago. However, widespread action to prevent abuse and treat victims has been slow to emerge. The first victim of child abuse was recorded in the United States in 1874. Within a year, New York State had passed the first child abuse law in the nation, and the Society for the Prevention of Cruelty to Children was founded. Almost a century later, the medical profession first offered a term to describe child abuse. Dr. C. Henry Kempe and colleagues described "the battered child syndrome" in a 1962 medical journal article. The article had a profound effect and generated many newspaper reports and magazine articles, and the topic of child abuse was soon a recurrent theme on television medical programs.

It was not until the late 1960s, however, that all U.S. states had child abuse reporting laws in place. In 1974, legislation required the states to report all forms of maltreatment, including neglect and sexual abuse, in addition to physical abuse.

Yet still today many states continue to have shortages in staff and resources in the area of child protection services, and there is a need for improved coordination among health, social service, law enforcement, and criminal justice agencies responding to incidents of child abuse. Child abuse remains a largely hidden epidemic among the nation's children.

HOW COMMON IS CHILD ABUSE?

More than three million reports of child abuse are made every year in the United States; however, those reports can include multiple children. In 2007, approximately 5.8 million children were involved in an estimated 3.2 million child abuse reports and allegations. An estimated 794,000 children were victims of maltreatment during 2007 at a rate of 10.6 children per 1,000. Furthermore, 1,760 children died in the United States in 2007 from abuse and neglect (a rate of 2.35 deaths per 100,000 children). In 2005 there were 899,000 victims of child abuse or neglect and 1,460 fatalities. Every 13 seconds an American child is reported as abused or neglected. Each day more than 2,000 children become victims of abuse or neglect. Between 2% and 3% of the total population under the age of 18 years may be abused. One study using self and parental reports estimated that approximately 8,755,000 children are victims of child maltreatment each year. This means that more than one-seventh of children between the ages of 2 and 17 years experience some form of maltreatment, including physical abuse, sexual abuse, psychological or emotional abuse, neglect, and custodial interference or family abduction.

A 2008 national youth survey found that more than one in ten children surveyed (10.2%) suffered some form of abuse or maltreatment (including physical abuse other than sexual assault, psychological or emotional abuse, child neglect, and custodial interference) during the past year and that approximately one-fifth (18.6%) experienced some form of abuse during their lifetimes. Both the past year and lifetime rates of exposure to abuse increased as children grew older, particularly for children aged 10 years and older; 1 in 6 children aged 14–17 years (16.6%) suffered abuse during the past year, and approximately 1 in 3 children (32.1%) suffered abuse during their lifetimes. Patterns of child abuse were similar for girls and boys, except for psychological or emotional abuse, for which the incidence was slightly higher for girls than for boys. Rates of sexual assault by a known adult (not limited to caregivers) were also higher for girls than for boys.

One study estimated that during 2007, 59% of victims experienced neglect, 10.8% were physically abused, 7.6% were sexually abused, 4.2% were psychologically maltreated, less than 1% were medically neglected, and 13.1%

were victims of multiple maltreatments. In addition, 4.2% of victims experienced other types of maltreatment, such as abandonment, threats of harm to the child, or congenital drug addiction. Another study reported that 14% of U.S. children experienced some form of child maltreatment. Of these, 48% were victims of physical abuse, 8% were victims of sexual abuse, 22% were victims of child neglect, and 75% were victims of emotional abuse. Approximately one-sixth to one-eighth of all maltreatment reports involve sexual assault, and 150,000–200,000 sexual abuse reports are filed annually in the United States. Child sexual abuse is discussed in greater depth in Chapter 3.

Over the course of the 1980s, as awareness and reporting of child abuse increased, the number of child abuse reports increased by approximately 200%. It is unclear from this, however, that the actual occurrence of child abuse had increased. Reporting can increase despite a stable incidence as social awareness is heightened by greater coverage of child abuse in the media.

Child homicide is among the top 5 causes of death in childhood and accounts for approximately 5% of all deaths among individuals aged less than 18 years. Approximately five children die every day as a result of child abuse. Research indicates that very young children (age four years or less) are the most frequent victims of child fatalities. The majority of infant victims are killed by parents and relatives. Remarkably, approximately 40% of the families involved were previously reported for child abuse.

Data for 2007 show that children younger than 4 years accounted for more than three-quarters (75.7%) of fatalities, and of these, children younger than 1 year accounted for 42.2% of fatality victims. These children are the most vulnerable for many reasons, including their dependency, small size, and inability to defend themselves (see earlier discussion on shaken baby syndrome). An estimated 1,200–2,000 childhood deaths occur each year as a result of maltreatment. Because deaths by abuse and neglect may be confused with natural causes that can occur at the same time as and perhaps as a result of abuse (e.g., pneumonia or malnutrition), some experts have suggested that the number of children dying of maltreatment in the United States may be as high as 5,000 per year. It is estimated that between 60% and 85% of child fatalities resulting from maltreatment are not recorded as such on death certificates.

The frequency of reporting abuse to protective services is greatly below the actual incidence. Studies have shown that perhaps only one in seven cases of severe physical abuse is reported. Several factors can influence whether a case of child abuse is reported or not. The socioeconomic class and race of the perpetrator partly determine whether a particular incident of abuse is reported. Abuse occurring in Black and Hispanic families is more likely to be reported than that in

White families, and those with the lowest incomes have higher rates of reporting than families earning $25,000 or more per year.

Many people admit to witnessing child abuse and doing nothing about it. The reasons for not reporting abuse include not knowing which agency to call and misconceptions regarding what will occur once a report of known or suspected abuse is made to the police or a child protective services agency. Many people incorrectly believe that by law abused children must be removed from their homes immediately, which is actually the least likely outcome. The public also generally believes that child abuse cannot be reported anonymously. In fact, in most states the reporter does not need to provide his/her name. Concerns also exist that the persons reported for abuse are entitled to know who made the report, when in reality they are not.

Child abuse, particularly fatal child abuse, has challenged the stereotype that violence in the home affects only poor or otherwise disadvantaged families. Child abuse occurs at all levels of society. Neglect and physical abuse increase in frequency with greater poverty, but may be found in the highest income homes as well. The frequency of sexual abuse is fairly constant across all income groups. One in ten parents has admitted to using severe violence with their children, including hitting, kicking, beating, threatening, or using knives or firearms. One survey found that 41% of responding parents reported having spanked or hit their child during the prior 12 months, 38% admitted having sworn at or insulted their child, and 51% indicated that they had failed to meet their child's emotional needs. Two percent of respondents admitted kicking, biting, or punching their child, whereas 6% said they had hit their child with an object.

One-fifth to one-third of all women report experiencing some form of child sexual abuse during their childhood, most often perpetrated by an adult male. In one study, 27% of women and 16% of men reported a history of child sexual abuse. This would suggest that up to 38 million adult Americans were sexually abused as children. The majority of the perpetrators were known to the victims, and one-third were family members. In less than one-third of all instances was the abuse perpetrated by a stranger. One-third of victims never reported the abuse and live with the history of abuse as a secret throughout their adulthood. Some experts believe that perhaps one-fifth of all Americans have been the victims of child sexual abuse.

The direct cost of child abuse and neglect in the United States totals more than $24 billion annually (including law enforcement, judicial system, child welfare, and health care costs). When indirect costs are considered, such as special education, mental health and health care, juvenile delinquency, lost productivity, and adult criminality, the figure increases to more than $94 billion annually in 2001 dollars.

The estimated annual cost resulting from child abuse and neglect in the United States for 2007 was 104 billion.

WHAT ARE THE SIGNS THAT A CHILD IS BEING ABUSED?

Victims of child abuse may have a wide variety of physical signs and symptoms, or in some circumstances, very few. These can range from broken bones, bruises, lacerations, and serious injuries that require hospitalization to very subtle manifestations. The trauma apparent on the child's body is often inconsistent with the explanation given by the parent or caregiver. A sign of possible abuse is that the story of the parent or caregiver changes with each retelling or involves an incident that was unwitnessed, such as a fall or hot water scalding of a child in a bath while the caretaker "stepped out for a moment."

Often there are multiple wounds in different stages of healing. There may also be welts in the shape or pattern of a recognizable object. These features may occur in combination with a failure of a child to grow and evidence of chronic malnutrition. A child may have dropped off the normal curve of growth by weight and height and fall near the lowest 5%–10% of his or her age group. There may be unexplained injuries to the teeth or mouth. A child may present with two black eyes and the parent reporting that there was only a single accidental blow or fall. In some instances children may have burns or evidence of poisoning.

Unusual patterns of bruising may be apparent in children who have been abused. For example, a bruise around the sides of the mouth and continuing along the cheeks may have been left by a gag. Bruises of various colors indicate they are in different stages of healing, and this suggests a long-term history of injury not consistent with a single fall or other accident as claimed by a parent. Blistering and swelling of the skin may occur around the wrist of a child who has been tied up, and over the long term, this may cause lasting changes to the pigment of the skin. Bite marks may be found on a child as well. Loop or cord marks on the back and buttocks may indicate that a child has been whipped with an electrical cord or a belt.

Several fingers may leave their impression as half-inch parallel columns on the face of a child who has been slapped repeatedly. Children who have been immersed in hot water will have typical burn patterns that are sharply segmented according to what parts of the body did or did not enter the water. Scalding from splashing hot liquids can appear anywhere on the body but is more common on the torso. Cigarette and cigar burns may be observed. Hair-pulling is a common form of abuse and may result in an area of traumatic baldness.

Broken ribs in the absence of major trauma such as a car crash are suspicious, as are fractures of the long bones of the legs or arms. Similarly, skull fractures after what are reported as short-distance falls may actually have occurred as a result of child abuse. Other injuries, such as to the organs of the abdomen and chest, may only be detected by a physician and may require diagnostic radiology.

In child sexual abuse, bruising and tearing of the genitals or the anus may be evident, and the child may complain of pain in these areas. A child may have inappropriate interest or knowledge of sexual acts. Nightmares and bed-wetting may occur. There may be fear of a particular person or family member (the abuser).

Neglect may be evident in a child as poor personal hygiene or clothing that is inappropriate to the weather. A neglected child may show extreme hunger. Victims of neglect often appear to have little or no parental or other supervision.

The psychological signs of abuse can be profound. Children who are the victims of abuse may be socially and emotionally withdrawn or apathetic. They may suffer from acute anxiety attacks, stress, and nightmares. Depression is not uncommon in victims. Bed-wetting, thumb sucking, and other forms of regressive behavior may be evident. Abused children may have trouble forming social relationships with adults and other children in the home or at school and may become antisocial. Often these children will begin to deteriorate in school performance and have little interest in recreational activities. Problems at school may increase, and the child may be unable to concentrate. Eating disorders, hypochondria, hostility, and destructive and self-destructive behaviors may occur in victimized children. Emotional extremes among victims are common, with excessive or no crying and behavior that is very aggressive or passive, highly fearful or fearless.

A child who has been victimized by abuse often will not be forthcoming in reporting abuse. Children typically experience shame or fear of reprisal from the abuser. Abusers may tell children that if they report the abuse they will be killed or otherwise hurt, or that their family may be harmed by the abuser. Inappropriate fear of adults may indicate that a child is a victim of child abuse.

WHAT ARE THE LONG-TERM CONSEQUENCES OF CHILD ABUSE?

Child abuse can produce long-term effects on an abused child. It has been estimated that every year 160,000 children suffer serious or life-threatening injuries as a result of child abuse. Approximately 15% of victimized children suffer from permanent physical abnormalities inflicted by abuse. Infants and younger children are the most likely to be afflicted with serious or life-threatening injuries resulting from child abuse.

Intracranial injury is the most important cause of morbidity and mortality in abused children. Children may experience severe or fatal head trauma. Nonfatal consequences of abusive head trauma include varying degrees of visual impairment (including blindness), motor impairment (including cerebral palsy), and cognitive impairments. Serious injury to the brain can occur without any evidence of external injury. Violent shaking of a child or the impact of a blunt object on the head can tear veins within the brain and create hemorrhages.

Scalds and burns of children can result in permanent disfiguring of the face and body and restrictions of the limbs and fingers. Cigarette and electrical burns may cause long-term scarring.

Direct injury to the eyes can result in hemorrhages and detachments of the retina, dislocation of the lens of the eye, and rupture of the eye globe. Blunt trauma to the chest and abdomen can seriously damage the internal organs, including the heart, liver, and spleen, and can cause internal hemorrhages. Hitting a child's back can injure the kidneys.

Abuse during infancy or early childhood can cause important regions of the brain to form and function improperly with long-term consequences on cognitive, language, and emotional development, as well as mental health. Seriously abused and neglected children suffer permanent neurological and physical damage, and may never progress to normal milestones in their development. These children may be unable to socialize normally with adults or other children. Their development of language, cognitive, and physical skills can be seriously impaired.

In addition to physical disabilities resulting from bone fractures and cognitive impairment resulting from brain damage, child abuse causes long-term psychological and emotional problems. One study found that as many as 80% of young adults who had been abused met the diagnostic criteria for at least 1 psychiatric disorder at age 21 years. These young adults exhibited many problems, including depression, anxiety, eating disorders, and suicide attempts. The stress of chronic abuse may cause a hyperarousal response in certain areas of the brain, which can result in hyperactivity, sleep disturbances, and anxiety. It also makes victims more vulnerable to post-traumatic stress disorder; conduct disorder; and learning, attention, and memory difficulties.

Children who have been physically abused are usually more aggressive with their peers than children who have not been abused. They may be affected by chronic fear and anxiety and an inability to manage even moderate levels of stress. A very high percentage (perhaps as many as 80%) of juveniles arrested for acts of delinquency have histories of child abuse and neglect. They also have more difficult interpersonal relationships and a higher frequency of depression. Experts believe that every child who is abused sustains lasting emotional and learning problems. Research has shown that abused youth were less likely to have graduated from high school and 25% more likely to experience teen pregnancy.

Early child maltreatment can have a negative effect on the ability of both men and women to establish and maintain healthy intimate relationships in adulthood. Abused adolescents are three times less likely to practice safe sex, putting them at greater risk for sexually transmitted diseases (including HIV/AIDS). Adults who were sexually abused as children have problems with sexual arousal and functioning. It is estimated that at least 30% of adults who were abused as children in turn mistreat their own children.

Children who experience maltreatment are at increased risk for adverse health effects and behaviors as adults, including smoking, alcoholism, drug abuse, eating disorders, severe obesity, suicide, sexual promiscuity, and certain chronic diseases. Those with a history of child abuse and neglect are 1.5 times more likely to use illicit drugs in middle adulthood. Children who have been sexually abused are 2.5 times more likely to abuse alcohol and 3.8 times more likely to become addicted to drugs. More than 60% of people in U.S. drug rehabilitation centers report being abused or neglected as a child.

In 2000 a study of 1,575 individuals found that those who were abused or neglected during childhood scored lower on IQ tests, held more menial and unskilled jobs, and were 1.6 times more likely to commit crimes as adults, to have attempted suicide, and to have developed antisocial personality disorders. Related research published in 2009 found that children who are punished corporally by parents scored five points lower in standardized intelligence tests.

Studies have found abused and neglected children to be at least 25% more likely to experience problems such as delinquency, teen pregnancy, low academic achievement, and drug use. A National Institute of Justice study indicated that being abused or neglected as a child increased the likelihood of arrest as a juvenile by 59%. Abuse also increased the likelihood of adult arrest for criminal behavior by 28% and of a person perpetrating violent crime by 30%. Fourteen percent of all men and 37% of all women in U.S. prisons were abused as children.

DOES ABUSE KILL CHILDREN?

Yes. The National Child Abuse and Neglect Data System defines "child fatality" as the death of a child caused by an injury resulting from abuse or neglect, or where abuse or neglect was a contributing factor. In 2007, 1,760 children ages 0–17 years died of abuse and neglect (rate of 2.35 per 100,000 children). Of these, children younger than 1 year accounted for 42.2% of fatalities, and 76% or more deaths occurred among children younger than 4 years. These children are the most vulnerable for many reasons, including their dependency, small size, and inability to defend themselves. Thirteen percent of fatalities were among 4- to 7-year-olds,

5% were among 8- to 11-year-olds, 5% were among 12- to 15-year-olds, and 2% were among 16- to 17-year-olds. Forty-one percent of child abuse deaths occurred among non-Hispanic White children, 26% occurred among Black children, and 17% occurred among Hispanic children. With the exception of 2005, the number and rate of fatalities have been increasing over the past 5 years.

In 2007, slightly more than one-third of fatalities (35.2%) were caused by multiple forms of maltreatment. Neglect accounted for 34.1%, and physical abuse accounted for 26.4%. Medical neglect accounted for 1.2% of fatalities. One or both parents were responsible for 70% of child abuse or neglect fatalities. More than one-quarter (27.1%) of these fatalities were perpetrated by the mother acting alone. Child fatalities with unknown perpetrators accounted for 16.4% of the total.

Fatal child abuse may involve repeated abuse over a period of time (e.g., battered child syndrome) or a single, impulsive incident (e.g., drowning, suffocating, or shaking an infant). In cases of fatal neglect, the child's death resulted not from what a caregiver did but from a caregiver's failure to act. The neglect may be chronic (e.g., extended malnourishment) or acute (e.g., an infant drowning after being left unsupervised in the bathtub).

Many researchers and practitioners believe child fatalities caused by abuse and neglect still are greatly underreported and misclassified or attributed to other, natural, or accidental causes of death. Studies in Nevada and Colorado have estimated that as many as 50%–60% of child deaths resulting from abuse or neglect are not recorded as such.

The Centers for Disease Control and Prevention reported in 1997 that American children are five times more likely to be victims of homicide than those in the rest of the industrialized world. Homicide is one of the top 5 causes of childhood death in the United States, and the homicide rate for children under the age of 15 years tripled between 1950 and 1993. Homicide accounted for 5% of all childhood deaths up to the age of 18 years. The number of homicides of children under age five years increased through the mid-1990s but then declined through 2005. Rates have remained stable or declined for all racial groups.

Victims of fatal child abuse are more likely to come from families with parents or caregivers who are young (under 20 years of age). The younger the child, the greater the risk for infanticide. Black and other non-White male children are usually at the highest risk. Most of the homicides that occur in early childhood are caused by battering. However, the percentage of deaths caused by firearms increases with age, and by age 15 years, the pattern of childhood homicide is dominated by firearms and the method of death reflects the adult pattern. Homicides involving victims under age 12 years are largely perpetrated by parents or caretakers, and those involving victims over age 14 years are perpetrated by friends, acquaintances, or gangs. Between 1976 and 2005, a parent was the perpetrator of most homicides in children under age 5 years—31% were killed by fathers, 29% were killed by mothers, 23% were killed by male acquaintances, 7% were killed by other relatives, and 3% were killed by strangers. Most of the children killed were male, and most of the offenders were male.

No single health, social service, or justice system exists to track and comprehensively assess deaths due to child abuse and neglect. It is not clear where the responsibility for review of cases of fatal child abuse lies. Many jurisdictions now use child death review teams to assess the causes of death and to investigate suspicious cases. Well-designed and properly organized child fatality review teams can help to define the underlying nature and scope of fatalities due to child abuse and neglect. The child fatality review process assists in identifying risk factors that may assist prevention professionals, such as those engaged in home visiting and parenting education, to prevent future deaths. In addition, teams are demonstrating effectiveness in translating review findings into action by partnering with child welfare and other child health and safety groups.

WHO PERPETRATES CHILD ABUSE?

Child abuse occurs at every socioeconomic level, across ethnic and cultural lines, within all religious denominations, and at all levels of education. The caretakers who most commonly abuse children are the child's biological parents (80% of incidents). However, stepparents, adoptive parents, foster parents, grandparents, siblings, other relatives, babysitters, teachers, or anyone with regular access to the household and taking care of a child may be a perpetrator of abuse. In 2007 more women (56%) were perpetrators of all forms of child abuse. This pattern may be associated with the fact that mothers more often have primary child caretaking responsibilities, especially in single-parent households. Approximately 39% of victims were abused by their mother acting alone, and 18% by their father acting alone. Another 17% were abused by both parents.

The racial distribution of perpetrators was similar to the race of their victims during 2007. Approximately one-half (48.5%) of perpetrators were White, 19% were Black, and one-fifth were Hispanic. The median age of perpetrators was 30 years for women and 33 years for men. Of the women who were perpetrators, 45% were younger than 30 years, compared with one-third of the men. Approximately 61% of all perpetrators were found to have neglected children. Approximately 13% were associated with more than 1 type of maltreatment. Ten percent physically abused children, and 7.1% sexually abused children.

Victims of physical and sexual abuse, compared with victims of neglect and medical neglect, were more likely to have been victimized by a male parent acting alone. In cases of sexual abuse, more than half (56%) of victims were abused by male parents, male relatives, or other males. Ninety percent of child sexual abuse victims know the perpetrator in some way; 68% were abused by family members.

Approximately 30% of abused and neglected children will later abuse their own children, and many abusers were themselves victims of abuse during childhood. This is a vicious cycle of violence, in which abused children become abusers and victims of violence become perpetrators of violence. The most significant predictor of whether a battered woman will physically abuse her child is whether she was abused by her mother (and not whether she has been battered by her partner).

Abusive parents are often individuals with low self-esteem. They may have become parents at a very young age, and, not uncommonly, they are single parents. Abusive parents tend to have many dependents. As a result of their youth and inexperience, they may possess inadequate knowledge of how to provide care for a child and are not mature enough to assume responsibility for a child's welfare. Substance abuse and mental health problems such as depression are more common among parents who abuse their children.

An episode of child abuse typically can be traced to some triggering or precipitating event, such as a family crisis or some act by the child. Child abuse perpetrators frequently appear to be in a period of acute or chronic stress resulting from unemployment, low income, a family death, drug/alcohol abuse, chronic health and mental health problems, or inadequate housing and crowded living conditions. Abuse may occur after a difficult pregnancy. Perpetrators often lack social support and are isolated socially. Families who do not have nearby friends, relatives, and other social support are also at risk.

Parents' lack of understanding of children's needs, child development, and parenting skills may increase the risk of perpetrating child abuse. Parental characteristics such as young age, low education, single parenthood, large number of dependent children, and low income are thought to contribute to the risk of abuse. Unrelated transient caregivers in the home (e.g., mother's male partner) may also increase risk.

Families in whom child abuse occurs tend to tolerate or condone corporal (physical) punishment as a method for shaping the behavior of a child. Abusive parents make unreasonable demands of children and often hold unrealistic expectations of what the child can and cannot do. They are usually extremely critical of the child. Conflict between the parents also may create a climate in which child abuse occurs.

Evidence suggests that a link exists between childhood and adult animal abuse and later violence, including child abuse and intimate violence. Research has shown that animal abusers are five times more likely than non-abusers to commit violent crimes against people. Animals are also frequent targets in domestic violence. Abused children may vent frustration on a pet; adults may harm family pets in a display of control or power. One study of battered women found that 57% of those with pets stated that their partners had harmed or killed those animals. One in four women said they stayed with a batterer because they feared leaving a pet behind. Clearly, pet abuse is a warning sign to families of potential violence against themselves.

There is no single profile of a perpetrator of fatal child abuse, although certain characteristics appear across many studies. Fatal child abuse, in which a child is killed by a caretaker or parent, occurs with greater frequency in families in whom the caregivers are aged 16–24 years. Frequently, the perpetrator is a young adult in his or her mid-20s, without a high school diploma, living at or below the poverty level, depressed, and who may have difficulty coping with stressful situations. In many instances, the perpetrator has experienced violence firsthand. Most fatalities from physical abuse are caused by fathers and other male caregivers. Mothers most often are responsible for deaths resulting from child neglect. Approximately one-third of child homicides are committed by parents, and one-third are committed by acquaintances. Twenty-six children were killed by their babysitter in 2005. Another 10% of child homicides are perpetrated by strangers.

WHICH CHILDREN ARE ABUSED?

Approximately 32% of all victims of maltreatment were younger than four years in 2007. Children under four years of age are at greatest risk for severe injury and death from abuse. An additional 23.8% were aged 4–7 years and 19% were aged 8–11 years. Victimization was split almost evenly between the genders. The youngest children had the highest rate of victimization. The rate of child victimization for boys in the age group of birth to 1 year was 22.2 per 1,000 male children of the same age group. The child victimization rate for girls in the age group of birth to 1 year was 21.5 per 1,000 female children of the same age group. The victimization rate for children in the age group of 4–7 years was 11.4 per 1,000 for boys and 11.6 per 1,000 for girls. The victimization rate for children in the age group of 16–17 years was 5.4 per 1,000 children of the same age group. Overall, the victimization rates decreased for older age groups. Of the victims who were sexually abused in 2007, 35.2% were in the age group 12–15 years, 23.8% were in the age group 8–11 years, and 23.3% were in the age group 4–7 years.

In 2007, Black children, American Indian or Native Alaskan children, and children of multiple races had the highest rates of victimization at 16.7, 14.2, and 14.0 per 1,000 children of the same race or ethnicity, respectively. Hispanic children and White children had rates of 10.3 and 9.1 per 1,000 children of the same race or ethnicity, respectively. Asian children had the lowest rate of 2.4 per 1,000 children of the same race or ethnicity. Approximately one-half of all victims were White (46.1%), one-fifth (21.7%) were Black, and one-fifth (20.8%) were Hispanic.

A child in a family of any income level, social class, race, ethnicity, and religion may be victimized. However, it seems that certain characteristics and health or developmental problems may increase a child's risk for abuse or neglect. Children who are the result of an unplanned pregnancy are at greater risk. Children of single parents are at higher risk of maltreatment. Sometimes children are abused because they were not of the desired gender. Some evidence indicates that the birth of twins, large families, and inadequate spacing of children heighten risk of abuse as well.

Children born during a severe family crisis are more likely to be abused, as are children who may be unwanted because they are the product of rape or incest, or because the child was conceived with a spouse who has subsequently separated or divorced from the caretaker parent. A child who is born prematurely or with any birth defects, chronic disease, physical or intellectual disabilities, mental health issues, or special needs may become a victim of abuse. The early occurrence of childhood illness, and particularly serious illness, may increase abuse risk.

In 2005, approximately 8% of child victims of abuse and neglect had a disability (including intellectual or learning disability; behavioral, psychological, or emotional disturbance; hyperactivity; visual impairment; physical disability; or another medical problem). Cerebral palsy is an example of a physical problem that can result in the parents' perception that their child is difficult to raise or different, and may increase risk of abuse. Children who are difficult to feed are more likely to be abused, as are those who have a defiant personality. Adopted children are at greater risk. Abuse tends to affect children who are perceived as too active or too passive. Despite these characteristics, the majority of abused and neglected children were normal children before the abuse began. Only a fraction of all abused children share one or more of these risk factors.

A Department of Justice study found that more maltreatment was reported among lower-income families. Children from families with an annual income of less than $15,000 had substantially more maltreatment of all types than children from families in other income groups. Maltreatment also was related to family size. Children living in large families (with four or more children) were physically neglected approximately three times more often than those living in families with one child and more than twice as often as those living in families with two or three children. Serious injuries were equally likely in families of all sizes.

ARE ONLY YOUNG CHILDREN ABUSED?

No. In domestic violence and child abuse, adolescents are often overlooked. It is assumed that the majority of victims of child abuse are young children; however, recent research has revealed that adolescence may be as abuse-ridden as early childhood. Adolescents experience high levels of abuse, including the most severe abuse that results in serious injuries and death. As occurs in the abuse of small children, the perpetrators of such violence are most frequently the parents of the child.

Youths 12–17 years of age constituted approximately 25% of abuse victims in 2007, greater than their fraction of the U.S. population. Victimization rates for adolescents aged 12–15 years were 6.9 per 1,000 for boys and 10.5 per 1,000 for girls. For those aged 16–17 years, the rates per 1,000 were 3.9 for boys and 7.0 for girls. Nonetheless, the highest victimization rates in 2007 were for the age group 0–4 years, and rates declined with increasing age.

IN WHAT SITUATIONS AND WHY DO PEOPLE ABUSE CHILDREN?

Research on the causes of child abuse and neglect has identified several factors that may predispose to abuse. These include poverty, social isolation, and family disruption. Despite much research, there is no single or simple explanation or theory for how these influences may combine to break down the usually nurturing and loving care provided to children by parents. Multiple antecedents and risk factors for child abuse have been identified. Adding to the complexity of understanding the causes of abuse is the fact that abuse can be the result of acts of commission or omission.

Acts of commission are deliberate and intentional. However, as noted earlier, harm to a child may or may not be the intended consequence. Intentionality only applies to the caregiver's acts and not to the consequences of those acts. For example, a caregiver may intend to hit a child as punishment (e.g., striking a child is not accidental or unintentional), but the intent was not to cause the child a broken arm. Physical abuse, sexual abuse, and psychological abuse all involve acts of commission. Acts of omission involve the failure to provide for a child's basic physical, emotional, or educational needs, or to protect a child from harm or potential harm. Just as occurs with acts of commission, harm to a child may or may not be the intended consequence. Failure to provide for a child physically, emotionally, and educationally; to ensure medical and dental care; and to provide supervision could all result in child abuse through acts of omission.

Part of the problem may be related to the fact that some experts estimate that up to 90% of American families use physical (or corporal) punishment to discipline children. Corporal punishment of children may contribute to violent behavior in children, including abuse of their own children as adults. The right of parents to discipline children in the manner of their own choosing is a basic element of our culture and beliefs about the autonomy of the family. This contrasts with several European countries where it is against the law to use corporal punishment, even against one's own children. Interestingly, very low levels of fatal child abuse are reported in these countries.

In one study, 40% of parents who used corporal punishment on their children said that it occurred when they had a bad day, and that it bore no relation to the child's behavior. Therefore, the rationale that this is an effective means of controlling bad behavior in children, itself questionable, is not supported by the use of physical punishment in everyday family situations. Researchers have demonstrated that the later into adolescence a child was physically punished, the more likely that person will abuse his or her own children as an adult. In homes where child abuse occurs, violence among siblings is not uncommon. Research indicates that children often learn about and imitate violence occurring between their parents. It may also be imitated between siblings.

Stresses experienced by parents both within and outside the home are thought to be closely tied to the onset of child abuse. Financial or job difficulties, lack of employment, alcoholism and drug addiction, illness, and marital problems such as divorce or separation may all contribute to abusive or neglectful treatment of children. One study found that children from families with annual incomes less than $15,000 were more likely to experience maltreatment than children from families whose incomes exceeded $30,000. Spouse abuse between parents often causes the turning of anger and assaults to the children. Abuse is more frequent in families with an absent biological mother or father. In 22 states reporting living-arrangement data, 26% of abuse victims were living with a single mother. Stepchildren are abused at four times the rate of natural children.

Teenage mothers with little in the way of parenting or coping skills and social support from family are at higher risk for abusing their children. This is particularly true for single teenage mothers. Any parent who lacks the needed emotional maturity to raise children is at risk for abusing them. Neglect may be the result of a combination of factors that lead to parental failure, including lack of financial resources, inadequate access to health care, substance abuse by the parents, or mental health problems such as depression. Many abusive parents suffer from intense feelings of inferiority and a frustrated need for love that may have origins in abuse during their own childhoods.

Illness shortly after birth, chronic health problems, and, particularly, admission to the neonatal intensive care unit or other prolonged hospitalization, may interrupt the normal process of parent–infant bonding. Children with this history are abused more frequently than those whose early life was normal. Children with certain behavioral characteristics that present a greater challenge to parents, such as hyperactivity or persistent crying, are more likely to be abused. Some research indicates that infant crying can serve as the final trigger for abuse from a caretaker. These children are often viewed as not responding well to the parent's efforts to be a good caretaker. This may result in neglect as the child is increasingly viewed as not worth taking care of.

A parent's expectations of the child may be unrealistic or inconsistent with the child's actual level of development and may precipitate abusive behavior. This is a form of role reversal, in which the child is treated as an adult while the caretaker expects his or her own needs and desires to be responded to by the child. When the child (predictably) fails to meet these needs, criticism and punishment result. From the caretaker's perspective, however, this is considered justified or appropriate disciplinary action.

Abusive behavior tends to occur in successive generations of families in a cycle of violence from parents to their children and then on to the next generation as these children become parents themselves. This generational repetition of abuse seems to occur in all forms of abuse and neglect. Abuse from this perspective is essentially a repetition of the pattern of child care that abusers experienced in early life. An estimated 40% of individuals who abuse children physically were abused as children. People often will reenact their parents' or early caretakers' behavior toward them in the care they provide to their own children.

Some experts believe that it is rare to encounter an abuser with no history of neglect or abuse if questioned appropriately. Adults who have had a positive early childhood experience can empathize with children in later years and form attachments to them. However, a personal history of neglect or abuse can become the basis of a caretaker's inability to provide care to children in an empathic manner, with sensitivity to the child's needs. These parents become poor providers of care and often are emotionally unavailable to their children. When stressed, the caretaker will give priority to his or her own needs while the child's needs are subordinated or ignored. Thus, child abuse is not a random act of violence, but often the result of a mix of current difficulties, a background of abuse in the abuser, and distorted expectations and standards for a child's behavior.

Child abuse does not usually occur every day or constantly. Periods of days, weeks, or months may pass between physical attacks or abusive episodes. Emotional abuse may occur more regularly, especially verbal assaults, yelling, and criticism. Abuse usually involves a caretaker with the psychological predisposition who is experiencing some additional stress in social isolation and a child who is perceived (inaccurately) as unsatisfactory in some way. The low self-esteem of abusers makes them dependent on their child for gratification, but their inflated expectations and the child's inability at this age to fulfill the abuser's needs set up the abuse. Then, even when a small stress arises, the parent's coping abilities are overcome, and a child's normal behavior, such as crying or making a mess, becomes a trigger for assault. Psychologists suggest that abusive parents seek gratification from their child as a substitute for their own parents and unhappy treatment as a child.

When a child is killed by a parent or caretaker through repeated physical abuse, there usually is no intent to kill. Death frequently occurs as an incidental and unexpected result of chronic or particularly severe abuse. The child's death is not desired, and the caretaker may be quite shocked and often does not understand what he or she has done that resulted in death. The abuser usually feels great guilt and remorse. Mild abuse can sometimes accidentally cause the death of a child, for example, if a child dies after being pushed and falling on an object that causes blunt trauma to the abdomen or head. Shaken baby syndrome (described earlier) also can cause serious injury or death that, because of the fragility of infants, occurs with relatively minor use of force from an adult's perspective.

IS CHILD ABUSE FALSELY ALLEGED OR MISDIAGNOSED?

Yes. The enactment of broad child abuse reporting laws and the establishment of mandatory reporters have done much to increase the recognition of child abuse. Many state laws include a penalty for failure to report child abuse and provide immunity from both criminal and civil liability to persons making reports in good faith. Most of the laws requiring the reporting of child abuse across the United States place the requirement to report suspected child abuse above all claims of professional–client privilege and privacy. Physicians, social workers, and other mandated reporters, therefore, weigh their decisions in favor of reporting, despite the potential for lasting damage to children and their families as a result of an erroneous report. These legal and reporting developments, necessary as they were, also have created a potential for incorrect reporting or overreporting.

Experimental studies have shown that children as young as 3–5 years old can accurately observe and report events happening to and around them. Studies of child sexual abuse indicate that less than 10% of children claiming to have been sexually abused have made a false disclosure. Even so, this level of incorrect accusations could represent a great deal of suffering for innocent families and their children. False allegations of child sexual abuse occur more frequently during custody disputes arising from divorce. Between 2% and 10% of all family court cases involving custody or visitation disputes involve an allegation of sexual abuse.

Up to one-fourth of children involved in cases of sexual assault that eventually yield a conviction or confession of the perpetrator recant their initial disclosure at some time during the investigation. Recanting or denial of previous allegations may occur as a result of pressure on the child victim from families seeking to protect the alleged abuser, particularly in cases of suspected incest. Recanting also can occur as a result of interviewers who inappropriately pressured a child to prove or disprove that abuse has occurred. Abused children commonly experience guilt and a sense of responsibility for the abuse and the consequences experienced by the abuser. It is critical that these feelings be assessed and dealt with during the investigation so that the child does not seek relief by changing his or her allegation.

There are great social and economic costs associated with an incorrect diagnosis of child abuse. The stigma of child abuse, whether an assault occurred or not, may have potentially serious and lasting psychological consequences on all parties. An allegation of child abuse subjects the child and family to investigation, medical and psychological examinations, possible court appearances, and often separation of the child from family members during the investigation. Family privacy is disrupted, family relations are disturbed, and the child and his or her caretakers are stigmatized.

The well-intended efforts of physicians, social workers, teachers, and others may, therefore, have negative effects in the instance of an incorrect allegation or diagnosis. In the United States each day approximately 500,000 children live apart from their biological parents, many as a result of a child abuse allegation. More than 50% of these children will be kept away from their homes for 1 year or longer, 60% will be placed in more than 1 setting, and some will have 15 or more "homes" during their childhood. Some will never again live with any permanent family.

The problem of misdiagnosis has the potential to undermine many of the gains in child abuse detection, treatment, and prevention so arduously attained over the past four decades. The aphorism of one bad act nullifying many good ones comes to mind, and in today's media-intensive environment, highly publicized cases of misdiagnosis (and what will be labeled professional "overzealousness") may inflict great damage on efforts to prevent the abuse of children.

Although it is necessary to expand child abuse detection efforts to ensure that underreporting does not occur, it is essential that the accuracy of diagnoses continues to be improved to minimize the risk of false accusations. This can be accomplished partly by reducing the fragmentation that occurs through the multiple systems that have been established for the detection, medical management, psychological intervention, and protection of abused children and for the prosecution of alleged assailants.

HOW CAN CHILD ABUSE BE PREVENTED?

At an individual or family level, a number of strategies can be used to reduce the risk of abuse. Never discipline your child when your anger is out of control. Participate in your child's activities and get to know your child's friends. Engage with and ask your child questions regularly. Listen carefully to your child and believe what he or she says. For example, when your child tells you he or she does not want to be with someone, this could be a warning sign. Be aware of changes in your child's behavior or attitude, and inquire about them.

Teach your child what to do if you and your child become separated while away from home. Never leave your child unattended, especially in the car. Make certain your child's school or day-care center will release him or her only to you or someone you have officially designated.

Teach your child the correct names of his or her private body parts. Explain to your child the difference in "good touches," "bad touches," and "confusing touches." Be alert for any talk that reveals premature sexual understanding. Pay particular attention when someone shows greater than normal interest in your child.

Perhaps first and foremost in the effort to prevent child abuse is the institution of an intensive and continuous program to educate the public and facilitate provision of help to caregivers before abuse becomes severe and entrenched. Media, school, and community-based initiatives all may have an impact. The ultimate goal is to prevent child abuse before it starts. Strategies that support parents, enhance family stability, and teach positive parenting skills are very important. Neighborhood-based programs may offer the best preventive and treatment services for abused children and their families. Such programs offer education, counseling, support, and treatment referral, and improve access to services that decrease stressors on a family that may lead to abuse (e.g., support in obtaining housing, employment, education, and transportation).

Positive parenting skills to nurture include good communication, appropriate discipline (setting household rules and monitoring), and the ability to respond to children's physical and emotional needs. Programs to prevent child abuse also improve parent–child relationships and provide parents with social support. Programs for parents can take many different forms and can involve one-on-one or group sessions. This approach recognizes that families cannot function normally without formal and informal support derived by living within a broader community. Neighborhood child abuse and parental education programs, working out of local facilities such as schools, churches, medical and mental health clinics, day-care centers, and even homes, can help build a sense of control and self-esteem within families.

Child abuse researchers generally agree that a coordinated program of regular home visitation by public health nurses, family therapy and individual counseling, and improved health care can reduce family risk of child abuse. Programs to provide support to parents before and immediately after the birth of a child, with the objective of preparing them emotionally and practically to parent, can help prevent child abuse. The content of these programs includes creating opportunities for stronger bonding of parents to their new child, setting reasonable expectations of children at differing stages of development, managing frustration, and guidance in nonviolent methods for disciplining children. Parents can be assisted in developing skills for positive interactions and communication with their newborn. Home visitation has been recommended for all new parents for a period of 1–2 years after the birth of their first child, and particularly if one or more of the risk factors discussed earlier are present.

These kinds of efforts can be targeted to families with the greatest risk of abusing children and who might be identified during pregnancy, the birth process, or the newborn period. Characteristics that might be used in screening for high-risk families include whether the parents used an affectionate, indifferent, or hostile tone of voice when speaking to the infant (or other children); whether the parents criticized the appearance of the newborn; whether the parents related to each other in a supportive or a combative manner; and whether eye contact was made and kept with the infant. Mothers could be taught child-care and homemaking skills and supported emotionally during the first difficult months of child-rearing. Rooming-in after the delivery of a child has been shown to decrease the risk of subsequent physical abuse, abandonment, and failure of a child to grow and thrive.

This approach assumes that child abuse is frequently predictable, and once predicted, its most severe forms can be effectively prevented. The view that a predisposition for child abuse can be screened for and identified in this manner is not universally held, but this kind of support for all new parents remains the ideal for many practitioners in the field of child abuse prevention. Such programs imply the need for major expenditures by local communities and social and human services agencies and government, which have historically been considerably below the demonstrated level of need.

Programs should focus on periods well beyond the birth as well, particularly during times when the family is facing mounting stress and before the first episodes of abuse. Education and support conveyed through child abuse and domestic violence telephone hotlines, and respite care to temporarily relieve parents of some of their burden are examples of potentially effective strategies. Adult education courses are another strategy for prevention of child abuse. More intensive courses should be provided to adults who have had negative childhoods before they become high-risk parents. Young adults can be provided an opportunity to learn or relearn interaction skills that should have been learned during their own childhoods. However, experts caution that prevention programs will not result in an immediate decrease in child abuse. The complexities of dysfunctional families are too great to expect rapid, dramatic, and readily measurable improvements.

WHAT DO I DO IF I LEARN THAT MY CHILD IS BEING ABUSED?

Most child abuse occurs in families, but it is possible for abuse to occur in other settings, such as schools, recreational and sports programs, camps, and day-care centers. If you suspect that your child is being abused outside the home, listen to and believe your child and convey to him or her your belief. Reassure the child that you will take action to ensure that the abuse stops. Be very clear that the abuse is not his or her fault; your child should not feel guilty about having been abused. Explain that abusing a child is wrong, and commend your child for communicating the problem to you. Seek medical assistance immediately, both to rule out any serious injury and to obtain documentation that may be needed for subsequent prosecution of the abuser. Your doctor should take color photographs of any visible injuries, but if he or she fails to, you should. Explain to your child why the photographs are being taken. Report the abuse to the authorities, including the police, if sexual abuse is alleged.

Contact the management or authorities in the institution or program where your child was abused. This may be the principal of a school or the owner/director of a camp or recreational facility. Inquire about what occurred, and listen to the explanation. Stay calm and avoid getting into an argument. Indicate firmly that any form of physical punishment of your child is unacceptable and will not be tolerated. If they are amenable, you may arrange a meeting to reconcile the child with them, during which apologies will be made to the child along with a commitment that abuse will not recur. Explore the behaviors that precipitated the abuse, if any, and as appropriate, work with your child to develop an understanding of the need and method for avoiding such acts in the future. Until the problem is fully resolved, do not return your child to the setting where he or she was abused.

WHAT DO I DO IF MY SPOUSE IS ABUSING MY CHILD?

If your spouse is abusing your child, you need to stop denying the problem and seek treatment immediately. You will need to reach out beyond your family for help. Generally, child abuse is not a problem that is easily and satisfactorily resolved within the family without some form of external assistance. Time is of the essence, because if the physical abuse of your child is serious, long-term consequences may result.

There is no simple or single approach to the treatment of child abuse. Treatment often involves working with each individual family member. Child abuse treatment teams usually include physicians, nurses, other health professionals, social workers, mental health specialists, attorneys, and community workers. Child abuse hotlines and crisis service centers exist in most communities, and you should reach out to them for help along with your spouse or, if necessary, alone. Referral resources are listed for all states at the end of this chapter. The general strategy of treatment is outlined later.

Treatment programs are not always successful. In terms of effectiveness, one study of 3,000 families treated for child abuse found that one-third of perpetrators continued to abuse or neglect a child. The study also found that the majority of families were just as likely to engage in abuse after treatment had concluded. Yet educational programs for physically abusive and neglectful parents also have shown some promising results. Drug therapy and psychotherapy are sometimes used to combat mental health problems that contribute to or result from abuse.

For the abused child, treatment can involve both positive and negative consequences. When foster care is used to protect a child from physically abusive caretakers, it may lead to permanent separation of the child from the family. The effect of such separation can be more traumatic for the child than remaining in an abusive home. An alternative to foster care is a family preservation program, which stabilizes the family and allows a child to remain at home. The program includes in-home health services, child care, counseling, and assistance in housing, food, and transportation. The evidence on whether these programs are superior to separating the child from the family is not yet clear.

WHAT DO I DO IF I AM ABUSING MY CHILD?

If you are having problems controlling your temper and managing your relationship with your child, your first step is to understand that you—not your child—are responsible for the abuse and that this behavior is not acceptable. You must seek help. If not, you are at risk of seriously injuring or even killing your child. Abuse may have long-term emotional and physical effects. You also could lose your family through separation, divorce, or incarceration. Child abuse is a crime.

You may be repeating a pattern of violence that you experienced yourself as a child. The good news is that you can break the cycle of violence and suffering. If you have a spouse who is not involved in the abuse, tell him or her that you fear you have a problem. Your spouse may already be aware of it, but your recognition of your own need for help can make all the difference in getting help from counselors and people around you. You can get support within your home to help you deal with your inability to control your temper with your child. Parenting classes, parent-effectiveness training, and information on child development can make a difference. Reach out for professional help in your community. Child abuse hotlines and crisis service centers exist in your community, and you should seek their help. It is better if you seek help for the abuse yourself rather than it being reported to the authorities by the child or your family. You must stop.

Therapy groups are made up of batterers like yourself in different stages of change, growth, and healing. In the group process you will need to take responsibility for your actions while your potential to change and overcome this problem will be emphasized. A method for achieving control of your anger will be outlined, and the group will offer support along the way. But you will be required to admit that the abuse is your fault, not the child's, and that violence against a child, under any circumstances, is wrong. The objective of treatment for abusers is to educate you about the nature and causes of child abuse, provide you with methods to modify your behavior, and train you to recognize and to more safely and appropriately manage your anger. Treatment for drug abuse or alcoholism, if you need it, will be integrated with therapy.

If a group setting is not an environment in which you feel you can participate, private therapy is available from counselors in most communities. Private counseling will involve many of the same elements as a group process, but without the reinforcement that others who share your experience and predicament can provide. Local mental health organizations, abuse prevention programs, and churches may offer such counseling, and social and human service agencies in your community can provide referrals.

WHAT DO I DO IF I AM A VICTIM OF ABUSE?

Abuse by parents or others is a very frightening and painful experience. If you are abused by anyone other than your parents—including teachers, coaches, brothers or sisters, other relatives (like an uncle), or other children—reach out and talk to your parents. They are in the best position to help you overcome this problem and stop the abuse. If you need help to stop abuse and your parents are not around or capable of helping you, you can contact one of the hotlines or crisis centers listed at the end of this chapter. If your parents are abusing you, contact your local child protective services agency, a child abuse hotline, or crisis center for assistance right away.

You must not blame yourself for the abuse. Physical and emotional abuse or neglect is never justifiable behavior for anyone, including parents. There is nothing wrong with you. That is not why you are being abused. You are being abused because you have been targeted by an individual with serious emotional and psychological problems and who wrongly blames you.

If you are being abused at home, find someone you can trust and talk to about the problem. This may be a family member or someone outside the family who has your well-being at heart. You may find a sympathetic person in a teacher, school counselor, or member of your local church or other community group. Your doctor is another individual who can help and put you in contact with someone who will help stop the abuse.

If violence at home is an immediate risk, go to a friend's house to call for help. Once you have brought the abuse to the attention of child protective services or some other trusted individual, always be honest and consistent in telling your story. Despite the efforts of an abuser to silence you, communicate the facts and do not change your story, because this only complicates the resolution of the problem. Stay hopeful. The situation can and will improve, but only after you take action to protect yourself and bring professional attention to an abusive situation.

WHAT HAPPENS AFTER CHILD ABUSE IS DISCLOSED?

Following a report of suspected child abuse to a child protection agency, an investigation will be conducted and measures taken to ensure the safety of (and provide treatment for) the child victim. Child protective services are provided by an agency authorized to act on behalf of a child when parents are unable or unwilling to do so. Across the United States these agencies are mandated by law to conduct investigations of reports of child abuse and neglect and offer rehabilitative services to families in whom abuse has occurred (or is likely to occur). Child protective services staff are responsible for determining whether the report constitutes an allegation of abuse or neglect and how urgently a response is needed.

The initial investigation involves gathering and analyzing information from and about the child and family. Protective service agencies may work with law enforcement and other agencies during this period. Following the initial investigation, the child protective services agency will conclude that there is either sufficient or insufficient evidence to support or substantiate the allegation of maltreatment or risk of maltreatment. If there is insufficient evidence to support the allegation, additional services may still be provided if concern remains that there is a risk of abuse or neglect in the future. These include further assessment of factors that may potentially contribute to maltreatment, case planning to alter the conditions or behaviors that could produce child abuse or neglect, and treatment planning for the family. If the child protective services worker determines that there is no actual abuse or neglect, the case may be closed.

If the allegation is confirmed, a treatment plan will be outlined for both the child and the abuser. A temporary or permanent restrictive or protective order (limiting access to the victim) may be placed on the abusive parent(s) by a court. The order may continue throughout the evaluation of allegations and the treatment period, during which the child may be placed in foster care. A social worker assigned to the case will investigate the charge, and if substantiated, a motion for preventive custody will be initiated. At a hearing the risk to the child is determined, and evaluation and treatment of the parent(s) may be ordered. The state does not need to prove that a specific person has been abusive, merely that the child was injured or molested and that the parents could not adequately explain this, and are, therefore, neglecting the child. Neglect, by itself, is grounds for temporarily removing the child from the home.

The court may permit a child to remain with the parents under the supervision of periodic visits by a social worker. If the home is seen as unsafe for the child, he or she may be placed temporarily in foster care or with a relative. The social service agency will develop a plan for treating the family and reducing the stresses it faces, which may include home support services, family therapy, home visits by a social worker, and financial aid. The child will receive therapy to help reduce the trauma of abuse and to understand and integrate what has happened. If treatment of the parents progresses well, the long-term outcome may or may not be to return the child to the parents. Depending on circumstances and treatment progress, parental rights may be terminated so that permanent alternatives for the child can be found. A legal guardian may be appointed and referral made to long-term foster care or a state adoption agency. Adolescents near the age of legal adulthood may be declared adults and freed from their parents' guardianship.

Treatment plans will be formulated as part of the process of investigating the abuse allegation and shaped by the decisions of the court. Treatment generally involves three sequential phases: acknowledgment of the abuse by the parents and family as a whole; increase in the parent's sensitivity and emotional availability to the child; and resolution. Each process may entail many counseling and therapeutic sessions with professionals and continue for months or longer.

Acknowledging the abuse includes recognizing the abuse, its impact on the child, the inability of the family to adequately protect the child, and the extent to which the parents are unavailable to the child emotionally. The second phase attempts to increase the emotional sensitivity and responsiveness of parents to their child and his/her emotional needs. The resolution phase begins a more adaptive pattern with the family and may include reuniting the family or permanently dissolving it. Because abuse is often a repetition of an abuser's own childhood abuse, treatment requires much work on early life experiences. It is important to know how the abuser's ability to care for a child has been compromised by his or her own past experiences. Many therapists believe that it is not possible to treat abusers without this understanding. On average, the three phases of the treatment process require approximately two years.

After the treatment plan has been implemented, protective services and other treatment providers will evaluate and measure changes in family behavior and conditions and the risk of maltreatment, and determine when services are no longer needed.

WHERE CAN I GET MORE INFORMATION AND HELP?

For information about and help in stopping child abuse, contact your local health department or doctor, local medical centers and hospitals, and other social service providers. These agencies can refer you to an organization that provides specific services for your needs. For information on child abuse treatment and prevention services in your community, look in the Yellow Pages under "Human Services Organizations" or "Social Service Organizations."

Contact your local police department or call 911 or the ChildHelp USA National Child Abuse Hotline at (800) 4-A-CHILD (24453) or (800) 2-A-CHILD (24453, TDD for hearing impaired).

Appendix 1 at the back of the book provides a state-by-state website listing of compensation and assistance programs for victims of violence and crime. You may find assistance by contacting one of your state programs. Appendix 2 is a bibliography for further reading on each of the violence topics discussed in this volume, organized chapter by chapter.

The following are national and state organizations and internet websites that offer information and services to victims, families, and professionals about child abuse treatment and prevention.

NATIONAL ORGANIZATIONS

ACTION for Child Protection
(704) 845-2121

American Academy of Pediatrics
(847) 434-4000

American Humane Association
(800) 227-4645

American Humane Society, Children's Division
(303) 792-9900

American Professional Society on the Abuse of Children (APSAC)
(877) 402-7722

Bureau of Indian Affairs, Indian Country Child Abuse Hotline
(800) 633-5155

Center for Effective Discipline
National Coalition to Abolish Corporal Punishment in Schools
(614) 221-8829

Childhelp
(480) 922-8212

Children's Defense Fund
(800) 223-1200

Children's Institute, Inc.
(213) 385-5100

Children's Safety Network
(617) 618-2918

Child Welfare Information Gateway
(800) 394-3366

Child Welfare League of America
(703) 412-2400

Defense for Children International
(914) 941-3059

Faith Trust Institute
(206) 634-1903

Family Resources Coalition
(352) 854-3001

Find the Children
(888) 477-6721

International Center for Assault Prevention
(800) 258-3189

Kempe Center for the Prevention and Treatment of Child Abuse and Neglect
(303) 864-5300

Missing Children in America
(888) 556-4774

National Association for Children of Alcoholics
(301) 468-0985

National Association of Counsel for Children
(888) 828-6233

National Center for Missing and Exploited Children
(800) THE-LOST or 843-5678; TDD (800) 826-7653

National Center for the Prosecution of Child Abuse
(703) 549-9222

National Center for Victims of Crime, National Crime Victim Helpline
(800) FYI-CALL (394-2255); TTY (800) 211-7996

National Center on Child Abuse and Neglect (NCCAN)
Department of Health and Human Services
(202) 245-0586 or (703) 385-7565

National Center on Domestic and Sexual Violence
(512) 407-9020

National Child Abuse Hotline
(800) 4-A-CHILD (422-4453)

National Children's Advocacy Center
(256) 533-KIDS (5437)

National Children's Alliance
(800) 239-9950

National Committee to Prevent Child Abuse
(312) 663-3520

National Council on Child Abuse and Family Violence
(202) 429-6695

National Court Appointed Special Advocate Association
(800) 628-3233

National Crime Prevention Council
(202) 466-6272

National Domestic Violence Hotline
(800) 729-SAFE (7233); (800) 787-3224 Hearing Impaired
National Exchange Club Foundation
(419) 535-3232

National Institute of Justice Criminal Justice Reference Service
(800) 851-3420

National Maternal and Child Health Clearinghouse
(703) 821-8955

National Organization of Parents of Murdered Children
(888) 818-POMC (7662)

National Organization for Victim Assistance
(800) TRY-NOVA (879-6682)

National Resource Center on Domestic Violence
(800) 537-2238; TTY (800) 553-2508

National Youth Crisis Hotline (reporting child abuse and help for runaways)
(800) 442-HOPE (4673)

Office for Victims of Crime Resource Center
Department of Justice Office for Victims of Crime
(800) 851-3420; TYY (877) 712-9279

Parents Anonymous
(909) 621-6184

Resource Center on Domestic Violence, Child Protection and Custody
(800) 527-3223

STATE CHILD ABUSE REPORTING AGENCIES, CRISIS CENTERS, AND HOTLINES

Alabama Department of Human Resources
www.dhr.state.al.us/page.asp?pageid=347
(334) 242-1310

Alaska—State of Alaska Office of Children's Services
http://hss.state.ak.us/ocs
(800) 478-4444

Arizona Department of Economic Security
https://egov.azdes.gov/CMSInternet/main.aspx?menu=154&id=2030
(888) SOS-CHILD (767-2445)

Arkansas Department of Human Services
www.arkansas.gov/dhs/chilnfam/child_protective_services.htm
(800) 482-5964

California Department of Social Services
www.cdss.ca.gov/cdssweb/PG20.htm
No statewide hotline; call your county child protective services child abuse hotline
or Childhelp (800) 422-4453 for assistance reporting

Colorado Department of Human Services, Division of Child Welfare
www.cdhs.state.co.us/childwelfare
Call county Child Welfare child abuse hotline (303) 866-5932 or
Childhelp (800) 422-4453 for assistance reporting

Connecticut Department of Children and Families
www.ct.gov/dcf/cwp/view.asp?a=2556&q=314388
(800) 842-2288

Delaware Department of Services for Children, Youth and Their Families
http://kids.delaware.gov/services/crisis.shtml
(800) 292-9582

District of Columbia Child and Family Services Agency
www.cfsa.dc.gov
(202) 671-7233

Florida Department of Children and Families
www.dcf.state.fl.us/abuse/report
(800) 96-ABUSE (962-2873)

Georgia Department of Human Resources Child Protective and Placement Services
Unit
www.dhr.state.ga.us
(404) 657-3416

Hawaii Department of Human Services
http://hawaii.gov/dhs/protection/social_services/child_welfare
(808) 832-5300

Idaho Department of Health and Welfare
http://healthandwelfare.idaho.gov/Children/AbuseNeglect/tabid/74/default.aspx
(800) 926-2588

Illinois Department of Children and Family Services
www.state.il.us/dcfs
(800) 25-ABUSE (252-2873) or (217) 785-4020

Indiana Family and Social Services Administration
www.in.gov/dcs/2454.htm
(800) 800-5556

Iowa Department of Human Services
www.dhs.iowa.gov/Consumers/Safety_and_Protection/Abuse_Reporting/
ChildAbuse.html
(800) 362-2178

Kansas Department of Social and Rehabilitation Services
www.srskansas.org/services/child_protective_services.htm
cell phone users (785) 296-0044
(800) 922-5330 (in Kansas, outside Topeka)
(785) 296-2561 (in Topeka, or outside Kansas)

Kentucky Cabinet for Health and Family Services
http://chfs.ky.gov/dcbs/dpp/childsafety.htm
(800) 752-6200

Louisiana Department of Social Services
www.dss.state.la.us/index.cfm?md=pagebuilder&tmp=home&pid=181
Hotlines by parish or call the Childhelp hotline (800) 422-4453

Maine Department of Health and Human Services
www.maine.gov/dhhs/ocfs/abuse.htm
(800) 452-1999

Maryland Department of Human Resources
www.dhr.state.md.us/cps/address.php
Child abuse reporting by county office or call the Childhelp hotline (800) 422-4453

Massachusetts Department of Social Services
www.mass.gov/dss
(800) 792-5200

Michigan Department of Human Services
www.michigan.gov/dhs
(800) 942-4357

Minnesota Department of Human Services
www.dhs.state.mn.us
Contact county social service agency or call the Childhelp hotline (800) 422-4453

Mississippi Department of Human Services
www.mdhs.state.ms.us/fcs_prot.html
(800) 222-8000

Missouri Department of Social Services
www.dss.mo.gov/cd/rptcan.htm
(800) 392-3738 or outside Missouri (573) 751-3448

Montana Department of Public Health and Family Services
www.dphhs.mt.gov/cfsd/index.shtml
(866) 820-5437

Nebraska Department of Health and Human Services
www.hhs.state.ne.us/cha/chaindex.htm
(800) 652-1999

Nevada Department of Health and Human Services
http://dcfs.state.nv.us/DCFS_ReportSuspectedChildAbuse.htm
(800) 992-5757

New Hampshire Department of Health and Human Services
www.dhhs.state.nh.us/DHHS/BCP/default.htm
(800) 894-5533 or (603) 271-6556

New Jersey Division of Youth and Family Services
www.state.nj.us/dcf/abuse/how
(877) NJ-ABUSE (652-2873)

New Mexico Children, Youth and Families Department
www.cyfd.org
(800) 797-3260

New York Office of Children and Family Services
www.ocfs.state.ny.us/main/cps
(800) 342-3720 or TDD (800) 369-2437

North Carolina Department of Health and Human Services
www.dhhs.state.nc.us/dss/cps/index.htm
Contact local Department of Social Services or call the Childhelp hotline
(800) 422-4453

North Dakota—Department of Human Services
www.nd.gov/dhs/services/childfamily/cps
Contact local county social services office or call the Childhelp hotline
(800) 422-4453

Ohio Department of Human Services
www.jfs.ohio.gov
(866) 635-3748

Oklahoma Department of Human Services
www.okdhs.org/programsandservices/cps/default.htm
(800) 522-3511

Oregon Department of Human Services
www.oregon.gov/DHS/children/abuse/cps/report.shtml
Report to local county or call the Childhelp hotline (800) 422-4453

Pennsylvania Department of Public Welfare
www.dpw.state.pa.us/ServicesPrograms/ChildWelfare
(800) 932-0313 or TDD (866) 872-1677

Puerto Rico Department of the Family
www.familia.gobierno.pr
(800) 981-8333

Rhode Island Department of Children, Youth and Families
www.dcyf.ri.gov/child_welfare/index.php
(800) RI-CHILD (742-4453)

South Carolina Department of Social Services
http://dss.sc.gov/content/customers/protection/cps/index.aspx
Contact county Department of Social Services office or call the Childhelp hotline
(800) 422-4453

South Dakota Department of Social Services, Child Protection Services
http://dss.sd.gov/cps/protective
(605) 773-3227

Tennessee Department of Children Services
http://state.tn.us/youth/childsafety.htm
(877) 237-0004 or (877) 54ABUSE (542-2873)

Texas Department of Family and Protective Services
www.dfps.state.tx.us/Contact_Us/report_abuse.asp
(800) 252-5400

Utah Department of Human Services
www.hsdcfs.utah.gov
(800) 678-9399

Vermont Department for Children and Families
http://dcf.vermont.gov/fsd/reporting_child_abuse
(800) 649-5285

Virginia Department of Social Services
www.dss.virginia.gov/family/childabuse.html
(800) 552-7096 or out of state (804) 786-8536

Washington Department of Social and Health Services
www.dshs.wa.gov/geninfo/gov/news/shtml
(866) END-HARM (363-4276)

West Virginia Bureau for Children and Families
www.wvdhhr.org/bcf/children_adult/cps/report.asp
(800) 352-6513

Wisconsin Department of Children and Families
http://dcf.wi.gov/children/CPS/cpswimap.HTM
Contact the county Department of Social Services or call the Childhelp hotline
(800) 422-4453

Wyoming Department of Family Services
http://dfsweb.state.wy.us
Contact local Department of Family Services Office or call Childhelp
(800) 422-4453

USEFUL INTERNET WEBSITES

Action for Child Protection: www.actionchildprotection.org
American Academy of Pediatrics: www.aap.org
American Bar Association Center on Children and the Law: www.abanet.org/child
American Professional Society on the Abuse of Children: www.apsac.org
Campaign for Our Children: www.cfoc.org
Centers for Disease Control and Prevention: www.cdc.gov
Child Abuse Prevention Network: http://child-abuse.com
Childhelp: www.childhelpusa.org
Children's Bureau, Administration for Children and Families: www.acf.hhs.gov/
    programs/cb
Children's Defense Fund: www.childrensdefense.org
Children's Institute International: www.childrensinstitute.org
Children's Safety Network: www.childrenssafetynetwork.org
Child Welfare Information Gateway: www.childwelfare.gov
Child Welfare League of America: www.cwla.org
Committee for Children: www.cfchildren.org
Defense for Children International: www.defenceforchildren.org
Don't Shake Jake Awareness Program: www.dontshakejake.org
Family Violence Prevention Fund: www.endabuse.org
Family Violence and Sexual Assault Institute: http://fvsai.org
Find the Children: www.findthechildren.com

FRIENDS National Resource Center for Community-Based Child Abuse Prevention: www.friendsnrc.org

International Center for Assault Prevention: www.internationalcap.org

Kempe Center for the Prevention and Treatment of Child Abuse and Neglect: www.kempe.org

Missing Children in America: www.missingchildreninamerica.com

National Association for Children of Alcoholics: www.nacoa.net

National Association of Counsel for Children: www.naccchildlaw.org

National Center for Missing and Exploited Children: www.missingkids.com

National Center for the Prosecution of Child Abuse: www.ndaa.org

National Center for Victims of Crime: www.ncvc.org

National Center on Domestic and Sexual Violence: www.ncdsv.org

National Children's Advocacy Center: www.nationalcac.org

National Children's Alliance: www.nationalchildrensalliance.org

National Coalition Against Domestic Violence: www.ncadv.org

National Coalition to Abolish Corporal Punishment in Schools: www.stophitting.com

National Council on Child Abuse and Family Violence: www.nccafv.org

National Court Appointed Special Advocate Association: www.nationalcasa.org

National Exchange Club Foundation: www.preventchildabuse.com

National Institute of Justice, National Criminal Justice Reference Service: www.ncjrs.gov

National Organization of Parents of Murdered Children, Inc.: www.pomc.com

National Scientific Council on the Developing Child: www.developingchild.net

National Shaken Baby Coalition: www.shakenbabycoalition.org

National Victim Assistance Academy: www.ojp.usdoj.gov/ovc/assist/vaa.htm

Office for Victims of Crime: www.ovc.gov

Parents Anonymous: www.parentsanonymous.org

Prevent Child Abuse America: www.preventchildabuse.org

Voices for America's Children: www.childadvocacy.org

CHAPTER 3

Sexual Abuse of Children

- What is child sexual abuse?
- What is incest?
- What is pedophilia?
- What is not child sexual abuse?
- How common is the sexual abuse of children?
- What are the signs that a child is being sexually abused?
- Does child sexual abuse have serious consequences?
- Can a child get HIV/AIDS or other sexually transmitted diseases from sexual abuse?
- Who usually abuses a child sexually and why?
- Which child can be a victim of sexual abuse?
- In what situations do child sexual abuse and incest occur?
- What do I do if I learn that my child has been sexually abused?
- What happens after I report that my child has been sexually abused?
- Can child sexual abuse be prevented by society?
- How can I prevent my own child from being sexually abused?
- What methods do child sexual abusers use to lure children?
- Is the internet used to victimize children?
- What do I do if I am sexually abusing or sexually attracted to a child?
- What do I do if I am a victim of sexual abuse?
- What happens to abusers who are caught?
- Can child sexual abusers be treated?
- Does child pornography contribute to child sexual abuse?
- Where can I get more information and help?

WHAT IS CHILD SEXUAL ABUSE?

Child sexual abuse is defined as the involvement of children or adolescents in sexual activity to which, by virtue of their age and developmental level, they cannot give consent. Child sexual abuse involves sexual relations between an adult and a child, whether the contact between adult and child is voluntary or coerced by the adult. The sexual activity is for the gratification of the older individual, and there is a large age disparity between the victim and the perpetrator. Sexual abuse of children may involve the inappropriate exposure of a child to sexual acts or materials, the use of children to sexually stimulate adults, and any other actual sexual contact between children and adults.

The major categories of child sexual abuse include incest, pedophilia (literally "love of children," often involving fondling but which may include penetration), exhibitionism, molestation, statutory rape and rape, child prostitution, and child pornography. Sexual abuse includes non-touching behaviors, such as an adult exposing his or her genitals or requesting that a child look at pornographic materials. Sexual handling of a child, or fondling, is also a form of child sexual abuse, as is genital contact, intercourse, and violent rape.

Sexual abuse often involves multiple episodes occurring over a period of time. It often progresses from the less physically intrusive (e.g., kissing, fondling) to the more invasive (e.g., genital or anal penetration). As the abuse becomes progressively more invasive, there is usually coercion of the victim to remain silent. Disclosures of sexual abuse by children often are delayed and may occur as a slip from the child after an argument between the child and the abuser, or only when the physical or emotional effects of abuse become evident. In the case of sexual abuse within the family, deliberate disclosures may occur only after the abuser or the child has left the home permanently or when the abuser begins to focus on another younger child.

Sexual abuse is usually characterized by three features. These relate to the differences between the abuser and the victim with respect to power, knowledge, and gratification. The abuser has more power and knowledge than the victim. Power differences imply that the relationship is not mutually conceived and undertaken and that the victim feels obligated to do what the abuser requests. The knowledge difference derives from the fact that the abuser is older (usually at least five years older if an adolescent abuser), more developmentally advanced, and more intelligent than the victim. The relationship is not mutually gratifying and is primarily a way for the abuser to obtain sexual gratification.

WHAT IS INCEST?

Incest is a form of child sexual abuse in which the perpetrator is a relative of the child victim. Incest typically occurs between a father and a daughter or a mother and a son. Incest can occur as well between other relatives, such as an uncle and nephew or niece, or between siblings. The most common form of incest is father–daughter incest. The least reported form of incest is mother–son incest.

WHAT IS PEDOPHILIA?

Pedophilia is, literally, the love of children. A pedophile is a person who derives sexual gratification exclusively from sexual acts with children. Pedophilia is diagnosed solely on sexual fantasies or urges—not acts. The *Diagnostic and Statistical Manual of Mental Disorders* of the American Psychiatric Association cites the following diagnostic criteria for pedophilia: over a period of at least six months, recurrent, intense sexually arousing fantasies, sexual urges, or behaviors involving sexual activity with a prepubescent child or children (generally 13 years or younger). The fantasies, sexual urges, or behaviors cause clinically significant distress or impairment in social, occupational, or other important areas of functioning. The person is at least age 16 years and at least 5 years older than the child or children (excluding an individual in late adolescence involved in an ongoing sexual relationship with a 12- or 13-year-old).

Pedophiles often claim that they have nothing but love and affection for children, although, unlike other adults, they mean this quite literally in the physical sense. Pedophiles are well organized in society, publicly and privately advocating for sex with children as not abnormal when voluntary on the part of the child. Pedophiles have a desire not only to have sex with children but also to do so in great numbers, and they can be highly promiscuous. As a result, pedophiles can have dozens, even hundreds of encounters with different children over the course of their lives.

Pedophiles do not recognize that this activity is deviant or that the subtle, covert methods by which they coerce and manipulate children into participating in sexual relations with them are wrong. The acquisition of sexual experiences with children is a dedication of their lives. The pedophile regards himself not as a child abuser but as a child lover, and he employs labels such as "transgenerational sex" to rationalize his behavior. He believes that he is in the vanguard of an important cultural trend. In the pedophile's mind, the only thing wrong about sex with children is society's misplaced condemnation of it. This distinguishes the pedophile from the family member who sexually assaults a child in a sustained incestuous relationship.

An incestuous father is typically secretive and would not participate in any form of advocacy or advertising of the fact that he is having sex with his own child. In contrast, pedophiles tend to collectivize into organized networks of communication—written, published, and electronic—and to seek mutual confirmation and sharing of the sexual experiences they have had with children. In many respects, this represents a need for validation of what they are doing, as well as a practical device for identifying and becoming involved with new children. Pedophiles try to convince themselves and others that they are actually doing good by providing children with the attention that neglectful parents often are unable or unwilling to provide. Victims of child sexual abuse may be drawn disproportionately from families in whom there has been a lack of close parental attention, supervision, and communication.

Ironically, some of the organizations that serve as forums for communication among pedophiles use terminology such as "children's rights" in articulating their philosophy that children should be allowed to have sex with adults. More often than not these organizations serve simply as contacts or forums for pedophiles and as an avenue for the exchange of child pornography. Pedophiles need a continuing source of new victims, and so they bond together in their search for the next sexual encounter with a child. The rights in which pedophiles are truly interested are not those of their child victims but their own rights to have sex with children. They attribute any psychological damage that may result from sexual abuse to the social taboo and condemnation victims experience after disclosure, rather than the emotional or physical injury caused directly by their sexual abuse and exploitation of the child.

WHAT IS NOT CHILD SEXUAL ABUSE?

Sexual abuse occurs when the adult has the power to impose sexual behavior on a child or to manipulate the child into compliance. The adult understands the social and personal implications of a child having sex with an adult; a child does not. The fact that children have no power or understanding about abuse means that they cannot give informed consent. Yet it is impossible for parents and others who care for children to avoid some degree of intimacy with them. Bathing, diapering, and dressing a child will involve contact with a child's genitals. Kissing and hugging a child are a natural expression of affection, something that children fundamentally need and desire from their parents. Children may become sexually stimulated when they receive intimate care. For example, it is not uncommon for a parent to notice that a baby boy gets an erection when his genitals are washed. It is also not abnormal for mothers who breastfeed or fathers who bounce their little girls on their laps to become sexually aroused. These are not deviant responses.

It would be disastrous for the emotional well-being of all parties if, because of our heightened attention and desire to decrease child sexual abuse, we were to limit the sharing of affection and intimacy between parents and children. Most parents know intuitively what is and is not an acceptable way of behaving with their children. Although it is normal for a father to bathe his daughter as a baby, it is inappropriate for him to help her in the bath when she is nine or ten years old. A father or mother who is accidentally exposed to an adolescent's genitals would not be abnormal in experiencing some arousal accompanied by embarrassment. But if intentional efforts are to be made to wander into circumstances when a child might be exposed, this leans toward abuse.

Physical affection and touching is an integral part of the loving bond between parents and children and should not be undermined by concerns about sexual abuse. However, voyeurism or touches and other physical encounters with a child that are intentionally pursued in the interest of being sexually aroused or gratified are abusive.

HOW COMMON IS THE SEXUAL ABUSE OF CHILDREN?

Most crimes that can be committed against an adult, such as rape, are far easier to perpetrate on a child. Approximately 70% of all reported sexual assaults (including assaults on adults) occur to children aged 17 years or less. The Department of Health and Human Services states that of 794,000 cases of child maltreatment reported in 2007, 7.6% or more than 60,000 involved sexual abuse. The Department of Justice reports that in 2008 the rate of rape/sexual assault was 1.6 per 1,000 among 12- to 15-year-olds and 2.2 per 1,000 among 16- to 19-year-olds. One in every 3–4 females is thought to be sexually abused before age 18 years. For males, the range is 3%–24% of all males, with most experts estimating that 1 in every 6–10 is sexually abused during childhood (before age 18 years). One report found that 5%–15% of all males and 15%–30% of all females reported some form of child sexual abuse. Twenty percent of children are estimated to be solicited sexually while on the internet.

A 2008 national youth survey found that 6.1% of all children surveyed had been sexually victimized in the past year and approximately 1 in 10 (9.8%) had been victimized over their lifetimes. Sexual victimizations included attempted and completed rape (1.1% past year, 2.4% lifetime); sexual assault by a known adult (0.3% past year, 1.2% lifetime), an adult stranger (0.3% past year, 0.5% lifetime), or a peer (1.3% past year, 2.7% lifetime); and flashing or sexual exposure by an adult (0.4% past year, 0.6% lifetime) or peer (2.2% past year, 3.7% lifetime).

The national youth survey further reported that in 2008 adolescents aged 14–17 years were most likely to be sexually victimized. Approximately one in six (16.3%) had been sexually victimized in the past year, and more than one in four (27.3%) had been sexually victimized during their lifetimes. The most common forms of sexual victimization were flashing or exposure by a peer, sexual harassment, and sexual assault. Girls were more likely than boys to be sexually victimized; 7.4% of girls reported a sexual victimization within the past year, and approximately 1 in 8 (12.2%) reported being sexually victimized during their lifetimes. In addition, girls aged 14–17 years had the highest rates of sexual victimization; 7.9% were victims of sexual assault in the past year, and 18.7% were victimized during their lifetimes.

It is estimated that there are 39–60 million survivors of childhood sexual abuse in America today. Approximately 31% of women in U.S. prisons state that they had been abused as children. Seven percent of girls in grades 5–8 and 12% of girls in grades 9–12 reported in a survey that they had been sexually abused. In a nationally representative survey of assault victims, 25.5% of females were first raped before age 12 years and 34.9% were first raped between the ages of 12 and 17 years. Forty-one percent of males were first raped before age 12 years, and 27.9% were first raped between the ages of 12 and 17 years. A 2005 survey of high school students found that 10.8% of girls and 4.2% of boys from grades 9–12 were forced to have sexual intercourse at some time in their lives. It is estimated that at least 2 of every 10 girls and 1 of every 10 boys are sexually abused by the end of their 13th year.

In general, boys are less likely to report sexual abuse than are girls. It seems that the closer the relationship between the assailant and the child, the less probable it is that the child will report the abuse. A pedophile involved in an incestuous relationship may commit from 35 to 45 acts against 1 or 2 children. Non-incest pedophiles may commit 1–2 acts against a much greater number of children, perhaps as many as 20 females or 150 male victims per pedophile.

Sexual abuse in day-care centers seems to be no more common than it is within families. In one study researchers estimated that of 7 million children attending day-care facilities in the United States, approximately 5 of every 10,000 are sexually abused. In contrast, it was estimated that 9 of every 10,000 children are sexually abused in their homes.

A 1994 survey of 453 pedophiles revealed they were collectively responsible for the molestation of over 67,000 children, an average of 148 children per pedophile. The typical child sex offender molests an average of 117 children, most of who do not report the offense. The incidence of substantiated child sexual abuse increased from 1977 to 1992, followed by a period of substantial decline in the 1990s. The number of child sexual abuse allegations has been increasing steadily since 1976, when data were first collected on abuse. From less than 6,000 cases reported that year, more than 130,000 cases were being reported 10 years later. Between 1976 and 1986, there was a 22-fold increase in sexual abuse reporting. From 1992 to 1998, cases of sexual abuse decreased by approximately one-third from 149,800 to 103,600. Possible explanations for these declines include a real decline in incidence or a drop in reporting or substantiation.

Researchers have evaluated several factors that may explain the decline in child sexual abuse cases over the past decade. The most optimistic explanation is that incidents of child sexual abuse are actually decreasing. Considerable public awareness of the problem has emerged over the past several decades. Prevention programs that seek to protect children are widespread. Many offenders have been incarcerated. Numerous treatment programs have been directed toward offenders to prevent them from reoffending, and laws have been passed in many states to improve the monitoring of sex offenders in the community. Cumulatively these efforts could have had the effect of reducing incidents of child sexual abuse. Improvement in family economic stability with the increasing affluence of the 1990s may have conveyed children some protection from sexual abuse victimization as well. The fact that other child welfare indicators show so much improvement makes the possibility of a real decline in child sexual abuse more plausible.

The evidence of an actual decline in child sexual abuse appears to be supported by parallel declines in various other violence indicators with some of the same origins. National rates of female victimization by intimate partners, rape victimization, and overall violent crime have been declining at levels comparable to the child sexual abuse rate over a similar time period. Trends in child sexual abuse could be expected to parallel trends in intimate partner violence.

Another possibility explored by researchers is that there has been a decline in the reporting of child sexual abuse as reporting behaviors have changed. Reluctance to report child sexual abuse may have increased as a result of a child abuse backlash. Some analysts have noted a more skeptical public attitude toward child sexual abuse in recent years, possibly arising from periodic false allegations and perceptions that innocent people are being unfairly stigmatized by professionals who are being overzealous in reporting possible cases of sexual abuse. As a result, victims may be more reluctant to seek help and professionals more reluctant to report their suspicions.

It also could be that the public or professionals are reporting less child sexual abuse because they are correctly distinguishing signs of sexual abuse from signs of other problems. When public awareness campaigns and prevention programs were initiated 30 years ago, many victims were identified whose abuse had previously gone unrecognized. The upsurge in cases during the 1980s likely included many cases in which abuse had occurred years before those annual reports. This reservoir of older cases may have been reduced, so recent statistics more accurately reflect actual new cases of abuse. Thus, a decline in total cases may have appeared even as the true incidence of yearly sexual abuse remained stable.

Much child sexual abuse is unreported by children, and therefore, not detected. Research on adults who were sexually abused as children suggests that the large majority of victims do not report their abuse at the time it occurs. Children often keep their history of child sexual abuse a secret because they fear their parents' rejection, punishment, and blame. In some cases, children do not understand what has occurred or are unable to verbalize it. Abusers may have threatened an abused child with violent retaliation should the child tell anyone about the abuse. Among older children there is often embarrassment about being abused.

It is not uncommon that when a child does confide in a trusted adult, the reports are dismissed as fantasy or lies. Learning of abuse is an embarrassing and painful experience for a parent. There may be a sense of having failed in protecting the child, and denial of the problem may be easier than taking appropriate action. Denial is especially strong when one of the parents is involved in an incestuous relationship. One study found that only slightly more than half of parents who discovered that a child had been sexually abused reported the crime to authorities. Other reports are as low as 38% of parents reporting. When asked why they did not report, parents typically state that they wanted to handle the situation by themselves, they did not want to get the abuser into trouble, or they wanted to put the incident behind them and forget about it. Fear of getting involved with law enforcement personnel and of disrupting the family were also common among parents. These responses suggest that many unreported cases of sexual abuse involve perpetrators within the family.

Because both the perpetrators and the victims of child sexual abuse are not likely to discuss their experiences, just like other forms of violence, child sexual abuse is greatly underdetected and underreported. Some experts estimate that perhaps 1 man in every 100 is a child sexual abuser. This would mean that there are more than one million child molesters in the United States. Several recent surveys, however, have indicated that even this estimate may be low. Remarkably, the higher estimate is that perhaps 1 in every 25–50 American men abuses children sexually. Because many child molesters abuse multiple children over the course of their lives, a magnifier effect occurs, and a substantial percentage of all children may be at risk of being sexually abused.

WHAT ARE THE SIGNS THAT A CHILD IS BEING SEXUALLY ABUSED?

It is not always obvious that a child has been sexually abused, and many children do not report that they have been victimized. More than 30% of victims never disclose the experience to anyone. Young victims may not recognize their victimization as sexual abuse. Approximately 80% of sexual abuse victims initially deny abuse or are tentative in disclosing. Of those who do disclose, approximately 75% disclose accidentally and more than 20% eventually recant even though the abuse occurred.

Some children may confide in their parents that they have been sexually abused. There is always some risk that a child is falsely reporting and has not actually been abused, but children rarely lie about such unusual and serious problems. False accusations by children occur in only 1%–4% of reports. You should operate on the assumption that your child is telling the truth and investigate the allegations.

There are sexual and nonsexual behaviors that suggest sexual abuse, as well as physical signs. Most of the physical signs and symptoms of abuse will be best detected by a physician who works specifically with children or abused children. A child who has experienced sexual abuse may have obvious injuries to the genitals or rectum. However, it is possible for sexual abuse to involve genital contact of a less physically traumatic nature, and so the absence of clear physical evidence does not mean that abuse has not occurred. Pregnancy in a young child may indicate abuse, as could the presence of a sexually transmitted disease.

Most sexual abuse of children does not involve a violent attack on the victim. There may be no physical injury evident. Fondling, oral sex, and exposing the child to pornography or to the perpetrator's genitals will produce no physical signs. Physical injury may occur with penetration, usually in and around the victim's genitals or anus. A discharge from a child's vagina or penis may be evident; bleeding, pain, itching, and chronic discomfort walking or sitting suggest sexual abuse.

Because of children's limited understanding of the nature of a sexual victimization, and particularly among young children, it may be extremely difficult to elicit a history of sexual abuse even when it is suspected. However, there are nonphysical and behavioral signs that should raise a parent's concern about the possibility of sexual assault. These signs are not specific only to child sexual abuse, and abuse may occur in the absence of any of these signs.

Children who are sexually abused may exhibit significant behavioral changes according to their age. Children up to age three years may exhibit fear or excessive crying; vomiting; feeding problems; bowel problems; sleep disturbances, including nightmares; and failure to grow and thrive. Children ages 2–9 years may exhibit fear of particular people, places, or activities; regression to earlier behaviors, such as bed-wetting or stranger anxiety; victimization of others; feelings of shame or guilt; sleep disturbances; social withdrawal from family or friends; and loss of appetite and eating disturbances. Symptoms of sexual abuse in older children and adolescents include depression, nightmares or sleep disturbances, poor school performance and inexplicable behavior with teachers or peers, promiscuity, substance abuse, aggression, running away from home, eating disturbances, early pregnancy or marriage, suicidal gestures, anger, and pseudo-mature behaviors.

Fear of a specific place, such as a day-care center or restrooms (where abuse often occurs), or fear of a specific person, such as a family friend or a relative, is an indication of something potentially wrong in how that child relates to an institution or person. Clinging to one or both parents more than is usual, exhibiting greater fear and anxiety, and behaving like a younger child are signs of possible child sexual abuse. Fear of returning home after school or play may indicate a problem at home, including abuse. Children may sometimes act out the sexual assault in play with dolls or friends or in graphic drawings of what has happened to them. Excessive attention to their own genitals and masturbation may indicate abuse, as well as unusual sexual knowledge or seductiveness with adults or friends.

DOES CHILD SEXUAL ABUSE HAVE SERIOUS CONSEQUENCES?

Yes. Consequences of child sexual abuse begin affecting children and families immediately and can continue throughout the life of the survivor. The way a victim's family responds to abuse plays an important role in how the incident affects the victim. Sexually abused children who keep it a secret or who disclose abuse and are not believed are at greater risk than the general population for psychological, emotional, social, and physical problems often lasting into adulthood.

There are many ways in which child sexual abuse affects its victims. A wide range of physical effects may include injury to the genital area (hemorrhage, vaginal and anal tears), pregnancy in adolescents, sexually transmitted diseases, changes in sleep and eating habits, and other physical complaints, including headaches, stomachaches, and bed-wetting.

Sexually abused children experience emotional problems, such as long-term guilt, shame, anxiety, fear, depression, and anger. Victims experience cognitive difficulties, such as problems concentrating and maintaining attention, and problems in school. These children often have very low self-esteem and difficult interpersonal relationships. Child sexual abuse victims generally have fewer social skills than do normal children. They may be extremely fearful children and experience a constant need to please others. Behavioral symptoms may include acting out hostile or aggressive impulses and antisocial acts, such as stealing or delinquency. Victims may withdraw socially or abuse alcohol and drugs. Self-destructive behaviors, such as self-mutilation and suicide attempts, may result. Victims may experience neurosis, multiple personalities, and character and psychotic disorders. Young child sexual abuse victims often revert to infantile forms of behavior, such as thumb sucking and bed-wetting, and may experience nightmares. These children are less confident and more socially withdrawn, and have poor self-images. They may participate in prostitution and be at increased risk for becoming a rape victim as an adult.

Many victims complain of anxiety as adults and a sense that their relationships with others are superficial and devoid of meaning. There is reason to believe that older victims suffer to a greater degree than those who were young at the time abuse ended. This is attributed to younger children not fully understanding the implications of the abuse. The psychological impact of abuse also seems to be greater if the abuse was perpetrated by a trusted person rather than a stranger. Brief incidents of abuse seem to have less negative effects than abuse sustained over a long period.

Victims of child sexual abuse are more likely to experience a major depressive disorder as adults. Young girls who are sexually abused are more likely to develop eating disorders as adolescents. Adolescent victims have difficulty in the transition to adulthood and are more likely to suffer later financial failure. Victims of child sexual abuse are more likely to be sexually promiscuous. Women who report childhood rape are 3 times more likely to become pregnant before age 18 years. An estimated 60% of teen first pregnancies are preceded by experiences of molestation, rape, or attempted rape. More than 75% of teenage prostitutes have been sexually abused. Several studies have suggested that adults with a history of victimization by sexual abuse are at higher risk of engaging in sexual behaviors that place the individual at greater risk for HIV/AIDS and other sexually transmitted diseases. For some survivors, sexual interaction becomes the primary focus of adult relationships. Victims may eventually have an abusive relationship with their own children.

Victims of child sexual abuse report more substance abuse problems, and 70%–80% of sexual abuse survivors report excessive drug and alcohol use. Young girls who are sexually abused are three times more likely to develop psychiatric disorders or alcohol and drug abuse in adulthood than girls who are not sexually abused. Among male abuse survivors, more than 70% seek psychological treatment for issues such as substance abuse, suicidal thoughts, and attempted suicide. Males who have been sexually abused are more likely to violently victimize others.

Adolescents who suffer violent victimization are at risk for being victims or perpetrators of felony assault, domestic violence, and property offenses as adults. Approximately 50% of women in prison state that they were abused as children. More than 75% of serial rapists report they were sexually abused as youngsters.

Researchers have described several ways of understanding the impact of sexual abuse on children. The "sexually abused child syndrome" involves sexual knowledge that is not appropriate to the child's age, as well as sexualized play and precocious behaviors. A child may be preoccupied with his or her genitals and masturbate excessively. There is evidence that the child has been coerced or under great pressure.

Doctors treating child sexual abuse victims believe that a number of the symptoms experienced by these children are similar to post-traumatic stress disorder. Post-traumatic stress disorder is a psychiatric diagnosis that involves reexperiencing of the traumatic event through memories, dreams, and, in children, repetitive play. In addition, children who experience the disorder following sexual abuse may repress thoughts and feelings. In young children there may be the loss of recently acquired developmental skills. Other symptoms include problems sleeping, irritability, difficulty retaining memories or maintaining concentration, and increased intensity of these symptoms when exposed to anything related to the trauma. Post-traumatic stress disorder seems to be more common among victims of father–daughter incest and in cases of severe abuse.

Research suggests that the aftermath following sexual abuse disclosure is as damaging to the child as was the abuse. Traumatic sexualization results from the inappropriate sexual relationship. Betrayal results when the child realizes that a loved and trusted person has harmed him or her. The child may feel further betrayed when other family members and individuals do not believe the allegations. The child is stigmatized when he or she realizes that the abuse is morally and socially unacceptable and often feels responsible for the abuse. Thus, although many ill effects result from the abuse itself, others are created by social factors that can be changed.

A "child sexual abuse accommodation syndrome" describes some of the child's reactions to abuse that appear contradictory or inconsistent. The sexually abused child may be very secretive because secrecy is made an imperative by the perpetrator. A sense of helplessness reflects that a child is helpless to resist or end abuse. The combination of secrecy and helplessness leaves children feeling they have no way out. Children may turn to prostitution, juvenile sex offenses, and substance abuse. They have pathological reactions, including multiple personalities. Some of these reactions are efforts to adapt.

A child's disclosure of sexual abuse may be delayed or unconvincing. It often will occur after the abuse has been chronic and going on for some time. The child may describe only a few episodes or facts so as to determine what the reactions of adults will be. If adults react with disbelief or anger, the history of abuse may never be disclosed completely. Sexually abused children may retract or recant what they have reported. The intensity of the reaction to a disclosure of abuse validates a child's fears that secrecy was necessary. The child's father may abandon the child and call the child a liar. He may be disgraced and put in prison if he is the abuser. The mother may not believe the child and can become very angry or even hysterical.

A family may be shattered and all the children placed in protective custody. The victim is usually blamed, directly or indirectly, for all the problems the family experiences. This stigmatized treatment is usually perceived by children, and they acquire a sense that they are what one expert described as "damaged goods." In view of all of these reactions, it is not surprising that retraction and recanting of allegations occur. Recanting is especially frequent among the victims of incest. Despite this, fabricated sexual abuse reports constitute only 1%–4% of all reported cases (and of these, 75% are falsely reported by adults and only 25% by children).

Treatment of adults who were abused as children involves changing their belief structures so they can recognize that they were not responsible for their victimization or the consequences to their families. Adults who were abused chronically as children—and with more serious acts such as penetration—are the most difficult individuals to treat. There is no consensus on the best method for treating sexually abused children, and research is ongoing. Despite the many problems that may affect a victim of child sexual abuse, most victims recover and lead normal and healthy lives. It takes work, and the victim needs support and professional help, but it is possible to turn this tragic experience around and limit its impact on one's life.

CAN A CHILD GET HIV/AIDS OR OTHER SEXUALLY TRANSMITTED DISEASES FROM SEXUAL ABUSE?

Yes. It is possible for a child who has been sexually abused to be infected with a sexually transmitted disease. Sexually transmitted infections have been reported in 2%–10% of sexual abuse cases. Gonorrhea, human papillomavirus (the name of a group of viruses that can cause genital warts and cervical cancer), and herpes have been diagnosed in sexually abused children. Transmission of HIV (the virus causing AIDS) through sexual abuse also has been reported. Although the frequency of HIV infection following child sexual abuse is unknown, increases in both HIV infection rates and reported sexual abuse in the U.S. population suggest that such transmission may increase. At present the incidence of HIV infection following sexual abuse appears low, in part perhaps because abuse would require penetration of the child's body (as opposed to fondling or kissing).

One study identified 28 U.S. children infected with HIV and a history of sexual abuse but no other risks for HIV infection. Two-thirds of the children were female, three-fourths were Black, and the average age was nine years. The perpetrator was male in 25 instances and of unknown gender in 3 instances. The abuser was the child's father in 42% of the cases, another relative in 25% of cases, and a friend of the parent in 17% of cases. One-third of these children had another sexually transmitted infection in addition to HIV.

When children have been sexually abused, it is appropriate for them to be medically evaluated for common sexually transmitted infections (e.g., gonorrhea and chlamydia) and selectively for HIV infection. The decision to test the child for HIV should be based on several factors, such as what is known about the abuser's risk for HIV; for example, is he an injection drug user? It is sometimes possible to obtain the results of a previous HIV test on the abuser (or request that he agree voluntarily to a new test) to avoid testing a child victim. If the abuser is negative for HIV, the child is unlikely to have been infected with the virus, but he or she will still require another test six months later to be certain.

If the abuser is known to be infected or to have engaged in high-risk behaviors, if the abuse occurred in a geographic area where HIV infection is highly prevalent, or if the sexually abused child has symptoms of HIV infection or another sexually transmitted infection, HIV testing is warranted. Your doctor can help you make an informed decision.

WHO USUALLY ABUSES A CHILD SEXUALLY AND WHY?

Across studies it appears that 80%–90% of children abused sexually are victimized by individuals they know, not by strangers. Most child sexual abuse victims are abused by a family member or close friend. Stranger assaults are rare. In a study of 4,000 perpetrators of child sexual abuse across the nation, only 10% of child sexual abusers molested children they did not know. Sixty-eight percent molested children within their own families—children they parent, nieces or nephews, or grandchildren. One study found that strangers were offenders in just 3% of sexual assaults against victims under age 6 years and in 5% of assaults against victims ages 6–11 years.

The majority of known sexual abusers are male, but females can be abusers as well. Some experts suggest that female abusers are underdetected because young male victims are socialized to believe that their experience of sex as a child is a positive event. A report from the states to the National Child Abuse and Neglect Data Systems (of the Department of Health and Human Services) found the following breakdown of sexual abuse perpetrators: mothers alone, 4%; fathers alone, 22%; both parents, 12%; other male relatives, 17%; 1 parent and another individual, 13%; and others, 28%. Male perpetrators were responsible for 56% of child sexual abuse.

Being abused as a child increases the risk that the individual will grow up to molest children (47% of abusers admit to having been molested as a child). Although not all child sexual abusers were sexually abused themselves as children, they often were physically or emotionally abused.

More than 70% of men who molest boys identify themselves as heterosexual in terms of sexual preference; 9% state they are both heterosexual and homosexual, and only 8% state that they are homosexual. A majority of men who molest boys are married, divorced, widowed, or living with an adult partner. Of pedophiles who primarily molest boys, 21% also molest girls; of those who molest girls, 53% also molest boys.

As adolescents, abusers often molest younger siblings. On questioning, pedophiles usually indicate that they began to be attracted to children sexually during their teenage years. Indeed, a large percentage of child sexual abusers are adolescents. In many instances, the desire for sex with children begins earlier. More than 40% of pedophiles first began molesting children before they were 15 years old; a majority began before they were 20 years old. It is estimated that approximately 70% of all child sex offenders are aged 35 years or younger. Yet it is important to differentiate between an 18-year-old with an underage partner and adult repeat offenders.

In 1995, local child protection service agencies identified 126,000 children who were victims of either substantiated or reported sexual abuse. Of these victims, 75% were girls and approximately 30% were between the ages of 4 and 7 years. Ninety-three percent of victims knew their attacker; 34.2% were family members and 58.7% were acquaintances. Only 7% of the perpetrators were strangers to the victim. Forty percent of the offenders who victimized children under age 6 years were juveniles themselves (under the age of 18 years).

These data indicate that abusers can range in age from being virtual children themselves (or adolescents) to adults. It is still not well understood why an individual prefers to have sex with a child. Research continues to shed light on this problem. Sociologists point out that many sexual abusers of children are users of prostitutes who may not care whether the prostitute is 13 or 23 years old. Indeed, sexual value is attached to youth. A common characteristic of child sexual abusers is a lack of adequate impulse control over sexual urges. Sexual abusers are not mentally ill, however. Less than 5% have significant psychological disorders. Incestuous parents tend to have a history of promiscuity and alcohol and drug abuse, and to have been sexually abused themselves as children. They are often in bad marriages where there is little sexual expression or gratification.

There are currently approximately 647,000 registered sex offenders in the United States (many of whom can be located on such websites as www.familywatchdog.us). Most perpetrators do not molest only a single child (especially if they are not reported and stopped). The average sex offender commits 117 assaults before being caught. Approximately 70% of child sex offenders have 1–9 victims, but at least 20% have 10–40 victims. An average serial child molester may have as many as 400 victims in his lifetime.

In 2008, the Center for Missing and Exploited Children reported that there were 686,515 registered sex offenders in the United States, or 223 per 100,000 on a population basis. Sixty percent of convicted sex offenders are under conditional supervision in the community (on parole or probation). In 1994 there were approximately 234,000 offenders convicted of rape or sexual assault under the care, custody, or control of corrections agencies. An estimated 24% of those serving time for rape and 19% of those serving time for sexual assault had been on probation or parole at the time of the offense for which they were in state prison in 1991. Of child molesters released from prison, 5.3% were rearrested for a new sex offense within 3 years of their release. Of released sex offenders who allegedly committed another sex crime, 40% perpetrated the new offense within a year or less from their prison discharge. The eventual rearrest rate for convicted child predators is 52%.

Many researchers believe that sexual attraction to children is a learned behavior. However, there is little understanding of how this behavior is learned. A common pattern appears to be that abusers were themselves sexually abused as children. Forty percent of molesters in some studies (and higher in others) have a history of sexual abuse during their childhood. Why victims become abusers as adults is not understood, except that in many cases a distorted pattern of sexual gratification begins in childhood.

Child molesters are thought to fall into two broad groups: regressed and fixated. A fixated abuser is an individual who never developed beyond a certain psychological stage and functions emotionally and sexually as a child or adolescent. The regressed abuser has returned, or regressed, to an immature stage of sexuality. Other types of child molesters exist as well, for example, homosexual abusers or those particularly attracted to small children. In some instances, child sexual abuse may result from violent rape, with motives similar to those described in Chapter 7 on sexual assault.

A regressed abuser is usually a man with a rather normal life history who has been involved with age-appropriate members of the opposite sex during each period of his life. As a teenager he would have dated teenage girls, and as an adult he would have been involved with adult women. He could be married and a parent, and prefers sex with adults rather than with children. Often heterosexual, the regressed abuser becomes sexually interested in children, most often girls, at some point in adulthood. It is thought that many fathers who sexually abuse their own children are regressed abusers, because to have fathered children, they were attracted to an adult woman at some time. It seems that the regressed abuser is affected by severe stress or a crisis that precipitates his turning to children for sexual gratification. For example, a father and husband who experiences deteriorating relations with or separates from his wife may begin an incestuous relationship with his daughter. The regressed abuser may imagine his child partner to be older than she really is to rationalize his behavior.

The origins of the desire to have sex with children in the fixated abuser are different. The fixated abuser's sexual attraction to children develops early in life, even during childhood. Sexual gratification from children becomes a major focus, and perhaps a compulsion. He may never experience sexual attraction to individuals of his own age group and is unlikely to marry and have children. As a result, incest within his own family is not possible for the fixated abuser, and he must turn to other people's children to fulfill his desire for sex with children.

Most pedophiles are fixated abusers. Although the fixated abuser, usually a man, will have sex with boys, he is not a homosexual and is not attracted to adult men. He is sexually excited by boys because they are children, not because they are male. Unlike the regressed abuser, the fixated abuser does not abuse as a reaction to a major stress or crisis, but with anticipation and premeditation. The fixated abuser rarely acknowledges or appreciates that what he is doing is child molestation. He would state that he is opposed to child abuse in any form, and he believes that voluntary sex with a child is normal, negative only insofar as it is condemned by society. Most fixated abusers deny they are committing a crime and regard an assault on a child as criminal. Some may recognize their compulsion and wish to stop abusing children, but cannot. These two general categories of abusers are not rigidly defined or mutually exclusive. Abusers may cross from one category to the other.

Women who abuse children sexually are more frequently single than married. If married, it is thought these women are trying to fulfill unmet emotional needs resulting from an absent or emotionally distant husband. Women abusers are typically the child's mother or stepmother and may be very emotionally dependent on the child.

One psychological characteristic thought to be prominent among child sexual abusers is narcissism (literally, love of oneself, often at the expense of meaningful relationships with others). Narcissists have an inflated perception of their abilities and appearance, and they often entertain grandiose fantasies about their future. However, this is simply a persona, and the narcissist is fundamentally insecure and deeply unsure about himself or herself. The narcissist is in constant pursuit of reinforcement of a fragile self-image. Through mostly superficial relationships, he or she strives to obtain the confirmation and admiration that his or her insecurity demands. The narcissist engages in relationships only insofar as he or she can obtain much needed affection and attention.

The narcissistic abuser derives substantial ego gratification from sex with a child. Physical pleasure derived from sex is an intense form of gratification, and the narcissist, who can never be loved enough, often equates love with sex, and thus, needs many sexual partners to meet his or her needs. Sex becomes a form of self-confirmation and reassurance. The narcissist finds in the sexual act evidence that he or she is desired and of value. The most uncritical, naive, and abundant sources of love in our society are children. The child sexual abuser with a narcissistic personality turns to children for affection, adulation, and self-confirmation, and the ease with which children can be manipulated and dominated allows such a person to obtain repeated and frequent gratification in ways that never could be matched by sex with age-appropriate adults. Whatever his or her questionable status among adults, an abuser is a controlling and authoritative figure with children.

This helps us to understand how child molesters are different from rapists. Rapists seek power and control and do not care for the love or admiration of those they victimize. They injure and humiliate their victims, regarding the rape as a single episode, not as a relationship. Child abusers seek to develop lasting relationships. They do not usually use physical violence or injure the child victim because the positive emotions that the abuser seeks will not be forthcoming if the child has been hurt. Many child sexual abusers seem to believe that a child enjoys the sexual relationship as much as they do and deny that a child may be suffering at their hands. The abuser believes he or she is above the prohibitions, rules, and laws set for others, and deals easily with the taboo against having sex with children. Being very self-centered, abusers overcome the usual inhibitions and rationalize away the pain and misery they create for their child victims and their families. They have little empathy with the victim, caring only that their own needs are met.

All of us are inherently narcissistic as infants, and as the center of our parents' attention receive abundant love and confirmation. During childhood we make a normal transition from the narcissism of the infant to a more mature state in which we acquire a level of self-confidence, self-admiration, and love for ourselves.

It has been suggested that victims of child abuse may have had this normal psychological growth process interrupted. Abuse may create an adult dependency on others for this important part of psychological well-being. The main source of ego gratification for the pedophile is affection and admiration obtained from children, unlike most of us who derive this meaning from our adult relationships and work. These individuals have a childlike self-image and continue to act in the self-centered and self-gratifying manner that an infant does, with the critical difference that their indulgence in sex with children is far from harmless.

WHICH CHILD CAN BE A VICTIM OF SEXUAL ABUSE?

Any child, irrespective of socioeconomic class, age, race, or ethnicity, can be a victim of sexual abuse. Both boys and girls are sexually abused, and although boys comprise only 10%–20% of reported incidents, it is believed that they are victims of much unreported abuse. In 2000, the Department of Justice released a report on sexual assault of young children as reported to the National Incident-Based Reporting System. The database captures reports from law enforcement agencies in 12 states and drew from approximately 61,000 sexual assault victims and approximately 58,000 offenders. For the period of 1991–1996, 67% of sexual assault victims were juveniles (under the age of 18 years), 34% involved a victim aged less than 12 years, and 1 of every 7 was aged less than 6 years. Juvenile victims of sexual assault were more likely to be male than were adult victims. Juveniles under the age of 12 years constituted approximately one-half of all victims of forcible sodomy, sexual assault with an object, and forcible fondling, and approximately one-eighth of all victims of forcible rape.

Older children make a conscious choice to enter into a sexual relationship with an adult (or adolescent). Abuse may begin at any age, and any child, from infancy to adolescence, can be a victim. Abuse commonly begins at approximately nine years of age (the median age) and before puberty, especially in a continuing relationship. More than 20% of children are sexually abused before the age of 8 years. Of the victims who were sexually abused in one report, 35.2% were in the age group 12–15 years, 23.8% were in the age group 8–11 years, and 23.3% were in the age group 4–7 years.

An estimated 15% of imprisoned rapists said their victims were 12 years old or younger, and 45% of those sentenced to prison for other sexual assaults (statutory rape, forcible sodomy, and molestation) said their victims were 12 years old or younger. The average victim age by gender differed, being 10.4 years for females and 8.6 years for males.

By gender, the rate of abuse has been reported higher for female victims (2.3 per 1,000 female children in the population) than for male victims (0.6 per 1,000 male children). Another study found that about one-half (51.5%) of sexual abuse victims were White.

Children are largely abused within their own homes, with 30%–40% of victims being abused by a family member across most studies. Another 50% are abused by someone outside of the family whom they know and trust. Approximately 40% are abused by older children whom they know. Less than 10% are abused by strangers. Many victims come from single-parent families, which create opportunities for abuse to occur because there is usually less supervision of a child. Absent or indifferent parents increase the likelihood that a child can become sexually involved with an adult.

Approximately 95% of teenage prostitutes have been sexually abused. It is estimated that children with disabilities are 4–10 times more vulnerable to sexual abuse than their non-disabled peers. Children who perceive themselves as unattractive are vulnerable targets for abusers because a negative self-image can be manipulated to the pedophile's advantage. Children from lower income families and those who do not have many friends in their age group are also more likely to be victimized. Poor performance or disinterest in school is often characteristic of sexually abused children. It is important to note, however, that victims of abuse may share none of these characteristics.

IN WHAT SITUATIONS DO CHILD SEXUAL ABUSE AND INCEST OCCUR?

Child sexual abuse generally falls into one of three patterns. A brief incident of abuse may involve only a single episode, such as a stranger exposing his genitals to a child on the street. Abuse can occur in ongoing relationships outside the family, which start gradually but can persist for years. Incest is the third pattern, in which the abuser is a member of the child's immediate family, with abuse continuing over many years. Seventy percent of all child sexual abuse lasts for longer than one year.

Another kind of sexual abuse that has been less often described is called ritual abuse. Ritual sexual abuse occurs in the setting of a religious or other belief system that includes, among other elements, sex with children. The belief systems can vary widely, but often involve sadism and satanic cults that rationalize sex with children.

Juvenile victims are more likely than adults to be sexually assaulted with other victims. One of five juvenile victims is victimized in incidents with more than one victim, whereas, only 4% of adult victims were assaulted with others. When this occurred, the other victims were mostly also children under age 12 years (90%). Approximately five of every six sexual assaults of young juveniles occurred in a residence. Assaults of older juveniles were much more likely to occur in other places.

Pedophiles may try to befriend children and bribe them with gifts. Children are attracted to pedophiles by the material benefits the relationship offers, which can include food, clothing, entertainment and recreational trips, electronics, sports equipment, cash, and virtually anything a child might desire. In this sense, the child is acting naively in the role of a prostitute, ultimately exchanging sex for one form of payment or another. Many pedophiles also use child prostitutes. There are many underage prostitutes working across the United States. The Los Angeles Police Department, for example, has estimated that there may be more than 5,000 male prostitutes under the age of 14 years in Los Angeles. Therefore, juvenile prostitution provides access for the pedophile who cannot cultivate an ongoing relationship with a victim. However, it is not the usual method of victimization.

Pedophiles seek environments where they can interact with children in ways that do not draw excessive attention to their actions, such as where sports events are staged, malls, or video game arcades. A common method by which pedophiles access children is by assuming roles in which they can be a temporary caretaker of children. In these settings, such as schools, day-care centers, and recreational facilities, pedophiles can interact with children without raising the usual suspicions that occur when an adult is closely involved with a child. In 2010, the sexual abuse crisis within the Catholic Church caused by priests accused of molestation reached global proportions, and the Boy Scouts of America faced allegations that children participating in activities under its aegis have been sexually abused. Computerized bulletin boards and other forums on the internet are being used as a technological tool for exchanging information with other pedophiles.

Parents may know the individual who is sexually victimizing their child. Ironically, parents sometimes appreciate the fact that another adult has taken an interest in their child and is providing what they believe to be supervision and guidance. Even when gifts begin to appear in the home from an adult "friend" of the child, parents often ask few questions. As for the child, the need to repay the debt, the desire to continue receiving nice rewards, and the custom of obeying adults all contribute to their willingness to initiate and sustain a sexual relationship.

In incest, when the abuser and the victim live in the same home, there is opportunity for many more instances of sexual abuse. Father–daughter incest may continue for years. There is no typical family in which incest occurs, and fathers who commit incest may be from any social or economic class. Generally, however, incest is more likely to occur in families with little communication. There may be a sexual incompatibility of the parents, with the father unwilling or unable to find another (adult) partner outside of the family.

Although the father ordinarily would never have sex with a child, abuse may be triggered by some trauma or stress, with such stresses most often affecting the abuser's relationship with his wife. For example, the wife may die, become chronically ill, or divorce him. Even a wife taking a job may cause emotional separation for the at-risk man so that his needs are not met, and he turns to one of his children for gratification. Other blows to self-esteem, such as the loss of his job, may provoke the susceptible father to begin an incestuous relationship with his daughter.

If, however, incest begins early in a child's life, the father is likely to be a pedophile and the abuse may not be precipitated by any crisis. Incestuous fathers who are pedophiles may begin abusing their children shortly after they are born. They also may abuse children who are not their own. The father may develop a gradual relationship with a child so that there is no discomfort with intimate touching, caressing, and, ultimately, sex. The incestuous father may try to create differences between the child and the mother to isolate the victim so that incest can continue for years.

Mothers of incest victims may subtly cooperate in the process, particularly if the mother was herself abused as a child. A role reversal may occur in which the daughter begins to act more like a wife, as the mother becomes increasingly uncertain of her family role. The daughter becomes the main female figure in the home, displacing the mother. The father justifies the incest in superficial ways, perhaps convincing himself that he is simply illustrating how much he loves his daughter or that he is helping her to learn about sex.

Abuse may have gone on for years before coming to the attention of parents and authorities. Usually it will continue unless stopped by the intervention of a parent or a professional. An incestuous relationship is most likely to end during the child's teenage years. As a teenager, the child comes to realize that a sexual relationship with her father is not normal. The daughter matures and, like her peers, becomes interested in boys her own age. Friends are discovering relationships and boys, yet she has been having sexual relations with her father for years. At this time the child often will appeal to the father to end the abuse, and if he agrees, he may turn to one of the other children in the family. Sometimes the father will resist ending the incestuous relationship. He will try to control his daughter's life and regulate her social contacts, especially with boys. In the end, to escape the abuse, she may either run away from home or disclose the abuse to a trusted adult.

In such relationships it is not unreasonable to question how the mother could not know what was going on in her home. Because of the horrendous nature of this act, many mothers engage in a severe form of denial, or what some experts consider to be unconscious sanction. For some mothers, the potential loss of their husband may be of greater concern than the incest. Often mothers will insist that they had no idea about the incest. But even if a mother suspects or knows what is going on, she may feel powerless and unable to change the status quo. A mother could fear physical retaliation from her husband. Children may withhold the truth from their mothers in the belief that they are protecting them from the pain that would be created by disclosure. Often the child fears that the mother will not believe the story, and frequently this is the case. When victims of incest do disclose a history of abuse, they may turn to a trusted adult outside of the family setting.

WHAT DO I DO IF I LEARN THAT MY CHILD HAS BEEN SEXUALLY ABUSED?

Listen to your child and stay calm. If you learn that your child has been abused, you must engage the matter fully and report any suspicions of abuse to the authorities who will investigate formally. In all discussions with your child, it is critical for you to convey that you believe him or her. However, other evidence besides a child's report should be sought before an allegation is rejected or confirmed. Although you may naturally react emotionally to the shock of this revelation, you should make it clear to your child that you do not blame him or her for the abuse and he or she is not at fault. Reassure your child and remain consistent in communicating your love. Express love and support for your child with words and gestures. Respect your child's privacy and potential fear or uncertainty about telling. Your child should feel comfortable talking about the incident, and not pressured. Tell your child that he or she will be protected from additional abuse and that any threatened retaliation on the part of the abuser will not be permitted.

Child sexual abuse should be reported immediately to the appropriate authorities in your community. Call your local police or sheriff's department (or 911) if the child has been abused by a family member, friend, or acquaintance, or if the abuse occurred in a licensed day-care setting, recreational facility, or school. If you are able to identify the assailant, you also may report the abuse to your local county department of children's protective or social services. Sexual abuse by a stranger should be reported to the police. Abuse of a child in a licensed day-care setting, school, or other institution should be reported as well to your state bureau of licensing for day-care centers or the Department of Education.

If your spouse is the abuser, you must separate the child from him. Your child must not receive the message that he or she is to blame; therefore, do not send the child away alone. Leave with your child, and stay together throughout the process to follow. Next steps may include getting your incestuous partner out of the home so that you and the child can return. Do not feel guilty for this breakdown of the family; it was not caused by you or the child, but by the abuser. A period of time away from the abuser will enable you to assess the situation with the help of professionals, other family members, and close friends, and allow therapy to begin. Subsequently, you may decide whether to try to be a family again (if therapy has progressed) or to seek permanent separation through divorce.

Never, at any time during this process, should you allow the abuser to be with your child in an unsupervised setting. If the abuse was perpetrated by a sibling, family therapy will be required followed by reconciliation in a supervised setting. Abuse by another relative, such as an uncle or cousin, should result in greatly reduced access to the child and then only in a supervised manner.

WHAT HAPPENS AFTER I REPORT THAT MY CHILD HAS BEEN SEXUALLY ABUSED?

Your child should receive immediate medical attention if you believe that he or she has been sexually abused. An examination by a qualified medical professional, preferably a pediatrician, is important to rule out possible internal injury or the presence of a sexually transmitted disease. A medical professional will collect forensic evidence that may be used in the criminal prosecution of an assailant. States laws require the reporting of child abuse by various professionals. These laws are intended to protect children and to ensure needed care and follow-up, as well as to prosecute and thereby prevent assailants from abusing other children.

Mandated reporters of child sexual abuse include child-care custodians (e.g., teachers, day-care center workers, foster parents, and social workers) and many health professionals (e.g., doctors, dentists, psychologists, and nurses). Public health practitioners, employees of child protective agencies, probation officers, sheriffs, and county welfare workers may be required by law to report suspected abuse. These individuals generally have your child's best interests at heart, and reporting will ensure that resources are mobilized to protect your child (and other children) and to control the abuser.

There are ways you can reduce the trauma experienced by your child after abuse has been discovered and while it is investigated. Investigative interviews can be reduced in number and repetition avoided by videotaping and allowing more than one professional in the room during the interview (yet limiting questioning to one person). The physical examination should be explained to your child as something to make sure he or she is not harmed, and the child's consent should be obtained. Each step should be explained fully beforehand to the child. If the child refuses, it may be necessary to delay the examination or to conduct it under mild sedation.

When an investigation confirms that sexual abuse has occurred, a team of professionals will determine what to do next. The two principal concerns are for the child's safety and rehabilitation. The family may remain intact, or the abuser may have to leave. Or the child may be removed from the home. Most professionals prefer to remove the abuser from the home rather than the child, but this is not always possible. Sometimes the child is best placed outside the family for protection, especially if the mother is unable or unwilling to protect and support the child. The child should be asked what he or she would like to happen. The preferences of the child are given great weight. If the child wants to be removed from the family, this should occur. However, the desired outcome after intervention and treatment is that the family will remain intact, if possible.

Therapy is available for victims of child sexual abuse, such as group therapy, individual treatment, counseling for pairs of family members (e.g., victim–mother, victim–father), and family therapy. Individual therapy may be provided for each family member. Therapy for family pairs is meant to heal specific relationships. Family therapy usually occurs after it is clear that reunification of the family is in the interest of the victim. Often a combination of therapies will be used. The objectives of therapy include dealing with the effects of the sexual abuse and to decrease the risk for future abuse. Group therapy exists for each family member, including the victim and the abuser.

Unfortunately, child victims of sexual abuse are put into an adult justice system that does not differentiate in its treatment of children and adults. The criminal justice system can view children with some skepticism, and there are special barriers to prosecuting victimizers of children. Children have special needs that the system does not respond to effectively. Relative to an adult, a child is less physically, cognitively, and emotionally developed, and less able to offer testimony and act as witness. Children have difficulty reasoning logically and often think in very literal and concrete terms, which may result in contradictory or confusing answers to questions. Children have a different and limited understanding of time, and their recall of events may not be understandable in adult terms. Great care must be used to question a child in terms the child can understand, such as whether an event occurred before or after school, or the season in which it occurred.

Children may answer questions incompletely because they believe that adults fully understand them. They have limited attention spans and may be uncomfortable when strangers ask them questions. Children often do not understand the different roles of professionals who are interviewing them. A child may not appreciate why they must tell and retell their histories to police, doctors, prosecutors, social workers, and others. A child's reaction to this repetition may range from frustration and tuning out to trauma, as the abuse is reviewed again and again.

There are serious implications for child victims whose cases are not legally prosecuted. Children who are sexually abused by a perpetrator who is unpunished may feel that adults did not believe them, and they may have (legitimate) fears of being victimized again. Victims of stranger abuse have some advantage insofar as they can receive support from their families, and with counseling, may overcome abuse. For victims abused by a family member, their best hope remains with the courts. A perpetrator may be placed under a no contact order or may receive treatment even if not successfully prosecuted. If the child is removed from the home and placed in foster care, which is usually the last resort of juvenile courts, the child may feel punished. Failure to prosecute leaves the abuser free to molest other children.

Throughout the process, which may be very difficult and highly emotional, it is important that you pay close attention to your own needs and feelings as well as those of your child. Support groups, counseling services, and advice from members of your local clergy and community are available to help you through this tragic experience. You may experience shock, anger, and disbelief; your emotional states can run from anxiety to depression and include disturbances in your sleep. Recognize that you cannot be of help to your child unless you take good care of yourself. Protect yourself physically and emotionally. Do not repress your feelings or resist the many emotions that will confront you as you learn about the abuse and manage the problem. Be sure, however, to communicate clearly and continually to your child that your anger, pain, and negative feelings are not directed at him or her.

CAN CHILD SEXUAL ABUSE BE PREVENTED BY SOCIETY?

The most common strategy used today to prevent sexual abuse of children involves teaching them how to protect themselves. Much educational material on preventing child sexual abuse has been created by rape/sexual assault crisis centers and counseling services, therapists, child abuse prevention services, and governmental agencies. These materials tend to focus on directing parents and children in methods that decrease the risk of abuse. Children's books, DVDs, television programs, comic and coloring books, and live theater are aids to help children know what they should do if approached by someone who suggests any unusual and potentially abusive activities or who makes them feel uncomfortable.

Children learn through such education that their bodies are their own property, and it is perfectly reasonable to refuse advances from adults who may want to abuse them. Children who are approached or have been molested learn to tell a trusted adult immediately. One approach suggests to children that "it's okay to say no." One problem with some of these materials is that they are not clear what it is that the child should say "no" to. Another approach avoids directly mentioning sexual acts by distinguishing between good and bad touches. A good touch might be a pat on the head or back or a hug, whereas, bad touches involve the genitals of either the child or an adult. An issue with some of these strategies is the authors' desire not to be explicit about sex. Adults are often not comfortable referring to penises and vaginas as such, preferring to talk about "private parts."

Many approaches tend to emphasize the risk to children from unknown adults and so minimize the far greater likelihood that they will be abused sexually by adults whom they know, including their own parents. Too much focus on strangers as potential abusers is a problem, because child sexual abuse is often perpetrated by someone who knows the child. Clearly, warning children about strangers can do little harm, except perhaps to provoke excessive fear of adults. Educational materials rarely instruct children about what they can and should do if they have been sexually abused by a relative or their father or mother. Incest is such a profoundly taboo topic in our society that it is not much discussed.

Parents sometimes oppose child sexual abuse prevention programs because of fear that they will promote sexual thoughts and actions in children. Many parents find incredible the idea that their child may be at risk for sex abuse from some family member, and so programs that try to prevent incest are likely to meet with resistance. Interestingly, resistance does not come from parents who are abusing their children. These parents do not usually believe that they are engaged in an abusive relationship, but a loving one. The resistance comes from non-abusive parents in the community. Teachers also may resist the introduction of child sexual abuse prevention programs into their schools because they feel this adds to their responsibilities, expanding an already overburdened curriculum. Most teachers do not see this as their role and feel that society frequently turns to them for solutions to problems having little to do with their educational mission.

Other obstacles and difficulties must be overcome to help children prevent their own sexual exploitation. One problem concerns memory recall of the prevention message. Children quickly forget much of the information conveyed in these programs, usually within a matter of months and often in less than a year. Also, it is difficult to create any sense of urgency that could compel a child to act if that child has no personal history of abuse. Abuse often does not seem pertinent to a child who has not experienced it and, when combined with the fact that programs are often vague to avoid discussing sex explicitly, their impact may be small. However, for a child who has been a victim of sexual abuse, prevention programs are readily understood and may help to identify children who have been abused. Often one or more children will come forward during a presentation to say that they have been sexually abused.

The view of some experts is that instructing children to merely refuse advances from a pedophile is far too simple a response to a very difficult and complex problem. There is a sense that it is inappropriate to place the primary responsibility for preventing sexual abuse on its victims without also implementing other measures. Improved reporting of child abuse is much needed to enable better detection of victims and abusers. Even though children who already have been victimized may not be helped directly by better detection, it reduces the risk for other children.

Most child abuse prevention experts believe that the responsibility for protecting children is ultimately in the hands of parents. Unfortunately, it seems that many parents who become abusive were not ready to become parents in the first place. Often these fathers and mothers never really wanted to have a child, and that fact is reflected in the way they treat them. If parents have been abused themselves as children, they have a poor model of how a parent should behave with a child. Sometimes impairment from drug or alcohol abuse undermines efforts to raise children. Efforts should be made to help such parents recognize their problems and seek appropriate treatment, guidance, and support for themselves, first as individuals, and second as parents, while society maintains vigilance for the welfare of their children.

Greater prevention efforts can reduce opportunities for abuse in institutions, such as schools, foster homes, and day-care centers, that are regulated by state and local governments. The professional and educational requirements for child-care workers in many U.S. day-care centers are modest at best. Less than one-fourth of child-care workers have professional training, and many are paid a minimum wage so that large day-care center chains can keep costs down. However, the result is that these low-paying jobs often attract less dedicated and qualified individuals, including pedophiles in search of a setting in which to abuse children. With shrinking state budgets, the number of day-care center inspectors and inspections has decreased. The majority of incidents of child abuse that occur in day-care centers are discovered by a child's parents. Countering this would require hiring more inspectors with additional public funds, an unlikely prospect in today's tight fiscal environment.

In schools it is possible that some teachers may sexually abuse the children to whom they have access. Incidents of this nature have been documented. There are legal obstacles to checking teachers for a record of sexual abuse or other criminal activity. Schools may claim that they are prohibited from investigating whether a teacher has an arrest record because of privacy protections. Teachers' unions have opposed attempts to examine the qualifications of teachers as well.

Another setting where child sexual abuse occurs is foster placement. Most children in juvenile institutions have not committed a serious offense. Children's shelters and foster-care centers are typically overcrowded, understaffed, and short of funds. Juvenile institutions pay very low wages and have difficulty attracting good employees. In this environment, it may be possible for pedophiles to get a job. During the 1980s, multiple cases of sexual abuse were reported in juvenile and child-care institutions in Oklahoma, Los Angeles County, and New York.

Because of the large numbers of children who need foster placement, several states have started to contract with private homes to take in children who have been abused and neglected by parents. There is a risk for abuse in these settings as well. Applicants to become foster parents are not thoroughly screened or well supervised. Although the majority of foster care providers seek to provide quality care, for others it is merely a source of income. For a pedophile, becoming a foster parent is an ideal method of acquiring easy access to children for sexual exploitation. Fingerprint checks are conducted on those who want to become foster parents, but they can only detect abusers who have been convicted in the past.

There are many private youth service and recreation organizations in the United States that have virtually no obstacles to deter child molesters from volunteer work. Several prominent organizations are lobbying to obtain legislation that will allow them to check applicants for arrest and conviction records. Parents need to be on guard, because it is quite possible for child molesters to secure employment with child-care service providers or volunteer jobs in local community-based youth organizations, and thereby gain access to children.

HOW CAN I PREVENT MY OWN CHILD FROM BEING SEXUALLY ABUSED?

The best way to prevent your children from becoming victims of child sexual abuse is to educate them about this problem and to make them feel comfortable in resisting the advances of an abuser. They must be taught to feel at ease in immediately communicating to you any effort by an individual to molest them. Discussions about child sexual abuse can be made a regular part of your effort to educate your child about safety in general. It is often difficult for parents to discuss sexuality and sexual exploitation with their children; nevertheless, it is essential to do so.

Parents have a legitimate concern about instilling excessive fear in their children. However, it is possible to educate your children about the potential for sexual assault and thereby reduce their risk without making them excessively fearful or suspicious of all adults. Many parents are uncomfortable with detailing the specifics of sexual relationships to young children. You can provide information to children about preventing their victimization by abusers without explicitly talking about sex, although some experts do not believe that this is the best approach. With young children who may not be able to understand sexual acts, this may be a more appropriate strategy. Tips for teaching your child to prevent sexual abuse follow in the next section.

Children can be taught that they should not tolerate anyone touching or doing anything to them that makes them feel uncomfortable. Empower your children to say no if they are asked, even by an adult, to do something that makes them ill at ease. Let them know that it is allright to refuse to do certain things or allow certain things to be done to them, even by relatives and close family friends. It is critical that these issues be explained to children in words that they can understand. Repetition of the message with young children is crucial. Make your child feel as if he or she can be at ease coming to you to talk about anything, including molestation.

Explaining to your child that adults also have to follow certain rules is very important. Teach children about the rule against adults touching a child's genitals (or "private parts"). Tell them that it is against the law for adults to do so. Let them know that anyone can potentially be a molester, that they should tell you or another trusted adult immediately if approached, and that they should not be embarrassed, ashamed, or afraid to report the abuse. At the same time, it is crucial that you educate your children about not making up stories about sexual abuse or making a false accusation.

There are other precautions parents can take to decrease the risk that their child may be sexually assaulted. Monitoring children's activities and knowing who they are with and what they are doing lessen the opportunities for an abuser to victimize a child. Become familiar with any adults and adolescents who have regular interactions with your children. It is important and appropriate for parents to question the motives of adults who spend a lot of time with their children. Do not presume that you could recognize an abuser, because there are no external signs of this pathology. It is imperative that you thoroughly assess babysitters, caretakers, and day-care providers. Do not only request references; check them out.

Most child sexual abusers have a recurrent pattern of assaulting children, and if they have been detected elsewhere, you may be able to find out. Websites list and locate registered sex offenders in communities across the United States (e.g., www.familywatchdog.us). Do not place your child in any child-care center that prohibits your making unannounced visits when your child is in attendance. Visit your child's day-care center regularly, and try to get a sense of what is going on in this vital environment for your child's well-being. Talk frequently with your child about what he or she experiences in your absence. Be attentive to anything that a child says or does that seems unusual, because you may be looking at an indicator of sexual abuse.

There are wide variations in the quality of care even among licensed day-care facilities. The greatest risk for abuse will be found at day-care centers that are unlicensed. Parents should avoid these; because they have never been inspected, there is no barrier to a child molester seeking employment. It is even possible for a child molester to establish a day-care center in his or her own home and remain unlicensed. Unlicensed day-care facilities are not always illegal; in many states, there is no need to acquire a license when less than six or ten children are cared for. Increasingly, day-care centers are fingerprinting and checking for criminal records among new employees.

A positive trend is the institution of day-care centers in the workplace by large corporations, where mothers or fathers are free to visit their child during work breaks. Such an arrangement reduces risk of abuse. Unfortunately, only a fraction of U.S. employers have established day-care at work. You may request that your employer create a day-care center at your place of work. For most parents, however, being educated about child sexual abuse—knowing what to look for, being alert, and taking care in selecting a day-care center for their children—remain the best methods for preventing abuse.

WHAT METHODS DO CHILD SEXUAL ABUSERS USE TO LURE CHILDREN?

Lures are techniques used by non-incest pedophiles to seduce children. In an effort to teach parents and children how to prevent child sexual abuse, experts have written books for parents to read with their children that describe specific lures used by child molesters (see Appendix 2, suggestions for further reading). The information was derived from interviews with individuals arrested for sexual assault of a child. Helping children to identify abuse lures while avoiding excessive fear and distrust is a balanced, non-alarmist approach to the problem. The emphasis is on teaching children, through parental participation and repetition, not to tolerate any adult crossing certain physical and sexual boundaries.

Experts have identified at least 15 categories of lures, most exploiting children's weaknesses and insecurities, or their childish desires and needs. Affection and attention given to a child, particularly one neglected by parents, is a very powerful lure. Pedophiles know that children who badly need affection and attention are among the easiest to abuse sexually. Children can be taught to tell the difference between real and artificial love, good and bad touches, and to be alert to affection that is tied to sexual advances (e.g., having private parts touched).

Molesters may request assistance from children, exploiting their good-natured desire to help others, to lure them into sexual abuse. Asking for directions, for assistance in carrying packages or home projects, or for help in finding lost pets are examples of this lure. Children should be taught that while helping others is good, adults should not be asking kids for help, and a child should always check with their parents first before helping an adult. Parents can demonstrate how to keep a safe distance from cars when directions are requested.

Children have a natural inclination to obey authority figures, such as police, fire, health, or utilities personnel. However, abusers may gain access to a home (and child) by posing as officials using false identification cards and badges. Although children should be taught to respect authority on the one hand, they can ask other adults nearby to help them when approached by an authority figure. This will help scare off those who are posing as officials to gain access to children. Children should be given the confidence never to allow anyone, even authority figures, to touch their (or force them to touch another person's) private parts. Particular caution should be given to plainclothes policemen and unmarked police cars. Children should seek and accept assistance only from uniformed officers and marked cars.

Bribery is another commonly used lure. Bribes can be used as payment for a child to go with a molester, for the actual performance of sex, and to keep it secret. Bribery can be used to coerce children by the abuser demanding a payment in return for a gift, but children should be taught that such payment is wrong and can hurt them. Parents should convey to children that gifts that are supposed to be kept secret are a warning sign. They should refuse such gifts and immediately tell their parents about the person who offered it.

Sexual abusers may try to appeal to a child's ego and desire for fame to lure them into an abusive situation. The abuser offers the possibility of life as an athlete, a movie star, a model, or a rock star. First the abuser compliments the child, and then invites him or her to an audition that is held privately and kept as a secret from parents. During the audition, sexual advances occur. Children should be taught that they must tell any talent scout to talk to their parents and that a legitimate scout would have no hesitation doing so. They should be alarmed when someone tries to keep their parents out of a talent search.

A false emergency may be used as another lure. The abuser tries to worry and confuse a child by telling him or her that someone the child knows is ill or has had an accident, and then offers to transport the child to the person. In this instance, the child's fear about the fake crisis overcomes reasonable suspicions about accompanying a stranger. Children should be taught to confirm an emergency by calling parents or going home, or as an alternative, seeking a trusted adult for assistance. Discuss possible emergencies with your children and what they should expect, including who might contact them.

Other lures are variations on these examples. They include using games such as wrestling or other sports as lures, particularly those that involve restraining a child. A local hero, such as a favorite teacher, an athletic star, or other celebrity that a child admires, may try to use his or her status to victimize a child sexually.

Molesters also may pose as employers, offering children or adolescents interesting and high-paying work opportunities as a lure for abuse. Parents should thoroughly investigate any jobs their children want to take, monitor their children's work time, and teach them not to enter a customer's house in door-to-door sales jobs unless accompanied by a trusted adult. Children should not attend job interviews alone, and parents should always meet the family for whom a child intends to babysit. Tell your children that other children may sometimes be recruited by a molester to bring them into an abusive situation or may themselves be molesters.

Pornography can be used to desensitize children to sexual scenes, particularly those between adults and children. Children must be made to feel comfortable telling their parents if any adult or other child shows them pornographic magazines or video content or asks that they pose for them. Drugs and alcohol also are used as lures by child molesters. Computer online services may use lures to access children for abuse. Combining bribery, drugs, hero worship, games, jobs, pornography, and other lures is made easier by internet communication and provides a molester anonymity until he actually meets the child. Parents should explain to children how lures can be offered through e-mail and online services, how to be on guard for them, and to tell parents of any communication that may be suspicious.

IS THE INTERNET USED TO VICTIMIZE CHILDREN?

Yes, the internet is a tool frequently used by abusers to identify and access children. In 2005, approximately one in seven young people received unwanted sexual solicitations online. Four percent of youth received sexual solicitations involving seeking an in-person meeting with the child, a telephone call, or sending the child mail, money, or gifts. Nine percent of young internet users have been exposed to distressing sexual material while online, and 9% report being harassed online.

In 2006 the CyberTipline operated by the National Center for Missing and Exploited Children received 62,480 reports of child pornography and 6,384 reports of online enticement of children to engage in sexual acts. Parents must be highly vigilant in limiting and monitoring children's use of new technology that can be used by predators and other violent perpetrators in diverse and often subtle ways. As in other forms of childhood violence, nonjudgmental and supportive parent involvement is the best preventive measure. Refer to the section on electronic aggression in Chapter 5 for discussion of the risks engendered with the expanding use of technology by youth and of methods for preventing their exploitation.

WHAT DO I DO IF I AM SEXUALLY ABUSING OR SEXUALLY ATTRACTED TO A CHILD?

Sexual arousal that may occur incidentally and innocently in a relationship with a child is not a problem if it is not sought after or planned and if not fulfilled by actions. Sexual attraction that leads to planning and taking action to engage a sexual relationship of any kind with a child is abuse. If you are sexually involved with a child, you may be rationalizing this behavior by telling yourself that the child likes and desires the sex or has asked for sex. You may be thinking that it is acceptable to have sex with a child because you are teaching him or her about sex. None of these rationalizations are true, and you are deceiving yourself. It is not acceptable to be sexually involved with a child. If you care at all for the child, you must stop having any kind of sexual interaction with him or her. Sexual relations cause psychological damage to children. Abuse may have long-term emotional and physical effects. You must stop. You can get help from a number of resources in your community. If you are afraid of going to jail for what you have done, it may be possible to avoid prison through a pretrial diversion program. It can make a great difference if you seek help for the abuse yourself rather than it being reported by the child or the family.

You may not realize that help is available. Being condemned socially and possibly put in prison are not inevitable. You can receive therapy and reduce the time spent in jail or avert it altogether. You must appreciate that your entire family may be hurt by abuse. In addition to potential imprisonment, there are fines and court costs as well as civil liability. Particularly if you have only recently begun abusing a child, you can be treated. You may have convinced yourself that the abuse will never be detected, but it is likely at some point that you will be caught. Take action now to help yourself and the child. Stop abusing and get professional help. Resources that you can contact for more information and referrals are listed at the end of this chapter.

WHAT DO I DO IF I AM A VICTIM OF SEXUAL ABUSE?

If you are being abused at home, find someone you trust and talk to him or her about the problem. This may be a family member, but could be someone outside the family who has your interest at heart. You may find a sympathetic person in a teacher, school counselor, or member of your church. Your doctor is another person who can put you in contact with a resource and services network that will stop the abuse. Go to a friend's house to call for help. Once you have reported the abuse to child protective services or a trusted person, always be consistent in telling your story. Despite the efforts of an abuser to silence you, do not change your story because this complicates your getting help to stop the abuse.

The situation can and will improve, but only after you take action to protect yourself and bring attention to the situation. If you are being sexually abused by a neighbor, relative outside the home, teacher, or other person, tell your parents immediately. Do not be ashamed, and do not feel guilty for the abuse; it is not your fault. It is the abuser who has the problem, not you. Your parents may be shocked at first, even angry, but this anger is not directed at you but at the person who molested you. Your parents can stop the abuse and get others to also protect you and help you understand what has happened and how you can feel better in the future.

If you are reading this book, you are probably a teenager. If you need help to stop abuse and your parents are not around or willing to help you, you can contact one of the agencies listed at the end of this chapter near where you live. If one of your parents is abusing you, contact your local child protective services agency or an abuse crisis hotline for assistance right away.

WHAT HAPPENS TO ABUSERS WHO ARE CAUGHT?

Child sexual abuse cases are settled more commonly by a guilty plea from the abuser than by adjudication or trial. A guilty plea is the desired outcome because the child is then saved from testifying at trial. A Department of Justice survey of 52 law enforcement agencies found that approximately 40% of child sexual abuse cases resulted in arrest. In another 42% of cases, the report had merit but could not be pursued because of insufficient evidence or lack of cooperation from the victim. Prosecution rates for child sexual abuse range from approximately 40% to 100%. Sexual assaults of children under the age of six years are the least likely to result in arrest. In providing an initial statement to police, in subsequent deposition, and through testimony at a preliminary hearing or grand jury, the child has an important role in the prosecution and in achieving a guilty plea.

Penalties for child sexual abuse vary. Abuse of younger children often results in more severe penalties. The level of force used in the abuse also is considered, and use of heavy force often results in a more severe penalty. The relationship between the abuser and the victim influences the court as well. Abuse by a parent, relative, or household member is considered a more serious crime than by perpetrators outside the home. Sexual abusers who have committed acts of penetration as opposed to fondling or other non-physical acts often receive longer criminal sentences.

Of sexual abuse assailants who are convicted, between 40% and 80% are sentenced to some form of incarceration. A study by the American Bar Association found that approximately two-thirds of convicted abusers are incarcerated. It also was found that individuals convicted of sex crimes against children were more likely to receive probation than those who commit similar crimes against adults. Up to one-half of convicted child molesters are required to participate in a sexual abuse treatment program. Sixty percent of convicted sex offenders in the United States are under conditional supervision in the community (on parole or probation).

In 1994, there were approximately 234,000 offenders convicted of rape or sexual assault under the care, custody, or control of corrections agencies. An estimated 24% of those serving time for rape and 19% of those serving time for sexual assault had been on probation or parole at the time of the offense for which they were in state prison in 1991. Of child molesters released from prison, 5.3% were rearrested for a new sex offense within 3 years of their release. Of released sex offenders who allegedly committed another sex crime, 40% perpetrated the new offense within a year or less from their prison discharge. The eventual rearrest rate for convicted child predators is 52%. In 2008, the Center for Missing and Exploited Children reported that there were 686,515 registered sex offenders in the United States, or 223 per 100,000 on a population basis.

CAN CHILD SEXUAL ABUSERS BE TREATED?

Although abusers can be treated, it is not yet clear whether treatment is successful in preventing further sexual assaults. Particularly in cases of incest, because the abuser's actions have been (presumably) precipitated by difficult relationships within the family, some judges and therapists have thought to control incest among fathers by using a program of psychotherapy. Not all therapists distinguish between assailants who commit incest and those who prey on children not related to them, and not all try to determine whether the sexual attraction to children is deeply entrenched or not. Whether the assailant is genuinely motivated to change his behavior is critically important to the success of any therapeutic program.

Several states have pretrial diversion programs for sexual abusers. These programs allow abusers who admit guilt and want help to receive psychotherapy instead of going to jail or prison. Such programs are used increasingly with abusers who have no prior convictions and when no force (or threat of force) was used against the child. Typically, the abuser has to move out of the child's home and have no further contact with that child (or any other) until allowed by the court. The parent is usually required to attend weekly individual or group treatment sessions. Treatment is geared toward helping the abuser understand why he sexually abuses children, what his arousal pattern is around children, and why he acts on the arousal. A plan is developed to prevent a relapse of sexual abuse.

Pretrial diversion recognizes that effective therapy is not usually possible in a prison setting, and imprisoning an incestuous parent is only likely to increase the guilt experienced by the child victim for reporting the abuse. Family therapy in a diversion program can change the behavior of an abusive father, a denying mother, and the child in an effort to salvage the family. Diversion programs also address precipitating stresses that may have contributed to the parent becoming abusive. Participation in alcohol treatment and marital counseling programs, as well as special counseling on interpersonal relations, may be included in sexual abuse therapy. Individual counseling is provided in separate sessions for the mother and the victim, and later in combination with the abuser and other family members.

A central element of any therapeutic approach to child sexual abuse is to ensure that the father recognizes and admits to the child that he—not the child—is at fault and fully responsible for the abuse. This reduces the child's burden of guilt. When the father is the abuser, the mother may experience resentment and anger toward the child for reporting the abuse or permitting it to occur. The child must be made to understand that the fault lies entirely with the abuser (and possibly with the other parent who did not protect the child).

The aim of therapy is to reduce the chance that an incestuous parent will abuse his child again. Short-term success may be readily achieved. However, the underlying narcissism of the abuser often remains unaffected by therapy. Over the long term, psychotherapy can affect narcissistic personality disorders, but they are very resistant to treatment. Without substantially altering this characteristic, the abuser may again offend. A real commitment and willingness to participate on the part of the abuser are required for psychotherapy to succeed. Therefore, the abusers most likely to be helped by psychotherapy are those who turn themselves in and seek help. Unfortunately, this is uncommon.

Other forms of therapy exist, such as behavior modification, which assumes that all behaviors, including the impulse to abuse children sexually, are learned and can be extinguished. Behavioral therapy is not concerned with the origins of a pedophile's activity or how current relationships may have contributed to abuse. Rather, it attempts to reeducate pedophiles. One tactic associates photographs of naked children with unpleasant stimuli (e.g., a painful electric shock or a drug that causes vomiting). Another strategy is used to decrease the abuser's fantasy obsession with children and move it toward adult women. Others try to recondition or desensitize the abuser to sexual arousal from children. A genuine desire to eliminate sexual attraction to children is required for the success of these approaches. Confirmed abusers serving long prison sentences are unlikely to be motivated to receive therapy.

In view of the low success rate of therapy, some experts believe that the best strategy to use with confirmed pedophiles is "incapacitation"—isolating them in jail. Although prison is not a therapeutic environment and few inmates obtain adequate therapy there, as a practical matter prison eliminates the possibility of an abuser victimizing additional children. However, although imprisonment serves the purpose of keeping child sexual abusers away from potential victims, because there is insufficient capacity in the prison system to hold the suspected number of pedophiles in the United States, prisons do not represent a complete solution to the problem. Evidence indicates that upon release from prison many pedophiles will again sexually abuse children. Unlike other violent criminal behavior such as assault and felonies, which criminals tend to outgrow in mid-life, there is reason to believe that pedophilia persists throughout the life of an abuser.

In Europe there has been an effort to find alternative solutions, such as chemical or surgical castration. The drug Depo-Provera, a progestin, is the leading method of chemical castration. In the United States these procedures have generated controversy from civil rights organizations as well as resistance from the medical community. Nonetheless, in 1996 the governor of California signed the first state bill enabling chemical castration by Depo-Provera to be used as a mandatory condition of parole for criminals twice convicted of certain sex crimes, including child molestation. In cases in which the victim is under 13 years of age, California judges may require first-time offenders to undergo chemical castration. After a second offense, treatment is mandatory. At least eight other states have since experimented with chemical castration. In Iowa and Florida, offenders may be sentenced to chemical castration in all cases involving serious sex offenses. As occurs in California, treatment is mandatory after a second offense. Louisiana Governor Bobby Jindal signed a bill in 2008 allowing Louisiana judges to sentence convicted rapists to chemical castration.

Female hormones, anti-androgen drugs, and contraceptives are used to reversibly decrease the male sex drive in abusers. The American Psychiatric Association conducted a study of their use in 48 men with histories of sexually deviant behavior and found them effective among 40 subjects in reducing the desire for deviant sexual behavior, lessening the frequency of sexual fantasies, and increasing control over sexual urges. No adverse side effects were evident. However, because hormonal treatment does not affect the psychological characteristic of narcissism, or need for power that underlies abusive behavior, it may be effective primarily in abusers who are highly motivated.

In some cases of incest, the mother may want to terminate her relationship with the abuser. Others will decide to try to work to salvage the marriage and family. This decision often is influenced profoundly by the motivation of the abuser to obtain therapy and how well he progresses. Good progress of therapy may be associated with the extent to which the abuser accepts responsibility for the abuse, as well as how far he has come to appreciate the harm that the abuse has caused the victim and his spouse or partner.

DOES CHILD PORNOGRAPHY CONTRIBUTE TO CHILD SEXUAL ABUSE?

Congress passed the first federal law prohibiting the production and sale of child pornography in 1978. Before this, there were approximately 300 child pornography magazines available in the United States. Although the law did not stop the exchange or possession of child pornographic material, it did halt the open sale of such magazines across the country. What remains of child pornography in the United States today is exchanged primarily among active pedophiles. Indeed, only pedophiles have objected to the law as a constraint on their expression of free speech.

It is unclear what effect pornography has on an individual. Debate has been intense as to whether viewing violent pornography actually contributes to violent sexual behavior. Many experts in the field do not think there is sufficient scientific evidence to support the view that exposure to pornography increases individual risk of perpetrating sexual violence. In Japan, for example, where violent pornography is abundant, there is a low incidence of rape and sexual assault. Researchers believe that an interest in child pornography may follow and flow from a sexual attraction to children rather than stimulate it. In this view pornography reinforces a pedophile fantasy but does not create the urge to molest children.

It is difficult to specifically define what does and does not constitute child pornography in the mind of a pedophile. Because advertising that contains children in bathing suits and underwear (or other non-pornographic materials) may stimulate a pedophile sexually as much as outright pornography, control of pornographic exploitation of children becomes very difficult. Some believe that the effort and resources required to eliminate the exchange of child pornography would be better spent arresting child molesters. Certainly existing laws have helped to reduce the use of children in creating pornography, itself a form of child sexual abuse.

WHERE CAN I GET MORE INFORMATION AND HELP?

For information about and help in stopping child sexual abuse, contact your local health department or doctor, local medical centers and hospitals, and other social service providers. These agencies can refer you to an organization that provides specific services for your needs. For information on child sexual abuse treatment and prevention services in your community, look in the Yellow Pages under "Human Services Organizations" or "Social Service Organizations."

To report child sexual abuse or an assault, call your local police department, or 911, or contact the ChildHelp National Child Abuse Hotline at (800) 4-A-CHILD (24453) or (800) 2-A-CHILD (24453, TDD for hearing impaired). The National Child Abuse Hotline may be reached at (800) 25-ABUSE (22873).

Sex offender registries that may be used to find and identify offenders residing in your community and state can be found at a number of sites on the internet, including www.fbi.gov/hq/cid/cac/registry.htm or www.nsopw.gov/Core/Conditions.aspx.

Appendix 1 at the back of the book provides a state-by-state website listing of compensation and assistance programs for victims of violence and crime. You may find assistance by contacting one of your state programs. Appendix 2 is a bibliography for further reading on each of the violence topics discussed in this volume, organized chapter by chapter.

The following are national and state organizations and internet websites that offer information and services to victims, families, and professionals about child sexual abuse treatment and prevention.

NATIONAL ORGANIZATIONS

ACTION for Child Protection
(704) 845-2121

American Academy of Pediatrics
(847) 434-4000

American Humane Association
(800) 227-4645

American Professional Society on the Abuse of Children (APSAC)
(877) 402-7722

Bureau of Indian Affairs, Indian Country Child Abuse Hotline
(800) 633-5155

Center for Child Protection and Family Support
(202) 544-3144

Childhelp
(480) 922-8212

Children's Defense Fund
(800) 223-1200

Children's Institute International
(213) 385-5100

Children's Rights of America
(770) 442-7865

Children's Safety Network
(617) 618-2918

Child Welfare Information Gateway
(800) 394-3366

Child Welfare League of America
(703) 412-2400

Clearinghouse National Center for Child Abuse and Neglect Information
(703) 385-7565 or (800) 394-3366

Faith Trust Institute
(206) 634-1903

Family Resources Coalition
(352) 854-3001

Generation Five
(510) 251-8552

Incest Survivors Resource Network International
(505) 521-4260

International Center for Assault Prevention
(800) 258-3189

Kempe Center for the Prevention and Treatment of Child Abuse and Neglect
(303) 864-5300

Missing Children in America
(888) 556-4774

National Association for Children of Alcoholics
(301) 468-0985

National Association of Counsel for Children
(888) 828-6233

National Association to Prevent Sexual Abuse of Children (NAPSAC)
(651) 340-0537

National Center for Missing and Exploited Children
(800) THE-LOST or 843-5678; TDD (800) 826-7653

National Center for the Prosecution of Child Abuse
(703) 549-9222

National Center for Victims of Crime, National Crime Victim Helpline
(800) FYI-CALL (394-2255); TTY (800) 211-7996

National Center on Child Abuse and Neglect (NCCAN)
Department of Health and Human Services
(202) 245-0586 or (703) 385-7565

National Center on Domestic and Sexual Violence
(512) 407-9020

National Child Abuse Hotline
(800) 4-A-CHILD (422-4453)

National Children's Advocacy Center
(256) 533-KIDS (5437)

National Children's Alliance
(800) 239-9950

National Committee to Prevent Child Abuse
(312) 663-3520

National Council on Child Abuse and Family Violence
(202) 429-6695

National Crime Prevention Council
(202) 466-6272

National Domestic Violence Hotline
(800) 729-SAFE (7233); (800) 787-3224 Hearing Impaired

National Institute of Justice Criminal Justice Reference Service
(800) 851-3420

National Organization for Victim Assistance (NOVA)
(800) TRY-NOVA or (800) 879-6682

National Resource Center on Child Sexual Abuse
(800) 543-7006 or (205) 534-6868

National Resource Center on Domestic Violence
(800) 537-2238; TTY (800) 553-2508

National Sexual Violence Resource Center
(877) 739-3895; TTY (717) 909-0715

Victims of Crime Resource Center
Department of Justice Office for Victims of Crime
(800) 851-3420; TYY (877) 712-9279

National Youth Crisis Hotline (reporting child abuse and help for runaways)
(800) 442-HOPE (4673)

Parents Anonymous
(909) 621-6184

Resource Center on Domestic Violence, Child Protection
and Custody
(800) 527-3223

Survivors of Incest Anonymous
(410) 893-3322

STATE CHILD ABUSE REPORTING AGENCIES, CRISIS CENTERS, AND HOTLINES

Alabama Department of Human Resources
www.dhr.state.al.us/page.asp?pageid=347
(334) 242-1310

Alaska—State of Alaska Office of Children's Services
http://hss.state.ak.us/ocs
(800) 478-4444

Arizona Department of Economic Security
https://egov.azdes.gov/CMSInternet/main.aspx?menu=154&id=2030
(888) SOS-CHILD (767-2445)

Arkansas Department of Human Services
www.arkansas.gov/dhs/chilnfam/child_protective_services.htm
(800) 482-5964

California Department of Social Services
www.cdss.ca.gov/cdssweb/PG20.htm
No statewide hotline; call your county child protective services child abuse hotline
or Childhelp (800) 422-4453 for assistance reporting

Colorado Department of Human Services, Division of Child Welfare
www.cdhs.state.co.us/childwelfare
Call county Child Welfare child abuse hotline (303) 866-5932 or
Childhelp (800) 422-4453 for assistance reporting

Connecticut Department of Children and Families
www.ct.gov/dcf/cwp/view.asp?a=2556&q=314388
(800) 842-2288

Delaware Department of Services for Children, Youth and Their Families
http://kids.delaware.gov/services/crisis.shtml
(800) 292-9582

District of Columbia Child and Family Services Agency
www.cfsa.dc.gov
(202) 671-7233

Florida Department of Children and Families
www.dcf.state.fl.us/abuse/report
(800) 96-ABUSE (962-2873)

Georgia Department of Human Resources Child Protective and
Placement Services Unit
www.dhr.state.ga.us
(404) 657-3416

Hawaii Department of Human Services
hawaii.gov/dhs/protection/social_services/child_welfare
(808) 832-5300

Idaho Department of Health and Welfare
http://healthandwelfare.idaho.gov/Children/AbuseNeglect/tabid/74/default.aspx
(800) 926-2588

Illinois Department of Children and Family Services
www.state.il.us/dcfs
(800) 25-ABUSE (252-2873) or (217) 785-4020

Indiana Family and Social Services Administration
http://www.in.gov/dcs/2454.htm
(800) 800-5556

Iowa Department of Human Services
www.dhs.iowa.gov/Consumers/Safety_and_Protection/Abuse_Reporting/
ChildAbuse.html
(800) 362-2178

Kansas Department of Social and Rehabilitation Services
www.srskansas.org/services/child_protective_services.htm
(800) 922-5330 (in Kansas, outside Topeka)
(785) 296-2561 (in Topeka, or outside Kansas)

Kentucky Cabinet for Health and Family Services
http://chfs.ky.gov/dcbs/dpp/childsafety.htm
(800) 752-6200

Louisiana Department of Social Services
www.dss.state.la.us/index.cfm?md=pagebuilder&tmp=home&pid=181
Hotlines by parish or call the Childhelp hotline
(800) 422-4453

Maine Department of Health and Human Services
www.maine.gov/dhhs/ocfs/abuse.htm
(800) 452-1999

Maryland Department of Human Resources
www.dhr.state.md.us/cps/address.php
Child abuse reporting by county office or call the Childhelp hotline
(800) 422-4453

Massachusetts Department of Social Services
www.mass.gov/dss
(800) 792-5200

Michigan Department of Human Services
www.michigan.gov/dhs
(800) 942-4357

Minnesota Department of Human Services
www.dhs.state.mn.us
Contact county social service agency or call the Childhelp hotline
(800) 422-4453

Mississippi Department of Human Services
www.mdhs.state.ms.us/fcs_prot.html
(800) 222-8000

Missouri Department of Social Services
www.dss.mo.gov/cd/rptcan.htm
(800) 392-3738 or outside Missouri (573) 751-3448

Montana Department of Public Health and Family Services
www.dphhs.mt.gov/cfsd/index.shtml
(866) 820-5437

Nebraska Department of Health and Human Services
www.hhs.state.ne.us/cha/chaindex.htm
(800) 652-1999

Nevada Department of Health and Human Services
http://dcfs.state.nv.us/DCFS_ReportSuspectedChildAbuse.htm
(800) 992-5757

New Hampshire Department of Health and Human Services
www.dhhs.state.nh.us/DHHS/BCP/default.htm
(800) 894-5533 or (603) 271-6556

New Jersey Division of Youth and Family Services
www.state.nj.us/dcf/abuse/how
(877) NJ-ABUSE (652-2873)

New Mexico Children, Youth and Families Department
www.cyfd.org
(800) 797-3260

New York Office of Children and Family Services
www.ocfs.state.ny.us/main/cps
(800) 342-3720 or TDD (800) 369-2437

North Carolina Department of Health and Human Services
www.dhhs.state.nc.us/dss/cps/index.htm
Contact local Department of Social Services or call the Childhelp hotline
(800) 422-4453

North Dakota Department of Human Services
www.nd.gov/dhs/services/childfamily/cps

Contact local county social services office or call the
Childhelp hotline
(800) 422-4453

Ohio Department of Human Services
www.jfs.ohio.gov
(866) 635-3748

Oklahoma Department of Human Services
www.okdhs.org/programsandservices/cps/default.htm
(800) 522-3511

Oregon Department of Human Services
www.oregon.gov/DHS/children/abuse/cps/report.shtml
Report to local county or call the Childhelp hotline
(800) 422-4453

Pennsylvania Department of Public Welfare
www.dpw.state.pa.us/ServicesPrograms/ChildWelfare
(800) 932-0313 or TDD (866) 872-1677

Puerto Rico Department of the Family
www.familia.gobierno.pr
(800) 981-8333

Rhode Island Department of Children, Youth and Families
www.dcyf.ri.gov/child_welfare/index.php
(800) RI-CHILD (742-4453)

South Carolina Department of Social Services
http://dss.sc.gov/content/customers/protection/cps/index.aspx
Contact county Department of Social Services office or call the
Childhelp hotline (800) 422-4453

South Dakota Department of Social Services, Child Protection Services
http://dss.sd.gov/cps/protective
(605) 773-3227

Tennessee Department of Children Services
http://state.tn.us/youth/childsafety.htm
(877) 237-0004 or (877) 54ABUSE (542-2873)

Texas Department of Family and Protective Services
www.dfps.state.tx.us/Contact_Us/report_abuse.asp
(800) 252-5400

Utah Department of Human Services
www.hsdcfs.utah.gov
(800) 678-9399

Vermont Department for Children and Families
http://dcf.vermont.gov/fsd/reporting_child_abuse
(800) 649-5285

Virginia Department of Social Services
www.dss.virginia.gov/family/childabuse.html
(800) 552-7096 or out of state (804) 786-8536

Washington Department of Social and Health Services
www.dshs.wa.gov/geninfo
(866) END-HARM (363-4276)

West Virginia Bureau for Children and Families
www.wvdhhr.org/bcf/children_adult/cps/report.asp
(800) 352-6513

Wisconsin Department of Children and Families
http://dcf.wi.gov/children/CPS/cpswimap.HTM
Contact the county Department of Social Services or call the Childhelp hotline
(800) 422-4453

Wyoming Department of Family Services
http://dfsweb.state.wy.us
Contact local Department of Family Services Office or call Childhelp
(800-422-4453)

USEFUL INTERNET WEBSITES

Action for Child Protection: www.actionchildprotection.org
American Academy of Pediatrics: www.aap.org
American Bar Association Center on Children and the Law: www.abanet.org/child
American Professional Society on the Abuse of Children: www.apsac.org
Campaign for Our Children: www.cfoc.org
Centers for Disease Control and Prevention: www.cdc.gov
Center for Sex Offender Management: www.csom.org
Child Abuse Prevention Network: http://childabuse.com
Child Welfare Information Gateway: www.childwelfare.gov
Child Welfare League of America: www.cwla.org
Childhelp: www.childhelpusa.org
Children's Safety Network: www.childrenssafetynetwork.org
Committee for Children: www.cfchildren.org
Family Violence Prevention Fund: www.endabuse.org
Family Violence and Sexual Assault Institute: http://fvsai.org
FBI National Sex Offender Public Website: www.fbi.gov/hq/cid/cac/registry.htm
Generation Five: www.generationfive.org
International Center for Assault Prevention: www.internationalcap.org
Kempe Center for the Prevention and Treatment of Child Abuse and Neglect:
    www.kempe.org
National Alliance to End Sexual Violence: www.naesv.org
National Association for Children of Alcoholics: www.nacoa.net
National Association to Prevent Sexual Abuse of Children: www.napsac.us
National Center for Missing and Exploited Children: www.missingkids.com
National Center for Victims of Crime: www.ncvc.org
National Center on Domestic and Sexual Violence: www.ncdsv.org
National Children's Advocacy Center: www.nationalchildrensalliance.org
National Children's Alliance: www.nationalchildrensalliance.org
National Committee for Prevention of Child Abuse and Family Violence: www.
    nccafv.org
National Institute of Justice, National Criminal Justice Reference Service: www.
    ncjrs.gov
National Resource Center on Domestic Violence: www.nrcdv.org
National Sex Offender Registry: www.nsopr.gov
National Sex Offender Registry: www.familywatchdog.us
National Sexual Violence Resource Center: www.nsvrc.org
National Victim Assistance Academy (OVC): www.ojp.usdoj.gov/ovc/assist/vaa.htm

Office for Victims of Crime: www.ovc.gov

Parents Anonymous: www.parentsanonymous.org

Prevent Child Abuse America: www.preventchildabuse.org

Rape, Abuse & Incest National Network: www.rainn.org

Safe NOW Project: http://safenowproject.org

SNAP (Survivors Network of Those Abused by Priests): www.snapnetwork.org

Survivors of Incest Anonymous: www.siawso.org

U.S. Department of Justice National Sex Offender Public Registry: www.nsopw. gov/Core/Conditions.aspx

Voices for America's Children: www.childadvocacy.org

CHAPTER 4

Youth and School Violence

- What are youth and school violence?
- How common are youth and school violence?
- Do youth and school violence inflict serious injury?
- Who is involved in youth and school violence?
- In what situations do youth and school violence occur?
- Are guns used in youth violence?
- What contributes to youth and school violence?
- Are there warning signs that your child may become involved in violence?
- Can youth violence be prevented or controlled?
- What can I do to raise nonviolent children?
- How can I help my child avoid becoming a victim of violence?
- Where can I get more information and help?

WHAT ARE YOUTH AND SCHOOL VIOLENCE?

Youth violence refers to harmful and injurious behaviors that start early in life and continue into young adulthood. This discussion will focus on youth through adolescence and into the college years (age 21 years). A young person can be involved in violence as a victim, an offender, or a witness. Youth violence includes various behaviors that have diverse impact. Bullying, slapping, or hitting tends to cause more emotional than physical harm. However, other violent actions, such as assault or rape, can result in serious injury and death.

School violence is one important form of youth violence. In many American communities, schools are no longer safe environments for students or teachers. Violence in schools is a serious public health problem and includes overtly violent acts such as homicide and battery, as well as concealed crimes such as child sexual abuse. Youth violence contributes substantially to the epidemic of violence in America. Reported levels of some of the most violent acts, including homicide, assault, and suicide, among young people across the United States have remained a very serious concern over the past several decades.

HOW COMMON ARE YOUTH AND SCHOOL VIOLENCE?

Youth violence is widespread in America. Young people are more likely than any other group to be victims of violent crime, yet teenage victims have the lowest rate of reporting to the police of any age group (36%). At least 40% of U.S. adolescents have witnessed violence, 17% have been victims of physical assault, 9% have been victims of physically abusive punishment, and 8% have been victims of sexual assault. In 2005–2006, 86% of public schools in the United States reported one or more violent incidents and thefts, amounting to 2.2 million crimes. In 2005, 5,686 young people aged 10–24 years were murdered, or an average of 16 each day. Homicide was the second leading cause of death for this age group. More than 720,000 violence-related injuries in young people aged 10–24 years were treated in U.S. emergency departments in 2006. Between 2001 and 2007, 116 students were killed in 109 separate school incidents. In 2008 the Federal Bureau of Investigation reported that persons under the age of 25 years accounted for 52% of those arrested for murder. In 2005, students aged 12–18 years were victims of approximately 1.5 million nonfatal crimes at school, including thefts and violent crimes. One percent of students reported violent victimization that year. It is estimated that youth violence costs the nation more than $158 billion every year.

A 2008 national youth survey found that 3 of 5 children and adolescents (61%) (birth to age 17 years) were exposed to violence, abuse, or a criminal victimization in the last year, including 46% who had been physically assaulted, 10% who had been maltreated by a caregiver, and 6% who had been sexually victimized. More than one-fourth (25.3%) witnessed a violent act, and 10% witnessed one family member assault another. More than one-third of the children experienced 2 or more different kinds of violence exposures in the past year, and 11% had experienced 5 or more. Approximately 1 in 10 (10.2%) was injured in an assault. Multiple victimizations were common: more than one-third (38.7%) experienced 2 or more direct victimizations in the previous year, and more than 1 in 10 (10.9%) experienced 5 or more direct victimizations in the previous year. As children grow older, their experience or incidence of victimization increases.

In the 2008 survey, children who were exposed to one type of violence, both within the past year and over their lifetimes, were at a much higher risk of experiencing other types of violence. A child who was physically assaulted in the past year was five times more likely also to have been sexually victimized and more than four times as likely to also have been maltreated during that period. A child who was physically assaulted during his or her lifetime would be more than six times as likely to have been sexually victimized and more than five times as likely to have been maltreated during his or her lifetime.

A national survey in 2007 found that 35.5% of high school students reported being in a physical fight during the prior year; 12.4% of these occurred on school property. Eighteen percent of high school students reported carrying a gun, knife, or club to school in the prior 30 days; 5.2% reported carrying a gun. Approximately 6% of students reported not going to school on 1 or more days in the 30 days preceding the survey because they felt unsafe at school or unsafe on their way to or from school. Approximately 8% reported being threatened or injured with a weapon on school property 1 or more times in the 12 months preceding the survey.

Historically, a steady increase in youth violence has occurred since 1980. From 1982 to 1991, the arrest rates for violent crimes committed by young people under the age of 18 years increased by 43%. An estimated 123,000 young people under age 18 years were arrested for violent offenses in 1991. This was the highest number in approximately 30 years. In the same year, approximately 3,400 young people were arrested for murder and non-negligent manslaughter. Arrests for robbery and aggravated assault also increased. Seventeen percent of all persons arrested in 1999 were under the age of 18 years. Approximately 38,000 juveniles were murdered between 1980 and 1997. In 2000, juveniles comprised 12% of all crime victims known to police, including 71% of all sex crime victims and 38% of all kidnapping victims.

Despite the violence that may affect young people at school, more youth victimizations happen away from school than at school. Nonetheless, personal safety and security have become major problems for school administrators over the past several decades. In the early 1990s, more than 2,500 school-aged children were killed by firearms in the United States each year. Approximately 13% of high school seniors reported being threatened with a weapon at school. The frequency of guns in schools increased to the point where many schools began to use metal detectors at entrances to prevent the admission of students with concealed weapons.

Over the 5-year period from 1994 to 1998, teachers were victims of 1,755,000 nonfatal crimes at school, including 668,000 violent crimes (rape or sexual assault, robbery, and aggravated and simple assault). This equals 83 crimes per 1,000 teachers per year, or approximately 10%–12% (341,000) of all elementary and secondary school teachers who were threatened with injury by a student (and 4% or 119,000 who were physically attacked). Between 1998 and 2003, teachers were the victims of approximately 183,400 total nonfatal crimes at school, including 64,600 violent crimes each year, a decline from prior years.

From 1990 to February 2002, the U.S. Bureau of Alcohol, Tobacco, Firearms and Explosives recorded 1,055 incidents of bombs being placed in schools. Of these incidents, only 14 were preceded by a warning to the school or authorities.

In 2006, 95,270 crimes were reported on university and college campuses, of which 3% were violent crimes (and 97% were property crimes). Of the violent crimes on campuses, 1,445 or 53% were aggravated assaults, 501 (18%) were forcible rapes, and 5 (0.1%) were homicides. In 2001, more than 97,000 students between the ages of 18 and 24 years were victims of alcohol-related sexual assault or date rape. Male college students were twice as likely to be victims of violence as females, and White students had higher rates of violent victimization than students of other races. Nine percent of violent victimizations against college students involved firearms, 7% involved knives, and 10% involved other type of weapons, such as blunt objects.

Despite these statistics and contrary to public opinion, violent crime (including homicides) in schools declined dramatically from 1994 to 2006 (with brief interruptions in the downward trend associated with highly publicized shootings that may have generated copycat violence). The rate at which juveniles committed serious violent crimes changed little between 1973 and 1989, peaked in 1993, and then declined to the lowest level since 1986. Rates of school-associated homicides decreased between 1992 and 2006, becoming more stable in recent years. The percentage of students who report being threatened or injured with a weapon at school has remained relatively stable since 1993, and the percentage who report carrying a weapon to school during the prior 30 days has been gradually decreasing. These declines cannot be attributed to a decline in the juvenile population, which increased during this period. Multiple factors are thought to have contributed to the decrease, including less violence associated with drug gangs, effective community-oriented law enforcement efforts, and school and community-based prevention efforts.

In sum, these data present a mixed picture of school safety. Although overall school crime rates have declined, violence, gangs, and drugs are still significant in some schools. In the aftermath of multiple school shootings around the nation, alarm about school and youth violence could not be higher. In late 1999, the Department of Justice's Office of Juvenile Justice and Delinquency Prevention offered the following insights and recommendations for a coherent approach to the problems of school and youth violence. The words are as pertinent in 2009 as they were a decade ago:

"In the midst of our national anxiety about recent violent tragedies in and around our schools and our search for solutions, we must be careful to act on the basis of fact, not fear, and to solve real problems, not imagined ones. Reliable data indicate that students are safer at school than away from school and commit fewer crimes during school hours than after school ends. . . . The real problem area is not the school itself but the world our children return to after the dismissal bell rings. In today's society, fewer and fewer children have a parent waiting for them at home when school lets out. As a result, youth often supervise themselves and younger siblings after school. . . . Most juveniles are responsibly engaged in an array of positive activities, such as sports, clubs, or homework, or they 'hang out' harmlessly with friends. However, for youth who have few activities available, whose friends are prone to negative behavior, or who experience other risk factors, the unsupervised hours between school and dinnertime offer ample opportunity to go astray . . . we should [also] not fail to recognize that during these afterschool hours, juveniles are most likely to become victims of crime, including violent crimes. . . . In this unsupervised time, youth are more vulnerable and more likely to be exploited, injured, and even killed."

Table 4.1 summarizes the most common forms of violence affecting youth during each period of development. Physical abuse is discussed in greater depth in Chapter 2, child sexual abuse is discussed in Chapter 3, and bullying is discussed in Chapter 5. Rape, dating, and sexual assault of adolescents are reviewed in Chapter 7.

DO YOUTH AND SCHOOL VIOLENCE INFLICT SERIOUS INJURY?

Yes. School and youth violence can and do result in serious injury and death. Physical fighting is a common form of interpersonal violence among adolescents. It is a prominent cause of injuries and homicides. Approximately 3 in 10 violent victimizations against youth ages 12–17 years result in an injury. Approximately 25% result in minor injuries, such as bruises or cuts. Older teens are more likely to experience serious injuries, such as gunshot or knife wounds, loss of consciousness, rape injuries, or injuries requiring two or more nights of hospitalization. In 2005, 3.6% of students in grades 9–12 reported that during the 30 days preceding the survey they had been in at least 1 physical fight that resulted in injury requiring treatment by a doctor or nurse (36% reported being in a fight during the prior 12 months anywhere and 14% were in a fight on school property). The Centers for Disease Control and Prevention has stated that physical

TABLE 4.1   PEAK RISK OF MOST COMMON VICTIMIZATIONS BY DEVELOPMENTAL PERIOD

Victimization in Infancy:	Assault by a sibling Assault with no weapon or injury Witnessing family assault
Victimization in the Toddler Years (Age 2–5 Years):	Assault by a sibling Assault with no weapon or injury Bullying (physical) Witnessing family assault
Victimization in Middle Childhood (Age 6–9 Years):	Assault by a sibling Assault with no weapon or injury Bullying (physical) Emotional bullying/teasing
Victimization in Preteens and Early Adolescence (Age 10–13 Years):	Assault with weapon Sexual harassment Kidnapping Witnessing family assault Witnessing intimate partner (and parental) violence
Victimization in Later Adolescence (Age 14–17 Years):	Assault with injury Assault by peer (non-sibling) Genital assault Dating violence Sexual victimizations of all types Sexual assault Sexual harassment Flashing or sexual exposure Unwanted online sexual solicitation Any maltreatment Physical abuse Psychological or emotional abuse Witnessing community assault Exposure to shooting School threat of bomb or attack

Adapted from: Finkelhor, D., H. Turner, R. Ormrod, S. Hamby, and K. Kracke. Children's Exposure to Violence: A Comprehensive National Survey. Washington, DC: Juvenile Justice Bulletin, Office of Justice Programs, U.S. Department of Justice, October 2009. NCJ 227744.

fighting is part of a spectrum of violent behavior that may ultimately result in homicide. In 2005, of the 28% of all school students ages 12–18 years who reported having been bullied at school during the prior 6 months, 24% sustained an injury as a result.

In 2005, 5,686 young people aged 10–24 years were murdered. Homicide was the second leading cause of death for individuals in this age group. Eighty-two percent of these young homicide victims were killed with a firearm. More than three-quarters of a million young people ages 10–24 years are treated in emergency departments every year for injuries sustained as the result of violence. Emotional, educational, and opportunity damage may result among the 6% of children who do not go to school regularly because of fear of violence at or on the way to or from school. In 2005–2006, there were 14 homicides and 3 suicides of school-age youth (ages 5–18 years) at school, or approximately 1 homicide or suicide of a school-age youth at school per 3.2 million students enrolled during that school year.

Genital assault is the intentional injury of the genitals with no sexual gratification on the part of the assailant and a desire simply to hurt the victim. The frequency of genital assault has been reported from one survey as 9.2% of boys and 1.0% of girls in the year before the interview. One-fourth of male victims were injured, and 2% required medical attention. The setting of genital assault often involved gang activity, bullying, and peer fighting. Victims experienced more depression and post-traumatic symptoms than children without a history of such assault.

In addition to causing injury and death, youth and school violence affect communities by increasing the cost of health care, reducing productivity, decreasing property values, and disrupting social services. The cost of youth violence has been estimated to exceed $158 billion each year.

WHO IS INVOLVED IN YOUTH AND SCHOOL VIOLENCE?

School and youth violence tend to cut across all social classes and exist in all areas of the country. The perpetrators of school violence can include fellow students as well as non-student peers. However, beyond the general population of young people, there are individuals with a history of high-risk behaviors who may be more likely than most to engage in violence. These include juvenile offenders, youth with a history of fighting, drug and alcohol abuse, and drug dealing. In addition, weapon carriers and gang members are more likely to participate in violent acts. Those who have either failed in or dropped out of school, and who are unemployed or homeless may be involved with violence.

One study found that deviant behavior in grade 7, poor grades, and weak social bonds predicted violent behavior, as did attendance at multiple elementary schools.

Youth victims describe their attacker as an acquaintance almost twice as often as adults do. For serious violent crimes, juvenile victims tend to know their offender (64% of the time), with the offender being a friend in 34% of instances, an acquaintance in 18% of instances, and a relative in 11% of instances. Younger students (ages 12–14 years) are more often the victims of school crime, and particularly violent crime, than older students (ages 15–18 years), and boys are twice as likely as girls to be victims of violence. Older students were more likely than younger students to be victimized away from school. In 2005, 10% of male students in grades 9–12 reported being threatened or injured with a weapon on school property in the prior year, compared with 6% of female students. In the same year, 43% of males said they had been in a fight anywhere, compared with 28% of females (18% of males and 9% of females reported being in a fight on school property). Hispanic students were more likely than White students to report being threatened or injured with a weapon on school property, and no differences were found between percentages of affected Black and White students.

When juveniles kill juveniles, the victims are generally acquaintances and are killed with a firearm. Victims in 70% of homicides by juveniles were killed with a firearm, and boys were far more likely than girls to kill with a firearm (73% vs. 41%). Black juveniles were more likely to commit murders with firearms than were other races (72% vs. 59% for Whites). Youths were most likely to kill persons of their own race 81% of the time. Between 1980 and 1997, most victims in homicides involving juveniles were male (83%), and slightly more were White (50%) than Black (47%). Juvenile murderers are more often male (93%) and often Black (56%), and 42% were age 17 years, 29% were age 16 years, and 17% were age 15 years. Boys tend to kill an acquaintance (54%), and girls tend to kill a family member (39%). From 1999 to 2006, higher rates of school-associated homicide were associated with males, students in secondary schools, and students in central cities. In 2007, school homicides were committed largely using guns (65%), by stabbing or cutting (27%), or by beating (12%).

Young people who commit violent acts share several common characteristics. With respect to their families, they appear to be less attached to and monitored by their parents. Violent young people have less commitment to school and less attachment to their teachers than nonviolent youth. More of their peers and friends are likely to be delinquent and to have participated in violence. These young people often live in high poverty areas where crime is more frequent. The 1996 Centers for

Disease Control and Prevention report on school-associated violent deaths found that victims were more often urban, minority, and male secondary school students. Firearms were responsible for three-fourths of the deaths. Teenage violence often coexists with emotional and behavioral problems. Violent youth were more likely than their peers to have poor mental health, use drugs, drop out of school, and be delinquent.

A history of inflicting or receiving a violent injury, as well as a criminal record, increases the likelihood that a young person will become involved with violence. Young people who have been relocated, for example, immigrants and those who live in highly mobile communities, may be placed in conflict and provocative situations and be more prone to fighting. A study conducted in 2000 found that in more than two-thirds of 37 recent school shootings, the perpetrators felt "persecuted, bullied, threatened, attacked, or injured." Young people with emotional problems or who were abused or neglected as children may be unable to settle conflicts without resorting to violence. Children who have witnessed violence (e.g., domestic violence and spousal abuse in the home) may view violence as a normal means for dealing with difficult social situations. Many of the accused boys in school shootings appeared to share a deep-seated sense of rage. Narcissistic traits (a lack of empathy and hypersensitivity to insult), low self-esteem, erratic coping skills, and depressive disorders also were common. Severe feelings of isolation—particularly from family members and girls—were noted, as were paranoia and suicidal tendencies.

It has been estimated that less than 15% of young people contribute to as much as 75% of youth violence. Most young people who are violent began committing violent acts as early as age 12 years. The origins of youth violence are difficult to assess. It seems that aggressive tendencies are usually acquired very early in life and then progress from common childhood fighting to more serious forms of violence. Conflicts with authority figures are common, and stubborn behavior in childhood may progress to outright defiance and complete rejection of authority during adolescence.

Youth gangs are frequently associated with violence among the young. Studies indicate that youth gang members are responsible for a disproportionate share of all offenses, violent and nonviolent. Obtaining a clear statistical picture of youth gangs in America is difficult because, although most gangs share some common elements—as self-formed, recurrently interacting groups, frequent crime involvement, communication through symbols, control of a particular territory or enterprise—there are no universally accepted criteria for identifying gangs and gang members. Subtle distinctions among active core members, fringe members, and "wannabes" often are lost in gang membership statistics. Also, because there is no uniform procedure for law enforcement agencies to purge the files of gang members who are no longer active, estimates of the number and ages of gang members in their jurisdictions may be inflated.

Nonetheless, the best data on America's gang problem come from the results of the annual National Youth Gang Survey, conducted by the Department of Justice in more than 3,000 police and sheriff's departments. The survey's recent findings suggest that the youth gang problem continues to be widespread and significant across the United States. In 1999, 44% of jurisdictions reported active youth gangs, down 4% since 1998 and 19% since 1996, but still very high. More than 26,000 gangs were estimated to be active in the United States in 1999, down 9% since 1998. Large cities accounted for 49% of all gangs and 60% of all gang members. More than 840,500 gang members were estimated to be active in the nation in 1998. In 2005, 24% of students aged 12–18 years reported that there were gangs at their schools, an increase from 21% just 2 years earlier (with students at urban schools more likely to report gangs at their schools than suburban or rural students, 36% vs. 21% vs. 16%, respectively). At urban schools from 2003 to 2005, the percentage of students reporting the presence of gangs increased from 31% to 36%.

Fifty percent of gang members in 1999 were aged 18–24 years, and 26% were aged 15–17 years. Studies have shown that the median age for beginning to associate with gangs is 13 years, and the median age for actually joining a gang— and for the first arrest—is 14 years. Gang members' racial/ethnic composition was Hispanic (47%), Black (31%), White (13%), Asian (7%), and other (2%). White participation in gangs is on the rise. This change may be associated with the proliferation of gangs in rural counties and small cities, where the White proportion of gang membership is much higher than in cities. The proportion of female gang members, although small, also may be increasing. With respect to socioeconomic status, 50% of gang members were reported as underclass, followed by working class (35%), middle class (12%), and upper-middle class (3%). Offense types reported to be most prevalent among gang members were larceny/theft, aggravated assault, and burglary/breaking and entering. An estimated 46% of youth gang members were involved in street drug sales to generate profits for the gang. There seems to be a clear progression in the seriousness of offenses committed by youth gang members, beginning with property crimes and moving within 1–2 years to violent crimes and drug crimes.

Public concern in recent years has focused on an apparent migration of gangs from large cities to small towns and rural areas. According to the Department of Justice, although it is true that gangs have proliferated over the past few years and the problem itself has spread from large cities to small towns and rural areas, this does not mean that the physical migration of gang members is the cause. Most studies have concluded that although such migration does occur, it does not actually play a major role in gang proliferation. Some well-organized gangs are believed to be engaged in interstate drug trafficking in an effort to expand their commercial base through member relocation. But overall there are relatively few migrating gang members, and most law enforcement agencies view their local gang problems as "home grown."

IN WHAT SITUATIONS DO YOUTH AND SCHOOL VIOLENCE OCCUR?

Serious juvenile crimes cluster in the hours immediately after the close of school. During this period juveniles injure the greatest number of victims. Violent victimization of juveniles occurs most frequently between 3 p.m. and 9 p.m., unlike adult victimizations, which are most common between 9 p.m. and midnight. One of five violent crimes involving juvenile victims occurs between 3 p.m. and 7 p.m. on school days. These data suggest that after-school programs have more crime reduction potential than juvenile curfews.

In the 2003–2004 school year, a greater percentage of teachers in city schools reported being threatened with injury or physically attacked than teachers in suburban, town, or rural schools. A greater percentage of secondary school teachers reported being threatened with injury (8%) by a student than elementary school teachers (6%). However, a greater percentage of elementary school teachers (4%) reported actually having been physically attacked than secondary school teachers (2%), and more public than private school teachers reported being threatened (7% vs. 2%) or physically attacked (4% vs. 2%) by students in school. Among teachers in city schools, those in public schools were five times more likely to be threatened with injury than those in private schools (12% vs. 2%) and four times more likely to be physically attacked (5% vs. 1%).

With respect to homicide, in most years the large majority of counties in the United States report no juvenile murders. Homicide by juveniles tends to cluster in a small geographic portion of the nation. In recent years, more than one-fourth of juvenile homicide offenses occurred within eight counties, whose major cities include Chicago, Illinois; Los Angeles, California; Houston, Texas; New York, New York; Baltimore, Maryland; Philadelphia, Pennsylvania; Detroit, Michigan; and Dallas, Texas.

The problem of youth and school violence is inextricably linked to the occurrence of bullying. Bullying is considered in-depth in Chapter 5 ("Bullying— Not Just Kids' Stuff"), and the reader is referred to that chapter for detailed information. Bullying, like other forms of violence, is a serious public health and personal problem in the United States. It may result in lasting emotional consequences for the victim and the bully, as well as physical injury to the victims. In 2005, 28% of all students aged 12–18 years reported having been bullied at school during the prior 6 months, of whom 24% sustained an injury as a result. Six percent of all students reported that they were afraid of attack or harm at school in 2005, and 5% reported being afraid of attack or harm away from school.

ARE GUNS USED IN YOUTH VIOLENCE?

Yes. Guns have become a weapon of choice for violent young people in America. The age at which persons most often commit homicide is 18 years, with those aged 18–20 years accounting for 22% of homicide arrests. Firearms are used in 86% of all homicides. Today's teen is more likely to die of a gunshot wound than of disease or other causes, and for every fatal shooting there are three nonfatal shootings. The handgun homicide rate for 15- to 24-year-olds increased 158% from 1984 to 1993. And although the homicide rate involving firearms steadily decreased between 1993 and 1997, the number of juvenile victims of gun violence was more than twice as high in 1997 than in 1984. Among homicide victims aged 10–24 years in 2007, 82% were killed with a firearm. Suicides and unintentional gunshot injuries claim the lives of even more young people than gun-related homicides.

The number of youth who report carrying a gun outside the home is significant. In a 1997 national survey of students in grades 9–12, 6% reported carrying a gun outside the home in the past 30 days, and 9% reported carrying a weapon to school. Between 1993 and 1997, the percentage of students in grades 9–12 who reported carrying a weapon on school property during the prior 30 days decreased from 12% to 9%. A 1992 survey of high school students in Seattle, Washington, sought to determine the prevalence of handgun ownership. The findings were startling. Thirty-four percent of students reported easy access to handguns, and 6% reported owning a handgun. Males were more likely to report both ready access to a gun and gun ownership. A previous study found that 40% of teenagers had carried a gun at least one time in the prior month. Large percentages of these adolescents carry a gun with them to school. Remarkably, one-third of gun-owning students in the Seattle study said that they had fired their weapons at some time at another person. In 2005, 19% of students in grades 9–12 reported they had carried a weapon anywhere, and 6% reported carrying a weapon on school property during the prior month.

Gang membership, selling drugs, suspension or expulsion from school, and assault and battery are associated with handgun ownership. Handguns are readily available for many urban high school students, and it seems that young people are willing to use them to inflict injury with little hesitation. In a 2007 survey, 5.2% of youth in grades 9–12 reported that they had carried a gun on 1 or more days in the prior 30 days, and 18% reported carrying some weapon (gun, knife, or club) on 1 or more days in the prior 30 days.

Inner-city youths in school are victimized with guns much more often than other students. Whereas 2% of the nation's students reported being victims of some sort of violence in one study, 23% of inner-city students had been victims of gun-related violence. The school environment, perhaps, does not generate gun-related violence as much as it is the place where violence is played out. Gun-related violence occurs in schools and on the way to and from schools because many students in school come from homes and communities where carrying and using guns is commonplace.

WHAT CONTRIBUTES TO YOUTH AND SCHOOL VIOLENCE?

The causes of youth violence are quite diverse and complex, and many of the factors contributing to violence among young people are poorly understood. All of the characteristics that increase the risk of encountering violent peers and settings will increase the likelihood that a young person will be involved with youth violence. It is clear that violence is a learned behavior. The values, attitudes, and interpersonal skills that a child acquires early in life are critically important in determining whether that child will be prone to violent behavior later in life. A child who has grown up in a social environment where violence has existed or been promoted, and who has not acquired the interpersonal skills needed to resolve conflicts and problems nonviolently, may be at increased risk for youth violence.

One of the first steps toward preventing violence, according to the public health approach, is to identify and understand the factors that place young people at risk for violent victimization and perpetration. Previous research shows that there are a number of individual and social factors that increase the probability of violence during adolescence and young adulthood. High rates of youth violence are mirrored by high rates of youth victimization, and violence and victimization tend to have common antecedents.

The role of child abuse in the origins of violence among young people may be significant. In America today there are few safe havens for many children. America's children are victimized in their homes, at their schools, and on the streets of their communities. Large numbers of young people everyday are assaulted, disabled, molested, and killed by their parents, relatives, caregivers, and others.

The most frequent reason for losing a teaching certificate or license among teachers is sexual impropriety. Approximately 4% of American children are abused or neglected each year, a figure that has increased 40% over the past 10 years. Child abuse as a predisposition for youth violence is a prime example of the view that violence begets violence. Among abused children, some of the most extreme violence occurs in older children. It is believed that large numbers of violent young people have histories of abuse as a child.

Our popular culture, including movies, television programs, and music, are saturated with heroes that use violence to successfully deal with difficulties in their environment. The American Psychological Association reported that an average child will have witnessed 8,000 murders and 100,000 other acts of violence on television before the end of elementary school. This has an undeniable effect on America's youth culture, where it has become "cool" and "macho" to carry a gun. More adolescents die each year from violence than from any illness.

Easy accessibility and availability of firearms contributes to the occurrence of violence among young people and in schools. The teenage arms race continues unabated, with climbing numbers of students stating that they have easy access to a handgun. Gun-related homicide is the second leading cause of death after car crashes for 15- to 19-year-old White adolescents and is the leading cause of death among Blacks in that age group. Much of the violence among young people is not necessarily gang-related or associated with drugs or crime. Quite often, it is simply a matter of young people getting angry at each other and managing these conflicts in a lethally violent way.

Another important contributor to school and youth violence results from inappropriate adult modeling and standards of behavior. The impact on children of adults and parents endorsing and using violence is profound. Adult acceptance and glorification of violence carries a great deal of weight with a young person who loves, trusts, and respects that adult.

Violence is used as a means for acquiring power and respect, as well as a method for resolving interpersonal conflicts and other problems. In gang disputes there are power struggles and retaliation that continually escalate the level of violence.

Alcohol and illegal drugs do not, by themselves, cause children to be violent, but they are believed to often lead to acts of violence. While the juvenile arrest rate for the possession of milder narcotics like marijuana decreased by two-thirds over the 1980s, the arrest rate during this period for the possession of heroin and cocaine increased by more than 700%. Is the dramatic increase in youth violence during this time coincidental or connected?

Because a disproportionate number of young victims of violence are poor and Black, this problem is closely tied to a number of other major social problems that affect the United States as a whole. The impact of widespread unemployment among the young, welfare, racism, ineffective schools, inferior housing, alcoholism and substance abuse, teen pregnancy, and the high frequency of single-parent households cannot be dissociated from the epidemic of youth violence in America.

Table 4.2, from the Centers for Disease Control and Prevention and the Department of Justice, summarizes the diverse risk factors that researchers have identified as potentially contributing to a young person becoming violent. The Department of Justice and numerous researchers on youth violence have recommended the development of community-based and other programs to address as many of these risk factors as possible.

The protective factors reducing the chance that an individual will become a perpetrator of youth violence flow from Table 4.2. They include individual, family, and social protective factors, such as high intelligence, strong school performance and school commitment, positive social orientation, and involvement with social and religious activities. Connectedness to family or adults outside the family and the ability to discuss problems with parents also seem to be important. Perceived high parental expectations about school performance and intolerant attitude toward deviance seem protective. Frequent shared activities with parents and consistent presence of a parent in the morning when waking, when returning from school, and at the evening meal or bedtime reduce the likelihood of involvement in youth violence.

ARE THERE WARNING SIGNS THAT YOUR CHILD MAY BECOME INVOLVED IN VIOLENCE?

Yes. There are warning signs that your child is becoming increasingly aggressive and may be at risk for violence. Following are some of the signs noted by the American Psychological Association and the American Academy of Pediatrics for children of different ages. If you observe these behaviors, you should discuss the problem with a health care or mental health professional or contact one of the resources at the end of this chapter for more information or referral to services in your local community. Not all children demonstrating some combination of these behaviors will require attention, nor is this a complete survey of all warning signs.

In the toddler and preschool child, you should take notice if he or she has numerous temper tantrums in a single day, or if several of the tantrums last more than 15 minutes at a time. It is important to observe whether the child can be calmed or consoled by parents or other members of your family. Does your child have many aggressive outbursts for no apparent reason? Is he or she impulsive and lacking any fear? Does the child refuse to listen to adults and follow their

TABLE 4.2 RISK FACTORS FOR YOUTH VIOLENCE

Individual Risk Factors	• History of violent victimization
	• Attention deficits, hyperactivity, or learning disorders
	• History of early aggressive behavior
	• Involvement with drugs, alcohol, or tobacco
	• Low IQ
	• Poor behavioral control
	• Deficits in social cognitive or information-processing abilities
	• High emotional distress
	• History of treatment for emotional problems
	• Antisocial beliefs and attitudes
	• Exposure to violence and conflict in the family
Family Risk Factors	• Authoritarian childrearing attitudes
	• Harsh, lax, or inconsistent disciplinary practices
	• Low parental involvement
	• Low emotional attachment to parents or caregivers
	• Low parental education and income
	• Parental substance abuse or criminality
	• Poor family functioning
	• Poor monitoring and supervision of children
Peer and Social Risk Factors	• Association with delinquent peers
	• Involvement in gangs
	• Social rejection by peers
	• Lack of involvement in conventional activities
	• Poor academic performance
	• Low commitment to school and school failure
Community Risk Factors	• Diminished economic opportunities
	• High concentrations of poor residents
	• High level of transiency
	• High level of family disruption
	• Low levels of community participation
	• Socially disorganized neighborhoods

Centers for Disease Control and Prevention, www.cdc.gov/ViolencePrevention/youthviolence/riskprotectivefactors/html; and Hawkins, J.D., I. Todd, T.I. Herrenkohl, et al., Predictors of Youth Violence. Office of Juvenile Justice and Delinquency Prevention, U.S. Department of Justice, April 2000.

directions? If these signs are common in your child and he or she engages in violent play or cruelty to other children, it may be wise for you to seek some professional assistance to guide you in shaping more positive behavior.

In the school-aged child, note whether he or she has difficulty paying attention and concentrating in school or disrupts the class frequently. Poor school performance, particularly by a child who is fighting a great deal with other school children, is another concern. Does the child react to criticism or disappointment with intense anger or a desire to exact revenge? Does he or she watch much violence on TV and in movies or spend much time playing video games with very violent themes? Is the child a social loner, perhaps rejected by other children because of fighting? Are the child's friends mostly aggressive, poorly behaved children? Is he or she violent to pets or other animals? When combined with a recurring refusal to listen to and follow the direction of adults, these signs should urge you to seek some assistance.

In the preteen or teenager, constant inattention to the feelings of others, mistreatment of others, and a reliance on violence or threats of violence is cause for concern. If your child expresses that he or she has been unfairly treated, is unwilling to listen to adults, has poor school performance, or is often skipping or suspended from school, these are important warning signs that merit attention. Does the child consistently get into fights? Does the child get caught stealing or destroying property? Has the child joined a gang? Is the child using drugs or drinking alcohol? These signs mean that your adolescent needs guidance, and you may need assistance in providing that guidance. In addition, the diverse risk factors listed in Table 4.2 identify key contributors to or risk factors for youth violence, many of which can be addressed by concerned and involved parents and family members.

CAN YOUTH VIOLENCE BE PREVENTED OR CONTROLLED?

In the United States, the current approach to school and youth violence is primarily to try to contain it effectively. Middle-class neighborhoods remain quite safe, but violence is epidemic in the homes, schools, and communities of the almost one-fifth of American children who live in poverty. Writing off this large fraction of our young people has been very costly. Americans have paid the price in more prisons, foster homes, crime, injury, and death, as well as in much greater fear for all.

No single approach can respond effectively to the problem of school and youth violence. This form of violence, like others, is too diverse and has too many underlying causes to be reasonably addressed by any single strategy. The Centers for Disease Control and Prevention and other organizations involved with the prevention of youth violence emphasize expanded teaching about violence, enactment and effective enforcement of regulations, and change in the physical environment.

Education is a key prevention strategy for youth violence. By providing information and new skills, a young person's attitudes and behaviors can be changed in a way that reduces their risk of behaving violently. Mentoring or role-modeling is an example of an educational strategy that may be effective. Mentors are adults who embody a standard of conduct for young people to follow and who offer them a positive alternative with caring, personal concern. It is critical that young people be exposed to alternatives to the many negative role models that are found in contemporary American culture. Mentors reinforce positive attitudes and behaviors that are expressed by young people. These adult role models can be any members of the community, including teachers, counselors, confidants, and friends. Mentoring can occur in any community center, school, church, or other location in your area. It is believed that mentoring relationships can help young individuals improve their self-esteem and ability to choose and engage nonviolent methods for managing interpersonal conflicts and other problems.

Young people can be taught skills to help them manage violent situations better. They can also be helped to develop the kind of self-esteem required to resolve differences without resorting to acts of violence. It is possible to teach individuals about the situations or actions that may produce violence, for example, associating with peers who have a history of violence, abusing alcohol or drugs, or owning a gun and other weapons.

Conflict resolution training is now offered in schools within many U.S. communities. Classes are available for young people to learn how to use conflict-resolution strategies. These classes provide an opportunity for young people to learn to empathize with other individuals and to learn how to control their impulses and anger while developing good problem-solving skills. This kind of teaching can be provided in any number of community settings, although the classroom in school is most typical. Classes in conflict resolution use role-playing in conflict situations, analyzing the students' responses afterward. Conflict resolution prevents the escalation of common disagreements to actual violence. When a level of understanding has been acquired about the origins and consequences of violent responses, students may then work on mediating conflicts that occur in the classroom or elsewhere on the school campus. Peer mediation centers and conflict resolution/negotiation curricula for high school students can be established within the schools of your community.

Teaching young people more effective social skills enables them to interact with other people in more positive and nonviolent ways. Social skills training programs emphasize improving the young person's communication skills and ability to maintain self-control, strengthening his or her resistance to pressure from peers, and forming better relationships with friends and adults. Conveying these skills to young people promotes standards of behavior and increases their sense of control over their actions. As a result, it is believed that young people may be less likely to use violence in managing difficult situations. Skills training courses can be offered in your local schools, in after-school programs, and in community or neighborhood organizations for young people.

Peer education programs use students to teach their peers about the prevention of violence. Because of the profound influence of peer relationships on young people, this strategy is a potentially effective one that may be able to change the behaviors of young people. Peer training programs have had some success in the areas of reducing youth alcohol and drug abuse and tobacco-smoking, and it should be possible to employ peers in community programs to prevent violence among young people. Some of these options are available to you as a parent through programs in your own community. Referral resources are listed at the end of this chapter.

Changes in the laws and rules that govern the behavior of young people can help to reduce gun violence. For example, schools in your community can prohibit weapons on campus. Students can be required to carry their books in see-through bags as opposed to solid ones through which weapons cannot be seen. Random locker searches can be implemented. Clothes in which weapons are easily hidden may be prohibited. Metal detectors can be placed at the entrances of schools.

Gun licensing laws can be made more restrictive, and better enforcement of laws against selling firearms to young people is needed. When you or other members of your community become aware that a gun dealer is selling weapons to underage young people, your local police department should be notified. They will enforce laws that prohibit such weapons sales. Because drinking alcohol contributes to violence, and because it is known that young people who have been drinking are more likely to get into physical fights, it is important that laws prohibiting the sale and public possession of alcoholic beverages among young people under the age of 21 years are enforced. In almost every state of the union the minimum drinking age is 21 years. If these laws are effectively enforced, alcohol-related violence among young people may be reduced.

In the effort to reduce gun violence among America's youth, the Department of Justice has summarized the strategic recommendations of numerous research, policy, and community-based organizations. Table 4.3 summarizes 12 gun violence reduction strategies, including efforts to reduce illegal youth access to guns, illegal carrying of guns, commission of gun-related crimes, awareness enhancement, and efforts to increase and coordinate services and resources for at-risk youth (especially those involved in the justice system). Clearly, a multidimensional problem such as youth gun violence demands a multidimensional response.

The Department of Justice identifies the following key elements of any comprehensive response to youth gun violence. Firearms suppression efforts are needed to reduce juveniles' access to illegal guns and prevent illegal gun trafficking. These efforts can be advanced through the development of special law enforcement units, using community allies to report illegal gun trafficking, targeting gang members, prosecuting those who possess illegal guns, and imposing sanctions on those who are involved in gun violence. Juvenile justice efforts must apply appropriate alternative sanctions and interventions to respond to the needs of juvenile gun offenders.

Communication efforts must unite law enforcement with neighborhoods and involve community policing and community supervision to educate at-risk and court-involved youth on the legal consequences of gun violence. The creation of positive opportunities must provide young people with beneficial programs, such as academic tutoring, mentoring, job training and placement, and after-school activities. Education efforts must teach at-risk youth how to resolve conflicts and resist peer pressure to carry or possess guns. Public information efforts should engage broadcast and print media to communicate the dangers and consequences of gun violence to juveniles, families, and residents. Community mobilization is needed to encourage neighborhood residents and youth to improve their communities.

Modifying the environment to reduce the risk of violence among young people may be an effective strategy. Child abuse, which predisposes a victimized child or adolescent to become a violent adult, can be prevented through home visitation programs. Home visitation is often conducted during the prenatal and early infant years when a child is in the home. It focuses on preventing health and development problems in children who are born to young mothers, to those who are unmarried, or to those with low incomes. Home visit programs are available in many U.S. communities.

Preschool programs, for example, Head Start, are believed to reduce inner-city crime and drug abuse, and their role in violence prevention may be considerable. Creating opportunities for recreation gives young people non-harmful outlets for their stress and anger, as well as chances to have meaningful social interactions. Other public health approaches to prevention include educational services that are different from the kinds of recreational activities that are traditionally offered to occupy young people. Programs could include tutoring after school, mentoring by successful adults in the community, and building self-esteem and support systems for both children and parents. Community activities that employ students or use them as volunteers associate young people with supportive adults who can act as role models and mentors. These programs exist to redirect the energies of young people from criminal and violent activities to more productive and nonviolent interests.

One experimental program involves intervening with victims of violence while they are still in the hospital emergency department. The theory behind this is that

TABLE 4.3　YOUTH GUN VIOLENCE REDUCTION STRATEGIES

Suppression Strategies	Targeted gun sweeps/hotspots analysis of gun crimes
	Tracing of illegal guns
	Tracking Brady Bill background checks
	Enhanced gang intelligence
	Home police/probation supervision of probationers
	Enhanced prosecution of youth committing gun-related crimes
	Street narcotics enforcement units
	Judicial reforms and sanctions
	Enhanced citizen reporting of illegal gun activities
Intervention Strategies	Enhanced assessment and case management of gun-involved youth
	Pre-release and aftercare programs
	Gang intervention strategies
	Youth and parents life skills training
	Job training and placement
	Street outreach workers
	Youth conflict resolution training
Prevention Strategies	Local ordinances and legislation restricting youth buying, selling, and carrying of guns
	Grassroots mobilization and rallies to increase community participation of residents and organizations in youth violence reduction efforts
	Gun violence educational programs in the schools to increase youth awareness of the personal and legal consequences of gun violence
	Mentoring programs for at-risk youth
	Peer training
	Counseling for victims of gun violence
	Community policing
	School safety programs

Reducing Youth Gun Violence: An Overview of Programs and Initiatives. Office of Juvenile Justice and Delinquency Prevention, U.S. Department of Justice, May 1996. Sheppard, D., H. Grant, W. Rowe, and N. Jacobs. *Fighting Juvenile Gun Violence.* Washington, DC: U.S. Department of Justice, Office of Justice Programs, Office of Juvenile Justice and Delinquency Prevention, Juvenile Justice Bulletin, September 2000. NCJ 182678 people who come in with injuries from violence are often perpetrators of violence. They may go back out on the street to seek revenge or else become involved in the same type of activities that resulted in their injury. By reaching injured people in the hospital, it may be possible to educate them about the risks of violence, how to resolve conflicts without resorting to violence, and the wisdom of avoiding violence. Emergency medicine physicians who encounter the victims of violence, however, have expressed skepticism about this approach.

It is uncertain whether increased security in and around schools will reduce levels of gun-related violence. Schools are using methods to make it more difficult to carry a firearm on campus. Schools where children are carrying firearms already have, in many cases, tight security measures. Approximately one-fourth of large urban school districts in the United States use metal detectors to reduce weapon-carrying in schools. Little difference has been found in the rates of violence between schools with and without conventional security measures, such as patrolled hallways and visitor check-ins. Public health practitioners tend to believe that a more direct intervention in the lives of youths at risk for school-related violence is needed.

It is clear that the problem of violence in inner-city schools cannot be isolated from the problem of violence in greater society. Violent neighborhoods and communities will produce violent schools whatever measures a school adopts. Public health scientists acknowledge that some of the core dimensions of violence and the factors contributing to violent behavior are not amenable to traditional preventive health strategies. Unemployment, poverty, lack of educational access, hopelessness, and exposure to violence all contribute to violent behavior and are not traditional targets of public health intervention. Inadequate health care also may contribute to levels of frustration and hopelessness. Without addressing these problems, the implementation of violence-prevention programs may be of limited impact.

Corporal or physical punishment of students by school teachers and administrators provides a model of behavior that condones fighting and physical injury as an acceptable way of dealing with people. Corporal punishment has been abolished in 23 states and in many large U.S. cities. It should be eliminated entirely, and parents should not physically punish their children or tolerate schools doing so.

Certainly there is some relationship between a history of being abused as a child or adolescent and the tendency to then be violent to others as an adult. Many studies have found that abused children are at higher risk of abusing their own children and of becoming violent juvenile delinquents and adult criminals. A cycle of violence that cuts across generations appears to exist. Thus, programs to reduce and prevent child abuse (discussed in Chapter 2) may have a beneficial impact in the area of stopping youth and school violence as well.

Domestic violence between a child's parents may promote violence as a reasonable method of solving problems among children who witness it throughout their childhood. It is known that in the large majority of homes where spouse abuse occurs, the children witness it. Programs for abusers; rapid intervention in cases of spouse abuse to get the mother and children away from a violent abuser; and mandatory arrest, prosecution, and incarceration policies may dramatically decrease the level of violence with which a child lives and his or her own subsequent likelihood of resorting to violence. In addition to modeling violence as a way of managing relationships and dealing with problems, spouse abuse in many families involves the assault of not only the mother but also the children. Domestic violence and spouse abuse are considered at length in Chapter 6.

A decade after the Columbine High School shootings, mass shootings at schools and other community settings still occur with alarming regularity. Columbine, as a result of its scale and ambition, served as a national wake-up call for school safety across the nation and prompted government and education officials to focus on how to prevent such rampages. A study of 41 shooters by the U.S. Department of Education and the Secret Service found that most planned their attacks in advance and told other students beforehand. Several key reforms have since been instituted, including better partnerships between law enforcement and schools. After Columbine, the federal government funded the placement of 7,000 police officers in schools across the United States, who often act in a consultative and mentoring role, as well as a responder role.

Today many schools encourage students to report suspicious individuals and behavior, and use anonymous tip lines that have resulted in the prevention of several attacks. Most attackers were later found to have been depressed, to have had difficulty coping with losses and personal failures, and to have felt persecuted, threatened, bullied, or injured by others. These problems went largely undetected because most attackers performed adequately academically. Teachers are now taught to focus on observations of potential importance, including body language, insults, and subtle behavior. More mental health professionals are in schools, and more states have anti-bullying laws. Better reaction plans have reduced police response time (at Columbine, 900 officers from 34 agencies took 4 hours to get to the school). Schools have emergency response plans and practice drills.

Despite several recent highly publicized school shootings, these approaches appear to have had an impact, with homicides in U.S. schools down 50% compared with the 7 years leading up to Columbine. In 2010, the successful response of a teacher to a shooter at a neighboring school to Columbine, which saved many lives, is further evidence that school readiness has increased significantly. Students are safer in school than elsewhere; in 2004 young people were 226 times more likely to be murdered outside of school than in school.

Finally, the importance of parents in preventing and reducing violence in schools and among young people cannot be overstated. The most valuable contribution to the reduction of youth violence will occur by improving the parenting skills and the quantity and quality of parents' interactions with their children. Better parent–child relationships can decrease the risk that a young person will experience behavioral problems and the kinds of antisocial behaviors that often lead to violence. Parenting programs focus on the emotional needs of parents and on their own behaviors that influence the social development of their children. Classes on parenting, available in most communities across the nation, can help to reduce the stresses and increase the competency of parents as they address their children's ongoing needs.

WHAT CAN I DO TO RAISE NONVIOLENT CHILDREN?

Children can be raised to resist violence. Research in psychology and public health has shown that violent behavior and aggression are learned in the first years of life. Parents, other members of the family, and educators have a critical role in teaching children how to deal with conflicts and difficult emotions without resorting to violence. Some researchers have suggested that it may be possible through the use of intelligent, caring, and consistent parenting to inoculate children against violence in much the same way as medicine inoculates them against communicable diseases. The American Psychological Association and the American Academy of Pediatrics have developed a series of recommendations to help parents promote the kind of communication, home environment, and behavior that will teach children to avoid violence in themselves and others.

Children require attentive and consistently loving relationships with parents. Children who lack strong bonds with a caring adult are at risk for becoming hostile and difficult to raise. A child whose parents are deeply involved in their lives from the earliest years is less likely to develop behavior problems and delinquency. It is a challenge for all parents to do this, to be constant in their love and guidance. Particularly if you are a young, inexperienced, or a single parent, the effort required is great.

If you have a child who seems unusually difficult to care for and comfort, discuss your questions with your child's doctor, another doctor, or a counselor or other provider of psychological services. These people can give you advice and refer you to local resources on parenting, such as support groups or classes that can teach positive ways to manage the difficult problems of bringing up children in a violent society. In raising children it is crucial to remember that your empathy and patience are essential when a child asserts his or her independence. Although this behavior may sometimes anger or frustrate you, avoiding hostile responses to your children is essential to modeling good behaviors for them.

Close supervision of children is the best method for providing the kind of guidance that will prevent behavioral problems. Research indicates that unsupervised children are at higher risk for problem behavior. As a parent, you should insist on knowing the whereabouts of your child at all times, and you should get to know your child's friends. If you are unable to look after your children yourself for a period of time, get a trusted neighbor or friend to do so for you. Every effort should be made to limit the amount of time, if any, that young children are at home alone. School-aged children should be encouraged to participate in supervised after-school activities, including sports and other forms of recreation.

Programs for children that are run by adults can be found in most local communities. To better appreciate how your children are interacting with others, accompany them to supervised play activities. It is important to teach children about how to resolve conflicts, such as insults and threats, without getting angry and hitting others. Through example and repeated explanation, children will come to understand what are, and are not, appropriate behaviors.

In violent neighborhoods, and where there is strong and negative peer pressure, the behavior of parents and siblings is a very important example for children to identify with and follow. Reflect your values in your actions. Explain to children about the choices that you are making as an adult, and why, so that they can understand their own choices. The constructive resolution of problems without violence should be praised regularly. Good behavior will be repeated when it is rewarded by your attention. You can teach your children how to resolve problems with a minimum of aggression by discussing tough situations with them, helping them imagine what might occur if violence would be used in solving a particular problem, and how the outcome improves if it is not. In this manner, a parent can illustrate to a child that problems are better solved with words, not hitting.

Corporal punishment of children, spanking and hitting them as a means of punishment, only illustrates that violence is a justified and appropriate way to solve problems (in this case, their misbehavior). From your example, children may learn that it is acceptable to punish others in the same way that they have been punished by you. The physical punishment of children to get them to stop unwanted behaviors is a strategy that is effective only temporarily. Children adapt to even the harshest of physical punishments. Such punishments soon become ineffective.

There are nonphysical methods of disciplining children that can help them to manage their emotions and to learn nonviolent methods for resolving problems.

Examples include giving children time-out periods in which they have to sit quietly and consider what they have done and what desirable behaviors are needed to return to pleasurable activities. One minute of time-out for each year of a child's age is a typical formula. Privileges and special activities can be reduced or eliminated as forms of nonphysical punishment and often have a great impact on children's behavior. Grounding children by not permitting them to play with friends or take part in school or other activities is useful in shaping the behavior of older children and adolescents. These punishments, as alternatives to physical punishment, must be applied consistently. When your child fails following a genuine effort to respond positively to this approach, be sure not to embarrass or humiliate him or her. Conveying love and caring at such times will make your efforts more effective the next time. Rather than severely punishing bad behavior, reward good behavior more consistently.

Consistency about the rules you create is very important. You must stick to the rules that you establish. Children need clear structure and expectations. Do not set rules and then fail to enforce them. It is possible to involve children in the setting of the rules they must live by. Explaining your expectations to children and the consequences for not following rules helps them to set limits on their behaviors.

Violence witnessed by children in the home, such as spouse abuse, does not mean that they will necessarily become violent, but it does increase their risk. Hostility and arguing between parents do not create a model environment in which children can grow. Violent behavior between siblings should be strongly discouraged. If there is physical or verbal abuse in your home, it is important for your children that you seek help. Various psychological and counseling services are available in most communities. Use them. These trained professionals will be able to understand the reasons why violence is occurring in your home and can help your family to reduce it. A certain amount of violence is an unavoidable fact in our society, whether at home, in school, or in the media. Parents have a critical role in helping children to understand these often frightening occurrences, and if necessary, professional resources are available in your community to help you in this difficult aspect of parenting (see the resource list at the end of this chapter).

A considerable body of research now indicates that watching many acts of violence on television, in the movies, and in video games, as well as hearing about violence in popular music, can influence children to act aggressively. It is your role as a parent to monitor and control the amount of violence that your children are exposed to in the media and popular culture. To control this problem, you may want to limit television-viewing time to no more than 1–3 hours per day. The content of these hours can be monitored fairly easily by you, as can the movies they see and the video games they play. Talk about the violence your children see in the media with them. You can help them understand the difference between the play-acting world of the media and the suffering and damage these same acts would cause in the real world.

When communicating with your children, do not do all the talking. Listen to what they have to say, and allow them to express their feelings and relate experiences. Do not be accusatory. Be clear about your expectations for their behavior, particularly about the use of drugs and violence.

HOW CAN I HELP MY CHILD AVOID BECOMING A VICTIM OF VIOLENCE?

There are ways that you can teach your children to reduce their chance of becoming a victim of violence. Specific precautions against violence can help them in this respect. A more detailed overview of recommendations can be found in Chapter 10 on stranger violence. Teach your children the safe routes for walking in your neighborhood. Suggest to them that they walk with a friend when possible and avoid areas that are not well-lighted or busy with other people. Tell them about the importance of reporting violence and crimes that they witness to you, so that you may, in turn, report it to the authorities.

Teach your children how to use the 911 telephone emergency number in your area. Help them to understand the importance of avoiding fights and reporting anyone who tries to victimize them. Explain why it is dangerous to speak with strangers, why they should not open the doors to their homes to unknown persons, and why they should not accompany strangers anywhere. Instruct your children about getting along with other people from different racial and ethnic backgrounds and that name-calling and criticizing others are hurtful and unacceptable behaviors. If your child has exhibited some of the aggressive tendencies and problem behaviors noted in the section on warning signs, you can obtain help from professionals and service organizations in your community. These resources can support your efforts to reduce the chance that your child will victimize others and that he or she will become a victim of violence.

WHERE CAN I GET MORE INFORMATION AND HELP?

For more information and resources on youth and school violence, you may contact a number of community service organizations, including your local school board, local health department, local medical centers and hospitals, and other social service providers. To find and contact youth violence prevention services in your community, look in the Yellow Pages under "Human Services Organizations" or "Social Service Organizations." These agencies can refer you to an organization that provides more specific services for your needs.

In emergency situations when immediate injury is a risk, you should contact your local police department or call 911.

Appendix 1 at the back of the book provides a state-by-state website listing of compensation and assistance programs for victims of violence and crime. You may find assistance by contacting one of your state programs. Appendix 2 is a bibliography for further reading on each of the violence topics discussed in this volume, organized chapter by chapter.

The following are additional national and regional resources that you can access via telephone or on the internet, many of which can refer you to local service providers in your community.

NATIONAL ORGANIZATIONS

Brady Center to Prevent Handgun Violence
(202) 289-7319

Centers for Disease Control and Prevention
National Center for Injury Prevention and Control
(800) CDC-INFO (232-4636)

Children's Creative Response to Conflict
(914) 353-1796

Children's Safety Network
Education Development Center
(617) 618-2918

Committee for Children
(800) 634-4449

National Center for Juvenile Justice
(412) 227-6950

National Center for Victims of Crime
(800) FYI-CALL (394-2255)

National Crime Prevention Council
(202) 466-6272

National Education Association
(202) 822-7974

National Gang Center
(850) 385-0600 or (202) 616-6500

National Institute of Justice Clearinghouse
National Criminal Justice Reference Service
(800) 851-3420

National Organization for Victim Assistance
(800) 879-6682

National Parent Teachers Association
(312) 670-6782 or (202) 289-6790

National Urban League
(212) 558-5300

National Youth Crisis Hotline (reporting child abuse and help for runaways)
(800) 448-4663

Project PEACE
(317) 232-9136

Violence Intervention Program
(323) 226-2095

Youth Alive
(510) 594-2588

USEFUL INTERNET WEBSITES

AfterSchool.gov: www.afterschool.gov
Centers for Disease Control and Prevention: www.cdc.gov
Children's Safety Network: www.childrensafetynetwork.org
Child Welfare Information Gateway: www.childwelfare.gov
Child Welfare League of America: www.cwla.org
Committee for Children: www.cfchildren.org

Communities in Schools: www.cisnet.org

Family Violence Prevention Fund: www.endabuse.org

Kidpower: www.kidpower.org

National Alliance for Drug Endangered Children: www.nationaldec.org

National Center for Juvenile Justice: www.ncjjservehttp.org/NCJJWebsite/main.html

National Center for Victims of Crime: www.ncvc.org

National Children's Alliance: www.ncaonline.org

National Education Association: www.nea.org

National Gang Center: www.nationalgangcenter.org

National Institute of Child Health and Human Development: www.nichd.nih.gov

National Parent Teachers Association: www.pta.org

National School Safety Center: www.schoolsafety.us

National Urban League: www.nul.org

National Victim Assistance Academy: www.ojp.usdoj.gov/ovc/assist/vaa.htm

National Youth Violence Prevention Resource Center: www.safeyouth.org

Office of Juvenile Justice and Delinquency Prevention: www.ojp.usdoj.gov/ojjdp

Office for Victims of Crime: www.ovc.gov

Safe Campuses Now: www.safecampusesnow.org

Security on Campus, Inc.: www.securityoncampus.org

Stalking Resource Center: www.ncvc.org/src

Stalking Victim's Sanctuary: www.stalkingvictims.com

Substance Abuse and Mental Health Services Administration (SAMHSA): www.modelprograms.samhsa.gov

Violence Intervention Program: www.violenceinterventionprogram.org

Voices for America's Children: www.childadvocacy.org

CHAPTER 5

Bullying—Not Just Kids' Stuff

- What is bullying?
- What is workplace bullying?
- How common is bullying?
- How do I know if my child is being bullied?
- Is bullying a serious problem?
- Who is a bully?
- Who gets bullied?
- Are only boys bullies or bullied?
- Where does bullying occur?
- Why do children bully?
- What is electronic aggression or cyber-bullying?
- How common is electronic aggression?
- Who is involved in electronic aggression?
- What can be done to stop and prevent bullying?
- Where can I get more information and help?

WHAT IS BULLYING?

Bullying is a pattern of repeated aggressive behaviors directed from one person or child to another, usually where there is a power difference. This aggressive behavior has a negative intent, for example, to cause the victim emotional distress. When one person targets another and inflicts pain on that person, and when the payoff is that person's humiliation, classic bullying behavior has occurred. Bullying typically involves a larger child or several children who pick on one child, rather than the usual aggressive acts of childhood that occur between individuals of relatively equal size, status, or number. The bullying victim has difficulty defending himself or herself. Bullying often occurs in a chronic pattern, over a long time in which a kind of relationship develops between a bully and his victim. Most bullies are boys, whereas, the victims are girls and boys in about the same numbers.

Among children, the bully's aggression can be physical, including pushing, shoving, hitting, kicking, and punching. Belongings often are taken from the victim. Bullying also can be verbal, involving name-calling, threats, insults, and ridicule. A bully not only says things directly to the victim but also spreads rumors about or insults the victim to other people. As bullies get older, their aggression increasingly takes the form of verbal threats and abuse, or social exclusion, rather than physical assault. Adult bullying also occurs, typically in the workplace, and involves a suite of aggressive, inappropriate behaviors characterized by repetition (occurring regularly), duration (enduring over time), escalation (increasing over time), and disparity in power (the target lacks the power to successfully defend himself or herself).

Hazing, an often ritualistic test requiring a person to perform meaningless tasks that can constitute harassment, abuse, or humiliation, may be a rite of initiation into a social group. Hazing can be considered a form of bullying. It occurs most commonly on college campuses, in secret societies, in the military, in fraternities and sororities, and on sports teams. The term can refer to either physical (sometimes violent) or mental (possibly degrading) practices. Where, exactly, hazing becomes degrading remains a gray area. Harmful abuse in hazing, even if accepted voluntarily by the victim, should not be tolerated (serious but avoidable injuries can and do occur with grave medical consequences).

WHAT IS WORKPLACE BULLYING?

Although bullying is often thought of in terms of its occurrence among and impact on children, it is a problem that extends across age groups and involves adults as well. Bullying is not an uncommon behavior in workplace settings, for example. According to the Workplace Bullying and Trauma Institute, workplace bullying is "repeated, health-harming mistreatment, verbal abuse, or conduct which is threatening, humiliating, intimidating, or sabotage that interferes with work or some combination of the three."

Workplace bullying is 3 times as prevalent as illegal discrimination in the workplace and 1,600 times more prevalent than workplace violence. Statistics also show that although only 1 employee in every 10,000 becomes a victim of workplace violence, 1 in 6 experiences bullying at work. Surveys show that 13%

of U.S. employees are currently bullied and that 24% have been bullied in the past. Women seem to be at greater risk of becoming a bullying target in the workplace; 57% of those reporting being targeted for abuse were women. Men are more likely to participate in aggressive bullying behavior (60%). However, if the bully is a woman, her target is more likely to be another woman (71%). Prevalence by race reporting currently experiencing or having ever experienced workplace bullying varied as follows: 52% of Hispanics, 46% of Blacks, 33% of Whites, and 31% of Asians.

Unlike the more physical form of school bullying that affects children, workplace bullying often takes place within the established rules and policies of the organization and society. Such actions are not necessarily illegal and may not even be against an employer's regulations. Nonetheless, the damage to the targeted employee and to workplace morale and productivity can be significant. Stress is the most predominant health effect associated with bullying in the workplace.

Research indicates that workplace stress has significant negative effects contributing to poor mental and physical health, and resulting in an increase in the use of sick leave. According to the National Institute for Occupational Safety and Health, mental illness among the workforce leads to a loss in employment amounting to $19 billion and a decrease in productivity of $3 billion, to which workplace bullying may be contributing. The International Labor Organization has estimated the annual cost of workplace bullying at $3.14 billion, excluding the cost of lost productivity.

In the United States, comprehensive workplace bullying legislation has not been passed by the federal government or by any U.S. state government. Since 2003, however, many state legislatures have considered bills. As of April 2009, 16 U.S. states have proposed legislation allowing employees to sue their employers for creating an "abusive work environment." The balance of this chapter focuses on childhood bullying.

HOW COMMON IS BULLYING?

Most children are never involved in bullying, either as a perpetrator or as a victim. Approximately 30%–40% of children (or more than 5.7 million), however, may regularly participate in bullying by assuming one of these roles. By early in their development, most children have acquired the internal restraints that prohibit bullying behavior. Research has shown that the level of bullying varies from country to country and from school to school. In the United States and Canada, it appears that 15%–20% of children are involved in an episode of bullying more than once or twice a school term. Children may be involved in such bullying either as the bully or as the victim. A study in Norway in the early 1980s found that 7% of students bullied others regularly. Studies of English children have reported that 22%–27% had been bullied, almost half once a week or more often. In 2005, 28% of U.S. students ages 12–18 years reported having been bullied at school during the prior 6 months. Of these students, 53% stated the bullying occurred once or twice during that period, 25% reported experiencing bullying once or twice a week, and 8% said they had been bullied almost daily.

A 2008 national survey reported that 13.2% of young people up to age 17 years had been physically bullied within the past year, and that more than 1 in 5 (21.6%) had been physically bullied during their lifetimes. The highest incidence occurs among 6- to 9-year-olds, who had rates of 21.5% past-year incidence and 28.0% lifetime incidence. Approximately one-fifth of children (19.7%) reported having been teased or emotionally bullied in the previous year, and approximately three in ten reported having been teased or emotionally bullied in their lifetimes. Teasing or emotional bullying followed a similar pattern to physical bullying among age groups, peaking among six- to nine-year-olds, approximately one-third of whom (30.4%) reported having been teased in the past year, and then falling steadily thereafter.

A study in 2000 by the National Institute of Child Health and Human Development found that more than 16% of U.S. school children reported that they had been bullied by other students during the current term. Overall, 10% of children said they had been bullied but had not bullied others; 6% said they had both been bullied and had bullied other children; and 13% had bullied others but had not been victims themselves. Thus, in total, 29% of U.S. school children (grades 6–10) reported frequent or moderate involvement with bullying as victim or perpetrator.

In the adolescent years, an estimated 8%–9% of U.S. children are the consistent targets of bullies. The percentage of children who are involved in bullying changes over the school year, peaking early in the year and decreasing by the end, as certain children are singled out as victims for bullying on a regular basis. Peak estimates are that one-half of all children are victimized by bullies on at least one occasion per school year. One study showed that at least 4% of bullies are armed with various kinds of weapons, including guns. An estimated 30% of 6th–10th graders in the United States were reported in 2001 to be a bully, a target of bullying, or both.

With respect to school bullying, the percentage of students bullied at least once per week appears to have increased between 1999 and 2005. It is not entirely clear whether this increase reflects more incidents of bullying at school or possibly greater awareness and reporting of the problem of bullying by educators and police. Nonetheless, between 2005 and 2007 student bullying remained one of the most frequently reported discipline problems at schools. In 2005–2006, 24% of public schools reported that student bullying was a daily or weekly problem. By school level, 21% of elementary schools, 43% of middle schools, and 22% of high schools reported problems with bullying.

HOW DO I KNOW IF MY CHILD IS BEING BULLIED?

There are warning signs that may indicate your child is a victim of bullying. A child who is being bullied may frequently come home with torn, dirty, or wet clothes or damaged books. He or she claims to "lose" things without providing a clear explanation of what actually happened. The child will have evident injuries, including bruises, cuts, and scratches, and cannot give a coherent explanation for what caused them. The bullied child is unusual in not bringing home friends or classmates, and in rarely spending time with classmates after school.

A bullying victim may be afraid or unwilling to go to school in the morning. He or she may take an indirect or illogical route to and from school to avoid a bully. The victimized child generally seems unhappy or depressed, and can have mood swings with sudden outbursts of anger. Physical symptoms from the bullying may exist, such as loss of appetite, headaches, or stomachaches. Sleep may be restless with frequent nightmares and possible crying out in sleep. To bribe the bully and prevent further aggression, a bullied child may steal or ask recurrently for extra money from family members.

IS BULLYING A SERIOUS PROBLEM?

Yes. Bullying, like other forms of violence, is a serious public health and personal problem. It may result in serious emotional consequences for the victim and the bully, as well as instances of physical injury to the victims. In 2005, of the 28% of all students ages 12–18 years reporting having been bullied at school during the prior 6 months, 9% were pushed, shoved, tripped, or spit on and 24% sustained an injury as a result. Males were more likely than females to report being injured by bullying. Six percent of students reported that they were afraid of attack or harm at school in 2005, and 5% reported being afraid of attack or harm away from school. The percentage of students reporting being afraid of an attack at school (including on the way to and from school) declined from 12% to 6% between 1995 and 2005. In 2005, 6% of students aged 12–18 years reported that they had avoided a school activity or 1 or more places in school in the prior 6 months because of fear of attack or harm.

Victims may experience a wide range of social and psychological difficulties during the bullying and later in life. While it is true that no one likes a bully, few people like a victim either. The failure or inability of victims to defend themselves against bullies appears to make other children very uncomfortable with them. The victims of bullies become more and more socially isolated from their peers in school. The National Association of School Psychologists estimates that bullying causes more than 160,000 children to skip school every day. Although the actual bullying can be quite physically painful, it is the resulting social isolation that may be the most damaging to victims. This social isolation and rejection can be a severe form of stress for these young individuals. The rejection may deprive them of opportunities to build their social skills. Research indicates that later in life, long after bullying has ceased, adults who were bullied as youths have higher levels of depression and poorer self-esteem than other adults.

The victims of bullies are often very lonely and may develop negative views of school that can affect their performance and future career options. Victims also may have physical symptoms, including headaches, stomachaches, and other problems. A 1996 report found a strong association between bullying and poor sleep, bed-wetting, and headaches and stomachaches. Children with these symptoms stated that they were bullied more often than their peers. Most important, their achievement as individuals can suffer because victimized children internalize the negative views that other children hold of them. As a result, they may lose confidence in their abilities and potential.

Recent research and thinking about the problem of bullying have shown, however, that the person most at risk of serious and long-term consequences from bullying is perhaps the bully himself or herself. These effects may not be obvious early on, but the negative results of bullying increase over time. Most bullies have a course of life that spirals downward as their bullying behavior interferes with their learning, friendships, career development, love life, achievement, and mental health. By the end of elementary school, approximately one-half of bullies are not in the grade they should be according to their age.

Bullies may become quite antisocial adults. Studies have indicated that male bullies are at much greater risk of committing crimes and abusing their wives and children than are children who are not aggressive. In addition, bullies will often create another generation of bullies in their own children. Chronic bullies appear to maintain these harmful behaviors into adulthood, which negatively affects their ability to develop and maintain healthy relationships.

There are researchers who believe that bullying is a trajectory that leads quite directly to criminal behavior. Long-term studies have shown that 60% of boys who were named as bullies in grades 6–9 have had at least 1 court conviction by the age of 24 years. Children who were aggressive in their childhood often continue to be so in adolescence and later in life. A study in England showed that those who were bullies at age 14 years often were still bullies at age 18 years and even at 32 years. As adults, bullies not only tend to commit more crimes and more serious crimes, but also have more driving offenses, are more frequently alcoholics, and have more antisocial personality disorders. Adult bullies tend to use mental health services more than the population at large.

Bullies tend not to achieve socially, economically, or professionally as adults because they have never learned productive social behaviors. This failure can interfere with virtually every major activity of life. They often have erratic work histories. The bullying behavior that makes them difficult to relate to among peers often has the same effect on co-workers. The great irony here is that in the long term, bullies suffer most from their own behavior. As such, the parents of children who exhibit this behavior should be very concerned about bullying. Their children are not only harming others but also harming themselves.

The physical injuries that may result from bullying have begun only recently to receive attention. Although the physical injuries are not clearly quantified, we know that bullying can have serious physical consequences for the victim, including a variety of injuries ranging from bruises and abrasions to more serious ones such as broken bones and internal organ damage. The victims of bullying also may commit suicide. This occurred in Georgia when a child agonized by teasing and victimization killed himself with a gun in front of his classmates. Five bullying-related suicides occurred in New Hampshire in 1993. A cluster of adolescent suicides resulted in Norway when three boys killed themselves to avoid being continuously and severely bullied by schoolmates. In 2010, Phoebe Prince, a 15 year old high school student in Massachusetts, committed suicide after chronic intense bullying by nine classmates.

School shootings have received a great deal of media attention in recent years, and bullying may have a significant contributory role in a number of these. An investigation undertaken by the U.S. Secret Service found that in more than two-thirds of cases, attackers in school shooting incidents "felt persecuted, bullied, threatened, attacked, or injured by others prior to the incident" and discredits the idea that school shooters are "loners" who "just snap." Although the report observes that "clearly, not every child who is bullied in school presents a risk for targeted violence in school," it also states that "a number of attackers had experienced bullying and harassment that was longstanding and severe. In those cases, the experience of bullying appeared to play a major role in motivating the attack at school." The report also observes that in a number of cases, attackers described experiences of being bullied approaching torment. The report concluded that "bullying played a major role in a number of these school shootings should strongly support ongoing efforts to combat bullying in American schools."

Thus, the combination of long-term psychological and social impacts of bullying on the victim and the perpetrator, as well as the potential for serious physical injury and even death for victims, indicates that bullying is a serious problem. It remains a public health challenge not only for schools and communities but also for families and particularly parents to help bullies change their behavior.

WHO IS A BULLY?

Most bullies are boys. Male bullies target both boys and girls, whereas, female bullies usually bully other girls, often using more subtle and indirect forms of aggression than do boys (such as spreading gossip or encouraging others to reject or exclude another girl). Bullies' aggression usually starts quite early, in the preschool years, and then increases in elementary and middle school. Bullies typically perceive provocation and hostile intentions where they do not exist. This becomes part of their rationalization for aggressive behavior. These children tend to process social information incorrectly, and the result is that they often seek revenge for benign acts on the part of others. They have low tolerance for frustration and exhibit little empathy for their targets. Male bullies often are physically larger and stronger than their peers, get into trouble more often, dislike and do poorly in school, and are more likely to drink alcohol and smoke than their peers.

Adults who bully appear to have personalities that are authoritarian and often have a strong need to control or dominate. Some researchers suggest that envy and resentment are motives for bullying. However, there is little evidence that bullies suffer from a deficit in self-esteem (which would undermine the ability to bully). Nonetheless, bullying also can be used to conceal shame or anxiety or to boost self-esteem because by demeaning others a bully may feel empowered. Researchers have identified other risk factors, such as quickness to anger and use of force, impulsiveness, addiction to aggressive behaviors, misinterpretation of others' actions as hostile, concern with preserving one's self-image, and involvement in obsessive or rigid actions.

Much attention has been paid to possible origins of bullying behavior in childhood. Children who come from homes where parents provide little emotional support for their children, who fail to monitor and supervise their activities, and who generally have little involvement in their children's lives are at greater risk for engaging in bullying. It seems that parents' discipline styles also relate to bullying behavior in their children. Overly permissive or harsh approaches to discipline may increase the risk of adolescent bullying.

It is thought that if aggressive behavior is not challenged in childhood, it can become validated and habitual. Bullies have favorable attitudes toward violence and use violence to solve problems. They often believe that aggression is the best solution to conflict, and they have a need to dominate. The other key element in the makeup of bullies is that they derive satisfaction from injuring others, and they lack the skills of relating to others in a socially positive manner. Because they do not understand the feelings of others, they tend to deny that others could be suffering as a result of their actions. They are blind to the feelings of others, and this becomes a major feature of their behavior and outlook.

WHO GETS BULLIED?

Studies suggest that the victim of a bully is not just any child. Most children who are bullied at one age tend to be bullied at a later age as well. Victims tend to be younger than the bully, usually physically smaller and perhaps weaker than their peers. This is not surprising, because these children have the greatest difficulty in resisting and fighting back against a bully. Also, victims have particular psychological characteristics. They tend to be more sensitive, cautious, and quiet than their childhood peers. They do not appear to "fit in" with their peer group. Victims are usually more anxious than average children, and they possess negative views of violence. These children are not only non-aggressive but also averse to confrontations of any kind. They may cry when attacked. As a result, victims project a certain vulnerability, and when faced with conflict, they experience acute fear. This fear is apparent to the bully, and combined with the victim's physical weakness, increases their risk of being victimized.

Bully victims do not fight back in most bullying situations, and they usually hand over possessions or otherwise gratify and reinforce the actions of the bully. Being basically unassertive, these children tend to be submissive even before they are ever targeted for bullying. They tend, in addition, to be socially incompetent. Throughout their lives, it is these characteristics that may identify them as potential victims to bullies. This description is not intended to blame the victim child for the aggressive behavior of bullies; it takes the addition of a bully to the mix for victimization to occur. But identifying features of the victim's character may help in assisting children to prevent their victimization. Victimized children's academic and other endeavors may suffer as they internalize the negative attitudes of others.

Studies have shown that victims frequently come from overprotective families in which they have very close-knit relationships with their parents. Early on, overprotectiveness in families tends to minimize a child's skills in handling conflicts in his or her social life. Perhaps this pattern persists into later life. These children have little confidence in negotiating through difficulties on their own. They often have not learned the skills necessary to avoid being exploited by other children.

In 2005 no differences were identified by gender in students' likelihood of reporting being bullied at school. However, among students who reported actually being bullied, males were more likely than females to report being injured during a bullying incident (31% vs. 18%). Females were more likely to report being the targets of rumors and sexual comments. Black and Hispanic students were more likely than White students to fear for their safety regardless of location. Nine percent of Black students and 10% of Hispanic students reported being afraid of an attack at school (including on the way to and from school) compared with 4% of White students. Away from school, 7% of Black students, 6% of Hispanic students, and 4% of White students reported a fear of attack.

ARE ONLY BOYS BULLIES OR BULLIED?

No. Girls can be bullies or the victims of bullies. The victims of bullying are girls and boys equally. Most bullies, however, are boys. Girls do not engage in physical aggression to the extent that boys do, or in verbal aggression such as name-calling, but they use what has been called relational aggression. Relational aggression involves hurting others by damaging or manipulating their relationships. This aggression includes spreading rumors in the peer group (so that others will reject the victim), telling others to stop liking the victim (socially excluding the victim), threatening to withdraw friendship from the victim, and giving a victim the "silent treatment." These tactics are used to coerce, retaliate against, or control the victim's behavior.

Among girls, bullying through relational aggression becomes more common as they enter the adolescent years. In particular, social exclusion is used with increasing frequency to manage conflicts with peers. Studies have shown that girls participate in relational aggression at approximately the same rate (22%) as boys bully physically (27%). Boys also use relational aggression, but it is far more common among girls. Such behaviors only have been detected recently because they are considerably more sophisticated and less readily identifiable than the physical and verbal aggression demonstrated by boy bullies. In addition, they may create less severe short-term problems in school or society.

WHERE DOES BULLYING OCCUR?

Bullying occurs virtually everywhere. It is not only a characteristic of Western cultures but also a serious problem in Japan, China, and other countries. It is just as common in rural as in urban settings and seems to have little to do with the size of the school or organization in which it occurs. Most bullying seems to occur in one special environment: school. Schools are well suited to this aggressive behavior because many areas are unsupervised and crowded, and because of the diversity of children found there.

In schools, bullying can and does occur in all areas of school. Most bullying tends to occur on the school playground and in school corridors, and more frequently during physical education class, at recess, in bathrooms, on school buses and at bus stops, in the midst of classes that require group work, and in after-school activities.

Bullying in school sometimes consists of a group of students taking advantage of or isolating one student in particular and gaining the loyalty of bystanders who want to avoid becoming the next target or victim of bullying. Bullies typically taunt and tease their target before physically bullying the target. Targets of bullying in school are often pupils who are considered unusual, strange, or different by their peers, thus, making the situation harder for them to deal with.

Bullying exists in a hidden world that is often just outside of the perception of adults. Most teachers do not realize or believe that bullying occurs in their school or their classroom. In fact, very often it does. Most parents do not know when their children are bullies or victims. Children often are convinced that their victimization is their fault or a result of something they have done. Victims are very secretive because they have been humiliated and are ashamed about being bullied. In addition, a child may be afraid of reprisals from the bully if he or she complains to a parent who then intervenes. Bullying is therefore a somewhat underground activity, but very pervasive nonetheless.

WHY DO CHILDREN BULLY?

Bullying is a tactic to obtain power and influence. Whether the bully is a boy or girl, this behavior has an objective. Its rewards are various: getting attention or material gain, building a reputation, or coercing another to act according to how the bully desires. Bullying also occurs because of its entertainment value for other children who are not involved but observe the aggression. In approximately nine-tenths of bullying episodes, other children are involved in some way.

When groups of children gang up on a particular victim, some researchers speculate that a process of social contagion or contamination occurs. Here the group is empowered by its size, and each individual's responsibility not to participate in aggression disappears. Children who would not normally partake in bullying get involved because of social conformity, peer pressure, and the importance of being part of a group, even a group that engages in antisocial and aggressive behavior. Research has suggested that a significant proportion of "normal" school children may not regard school-based violence (student-on-student victimization) as negative and as unacceptable as their parents and adults generally do. Some children may appear to derive enjoyment or a sense of belonging to a particular kind of social dynamic from even victim status. They may thus not perceive any reason to prevent bullying if it brings them some form of secondary gain in this manner.

Bullying seems to originate partly in parental behaviors and neglect. Although most kids are aggressive at some point in childhood, it seems that aggressive behavior within the family reinforces bullying. Bullies often are aggressive as small children and receive harsh punishment from parents. This further teaches the child how to be aggressive and how to use punishment as a method for managing his or her environment. It also fosters resentment. The bully is often the product of an inconsistent parenting pattern in which a child's undesirable behaviors are rewarded and punished in a changing, unpredictable manner. Superimposed on this may be a lack of parental monitoring of the child's behavior, which the child interprets as a lack of caring. Some children are thought to bully because they have been isolated and have developed a deep need for belonging, but lack the social skills to effectively keep friends. The bullying here is a compensatory mechanism.

Physical punishment combines with inconsistent or neglectful parenting to reinforce antisocial and aggressive behaviors. The best way to reduce the chance that a child will become a bully is to apply nonphysical and nonthreatening sanctions in a consistent and predictable manner when rules are broken. It is possible to rear children in a way that reduces their risk of becoming a bully.

The underlying reason why bullying is so common is that the bully believes that aggression is a reasonable method for solving problems and conflicts. The bully's behavior derives from a need to dominate situations and people and from the satisfaction and rewards they receive from injuring others. In some circumstances, once this dynamic is established, victims may participate willingly because the bullying relationship is a social group within which they receive attention, notwithstanding the negative character of this attention. Sadly, for some children, this is preferable to receiving absolutely no attention; being a victim and suffering at the hands of a bully may be a way in which a child has his or her value confirmed.

Some researchers believe countries that glorify and have a greater tolerance for violence as a solution to problems create cultures in which bullying is more likely to appear and pervade social relations in childhood. In the United States, bullying often is not taken very seriously by parents (and occasionally school personnel). It often is dismissed as a passing and generally harmless stage of childhood, usually attributed to boys (and not involving girls), and having little, if any, lasting effects. It should be clear from the preceding discussion that these perceptions are incorrect. They persist insofar as they are myths that allow schools and families to ignore and remain indifferent to this serious problem.

WHAT IS ELECTRONIC AGGRESSION OR CYBER-BULLYING?

Cyber-bullying is a form of electronic aggression in which youth and others use technology and electronic media to embarrass, harass, or threaten peers. Increasing numbers of adolescents are becoming victims of this new form of violence, sometimes referred to as "cyber-bullying," internet harassment, and internet bullying. Cyber-bullying is the use of information and communication technologies involving e-mail, cell phone and pager text messages, instant messaging, defamatory personal websites, blogs, online games, and defamatory online personal polling websites to support deliberate, repeated, and hostile behavior by an individual or group intended to harm others. Electronic aggression is any kind of aggression perpetrated through the use of technology.

Young people are among the most avid and advanced users of new media technology, including cell/mobile phones and communication devices, personal data assistants, and the internet. New forums for communication are multiplying rapidly, including text messaging, chat rooms, and social networking sites (e.g., MySpace, Facebook, and Twitter). These new avenues of communication and participation in communities have enabled young people to easily develop new relationships and new kinds of relationships, occasionally with individuals whom they (and their parents) have never met in person. The Centers for Disease Control and Prevention (CDC) has defined electronic aggression as "any type of harassment or bullying (teasing, telling lies, making fun of someone, making rude or mean comments, spreading rumors, or making threatening or aggressive comments) that occurs through e-mail, a chat room, instant messaging, a website (including blogs), or text messaging."

New technology clearly has many benefits for young people, allowing them to communicate with family and friends regularly, to connect socially, and to gain access to the wealth of information and knowledge available through the internet. However, when used to bully or intimidate, electronic media become a vehicle for aggression and possible violence that can produce emotional distress, problems at school, and even physical injury.

HOW COMMON IS ELECTRONIC AGGRESSION?

In 2000, 6% of internet users said they had been the victim of online harassment. By 2005, this percentage had risen to 9%, a 50% increase. The CDC reports that across studies between 9% and 35% of young people state that they have been the victim of electronic aggression. This range falls to between 4% and 11% when limited to a specific similar timeframe, such as at least monthly or at least once in the last 2 months. The percentage of young people who admit they perpetrate electronic aggression also varies considerably across studies (4%–21%), with 4% acknowledging behaving aggressively electronically at least monthly or at least once in the past 2 months.

Electronic aggression occurs commonly on social networking websites and in chat rooms. The CDC reports that 25% and 23% of victims of electronic aggression stated it occurred in a chat room and on a website, respectively. However, instant messaging is the most common vehicle for perpetrating electronic aggression; 56% of perpetrators of electronic aggression and 67% of victims stated that the aggression was mediated through instant messaging. Victims also reported experiencing electronic aggression through e-mail (25%) and text messages (16%). Differences also were reported with respect to whether the victim knew the perpetrator from prior in-person encounters or exclusively online. Instant messaging was the method of harassment more frequently when an in-person past encounter existed, and e-mail, chat rooms, and online gaming websites were used more frequently when the relationship was only online. Personally knowing the perpetrator tended to produce a relationship more like that which occurs in face-to-face bullying, with a pattern of recurrent harassing incidents. It also was associated with sending or posting messages for others to see.

The rates of internet harassment for young people who are home-schooled compared with those who attend public and private schools are fairly similar, suggesting that cyber-bullying is not simply an extension of in-person bullying at school. Most electronic aggression is perpetrated and experienced away from school and during off-school hours.

WHO IS INVOLVED IN ELECTRONIC AGGRESSION?

Preliminary evidence suggests that electronic aggression may peak around the end of middle school and the beginning of high school. It is still unclear if the prevalence of electronic aggression varies by race or ethnicity. Between 7% and 14% of surveyed youth reported being both a victim and a perpetrator of electronic aggression, an overlap also seen in other forms of violence. Individuals who report perpetrating electronic aggression are more likely to also report perpetrating face-to-face bullying.

Electronic technology enables perpetrators to hide their identity, by sending or posting messages anonymously, by using a false name, or by assuming someone else's on-screen identity. Therefore, unlike the physical aggression or bullying that occurs at schools, victims and perpetrators may remain anonymous and unidentified. Between 13% and 46% of victims of electronic aggression report not knowing their harasser's identity, and 22% of young people who admit to perpetrating electronic aggression report not knowing the identity of their victim. In the school environment victims can respond to a bully or seek adult involvement and assistance. However, when aggression is mediated electronically the victim is often alone when receiving aggressive e-mails or text messages, and the only defense may be to turn off the computer, cell phone, or device. If the electronic aggression takes the form of posting a message or an embarrassing picture of the victim on a public website, the victim may have no ability to respond at all. When the perpetrator was known, in 47% of instances it was another student at school and in 12% of instances it was a sibling.

The CDC reports that youth who are victims of internet harassment are significantly more likely than those who have not been victimized to use alcohol and other drugs, to have school detentions or suspensions, to skip school, and to experience emotional distress or in-person victimization. They are also more likely than non-victims to have poor parental monitoring and weak emotional bonds with their caregiver. Caregivers report that they can become even more fearful, frustrated, and angry about the incidents of electronic aggression than their victimized children.

Perhaps the most publicized case of cyber-bullying occurred in 2006 when 13-year-old Megan Meier committed suicide after cyber-bullying and an online emotional attack. This bullying was perpetrated by a classmate's parent posing as a new (male) online friend. Less extreme but nonetheless still harmful forms of cyber-bullying are suspected to be relatively common and in line with levels of face-to-face in-person bullying. Although research on this area of bullying is still developing, parents should be actively engaged in ensuring that their children are not involved in perpetrating this form of bullying or at risk for victimization.

WHAT CAN BE DONE TO STOP AND PREVENT BULLYING?

The parents of a child who is being victimized by a bully should be involved in the prevention of bullying. Parents of children who are victims should not view bullying as an unavoidable part of growing up. These parents can help their child by consistently trying to improve his or her confidence and comfort in behaving assertively. If bullied children have practice at handling conflict, their confidence in skillfully negotiating difficult situations will increase. Parental example and direct discussion with the child are important in achieving this skill. Once involved in a bullying relationship, the best defense for the child victim is to avoid the bullying. Although not always possible, avoiding common areas of recreation or routes to and from school can reduce the number of times that a child may encounter the bully.

When faced by the bully, a child should walk away. Children should be made to understand that there is no advantage in allowing themselves to be insulted or physically abused. Silent acceptance of bullying does not equate with strength. Using humor can sometimes defuse a bully who is about to begin intimidation. And, a strong assertion by the victim that he or she wants to be left alone, combined with walking away from the bully, can disinterest the bully. A child can also recruit a friend as a preventive measure; a bully will usually not feel comfortable or be able to assert his dominance when the victim is accompanied by someone who supports the victim. To decrease the victim's isolation and lessen the interest of a bully, a victim should develop good friendships with nonaggressive children.

Once bullying has been discovered either by the school or by the victim's parents, the school can play a central role in contacting the parents of both the victim and the bullies to inform them and to establish cooperative communication. Many parents of bullies are not aware of their children's behavior at school and that their child is a bully. A victim's parents usually should not contact the bully's parents directly, and the school can act as an intermediary and neutral ground to arrange a meeting attended by the students and their parents. The objective of such a meeting is to bring about a thorough review and discussion of the situation and to arrive at a concrete plan of action with commitments for change made on the part of the bully and his family. From the first moment when a bullying situation has been identified, it is imperative that the victim of bullying be guaranteed effective protection by the school.

When the situation is communicated, a number of parents of bullies want to bring about positive change. However, some bullies' parents try to trivialize the problem or take a defensive stand. They may refuse to come to meetings intended to address the problem. Even when it is not possible to establish positive communication with the victimizer's parents, an effort to do so still must be made. The initial meeting should not be a one-time event but must be followed up with regular meetings so the situation can be further evaluated and monitored, and information can be exchanged between parents and teachers.

It is critical to check that decisions and commitments that have been made are being translated into action. In some instances it is clear in advance that the relationship between the bully's and the victim's families is tense and hostile. In such situations, meetings can be arranged with one family at a time before arranging a joint meeting. It may be necessary to involve the school social worker, counselor, or psychologist in meetings where the level of hostility is high.

Of course, before a parent can do anything for a child who is a bully victim, the bullying must be detected. It is, therefore, important to ask children how they are being treated by peers and to subtly try to assess the status of their child's relationships with peers at school and elsewhere. Children are often too humiliated and ashamed to broach this topic spontaneously, and it must be carefully elicited from them. Children should be specifically asked about cyber-bullying, and their use of the internet and other communication technologies should be monitored by parents.

Attitudes can change an environment for the better when a number of children, especially children who are not involved as a victim or perpetrator of bullying, begin to disapprove of bullying and spread the word about how bad bullying actually is for the bully himself or herself. Education leading to awareness about its long-term consequences and negative impact on an individual's future may cause bullies to be self-reflective and to limit the acting out of their aggression.

Children who have been victimized also can participate in groups that improve general social skills. It is important, however, that parents understand that children will not by themselves be able to resolve a typical bullying situation. The profound influence of a peer group and the importance of reputation and status often ensure that a bullying problem will not work itself out spontaneously. Therefore, parents should always intervene in these difficult, sometimes complex, situations. They should contact their child's teachers and work with them in a concerted effort to educate children and to stigmatize bullying behavior. As the parent of a child who is being bullied, you should talk to other parents, because it is more than likely that other children in the community also are being bullied. Collectively, parents and the school can communicate a consistent message that bullying behavior is absolutely not acceptable.

Help your child join other groups of children in sports, music, or other leisure time activities. Encourage your child to make contact with (and perhaps bring home) a friendly student from the same or another class. Because socially excluded children often lack relationship-building skills, it is important that you or a school counselor assist your child with advice about making friends with peers. Sometimes a victim of bullying behaves in a way that irritates and provokes those around him or her. In such cases, you can help your child find more suitable ways of reacting and interacting in peer social settings.

If your child is a bully, you need to be involved directly in positively shaping his or her behavior. Make it clear that you take bullying seriously and find it unacceptable. Set firm prohibitions against bullying. If both parents and the school consistently react negatively to bullying, a child is more motivated to change. Establish rules for family and social interactions. When the rules are followed, offer praise; if your child breaks the rules, consistently enforce a negative consequence (e.g., withholding allowance or other benefits/privileges). Non-physical, non-hostile negative consequences (or sanctions) must be applied when agreed-on rules have been broken.

Spend quality time with your child every day because this helps change aggressive behavior. Gain detailed knowledge of who he or she is spending time with and what they are doing. Help your child identify a pursuit in which his or her energy and need to dominate can be applied in a more positive manner. Explore any talents your child may have that can be developed to enhance his or her self-esteem. If after some time these measures and the plan established with the school have not produced noticeable changes in your child's behavior, you should consider seeking the assistance of a mental health professional.

If bullying behavior persists, it is reasonable to demand the transfer or expulsion of a bully to other classes or schools, or perhaps to temporarily isolate him or her to protect your child. As a last resort, if none of these strategies produce the desired effect, a victimized child should be transferred to another school. A child who has been chronically and viciously intimidated may thrive and excel in another setting where there is less bullying. Parents of a child engaged in personal or cyber-bullying should engage that child to determine the underlying causes of perpetrating aggression and to prevent it.

Schools can change their environments to reduce bullying by raising awareness about the issue, increasing teacher and parent involvement and supervision, articulating clear rules and strong social norms against bullying, and providing strong support and protection for all students. These can and should involve virtually everyone associated with the school, including custodial and cafeteria workers, administrative staff, students and parents, and educators. It is possible to change student culture by educating students and soliciting pledges from them against bullying and commitments to help those who are bullied and include students who are left out.

States across the nation are increasingly considering or implementing laws to address and deter school bullying. Presently, California, Oregon, Maine, Minnesota, and Washington have laws on the books prohibiting bullying of students based on sexual orientation and gender identity. An approach that seeks to prevent bullying using law enforcement may be useful but, as in other forms of violence, will need to be complemented by social, community, familial, and public health methods as well.

With respect to cyber-bullying or electronic aggression, the usual response of using blocking software to prevent access to certain websites is a partial but incomplete one for a number of reasons. These kinds of software do not apply to cell phones, and young people often can bypass them. They also undermine the many benefits of internet use for youth. The CDC has recommended a combination of blocking software, educational classes about appropriate electronic behavior for students and parents, and regular communication between adults and youth about their experiences with technology.

Parents should talk to their children, visit and learn about the websites where their children are spending time, and know who they are spending that time with (much as one might do for in-person relationships and associations). Because children will fear having their internet privileges revoked for being victimized, it is important that parents be non-punitive and supportive in engaging their children around this issue. Rules should be established for appropriate use of electronic technologies. Other parents may have useful ideas and experiences to share in this regard.

For all forms of bullying, educators should be encouraged to review existing policies and develop innovative preventive strategies in collaboration with law enforcement and public health experts. Educators and school administrators should be provided continuous training to better understand, detect, and interrupt bullying and to protect victims.

WHERE CAN I GET MORE INFORMATION AND HELP?

For resources on bullying prevention in your local community, you may contact a number of service organizations, including your local school board, local health department, local medical centers and hospitals, and other social service providers.

For more information about how to prevent bullying and what to do if your child is victimized by a bully, you may access the national and regional organizations in the list that follows either via telephone or on the internet. Many organizations also can provide referrals to local agencies in your community that may be useful in managing this problem.

Appendix 1 at the back of the book provides a state-by-state website listing of compensation and assistance programs for victims of violence and crime. You may find assistance by contacting one of your state programs. Appendix 2 is a bibliography for further reading on each of the violence topics discussed in this volume, organized chapter by chapter.

In emergency situations when immediate injury is a risk, you should contact your local police department or call 911.

NATIONAL ORGANIZATIONS

Brady Center to Prevent Handgun Violence
(202) 289-7319

Centers for Disease Control and Prevention
National Center for Injury Prevention and Control
(800) CDC-INFO (232-4636)

Children's Creative Response to Conflict
(914) 353-1796

Children's Safety Network Education Development Center
(617) 618-2918

Committee for Children
(800) 634-4449

International Bullying Prevention Organization
(800) 293-9071

National Center for Juvenile Justice
(412) 227-6950

National Center for Victims of Crime
(800) FYI-CALL (394-2255)

National Crime Prevention Council
(202) 466-6272

National Education Association
(202) 822-7974

National Gang Center
(850) 385-0600 or (202) 616-6500

National Institute of Justice Clearinghouse
National Criminal Justice Reference Service
(800) 851-3420

National Organization for Victim Assistance
(800) 879-6682

National Parent Teachers Association
(312) 670-6782 or (202) 289-6790

National Urban League
(212) 558-5300

National Youth Crisis Hotline (reporting child abuse and help for runaways)
(800) 448-4663

Project PEACE
(317) 232-9136

Violence Intervention Program
(323) 226-2095

Youth Alive
(510) 594-2588

USEFUL INTERNET WEBSITES

AfterSchool.gov: www.afterschool.gov
Bullying.org: www.bullying.org
Centers for Disease Control and Prevention: www.cdc.gov
Child Welfare Information Gateway: www.childwelfare.gov
Child Welfare League of America: www.cwla.org
Committee for Children: www.cfchildren.org
Communities in Schools: www.cisnet.org
Cyberbullying.org: www.Cyberbullying.org
International Bullying Prevention Organization: www.stopbullyingworld.org
Kidpower: www.kidpower.org
National Alliance for Drug Endangered Children: www.nationaldec.org
National Center for Victims of Crime: www.ncvc.org
National Children's Alliance: www.nationalchildrensalliance.org
National Institute of Child Health and Human Development: www.nichd.nih.gov
National School Safety Center: www.schoolsafety.us
National Youth Violence Prevention Resource Center: www.safeyouth.org

Office of Juvenile Justice and Delinquency Prevention: www.ojjdp.ncjrs.org
Office for Victims of Crime: www.ovc.gov
Safe Campuses Now: www.safecampusesnow.org
Security On Campus, Inc.: www.securityoncampus.org
Stop Bullying Now: www.stopbullyingnow.com
Substance Abuse and Mental Health Services Administration (SAMHSA):
   www.samhsa.gov
Voices for America's Children: www.childadvocacy.org

CHAPTER 6

Spouse Abuse, Domestic Violence, and Intimate Partner Violence

- What is domestic violence or violence between intimate partners?
- What is spouse abuse?
- How common are domestic or intimate partner violence and spouse abuse?
- What are the signs of domestic violence?
- Can intimate partner violence have potentially serious effects?
- Who violently victimizes women?
- Who abuses their spouse or intimate partner?
- What kind of woman is abused by an intimate partner?
- Can men be battered?
- In what situations is abuse of a spouse or an intimate partner likely to occur?
- Are guns involved in domestic violence?
- How common is stalking?
- What is electronic aggression or cyber-stalking?
- Why does domestic violence persist?
- Isn't domestic violence against the law?
- How can society prevent violence against intimate partners and spouses?
- What can I do if a family member or friend is being abused?
- What should I do if I am an abused spouse or intimate partner?
- What can I do to stop abusing my spouse or intimate partner?
- Where can I get more information and help?

WHAT IS DOMESTIC VIOLENCE OR VIOLENCE BETWEEN INTIMATE PARTNERS?

Domestic violence is a pattern of abusive behavior that is used by one partner to gain or maintain power and control over another intimate partner. Domestic violence can be physical, sexual, emotional, economic, or psychological actions or threats that seek to influence another person. According to the Department of Justice this may include any behaviors that intimidate, manipulate, humiliate, isolate, frighten, terrorize, coerce, threaten, blame, hurt, injure, or wound another individual. Domestic violence occurs between members of a family or partners in an intimate relationship.

Domestic violence includes a range of crimes (i.e., murders, rapes, robberies, or assaults) committed by spouses, ex-spouses, other partners, boyfriends, or girlfriends. Physical abuse is a pattern of coercive behavior that usually involves repeated beatings and injury. It also may include emotional or psychological abuse, sexual assault, social isolation, and intimidation of the victim. Sexual abuse is the coercing or attempt to coerce sexual contact or behavior without consent. Sexual abuse includes (but is not limited to) marital rape, attacks on sexual parts of the body, forcing sex after physical violence has occurred, or treatment in a sexually demeaning manner. Emotional abuse undermines an individual's sense of self-worth and self-esteem, often involving constant criticism, humiliation, name-calling, threats, social isolation, or attempts to damage an individual's relationship with his or her children. Psychological abuse causes fear by intimidating others; threatening physical harm to self, a partner, children, or a partner's family or friends; destroying pets and property; and forcing isolation from family, friends, school, or work. Economic abuse makes an individual financially dependent by maintaining total control over financial resources, withholding access to money, or forbidding attendance at school or employment.

Intimate violence does not involve other relatives, such as a parent or child, acquaintances, or strangers. Violence between intimates is also called battering. Most intimate violence is assault, which is the intentional infliction of injury on another person. Battering is not only recurrent but also often escalates in intensity and frequency over time. The abuse may include efforts to intimidate and control the victim, most often the woman, by limiting her access to money, friends, transportation, health care, and educational and work opportunities. Domestic violence is a crime, but until the mid-1970s, assaults against spouses were only misdemeanors in most states. Emotional abuse often precedes or accompanies physical assaults. Abusers ignore the victim's needs and continually blame him or her for problems that arise in everyday living.

WHAT IS SPOUSE ABUSE?

Spouse abuse is violent victimization of one partner, most often the woman, by the other partner within a marriage. Although intimate violence can occur between spouses, ex-spouses, boyfriends and girlfriends, and same-sex partnerships, spouse abuse is a specific form of intimate violence in which the individuals involved are a husband and wife. Spouse abuse is also known as spouse-battering or wife-beating (although husbands can be battered as well).

All couples bicker or fight occasionally, sometimes including a slap or other physical blow. However, intimate violence and spouse abuse are not the same as an occasional fight between partners in a relationship. Recurrent fighting may evolve into abuse. Fights between couples are typically driven by a disagreement over a specific issue of some importance to one or both individuals. In abuse, this is not usually the case. Intimate violence is precipitated by unimportant and insignificant actions or omissions or by nothing at all. It is characterized by irrational and spontaneous episodes of anger and rage, and efforts by one partner to control and coerce the other.

HOW COMMON ARE DOMESTIC OR INTIMATE PARTNER VIOLENCE AND SPOUSE ABUSE?

Quantifying the level of intimate violence is a complex task. How researchers define terms and pose survey questions affect subjects' responses greatly and often produce different results depending on the instruments used, the focus of the survey (crime, safety, health), and the severity of injuries. This is reflected in some of the figures that follow.

Studies have indicated that women in the United States are more likely to be assaulted, raped, or killed by a current or ex-partner than by all other types of assailants combined. Intimate violence perpetrated against women includes marital rape and cohabiting and dating violence. The National Crime Victimization Survey in 2008 reported 504,980 incidents of intimate partner violence against females (a rate of 3.9 per 1,000) and 88,120 incidents against males (a rate of 0.7 per 1,000). In one major 2005 Department of Justice survey, 389,100 women and 78,180 men reported having been victimized by an intimate partner, accounting for 9% of all violent crime. An estimated 1.3 million women and 835,000 men are physically assaulted by an intimate partner annually in the United States. These figures do not consider the many victims who are victimized more than once, which could increase the annual number of victimizations to as high as 4.8 million intimate partner physical assaults and rapes against U.S. women and up to 2.9 million assaults against U.S. men. Women accounted for 85% of domestic violence victims from 1993 to 2001 and for 83% in 2005. One in every four women will experience domestic violence in her lifetime. Violence has been a stated reason for divorce in one-fifth of all middle-class marriages.

The Federal Bureau of Investigation estimates that an American woman is victimized by an intimate partner every 1.3 minutes and that a man is victimized every 6.7 minutes. Six of every ten married couples have experienced violence between partners at some time during their marriage, and domestic violence may commonly touch as many as one in four of all American families. A 1993 national poll found that 34% of adults reported having witnessed a man beating his wife or girlfriend, and 14% of women reported that a husband or boyfriend had been violent with them. Seventy-four percent of Americans personally know someone who is or has been a victim of domestic violence, and 30% report that they know a woman who has been physically abused by her husband or boyfriend in the past year.

Intimate partner violence resulted in 1,544 deaths in 2004. Of these deaths, 25% were males and 75% were females. One-third of all female homicide victims were killed by their intimate partners, and 2% of male murder victims were killed by their wives or girlfriends. A woman is twice as likely to be shot by her husband as to be shot, stabbed, bludgeoned, strangled, or otherwise killed by a stranger. This suggests that many women may be safer on city streets than in their own homes. In 2006, lesbian, gay, bisexual, or transgender people experienced 3,534 incidents of domestic violence, 4 of which culminated in homicide.

Women experience more intimate partner violence than do men. A victim survey published by the Department of Justice in 2000 found that women were significantly more likely than men to report being raped, physically assaulted, or stalked by a current or former intimate partner, whether the time frame considered was the person's lifetime or the previous 12 months. Of all women who reported being physically assaulted or raped since age 18 years, 76% were victimized by a current or former husband, cohabiting partner, boyfriend, or date.

The Centers for Disease Control reported in 2006 that 1 of every 11 adolescents reports being a victim of physical date violence. Approximately 1 in 5 high school girls reported being emotionally abused by a boyfriend, and 20% have been physically or sexually abused by a dating partner. Victims of dating violence are at increased risk for injury and more likely to engage in binge drinking, suicide attempts, physical fights, and high-risk sexual activity.

The Department of Justice reported that approximately 25% of surveyed women and 7.6% of surveyed men said they had been physically assaulted or raped by a current or former spouse, a cohabiting partner, or a date at some point in their lifetime; 1.5% of women and 0.9% of men said that such an assault by an intimate had occurred in the previous 12 months. Violence against women is primarily intimate partner violence; 64% of the women who reported being raped, physically assaulted, or stalked since age 18 years were victimized by a current or former husband, cohabiting partner, boyfriend, or date. Of the remainder, 16.4% were victimized by an acquaintance, 14.6% were victimized by a stranger, and

6.4% were victimized by a relative other than a husband. In comparison, only 16.2% of the men who reported being raped or physically assaulted since age 18 years were victimized by an intimate perpetrator, and 50.4% were victimized by a stranger.

The most frequently reported intimate partner violence was physical assault. Battered women may occur in up to 60% of all raped women over 30 years of age. Battering contributes to other forms of violence affecting women as well. For example, battered women are thought to account for up to 25% of women who attempt suicide. In several studies, rape has been reported to occur in more than one-half of violent marriages, and estimates are that 14% of married women have been raped by their current or former husband. Some estimates suggest that one-fourth of pregnant women are abused, and perhaps one-fourth of all battered women in the United States are abused while pregnant. The March of Dimes reports that battering during pregnancy is the leading cause of birth defects and infant mortality. In 2005, 56% of women with physical disabilities reported abuse, of which 87% was physical, 66% was sexual, and 35% was refusal of help with a personal need.

In 2008, 1,553 of 2,000 (78%) U.S. domestic violence programs participated in the National Census of Domestic Violence Services. During the 24-hour survey period, 60,799 victims were served, 30,433 domestic violence victims found refuge in emergency shelters or transitional housing provided by local domestic violence programs, and 21,683 hotline calls were answered. Approximately 2.2 million people called a domestic violence crisis hotline in 2004 to escape crisis situations, seek advice, or assist someone they thought might be victims. Overall, however, reported intimate violence declined between 1993 and 2005 from a rate of 5.8 to 2.3 episodes per 1,000 persons. Intimate homicides also decreased between 1976 and 2005, particularly for males.

Yet as staggering as these statistics are, domestic violence against women and intimate partner violence are most likely underreported. Some estimates of non-reporting are as high as 90% of battering incidents. All forms of family violence are difficult to measure because they mostly occur in the privacy of the home, which, along with the perceived autonomy of the family, can act as a hurdle to victims reporting abuse and seeking help. It has been estimated that only one-half of intimate violence victims report the assault to the police. More than 50% of physically abused victims are thought not to discuss their battering with anyone.

Victims may be reluctant to report intimate partner violence because they are ashamed or they fear reprisal from the abusive partner. There are strong social and familial pressures not to report. Denial of the serious nature of the abuse – of violence at the hands of someone who supposedly loves the victim – is thought to contribute significantly to underreporting. A Department of Justice survey found that six times more women victimized by intimates than by strangers did not report it to police because they feared reprisal from the known assailant. Four of every ten wives who did not call the police following an episode of domestic violence were victimized again in less than six months. Among women who did call the police, the rate of recurrent battering was approximately one-third of those who did not call. For male victims, cultural norms require men to present a strong façade and to minimize female-perpetrated abuse, which also may affect reporting.

Violence perpetrated against women by intimates is often accompanied by emotionally abusive and controlling behavior (including control of the family's finances and where the woman goes and what she does). In a 2000 report, women whose partners were jealous, controlling, or verbally abusive were more likely to report being physically assaulted, raped, and stalked by their partners. Having a verbally abusive partner was most predictive that a woman would be victimized by an intimate partner. In these cases, the violence is a part of a consistent pattern of dominance and control in which the woman is the victim of multiple forms of abuse.

Because most victimization of women is perpetrated by current and former intimates, and because women are more likely to be injured if their assailant is an intimate, violence prevention for women must clearly focus on how they can protect themselves from their partners. The United States is yet a long way from providing adequate preventive services to those at risk of intimate partner violence. This is perhaps most compellingly illustrated by the remarkable fact that although there are 3,400 animal protection shelters in the United States, there are only 1,500 shelters for battered women.

WHAT ARE THE SIGNS OF DOMESTIC VIOLENCE?

Domestic or intimate violence may be the reason a woman has unexplained bruises, lacerations, dislocations, bone fractures, or a number of injuries that are in various stages of healing. Most often these will appear on the head, face, and chest. Bruises, slap marks, and lacerations around the eyes, mouth, and other parts of the face may indicate abuse. Multicolored bruises indicate that the injuries were sustained over time. The extent or the type of injury is not consistent with the explanation provided by the woman. Histories of being "accident prone" or "doctor shopping" and missed medical appointments may indicate an attempt to conceal abuse.

The victim may be fearful, hesitant, embarrassed, and evasive in discussing the cause of her injury. Often there has been considerable delay before the victim seeks help for an injury. The abusive partner typically will accompany the woman when she seeks care and try to answer questions for her. He may be openly hostile and impatient with her. Suspicion should increase when the victim is not allowed to speak for herself in the presence of the caregiver. Domestic abuse is likely if the woman fears returning to her home or expresses concern for the safety of her children. Battered women often have feelings of guilt and are depressed.

Questions asked by professionals to assess whether abuse is occurring focus on whether the woman is in a relationship in which she or her children have been threatened or injured physically, or if the abuser has destroyed things she cherished. The victim should be asked whether her partner ever forced her to have sex or to engage in sex that made her feel uncomfortable. She should be asked if she ever fears her partner or if her partner has ever prevented her from leaving the house, contacting friends or family, getting a job, or continuing her education. The victim should be asked if a gun is kept in the house and if it has ever been used to threaten her.

CAN INTIMATE PARTNER VIOLENCE HAVE POTENTIALLY SERIOUS EFFECTS?

Yes. Intimate violence against women can and often does seriously harm the victim. Estimates are that from one-third to more than half of women assaulted by intimates are seriously injured and at least 25% receive medical care. Domestic violence in the United States during a typical year may result in 21,000 hospitalizations, 100,000 admission days in a hospital, 29,000 emergency department visits, and 39,000 physician visits. The U.S. Department of Health and Human Services reports that more than one million women seek medical assistance for injuries caused by battering each year. Other estimates are that four million women are so seriously battered each year that they seek police or medical attention.

Violence may be the second leading cause of injuries to women overall and the leading cause of injuries to women aged 15–44 years. One of the most common reasons women go to emergency departments for treatment is to receive care for injuries inflicted by a male intimate (estimates range from 19% to 30% of visits). One study found that women who have experienced any type of personal violence reported a greater number of chronic physical symptoms than those who have not been abused (even when the last episode was 14–30 years ago). Abused women have a higher rate of miscarriage, stillbirth, premature labor, low birth weight babies, and fetal injury.

Injuries from violence are twice as common when assailants are intimates of the women (59%) as opposed to strangers (27%). Injuries are twice as likely to require medical attention when the attacker is an intimate (27% vs. 14% for a stranger). It is believed that battering contributes to one-fourth of all suicide attempts by women. The Centers for Disease Control and Prevention report that more women receive emergency department treatment for battering each year than all victims of muggings, rapes, and car crashes.

Intimate violence also can kill. Between 1976 and 2005, approximately 11% of all murder victims were killed by an intimate and 54% were killed by a non-intimate (in 35% the victim–offender relationship was unknown). Approximately one-third of female murder victims were killed by an intimate between 1976 and 2005, and this proportion is increasing. Female murder victims were more likely to have been killed by an intimate partner than were male victims across all age groups. Among female homicide victims in 2007 for whom the relationship to the perpetrator was known, 32.9% were murdered by their husbands or boyfriends. Intimate murders over the past 30 years were committed more often by spouses, but in recent years the rate by spouses has declined such that by 2005 it was almost equal to the rate committed by boyfriends and girlfriends. The number of women killed by intimates was stable for approximately two decades and after 1993 declined to its lowest level in 2004.

According to the Department of Justice, of the estimated 4.8 million intimate partner physical assaults and rapes perpetrated against women annually in the United States, approximately 2 million will result in an injury to the victim and more than a half-million will result in some form of medical treatment. Of the 2.9 million intimate partner assaults against men, 580,000 will result in injury and 125,000 will result in medical treatment. The risk of injury increases among female rape and physical assault victims when their assailant is a current or former intimate: Women who were raped or physically assaulted by a current or former spouse, cohabiting partner, boyfriend, or date were significantly more likely than women who were raped or physically assaulted by other types of perpetrators to report being injured during their most recent rape or physical assault. Women victims of physical assault were more than twice as likely as male victims to be injured during their most recent victimization.

Risk of injury to female rape victims increased if the perpetrator was Hispanic, used drugs or alcohol at the time of the assault, was a spouse or cohabiting partner (rather than a date), or had threatened to harm or kill them or someone close to them at the time of the assault. When only assaults by intimates are considered, 42% of women and 20% of men were injured. In another study, 50% of female victims and 32% of male victims were injured by an intimate partner.

Most of the women who were injured during their most recent intimate partner assault or rape sustained relatively minor injuries, such as scratches, bruises, and welts.

Some 70% of girls and 52% of boys who are abused report an injury from a violent intimate relationship, and 8% of boys and 9% of girls have been to an emergency department for an injury received from a dating partner. Victims of dating violence are also at greater risk of engaging in binge drinking, suicide attempts, physical fights, and high-risk sexual activity. Rates of drug, alcohol, and tobacco use are twice as high among girls who report physical or sexual dating violence as compared to those who report no violence.

Women who have experienced serious abuse face overwhelming mental and emotional distress. Approximately half of the women reporting serious domestic violence also meet the criteria for major depression; 24% suffer from post-traumatic stress disorder, and 31% suffer from anxiety. Similar to other victims of abuse or rape, women who are battered can experience post-traumatic stress disorder. Post-traumatic stress disorder is a diagnosis that was first used to understand the long-term psychological consequences of living through violent conflicts (e.g., warfare among soldiers). It includes psychological numbing, intense and intrusive reexperiencing of the trauma, avoidance of anything associated with the trauma, and severe psychological distress.

Experts have described a variation of post-traumatic stress disorder that applies to battered women. This "battered woman syndrome" involves a source of extreme stress, such as spouse abuse; undesired reexperiences of the abuse through nightmares, flashbacks, or vivid memories; emotional numbing; and high levels of anxiety, phobias, panic attacks, and sexual difficulties. This syndrome is not a mental illness as much as an effort to adapt to an unpredictable and terrifying situation. Professional counseling is necessary for women who experience this syndrome.

Beyond these immediate effects on the battered woman, children in a home where domestic violence occurs are influenced by what they observe. These children are more likely to be abused themselves by one or both parents. Battered women abuse their children more often than non-battered women. Between 50% and 70% of men who abuse their intimate partners are abusive with their children as well. In addition to the obvious anguish of a child who observes his or her mother being repeatedly abused, there may be psychological consequences. Domestic violence desensitizes children to violence, shows them that violence is an acceptable way to manage or respond to problems, and increases their risk of becoming violent adults. It has been estimated that children regularly witness the violence in more than 70% of homes where a mother is battered.

At a societal level, it is estimated that 25% of workplace absenteeism, employee turnover, reduced productivity, and excessive use of medical benefits result from domestic violence. Victims of intimate violence lose approximately 8 million days of paid work—the equivalent of more than 32,000 full-time jobs— and approximately 5.6 million days of household productivity each year. In 2004, it was estimated that the costs associated with intimate violence exceeded $8.3 billion a year (including $460 million for rape, $6.2 billion for physical assault, and $461 million for stalking). Updated to 2009 dollars, the cost of domestic violence exceeds $10 billion (including medical care, mental health services, and lost productivity and time away from work).

WHO VIOLENTLY VICTIMIZES WOMEN?

Research in the United States on violence against women has found that fear of attacks by strangers, which tends to dominate public concern, is exaggerated. Although attacks by strangers against women do occur, women are primarily at an elevated risk of being victimized violently by an intimate, acquaintance, or relative. In 2008, female victims knew the offender in approximately 70% of assaults. Twenty-three percent of assailants were intimates, 38% were friends or acquaintances, and 9% were other relatives. Most are attacked by lone assailants. In only 32% of instances was the assault perpetrated by a stranger.

Violent crime against women usually involves an assailant of the same race as the victim (80% for Whites and 90% for Blacks). Alcohol and illegal drug use are often factors in violence against women, and guns and other weapons are frequently present. One-quarter of all violent acts targeted at women involve the use of a weapon. One-third of strangers and one-fifth of intimates used a weapon against a victimized woman.

Although the majority of violence against women is perpetrated by men, one-fourth of violent crimes (including simple and aggravated assaults, rapes, and robberies) were committed by female assailants.

WHO ABUSES THEIR SPOUSE OR INTIMATE PARTNER?

Some data have suggested that women are just as likely as men to engage in partner aggression. Collecting various types of counts from men and women does not yield an accurate understanding of battering and serious injury occurring from intimate partner violence. National surveys supported by various agencies of the federal government that examine serious assaults do not support the conclusion of similar rates of male and female spousal assaults. Although there is little doubt that women, and perhaps substantial numbers of women, are abusers, a review of the research found that violence is instrumental in maintaining control and that more than 90% of systematic, persistent, and harmful intimate violence is perpetrated by men. Individuals who seek to control their partners are much more likely to be physically assaultive, whether male or female. Nonetheless, women are significantly more likely than men to report being victims of intimate partner violence, whether it is rape, physical assault, or stalking.

Thus, violence against women is predominantly male violence, and intimate partner violence is perpetrated primarily by men, whether against male or female intimates. Women living with female intimate partners experience less intimate partner violence than women living with male intimate partners. Men living with male intimate partners experience more intimate partner violence than men living with female intimate partners.

Among perpetrators of intimate violence, half grew up living with both parents and 12% had lived for some time in a foster home. More than one-fifth reported a history of physical or sexual abuse. Approximately one-third had parents who abused alcohol or drugs. One-third had a family member who served time in prison or jail. Two-thirds of individuals incarcerated for harming intimates had a criminal history.

One study of persons who had killed their spouses found that 60% were male and three-fourths were under age 30 years. Over half had a prior criminal history. Most of the victims were killed at home. One-quarter of the murdered spouses precipitated the killing by provoking the murderer with a deadly weapon, a nonlethal weapon, or other physical fighting such as hitting. More than half of the murderers had been drinking alcohol at the time of the killing, as were approximately half of the victims.

Seventy percent of men who were raped since age 18 years were raped by a male, and 86% of men who were physically assaulted since age 18 years were assaulted by a man. Prior research on violence in same-sex relationships suggested that same-sex couples are about as violent as heterosexual couples. The Department of Justice survey found that same-sex cohabitants reported significantly more lifetime intimate partner violence (39% for women; 23% for men) than did opposite-sex cohabitants (22% for women; 7% for men).

Men who abuse women share a number of common characteristics. They are usually emotionally dependent on the woman they are abusing. Psychologically, the man wants to deprive his spouse of all power and control, but at the same time he expects her to remedy his problems. The abuser creates impossible-to-meet expectations, and when unmet, he becomes angry and violent. He fails to accept responsibility for his own emotional state, or the resulting violence, and blames the victim for both. In this sense the abuser is emotionally immature and vulnerable.

Abusers often have very low self-esteem and a poor self-image. They tend to compensate for this with excessive masculine behavior and rigid views of gender roles, often believing that men are superior to women. Abusers usually deny or minimize the violence. Although financial difficulties, unemployment, or other stresses may contribute to domestic violence, stress does not by itself create the predisposition for violence in nonviolent men.

Many abusive men came from families who were emotionally cold and distant. In some cases, the abuser comes from a violent home where spouse abuse occurred, so violence may be viewed as normal behavior. He may have been abused himself. Substance abuse is common among men who abuse their partners. Perhaps up to 50% abuse alcohol or drugs. Although alcohol is not the cause of violence against women, a significant relationship exists between male perpetrator problem drinking and violence against intimate female partners. Severe drinking problems by intimate males increase their risk for lethal and violent victimization of their women. More than two-thirds of the offenders who commit or attempt homicide used alcohol, drugs, or both during the incident; less than one-fourth of the victims did. Other mental health problems are common. Depression and a sense of having been victimized or persecuted are often evident among abusers.

Abusive men usually suffer from a lack of empathy for other people, particularly their partner. The man is often jealous toward other men and anyone who competes with him for attention and support from a woman. The abusive man is deeply fearful that he will be abandoned by the victim, and when he perceives this as a real possibility, his rage and violence intensify. Despite all of these abnormal sentiments and perceptions, the abusive man often seems entirely normal to people who encounter him outside of the home.

There are several predominant kinds of abusers. The first kind is men who do not necessarily get angry when they become violent. They do not fly into a rage and then become violent, but appear to be quite calm as they beat up their partner. It is believed that these men may have lived in homes where violence between the parents was common. Another type of abuser is antisocial and may have a personality disorder. This man is violent not only with his partner but also with other people away from home. However, most (perhaps four in five) abusive men are violent only at home with their wives or partners. Their ability to maintain good jobs and working relationships often invokes surprise when it is learned that they are batterers. Abusive men are adept at hiding their violent tendencies.

WHAT KIND OF WOMAN IS ABUSED BY AN INTIMATE PARTNER?

Domestic and intimate violence has no social, racial, ethnic, religious, educational, or economic boundaries. Every social group and stratum in American society are affected by this form of violence. Although women of all races and ethnicities are vulnerable to attacks by intimates, the average annual rate of nonfatal intimate partner violence from 1993 to 2004 was highest for American Indian and Alaskan Native females and higher for Black females than for White females (and for Black males vs. White males as well). Average annual rates of intimate partner victimization between 1994 and 2004 are approximately the same for non-Hispanic and Hispanic females and males.

Other studies have found that Hispanic women were significantly more likely than non-Hispanic women to report that they were raped by a current or former intimate partner at some time in their lifetime. Asian/Pacific Islander women and men tend to report lower rates of intimate partner violence than do women and men from other minority backgrounds. In 2006, dating violence occurred more frequently among Black students (13.9%) than among Hispanic (9.3%) or White (7%) students.

As of 2005, women between the ages of 20 and 24 years experience the highest rates of violence by intimates. Most victims of spouse abuse are between 25 and 40 years old. Approximately 40% of female victims of intimate partner violence lived in households with children under age 12 years (approximately 27% of U.S. households are home to children aged less than 12 years).

Both females and males who were separated or divorced faced the greatest risk of nonfatal intimate partner violence, whereas, persons who were married or widowed reported the lowest risk of violence. Divorced or separated women have more than twice the rate of women who never married and ten times the rate of married women. Numerous studies have shown that unmarried, cohabiting couples have higher rates of intimate partner violence than do married couples, as do couples with large disparities in income, education, or job status.

Risk of intimate violence varies according to where victims live. Between 1993 and 2004, residents of urban areas experienced the highest level of nonfatal intimate partner violence. Residents in suburban and rural areas were equally likely to experience such violence, at rates approximately 20% lower than their urban counterparts.

For nonfatal intimate partner victimization from 1993 to 2004, persons living in households with lower annual incomes experienced the highest annual rates of victimization; persons living in households with higher incomes had lower rates of victimization than those with less income. Individuals with lower annual income (less than $25,000) are at a 3-fold higher risk of intimate partner violence than people with annual income over $50,000. Another study found that 1 of 4 women with incomes above $50,000 reported intimate violence at some point in life versus 37% of women with incomes of $16,000 or less. Women residing in rental housing were victimized at an annual rate three times greater than those living in owned housing. A 2004 study found that women living in disadvantaged neighborhoods were more than twice as likely to be the victims of intimate partner violence compared with women in more advantaged neighborhoods.

Pregnancy can increase the risk of assault and homicide against women by intimate partners. Battering is the leading killer of pregnant women (not complications of childbirth). Between 3.9% and 8.3% of all pregnant women experience violence.

Research has not identified a specific psychological or cultural profile of a battered woman. Low academic achievement increases risk of intimate violence. College graduates have the lowest rates of violence committed by an intimate; graduates have half the level of women with incomplete high school educations or some college education. Chronic health problems and illness may place women at increased risk of being a victim of domestic violence. Depression increases risk, as does having low self-esteem, having few friends, and being socially isolated.

There is a relationship between victimization as a minor and subsequent victimization: Women who reported they were physically assaulted as a child by an adult caretaker were twice as likely to report being physically assaulted as an adult. One survey found that 40% of surveyed women and 54% of surveyed men reported being assaulted by a parent, stepparent, or other adult caretaker as a child. Women in abusive relationships are also more likely to have been sexually abused or neglected as children. Typically this sexual abuse was incestuous, occurring within the family. Adult victims also may have witnessed domestic violence in their childhood home. Women who reported they were stalked before age 18 years were 7 times more likely to report being stalked as an adult.

The victims of intimate violence tend to have married early in life and have small children. Early parenthood is a risk factor. Women who had children by age 21 years were twice as likely to be victims of intimate partner violence as women who were not mothers at that age. Men who had fathered children by age 21 years were more than 3 times as likely to be abusers as men who were not fathers at that age.

Although the self-image of intimate violence victims may have deteriorated under the effects of chronic abuse, they are not the passive and docile individuals usually associated with domestic abuse. Victims of domestic violence are not masochistic personalities who enjoy the violence against them. Many initially resist the violence but find that this is futile. Within their partner relationship, however, the woman may be more competent and capable in a general sense than the man and often contributes equally to maintaining the household. Indeed, this sense of responsibility for maintaining the family or the relationship with the abusive partner is one of the more complex factors that keep women in these violent relationships. They often have traditional and rigid notions of relationships and feel strongly the social imperative to be in a relationship with a man.

Before the abuse, victims share few characteristics, but after the abuse has begun several features become more common. One of these is that victims often acquire a helpless attitude that is a learned response to a highly stressful situation. Such behaviors may appear to be unhealthy, but experts believe that they are coping strategies. Most often, these women do not believe that there is anything they can do to help themselves or to stop the violence. They are more afraid than angry. Victims sometimes believe that their violent partner will find them no matter where they go if they leave. Women who stay in abusive relationships over many years tend to be more emotionally dependent and have a high need for approval and affection.

CAN MEN BE BATTERED?

Yes. Men are abused by partners. Battering of men can occur in homosexual relationships, and in certain circumstances men are battered by women. The Department of Justice has estimated that up to 835,000 men are assaulted by an intimate every year. Men stay in abusive relationships for many of the same reasons that women do; they are afraid of retaliation, believe that the abuser will improve, feel both dependent on the abuser and depended on by that individual, and may fear breaking up the family. They feel helpless.

The psychological experiences of men and women who are victimized by intimate violence are not dissimilar and can include fear and anxiety, depression, loss of self-esteem, dependence, anger, guilt, and indecision. The major difference between male and female victims is that men suffer fewer and less severe physical injuries as a result of the violence. This is more often the case in heterosexual relationships because women are generally unable (or less willing) to inflict the kind of bodily damage that a man can.

The relationship between a female abuser and a male victim is similar to that in which the man is abusive. An abusive woman tries to control the man, is jealous and possessive, and violence can occur with or without warning. Men also will leave an abusive relationship sooner than women, possibly because they are better able financially to leave.

Men who are battered face special problems related to the stereotypes that society projects onto them. An abused man may be met with disbelief and ridicule from family, friends, and even the police. Our society has the notion that a man should be able to defend himself against the threats and assault of a woman. Therefore, battered men may experience shame and embarrassment. Cases in which a man is battered by a woman tend to be sensationalized by the media, which creates a perception that men are as likely as women to be abused (whereas, in reality women are three times more likely to be a victim of intimate violence). Fewer professional services and resources are available to battered men, but this is changing as it becomes more socially acceptable for men to seek help for domestic violence. A battered man can and should seek professional assistance in dealing with this problem. Psychologists and counselors who provide care for battered men can be found in most communities.

IN WHAT SITUATIONS IS ABUSE OF A SPOUSE OR AN INTIMATE PARTNER LIKELY TO OCCUR?

Most physical assaults perpetrated by intimate partners consist of pushing, grabbing, shoving, slapping, and hitting. Two-thirds of all intimate partner violence against women and 68% against men involve a simple assault. Differences between female and male rates of physical assault by an intimate partner become greater as the seriousness of the assault increases. Although women were only 2–3 times more likely than men to report being pushed or shoved, they were 7–14 times more likely to report that an intimate partner beat them up, choked or tried to drown them, or threatened them with a gun.

The violence perpetrated against women by intimates is typically chronic in nature. Two-thirds of the women responding to the Department of Justice survey said they were physically assaulted multiple times by the same intimate partner, and approximately one-half said they were raped repeatedly. Female physical assault victims averaged 6.9 assaults and female rape victims averaged 4.5 rapes by the same intimate partner; 60%–70% of these victims said their victimization lasted a year or more, the average victimization lasting 3.8 years for rape victims and 4.5 years for physical assault victims. Much of the violence perpetrated against men by intimates is also chronic, with two-thirds of physically assaulted men saying that they were assaulted more than once by the same intimate partner (on average 4.4 assaults lasting on average 3.6 years).

Approximately two-thirds of all intimate partner violence against women and one-half against men occurred in the victim's home. Intimate violence occurred most often between 6 p.m. and 6 a.m. One in five women killed or severely injured by an intimate partner had no advance warning – the fatal or life-threatening incident was the first physical violence they had experienced from their partner. Termination of a relationship seems to pose an increased risk for, or escalation of, intimate partner violence for both women and men. A woman's attempt to leave an abuser was the precipitating factor in 45% of the murders of women by their intimate partners.

Domestic violence typically begins with minor and occasional assaults and escalates with more severe and frequent abuse. In the beginning the abuse usually starts with the abuser degrading the partner with insults and criticism. Over time the abuser seeks increasingly to isolate the victim, often expressed as jealousy. Jealousy is directed not only at other potential romantic interests but also at work colleagues, friends, and others. The abuser will try to make the victim entirely dependent on him for financial support, controlling all access to money and other resources. An effort may be made to make the victim dependent on alcohol or drugs to further his control over her. The abuser himself may be drug or alcohol dependent.

Domestic violence typically involves a cycle that occurs over and over again. In the first part of the cycle, the man becomes increasingly tense, usually evidenced by bitter criticism or insults directed at the woman. Sensing this, the woman tries to avoid triggering more anger in the man. The man becomes more abusive and may escalate from insults to slapping and other forms of violence that do not usually injure the woman. Women may not challenge this behavior in the hope that it will go away, but this in itself may contribute to the risk of violence by giving the abuser the control he seeks. The next phase often involves physical abuse in which the man is extremely angry for reasons not usually evident; he can become quite irrational and uncontrollable.

After the violence, the cycle usually concludes with the man acting sorry for what he has done and seeking forgiveness. The abuser promises he will change and gives the woman attention or gifts as evidence of his affection and remorse. Unfortunately, many women are convinced by this show of affection; they want to believe that this peaceful, loving man is the "real" person. Women may deny the recurrent nature of the abuse, convincing themselves that it may really be over each time he begs forgiveness. The man manipulates her into staying and tolerating the violence. But the violence almost never ends by itself, and the cycle repeats, with increasing anger and violence, followed by forgiveness and reconciliation. Throughout the cycle there is chronic emotional and psychological abuse and often continual threats to injure or kill the woman.

Risk factors have been identified for homes and situations in which intimate violence is most likely to occur. Not all homes in which these characteristics are found will have domestic violence, and homes that do not evidence these traits are not necessarily at no risk of abuse. Homes where the male is between 18 and

30 years old, unemployed, uses drugs, and did not graduate from high school are at elevated risk of violence between partners. If the man witnessed violence between his parents, or if either parent is abusive toward their own children, intimate violence is more likely.

Unmarried cohabiting couples are at a higher risk for violence, as are homes where the income is below the poverty level and there are significant disparities between partners in income, job status, or education. However, it is thought that middle- and upper-class families tend to deny or conceal domestic violence more than low-income families. Perhaps the most significant risk is a history of domestic violence in the home.

Female victims of intimate violence seek medical attention for abuse injuries more frequently after separation from an abusive partner, rather than while cohabiting with the assailant. Approximately three-fourths of emergency department visits by battered women and calls to law enforcement for intervention in domestic violence occur during the period following separation. Half of homicides of female spouses and partners were committed by men after separation. Newer marriages also seem to have a higher rate of violence between spouses.

Financial considerations are important factors in abusive situations. Severe poverty and its associated stressors increase the risk for intimate partner violence— the lower the household income, the higher the reported intimate partner violence rates. Women are often afraid that they cannot survive financially outside of the abusive relationship, perhaps because the abuser has effectively controlled her, not permitting her to hold a job or acquire needed education. The abuser also may try to control access to money and prevent the woman from accumulating any savings that could be used to aid her departure.

Stress from financial difficulties, unemployment, or other problems may contribute to a man becoming abusive, but finances, per se, do not cause nonviolent men to become abusive. The abusive situation results from an abuser who, in addition to some stress, has a strong need to control and dominate his partner and depends on her for basic psychological rewards and meaning. Domestic violence involves a man who blames his partner for all of his failures and dissatisfactions in life and derives his emotional well-being almost entirely from this single relationship.

Women who are living in an abusive and violent situation may be slow to leave the relationship, which often confuses friends and relatives who care about them. In fact, at some point, most women do end up leaving an abusive partner. Some women leave immediately. Others may take months or years to do so. The obstacle to leaving is the combination of psychological characteristics and situational factors that work to keep the woman in the relationship. She often feels responsible for the man's happiness because he is so dependent on her emotionally, and when not abusive, he may be her only or primary source of love. She is fearful for herself and if a mother as well, probably for her children. She may be deprived of the financial and psychological tools of independence, of transportation, perhaps even of the ability to cultivate relationships of trust with other adults to whom she can turn in her time of need and on whom she can depend.

Abused women become emotionally numb and physically and emotionally exhausted. Many believe they cannot leave the relationship, that they would be found anywhere by the abuser, or even that they in some way deserve the abuse. But the man's positive, loving reinforcement following his episodes of violence, along with the woman's own learned helplessness, are perhaps the most potent factors prolonging the time before a woman ultimately seeks help and escapes the relationship. In abuse that continues over a long period there usually is some final act of violence that precipitates the departure. Threats to the children are an example, or the woman may have acquired confidence from a new job or some other accomplishment that motivates her to leave.

ARE GUNS INVOLVED IN DOMESTIC VIOLENCE?

Yes. Weapons, including guns, are involved in domestic violence and increase the seriousness and potential lethality of injuries that may result from it. Approximately one-fourth of attacks on women in general involve the use of a weapon, and approximately one-third of these are firearms. When women are victimized by assailants with weapons, strangers are more likely to use a gun and intimate partners are more likely to be armed with knives or other sharp objects. Among female victims of intimate partner violence, 4% report having been threatened with a gun by an intimate partner, and 1% sustained firearm injuries in these assaults. In one study, 1 in 4 abused pregnant women aged 14–42 years reported that their batterer owned or had access to a gun.

A majority of intimate partner homicide victims are killed with a firearm. From 1990 to 2005 more than two-thirds of spouse and ex-spouse intimate victims were killed by perpetrators with guns (69% by husbands, 86% by ex-husbands, 45% by boyfriends, 68% by wives, 77% by ex-wives, and 56% by girlfriends). Boyfriends were more likely than any other group to be killed by a knife, and girlfriends more likely to be killed by force. Family and intimate assaults with firearms are at least 12 times more likely to result in death than non-firearm assaults.

From 1976 to 2002, a woman was 2.2 times more likely to be shot and killed by her male intimate than killed in any other way by a stranger. Handguns accounted for most of these deaths. Women killed by a spouse, intimate acquaintance, or close relative are seven times more likely to live in homes with one or more guns. One study of women physically abused by current or former intimate partners revealed a five-fold increased risk of the partner murdering the woman when the partner owned a firearm. Investigators at the Centers for Disease Control and Prevention compared the risk of death and nonfatal injury occurring in family assault that did and did not involve firearms. Firearm-associated assault is 3 times more likely to result in death than assault involving knives or other cutting instruments, and 23 times more likely to result in death than assault involving other weapons or bodily force.

In 1994, Congress expanded the list of people prohibited from purchasing and possessing a firearm to include individuals subject to a court order restraining them from "harassing, stalking, or threatening an intimate partner." Under federal law established by the Lautenberg Amendment in 1996, an individual convicted of a domestic violence misdemeanor is prohibited from purchasing a firearm. In states with laws that restrict intimate partner abusers from possessing firearms, intimate partner homicide rates decreased by 9%–12%. From 1998 to 2001, 14% of the 200,000 denials for gun purchases generated by National Instant Criminal Background Check System were the result of domestic violence misdemeanor convictions.

HOW COMMON IS STALKING?

The Department of Justice reports that more than 1 million women and approximately 400,000 men are stalked each year in the United States. As of 2006, 8% of women and 2% of men in the United States have been stalked at some point in their lifetime. In 27.6% of these incidents, the stalker was a current or prior intimate partner. In 2000, 5% of women and 0.6% of men surveyed by the Department of Justice reported having been stalked by a current or former spouse, cohabiting partner, or date at some time in their lifetime. According to these estimates, more than a half-million women and 185,000 men are stalked by an intimate partner every year in the United States.

Most stalking victims are female (78%), and most perpetrators are male (87%). In 2004, 20% of university undergraduates had been stalked or harassed by a former dating partner. The average duration of stalking is 1.3 years, with two-thirds of stalkers pursuing their victims at least once a week. Twenty percent of the time stalkers used a weapon to harm or threaten their victims. More than 50% of stalkers had some (not necessarily intimate) prior relationship with the victim, also known as intimate stalking. One-third of stalkers were repeat offenders. One-seventh of stalkers were clinically psychotic at the time of stalking.

In 81% of stalking incidents of women by a current or former husband or cohabiting partner, the victim was physically assaulted. Thirty-one percent were also sexually assaulted by that partner. Stalking is a significant risk factor for homicide of women within an abusive relationship. The overall rate of violence experienced by stalking victims was 39% in 13 studies of 1,155 cases. Serious violence was associated with a history of sexual intimacy with the stalker, the stalker appearing previously at the victim's home, the absence of a criminal record, and a shorter duration of stalking.

Stalking victims, whether stalked by an intimate partner or not, experience much higher rates of anxiety, insomnia, problematic social relationships, and severe depression than the general population.

WHAT IS ELECTRONIC AGGRESSION OR CYBER-STALKING?

Electronic aggression is any kind of aggression perpetrated through and using technology to support deliberate, repeated, and hostile behavior by an individual or group intended to harm others. As more and more people gain access to the internet, there is growing awareness about a new form of stalking called "cyber-stalking." Cyber-stalking involves recurrent harassment or threats to an individual through the inappropriate use of information and communication technologies involving e-mail, harassment in live chat exchanges, cell phone and pager text messages, instant messaging, defamatory personal websites, blogs, signing a victim's code name or e-mail address after leaving inappropriate messages on message boards or guest books, sending viruses, or electronic identity theft.

Other methods of harassment include a stalker using e-mail to send spam (large volumes of unsolicited junk mail), "flaming" or online verbal abuse, sexual harassment, and repeated attempts at "private chats." Electronic identity theft is use of the internet to gain personal information. There are online services that will sell your social security number, financial history, personal information, and a detailed map to your house to any buyer. Cyber-stalking can have an objective of sexual assault and can involve the use of explicit sexual content, pornography, and communication to sexually harass a victim.

In 2000, 6% of internet users said they had been the victim of online harassment. By 2005, this percentage had risen to 9%, an increase of 50%. Electronic aggression occurs commonly on social networking websites and in chat rooms. The Centers for Disease Control and Prevention reports that 25% of victims of electronic aggression stated it occurred in a chat room and 23% on a website. However, instant messaging is the most common vehicle for perpetrating electronic aggression; 56% of perpetrators of electronic aggression and 67% of victims stated that the aggression they perpetrated or experienced was through instant messaging. Victims also reported experiencing electronic aggression through e-mail (25%) and text messages (16%).

Cyber-stalking can be as harmful and terrifying as real-life stalking but is more difficult to prove and to control. Much as occurs with in-person stalking, a former intimate partner can be a cyber-stalker. The anonymity of the internet works to conceal and protect the stalker, but there are safety procedures to help anyone online and those being cyber-stalked. One should not give out personal information online and not use one's real name or nickname online. If you are being cyber-stalked, change e-mail accounts. If you cannot change accounts, look into filter programs. Within a chat room, use gender-neutral nicknames, do not use real e-mail addresses, be careful with profiles, use ignore options, and do not answer individual chat requests. Notify the chat administrator or room moderators of abuse. If you are being harassed through e-mail or a chat room, notify your internet provider.

WHY DOES DOMESTIC VIOLENCE PERSIST?

Unfortunately, American society embraces a number of social and cultural values that allow domestic violence and spouse abuse to proliferate. The entertainment industry implicitly and explicitly validates violence against women. Stereotypes of women's roles and of marriage tolerate, even facilitate, domestic violence. The notions that intimate violence is infrequent and of minor impact are myths. The idea that most victims regard the privacy and independence of the family as sacred and that they do not want assistance is also incorrect and perpetuates abuse. A "blame-the-victim" perspective suggests, contrary to the facts, that women who are victimized by intimate violence are those who nag their partners, who get angry easily and fight with them, or who stand up for themselves and thus provoke an "understandable" response from frustrated partners. Another myth is that domestic violence is restricted to lower-income families who are stressed by poverty and whose members have little formal education. On the contrary, domestic violence affects all types of American families.

Abusers perceive themselves as lacking power in their environment and compensate by exerting power over intimate partners and other members of the family. Abuse results from one partner having a need to be in complete control of the other. The abuser finds that the victim cannot retaliate and uses the victim as a scapegoat against whom to ventilate his hostilities. In intimate violence, there is a tendency for the abuser to blame the victim for everything that has gone wrong in his life.

Intimate abusers often come from families where violence was a frequent and accepted behavior, so they may believe that violent behavior is a reasonable method for solving problems. Indeed, witnessing violence between one's parents or caretakers is the strongest risk factor for transmitting violent behavior from one generation to the next. Boys who witness domestic violence are twice as likely to abuse their own partners and children when they become adults.

Police departments around the nation are not uniform in their approach to domestic violence. Some departments (and individuals) remain indifferent or ignorant about the problem. In the judiciary, there are prosecutors who do not want to pursue charges against an abuser and judges who offer lenient sentences or release abusers without punishment or placement in a treatment program.

ISN'T DOMESTIC VIOLENCE AGAINST THE LAW?

Not everywhere. Many states and the District of Columbia have laws that mandate the arrest of a perpetrator of domestic violence. To legally arrest a suspect, however, the police must first acquire a warrant from a judge. They can arrest a suspect without a warrant only if they can demonstrate at the time of arrest that they had probable cause to believe the suspect had committed the crime.

An arrest without a warrant and based on such probable cause is authorized in most states and the District of Columbia. Police in these states often are instructed to communicate to the victim that she has certain rights, including the ability to obtain a protection order (to keep a perpetrator away from a victim) and about the availability of abuse shelters, emergency facilities, and transportation to these.

HOW CAN SOCIETY PREVENT VIOLENCE AGAINST INTIMATE PARTNERS AND SPOUSES?

In the past 20 years, a new national awareness of intimate violence against women has emerged. Today less stigma is attached to those who recognize and admit there is violence within their families and who seek professional assistance. The sanctity of privacy in the home and family is being challenged as more people come to view domestic violence as a serious social problem that will not resolve by itself. The first battered women's shelter in America was opened more than three decades ago in St. Paul, Minnesota. Since that time, 1,500 shelters for battered women have been established across the nation. Before the 1970s, the focus was on the danger of assault and rape by strangers or acquaintances. Violence in the family was thought to be infrequent, resulting from isolated cases of mental illness in rare individuals rather than a broader problem within society. Over the past 15 years, data on the prevalence of intimate violence have been gathered that evidence a major and profound public health and safety problem.

Society's responses to domestic violence have included advocacy; the provision of crisis, medical, and mental health care services; increased prosecution of perpetrators in the criminal justice system; and expanded research to identify causes and prevention strategies. For example, hotlines to private and public sector agencies have been established for victimized women in many U.S. cities. Rape laws have been amended to protect victims from assault by marital partners. Nearly every state has established legislation addressing violence between adult intimate partners. Increasing prosecution of family assailants is critical to prevention, because it is estimated that up to 90% of assailants are never prosecuted (and one-third of cases that would be treated as felonies if committed by strangers are filed as misdemeanors, a much lesser crime).

Increasing public awareness and intolerance of intimate partner violence are greatly needed, particularly among youth and certain cultural and socioeconomic segments at increased risk for victimization. Among youth for example, acceptance of dating violence among friends is one of the strongest predictors of future involvement in dating violence. Adolescents often believe that unhealthy relationships are the norm. The media often portrays unhealthy examples of relationships (in part because conflict is central to creating drama). But individuals without the educational background or experience to know better may incorporate such destructive relationships as norms, if not models, not warranting resistance. Adolescents who have not learned that the qualities of an appropriate, healthy relationship include mutual respect, good communication, and honesty (with no abuse) have greater difficulty establishing nonviolent relationships.

Many experts believe that domestic violence must be treated as a crime if prevention and control efforts are to be successful. In this view, assailants should be arrested, removed immediately from the home, and possibly jailed for at least one night to shock them into recognizing that this form of behavior is unacceptable and will have legal consequences. A powerful message must be sent to abusers that further violence against their intimate will not be tolerated. It seems the most successful programs for abusers combine some jail time, individual counseling, and participation in a men's battering group. The latter two educate the man about intimate violence and provide behavior modification, training in anger management, and treatment for substance abuse (if needed).

A protection order may be an important element in preventing recurrences of intimate violence. A protection order can be civil or criminal and is a legally binding court action to prohibit an abuser from contacting, abusing, or harassing his victim. Each state has a procedure for obtaining a protection order. A protection order can be issued on an emergency basis to the woman without having the abusive partner in court. If an abuser disobeys the order, he can be arrested and incarcerated, and police will be more aggressive in responding to an abuser if he is violating such an order. The violation of an order often involves mandatory arrest and jail time. Although the orders may expire after a month or two, they can be extended or made permanent for a period of up to three years in some jurisdictions. Protection orders can be renewed as often as necessary. The order may require the abuser to leave the home and may temporarily determine the custody of children, as well as define what child or spouse support the abuser must pay.

A criminal court may issue a protection order during the trial or sentencing of an abuser as a condition of obtaining bail and release before a trial. Divorces can involve an order, and an attorney or the prosecutor in a community can educate victims about the options available in their specific circumstances. There are often local services that help victims obtain such a protective order. The benefits of protection orders go beyond keeping the abuser away from the victim. They also can facilitate the victim's introduction to resources available in her local community.

Studies show that access to domestic violence shelter services by victims leads to a 60%–70% reduction in the incidence and severity of reassault during the 3- to 12-month follow-up period compared with women who did not access a shelter. Shelter services led to greater reduction in severe reassault than did seeking court or law enforcement protection, or moving to a new location.

An important part of preventing intimate partner violence is early detection of abuse so that assistance, counseling services, and, if necessary, law enforcement can be provided in support of a victim. Because domestic violence victims are often purposely socially and physically isolated by abusers, detection can be difficult. One setting in which detection may be possible is the emergency department, where victims must seek care when seriously injured from violent victimization.

Insofar as a victim of intimate violence is seen at and treated by an emergency department or a physician's office, failure to detect and engage a victim when seeking such medical care is a critical missed opportunity. For example, one study found that 44% of women ultimately murdered by their intimate partner had visited an emergency department within the 2 years before the homicide. Of these women, 93% had at least 1 injury visit. With respect to visits to primary care and office-based physicians, more frequent communication about domestic violence is essential. Research has shown that although 96% of patients believe physicians should generally inquire about family conflict, two-thirds reported that their own physician never asked them about intimate partner violence. Sixty-seven percent of individuals whose physician has inquired about family conflict reported that the same physician did indeed help them receive assistance. Increasing the training and vigilance of health care providers to detect and report intimate partner violence is imperative for effective prevention.

Some experts suspect that the dynamics of relationships in which intimate violence occurs rarely can be improved. In this view, the violence becomes so entrenched in the pattern of relating between the partners that it can never be eliminated entirely. Here the best hope may be to reduce its frequency and intensity. In some relationships, the only option may be to end the relationship entirely. In others, the physical assaults may cease, but the emotional and psychological abuse persist. Unfortunately, women often return to an abusive relationship because they cannot shed themselves of the hope that the relationship can be salvaged and the violence will end.

WHAT CAN I DO IF A FAMILY MEMBER OR FRIEND IS BEING ABUSED?

Perhaps the most important thing that you can do for your friend is to remain accessible and offer yourself as a resource. Above all, get involved and stay involved. Try to educate and encourage the victim to report the abuse and seek counseling and crisis services. If the abuse is severe or escalating in intensity and your friend is unable to, report it yourself. Providing your friend with emotional support is critical to regain the self-esteem that intimate violence robs from its victim. You should serve as a constant reminder that the abuse is not her or his fault and that she or he has a right to a safe and sane existence.

Providing your friend and her children occasional temporary shelter when the abuse becomes intolerable and assisting in the search for new housing and job opportunities can be invaluable to an abused victim. You can give your relative or friend information about abuse and refer her to a telephone hotline and specific local community resources on domestic violence. Contact the local shelter and domestic violence coalition on her behalf, and find out what policies are followed by the local police department and the office of the district attorney that prosecutes domestic violence cases. Keep a supply of money, clothes, and other emergency items for her at your home in case she needs to flee her home suddenly.

The moment of departure from an abusive relationship is dangerous and potentially violent because the abuser fears losing his victim and control, so your support and assistance will be important. It will not help to try and accelerate the process of leaving an abusive situation by pushing a victim excessively. Generally, a person must be ready to go on her own accord. But you can be instrumental in moving her toward this decision point. If you are too forceful in trying to extricate her from the relationship before she is ready, she may feel that she has no choice but to avoid you. Do not drive her away with simplistic or self-righteous rhetoric about a situation with which you may have no firsthand experience. Keep in regular contact with your abused friend, but not in a manner that raises the abuser's suspicions (e.g., telephoning or stopping by when he is around). You also can provide transport for an otherwise trapped victim to a shelter. Information and program services resources are listed at the end of this chapter.

If you have a friend or relative who is an abuser or is becoming increasingly abusive of his intimate partner, try to convince him that he has a real problem. Explain the nature—and consequences—of domestic violence as described earlier, and the risk it entails to the relationship. Advice from a trusted friend or relative can have real value in getting an abuser to seek assistance. Urge him to seek help, and if he wants, accompany him to his first encounter with a services program for abusers. If you are unable to convince him by yourself that he needs help, recruit his other close friends and relatives to talk to the abuser. Tell him that if he does not obtain help on his own, sooner or later the legal system will force him to get treatment under court order, and this may follow only after he has destroyed the relationship with his partner and possibly served time in jail.

WHAT SHOULD I DO IF I AM AN ABUSED SPOUSE OR INTIMATE PARTNER?

If you are being abused by your partner, you must make the decision to seek help and stick with it. The first step is to educate yourself about intimate partner violence and battering. Contact your local domestic violence coalition or crisis hotline for battering victims to get information about and help for your situation (a list of contacts and website resources conclude this chapter). You must come to recognize it is not your fault that your partner beats or otherwise abuses you and that there is no provocation that justifies such violence. You have a right to personal safety and a happy, healthy relationship.

If the violence against you is severe, you must leave as soon as possible. Domestic violence shelters can give you a place to live temporarily, and they have services to help you move out permanently (if necessary). A domestic violence organization in your community also can refer your partner to groups for abusive men if he is willing and ready to receive help. Through individual or group therapy, men can be taught to recognize their responsibility for violence and to take steps to halt it. More information about treatment for men who abuse women is covered in the next section.

There are ways to protect yourself from an abusive spouse. You can protect yourself physically by fighting back. The risk this entails is that you may further enrage your partner and escalate the violence to a more dangerous level. Verbal defense, such as trying to convince your spouse to stop an assault or to prevent one, is a more passive measure that may be easier and safer to engage. Eluding a spouse at times when it appears that violence can be easily triggered (by leaving the room or the home) can be preventive. A Department of Justice survey reported that more than one-half of women who tried to protect themselves against an abusive intimate partner thought that their efforts helped the situation. One-fourth, however, believed that their actions made the problem worse.

A new strategy has been employed using panic buttons placed in the homes of victims. When an abuser violates a protection order or is stalking a victim around the home, this electronic device can be activated to notify police to come to the victim's aid (the police arrive in a matter of minutes). Inquire if police in your community have this option available. Do not purchase a gun, and try to get rid of all guns in the home because these may be turned against you. If a missing gun might enrage your partner, hide the bullets.

If you feel acutely threatened, and if your partner is so violent that he could seriously injure you, do not hesitate to call the police to help you. Call 911 if you fear injury and certainly if you fear for your life. In the past, police often did not arrest abusers because they believed it only made the problem more difficult by fragmenting the family and damaging the man's reputation. This has changed, and today arrest is much more common—and in many states legally required. The U.S. Attorney General has recommended that arrest be the standard procedure of police when responding to domestic violence calls. Some police departments have been sued for not arresting an assailant who abused an intimate partner. Many states require arrest when there is probable cause or evidence (such as a woman's injuries) that a crime has been committed. Police are required to stay at the scene of a domestic violence call until it is determined that the victim is safe.

Most states have laws requiring that the abuser be jailed immediately on arrest to protect the victim. This is followed by arraignment in court. The court may set bail, deny the abuser release, or issue a restraining (or protective) order that prohibits contact with the victim. The abuser may be enrolled in a treatment program as a condition for staying out of jail, usually when a protective order also has been issued. This course of action, involving an arrest, may be the best for getting an abuser to recognize that violent behavior is unacceptable and illegal, and will not be tolerated by society.

After a brief stay in jail, an abuser may be ready to receive the kind of private counseling or group therapy that can change his behavior. The system strives to be fair, and those who really want to change and are willing to make an effort will be given an opportunity through counseling to do so. Abusers who are unwilling to receive treatment will be dealt with as criminals and incarcerated to prevent them from committing future acts of violence. Research indicates that arresting abusers can reduce repeat violence by up to 50%. Police can be helpful by referring a case to prosecutors to obtain a protection order. Police also will transport a victim to a hospital (if necessary) or shelter.

However, calling the police is not a victim's only recourse. As a victim you may not be ready or able to leave or to call the police for help even if you need it. You may be torn by a sense of loyalty to your partner—not wanting to betray him— and your desire to protect yourself from further beatings and abuse. But protecting yourself from an abusive partner is not a betrayal of him. You must recognize that it is he who is at fault and to blame for this situation, not you, and your getting help is a normal and natural consequence of his violent behavior toward you. Educate yourself about the problem by obtaining information, reading books, calling a crisis hotline, and talking to friends who can help you.

Try to find one or more trusted friends to whom you can turn in moments of crisis and when you need emotional support and practical assistance. Keep their telephone numbers and those of local shelters for battered women where you can get to them if you have to leave the house quickly. Make spare copies of car keys and hide them. Try to save some money to cover taxi fare and a night in a motel until you can get to a shelter.

Know where the closest pay phone is to your home, as well as a store or restaurant that is open 24 hours a day. Be sure to ask someone to back you up in your efforts and to help you and your children find a place to stay temporarily, where you can keep money, clothes, and other emergency items. Ask someone to assist you in getting professional help. He or she can find out what services are available in your community and what the response of local police and prosecuting attorneys will be to your request for help.

When you are ready to leave the abusive situation, be sure to take important documents such as your driver's license, your and your children's birth certificates, passports, financial statements and other papers, bank account books, and credit cards. Take possessions of special sentimental value with you because the abuser may destroy them. Bring your children with you. If this is not possible, go back for them quickly and only with a police officer, or get them from school. Never tell the abuser that you are leaving, because this will precipitate or worsen a violent episode. Make up a routine excuse for going out, or leave when he is not there.

Your doctor can play an important role by intervening before domestic violence reaches life-threatening levels. A doctor will screen for physical and sexual assault and will design treatment plans. Health and social service professionals will follow a protocol to assess your history of current or past victimization. Health care providers will have links with a variety of resources in your community, including battered women shelters and crisis services, abuse hotlines, rape crisis centers, and treatment programs for men who abuse women. If you have been victimized, it is in your best interest from both a health and a legal point of view to have any possible injuries assessed and documented by a doctor. Internal injuries may not be immediately apparent to you. Just the fact that you sought medical attention may be important if legal proceedings are pursued later.

In addition to health care providers, other resources in the community in which you live can be found in the white and yellow pages of your telephone directory. Look for listings under the headings "Shelters," "Women's Services," or "Social Services." Referral resources are provided at the end of this chapter, and you can call the National Domestic Violence Hotline at (800) 799-SAFE (7233) or (800) 787-3224 TTY to find help in your local community.

In the United States, there are more than 1,500 shelters and many private homes and temporary facilities in community centers and churches that provide services for abused women. Most shelters will accommodate an abused woman for up to 30 days, and the average stay lasts approximately 2 weeks. Many shelters organize support groups, provide individual counseling, and help with finding permanent housing and locating a new job. Therapy and counseling for women who have been abused should not be misinterpreted as suggesting that such women are sick or that something is wrong with them. Counseling is not intended to blame the victim. Rather it is recognition of the fact that intimate violence is a traumatic and potentially damaging experience, emotionally as well as physically, and that help often is needed to produce positive change, to integrate the impact of the abusive relationship, and to move on.

Services also are available to women who want to use them while they remain in their homes with their families rather than move to a shelter. Abused women who spend some time in a shelter or private safe house tend to leave their abusers more often than those who do not. In shelters, victims can find not only temporary escape from physical abuse but also a community of others who have had similar experiences. Victims will find encouragement and the emotional strength to end their isolation and sense that there is nothing they can do to help themselves. The shelter can serve as a way to engage resources that are available to women to stop abuse and, if necessary, to leave their abusers.

Counseling for couples is also available, in which the victim and her abuser attend therapy sessions together. This approach is somewhat controversial because of the chance that it could precipitate more violence or be used to intimidate the victim. Care should be used in the selection of a counselor or a support group. Find one that improves your outlook and gives you hope.

Financial assistance is available from federal programs, such as Aid to Families with Dependent Children and the food stamps program. These can usually be found under "Social Services" in the phone book. Do not hesitate to use these resources until you can support yourself financially. Shelters can help with job searches and locating job-training programs. Getting new job skills and a new job can dramatically affect a victim's emotional outlook, well-being, and sense of accomplishment. Although these strategies may seem overwhelming at first glance, it can be done. There is no need to remain a victim of abuse because of financial or other kinds of dependence on an abusive partner.

WHAT CAN I DO TO STOP ABUSING MY SPOUSE OR INTIMATE PARTNER?

If you recognize that you have a problem and want to change, you can be helped. The first step is to realize that you, not your spouse or intimate partner, are responsible for the violence in your relationship and that this behavior is not acceptable. You can turn this situation and your life around and establish a peaceful home. If you do nothing, you are at risk of seriously injuring your partner. You also could lose your family through separation and divorce or your own incarceration. Battering is a crime. Eventually you could kill your partner. You may be repeating a pattern of violence that you experienced yourself as a child victim of abuse or as a witness to your father abusing your mother. You can and must break the chain of violence and suffering.

Reach out for professional help in your community. Men's groups that can help exist. These groups are made up of batterers like yourself who are in different stages of change, including some well along the road to successfully eliminating violence from their relationships. The groups discuss some of the stereotyped and unhealthy views and expectations that society places on men, including those that include violence as a normal response. Here you will learn that you are not alone in living with the problem of domestic violence and that the confusion, anger, and fear that you have experienced are not unusual. Other men in the group will have experienced similar difficulties in intimate relationships as you have.

Violence is a learned behavior, and in therapy you can learn ways to avoid it and enrich your relationships. You will be taught methods to resolve conflicts nonviolently and to help control your rage and impulse to punish. Programs for abusers are thought to be most effective if begun right after the first time abuse comes to the attention of the authorities. Counseling initiated after a few assaults may be more likely to succeed than that begun after many years of abuse. Remember that if you plead guilty or are found guilty of battering you may be required to accept treatment or go to jail through a pretrial diversion program.

The objective of treatment will be to educate you about the nature and causes of intimate abuse, provide you with methods to modify your behavior, and teach you about the safe and appropriate management of your anger. In the group process you will be required to take responsibility for your actions and violence, but the emphasis will be on your potential to change and overcome this problem. A method for achieving change will be outlined, and the group will offer support along the way. But you will be required to admit that the violence is your fault, not your partner's, and that abuse under any circumstances is wrong. Developing respect for and equality with your intimate partner will become the foundation for a new and healthy relationship.

Group or individual treatment programs usually involve sessions over a six-month period. It appears that longer programs have a greater impact and better outcome for the abuser than those involving only a few sessions. Treatment for drug abuse or alcoholism, if you need it, will be integrated with therapy. After the group program is over, you will be required to participate in follow-up or monitoring of your progress and possibly occasional group sessions; if you do not cooperate, the court may impose probation or an order prohibiting contact with your partner.

If do not feel you can participate in group sessions, private therapy is available from counselors in most communities. Private counseling involves many of the same elements as a group process but lacks the reinforcement and support that others who share your experience and problems can provide. Local mental health organizations, churches, social service agencies, and those that help battered women can provide referral to services for men who batter. Most important, don't delay. The sooner you get help, the greater the likelihood that you can change your behavior and stop the violence. Get help immediately and save your family.

WHERE CAN I GET MORE INFORMATION AND HELP?

For information about domestic violence and help for spouse or intimate partner abuse, contact your local health department or doctor, local medical centers and hospitals, and other social service providers. These agencies can refer you to an organization that provides specific services for your needs. For information on shelters or services in your community, look in the Yellow Pages under "Human Services Organizations" or "Social Service Organizations."

In addition, and especially if you fear violence that could result in injury, immediately contact your local police department or call 911 or the National Domestic Violence Hotline at (800) 799-SAFE (7233) or (800) 787-3224 TTY.

Appendix 1 at the back of the book provides a state-by-state website listing of compensation and assistance programs for victims of violence and crime. You may find assistance by contacting one of your state programs. Appendix 2 is a bibliography for further reading on each of the violence topics discussed in this volume, organized chapter by chapter.

The following are national and state organizations and internet websites that offer information and services to victims, families, and professionals about domestic and intimate violence.

NATIONAL ORGANIZATIONS

Abusive Men Exploring New Directions (AMEND)
(303) 832-6363

Asian Task Force Against Domestic Violence
(617) 338-2350

Battered Women's Justice Project
(800) 903-0111

Break the Cycle
(310) 286-3383

Centers for Disease Control and Prevention
National Center for Injury Prevention and Control
(800) CDC-INFO (232-4636)

Domestic Abuse Intervention Project
(218) 722-2781

Domestic Abuse Project (DAP)
(612) 874-7063

EMERGE: Counseling and Education to Stop Male Violence
(617) 547-9879

Family Violence Prevention Fund
(415) 252-8900

Institute on Violence, Abuse, and Trauma
(858) 527-1860

National Battered Women's Law Project
(212) 741-9480

National Center on Sexual and Domestic Violence
(512) 407-9020

National Center for Victims of Crime, National Crime Victim Helpline
(800) FYI-CALL (394-2255); TYY (800) 211-7996

National Clearinghouse for the Defense of Battered Women
(800) 903-0111

National Coalition Against Domestic Violence
(303) 839-1852 or (202) 745-1211; (303) 839-8459 TTY

National Crime Prevention Council
(202) 466-6272

National Domestic Violence Hotline
(800) 799-SAFE (7233); (800) 787-3224 TTY

National Institute of Justice
National Criminal Justice Reference Service
(800) 851-3420

National Network to End Domestic Violence
(202) 543-5566

National Online Resource Center on Violence Against Women
(800) 537-2238; (800) 553-2508 TTT

National Organization for Victim Assistance
(800) TRY-NOVA (879-6682)

National Office for Victims of Crime Resource Center (NVRC)
Office for Victims of Crime, Office of Justice Programs
Department of Justice
(800) 851-3420; TYY (877) 712-9279

Resource Center on Domestic Violence, Child Protection and Custody
(800) 527-3223

Texas Council on Family Violence
(512) 794-1133

Women in Crisis, Inc.
(212) 242-4880

YWCA Center for Safety and Empowerment
(888) 822-2983

STATE DOMESTIC VIOLENCE COALITIONS, CRISIS CENTERS, AND HOTLINES

Alabama Coalition Against Domestic Violence
www.acadv.org
(800) 650-6522

Alaska Network on Domestic Violence and Sexual Assault
www.andvsa.org
(907) 586-3650

Arizona Coalition Against Domestic Violence
www.azcadv.org
(800) 782-6400

Arkansas Coalition Against Domestic Violence
www.domesticpeace.com
(800) 269-4668

California Partnership to End Domestic Violence
www.cpedv.org
(916) 444-7163 or (800) 524-4765

Colorado Coalition Against Domestic Violence
www.ccadv.org
(888) 788-7091

Connecticut Coalition Against Domestic Violence
www.ctcadv.org
(888) 774-2900

Delaware Coalition Against Domestic Violence
www.dcadv.org
(800) 701-0456

D.C. Coalition Against Domestic Violence
www.dccadv.org
(202) 299-1181

Florida Coalition Against Domestic Violence
www.fcadv.org
(800) 500-1119

Georgia Coalition Against Domestic Violence
www.gcadv.org
(404) 209-0280

Hawaii State Coalition Against Domestic Violence
www.hscadv.org
(808) 832-9316

Idaho Coalition Against Sexual & Domestic Violence
www.idvsa.org
(888) 293-6118

Illinois Coalition Against Domestic Violence
www.ilcadv.org
(217) 789-2830

Indiana Coalition Against Domestic Violence
www.violenceresource.org
(800) 332-7385

Iowa Coalition Against Domestic Violence
www.icadv.org
(800) 942-0333

Kansas Coalition Against Sexual and Domestic Violence
www.kcsdv.org
(785) 232-9784

Kentucky Domestic Violence Association
www.kdva.org
(502) 209-5382

Louisiana Coalition Against Domestic Violence
www.lcadv.org
(225) 752-1296

Maine Coalition to End Domestic Violence
www.mcedv.org
(207) 430-8334

Maryland Network Against Domestic Violence
www.mnadv.org
(800) 634-3577

Massachusetts Coalition Against Sexual Assault and Domestic Violence
www.janedoe.org
(617) 248-0922

Michigan Coalition Against Domestic and Sexual Violence
www.mcadsv.org
(517) 347-7000

Minnesota Coalition for Battered Women
www.mcbw.org
(800) 289-6177

Mississippi Coalition Against Domestic Violence
www.mcadv.org
(800) 898-3234

Missouri Coalition Against Domestic and Sexual Violence
www.mocadv.org
(573) 634-4161

Montana Coalition Against Domestic & Sexual Violence
www.mcadsv.com
(888) 404-7794

Nebraska Domestic Violence Sexual Assault Coalition
www.ndvsac.org
(402) 476-6256

Nevada Network Against Domestic Violence
www.nnadv.org
(800) 230-1955

New Hampshire Coalition Against Domestic and Sexual Violence
www.nhcadsv.org
(866) 644-3574

New Jersey Coalition for Battered Women
www.njcbw.org
(609) 584-8107

New Mexico State Coalition Against Domestic Violence
www.nmcadv.org
(800) 773-3645

New York State Coalition Against Domestic Violence
www.nyscadv.org
English: (800) 942-6906
Spanish: (800) 942-6908

North Carolina Coalition Against Domestic Violence
www.nccadv.org
(888) 232-9124

North Dakota Council on Abused Women's Services
www.ndcaws.org
(888) 255-6240

Ohio Domestic Violence Network
www.odvn.org
(800) 934-9840

Oklahoma Coalition Against Domestic Violence and Sexual Assault
www.ocadvsa.org
(405) 524-0700

Oregon Coalition Against Domestic and Sexual Violence
www.ocadsv.com
(503) 230-1951

Pennsylvania Coalition Against Domestic Violence
www.pcadv.org
(800) 932-4632

Puerto Rico Coalition Against Domestic Violence and Sexual Assault
Coordinadora Paz Para La Mujer
pazmujer@prtc.net
(787) 281-7579

Rhode Island Coalition Against Domestic Violence
www.ricadv.org
(800) 494-8100

South Carolina Coalition Against Domestic Violence and Sexual Assault
www.sccadvasa.org
(800) 260-9293

South Dakota Coalition Against Domestic Violence & Sexual Assault
www.sdcadvsa.org
(605) 945-0869

Tennessee Coalition Against Domestic and Sexual Violence
www.tcadsv.org
(800) 289-9018

Texas Council on Family Violence
www.tcfv.org
(800) 525-1978

Utah Domestic Violence Council
www.udvac.org
(801) 521-5544

Vermont Network Against Domestic Violence and Sexual Assault
www.vtnetwork.org
(800) 228-7395

Virgin Islands Domestic Violence/Sexual Assault Women's Coalition of St. Croix
wcscstx@attglobal.net
(340) 773-9272

Virginia Sexual and Domestic Violence Action Alliance
www.vadv.org
(800) 838-8238

Washington State Coalition Against Domestic Violence
www.wscadv.org
(800) 562-6025

West Virginia Coalition Against Domestic Violence
www.wvcadv.org
(304) 965-3552

Wisconsin Coalition Against Domestic Violence
www.wcadv.org
(608) 255-0539

Wyoming Coalition Against Domestic Violence and Sexual Assault
www.wyomingdvsa.org
(800) 990-3877

USEFUL INTERNET WEBSITES

Abusive Men Exploring New Directions (AMEND): www.amendinc.org
Asian Task Force Against Domestic Violence: www.atask.org
Battered Women's Justice Project: www.bwjp.org
Centers for Disease Control and Prevention: www.cdc.gov
Commission on Domestic Violence: www.abanet.org/domviol
Domestic Abuse Intervention Programs: www.theduluthmodel.org
Domestic Violence Resource Center: www.dvrc-or.org/domestic
EMERGE—Counseling and Education to Stop Male Violence: www.emergedv.com
Family Violence Awareness Page: www.famvi.com
Family Violence Prevention Fund: www.endabuse.org
Feminist.com: www.feminist.com/antiviolence/facts.html
Institute on Domestic Violence in the African American Community:
   www.dvinstitute.org
Institute on Violence, Abuse, and Trauma: www.ivatcenters.org
National Center for Victims of Crime: www.ncvc.org
National Clearinghouse for Defense of Battered Women: www.ncdbw.org
National Coalition Against Domestic Violence: www.ncadv.org
National Center on Domestic and Sexual Violence: www.ncdsv.org
National Maternal and Child Health Clearinghouse: www.healthywoman.org
National Network to End Domestic Violence: www.nnedv.org
National Online Resource Center on Violence Against Women: www.vawnet.org
National Resource Center on Domestic Violence: www.nrcdv.org
National Sexual Violence Resource Center: www.nsvrc.org
National Victim Assistance Academy: www.ojp.usdoj.gov/ovc/assist/vaa.htm
National Violence Against Women Prevention Research Center:
   www.musc.edu/vawprevention
MEDLINEplus: www.nlm.nih.gov/medlineplus/domesticviolence.html
Office of Justice Programs, United States Department of Justice: www.ovw.usdoj.gov
Office for Victims of Crime: www.ovc.gov
Office on Violence Against Women: www.usdoj.gov/ovw
Rape, Abuse & Incest National Network: www.rainn.org
Stalking Resource Center: www.ncvc.org/src
Stalking Victim's Sanctuary: www.stalkingvictims.com
Violence Against Women Online Resources: www.vaw.umn.edu/sxasault.asp
Women's Health and Violence Resource: www.womenshealth.gov
Women's Justice Center: www.law.pace.edu/bwjc

CHAPTER 7

Rape and Sexual Assault of Adults

- What is sexual violence?
- What is rape?
- How common are rape and sexual assault?
- What are the consequences of rape and sexual assault?
- Who is a rapist or sex offender?
- Who gets raped or sexually assaulted?
- Can men be raped?
- In what situations do rape and sexual assault occur?
- Why do men rape?
- Can a man rape his wife?
- Are alcohol and drugs associated with rape?
- What is date rape?
- How can I protect myself from drug-facilitated rape?
- How can I tell if I have been drugged and raped?
- What should I do if I think I have been drugged and raped?
- What can I do to prevent being raped or sexually assaulted?
- What should I do when I am sexually assaulted?
- What should I do after I have been raped?
- What do I do if I feel the urge to rape?
- What is sexual harassment and how can I prevent it?
- Where can I get more information and help?

WHAT IS SEXUAL VIOLENCE?

Sexual violence describes any sexual activity where consent is not obtained or freely given. Not all of sexual violence necessarily involves physical contact between the victim and a perpetrator. Researchers have categorized four primary forms of sexual violence: (1) a completed sex act (penetration of the penis, a hand, a finger, or other object into the anal or genital opening; contact of the mouth and penis, vulva, or anus; or contact between the penis and the vulva or the penis and the anus involving any, even slight, penetration); (2) an attempted but not completed sex act; (3) abusive sexual contact involving intentional touching directly or through clothing of the genitals, anus, groin, breast, inner thigh, or buttocks; and (4) non-contact sexual abuse without a physical component, including voyeurism, peeping, intentional exposure, verbal or behavioral harassment or intimidation, threats of sexual violence, and taking or circulating nude photographs without consent.

In some states, the word "rape" is used only to define a forced act of vaginal sexual intercourse, and an act of forced anal intercourse is termed "sodomy." In certain states, the crime of sodomy also includes any oral sexual act. A number of states now use gender-neutral terms to define acts of forced anal, vaginal, or oral intercourse. Some states no longer use the terms "rape" and "sodomy" at all and describe all sex crimes as sexual assaults or criminal sexual conduct. Both rape and sexual assault include situations when the victim cannot refuse or say "no" because he or she is disabled, unconscious, drunk, or high.

Victims of sexual violence can be male or female, adult or child. Sexual violence is a serious problem in the United States. This chapter will focus on rape and sexual assault of adults, whereas Chapter 3 discusses sexual abuse of children.

WHAT IS RAPE?

Although the legal definition of rape has been considered and reconsidered over decades, there is no single, commonly accepted definition today. Many state laws now define rape as sexual penetration of an adult or adolescent without consent and by physical force, threat of bodily harm, or inability to consent because of mental illness, retardation, or intoxication. Rape is an assault on the physical, psychological, social, and sexual dimensions of a victim's life.

The Federal Bureau of Investigation (FBI) defines rape as the carnal knowledge (involving vaginal penetration) of a woman by force and against her will by a man who is not her husband. Attempts to commit rape by force or the threat of force are included in this definition, but many other kinds of sexual assault are not. For example, penetration by an object or sexual activity between husband and wife without consent are excluded from this definition. Most states define forcible rape as the FBI defines it, with some modifications. Date rape is sexual intercourse within a relationship, but without consent. Acquaintance rape involves individuals who know each other, including assailants who are the victim's relatives, neighbors, or friends. Marital rape involves spouses. Stranger rape involves people who have no relationship to each other.

The Department of Justice uses a much broader definition of rape, which allows each victim to define rape for herself, stating "if she [the victim] reports that she has been the victim of rape or attempted rape, she is not asked to explain what happened." Thus, although rape may sometimes be defined very narrowly, as vaginal penetration by the male sex organ, in recent years the definition of rape has broadened to take into consideration the perpetrator's intent and the impact on the victim (rather than merely the specific acts involved). The law also rarely distinguishes between the impacts of rape as a crime versus as an injury and does not consider the degree of injury to the victim.

Aggravated rape has been described as a rape committed by one or more strangers, by force, or with a weapon. Simple rape is forced sex without consent by only one man, known to the victim, who does not beat or attack her. Under some state laws, rape has not occurred if the assailant is an acquaintance or relative, yet it is well known that rape occurs among persons who are related.

HOW COMMON ARE RAPE AND SEXUAL ASSAULT?

In the United States, 1 in 6–10 women and 1 in 33–50 men have experienced an attempted or completed rape at some time in their lives. Estimates run as high as 17.7 million U.S. women having been the victims of an attempted or completed rape and 2.78 million men having been the victims of sexual assault or rape. A national survey published in 2007 found that 10.6% of women and 2.1% of men reported experiencing forced sex at some point, and 2.5% of women and 0.9% of men reported experiencing some form of unwanted sexual activity in the previous 12 months. The Department of Justice states that 20%–25% of women have reported experiencing an attempted or a completed rape while in college. Ninety-two percent of rape or sexual assault victims in 2005 were female.

The National Crime Victim Survey estimates that in 2008 there were 203,830 rapes and sexual assaults in the United States (including crimes both reported and unreported to police), a decline of 18% from 2007. In 2008, 89,000 forcible rapes were reported to the FBI. For the decade 1999–2008, the estimated rate of rape and sexual assault decreased from 1.7 per 1,000 persons aged 12 years or more to 0.8 per 1,000, a decrease of 52.6%. The rate of rape for women (1.3 per 1,000) far exceeded that of men (0.3 per 1,000). In 2005, 191,670 victims aged 12 years or more reported rape and sexual assault to the police. The National Violence

Against Women Survey estimated in 2006 that more than 300,000 women and approximately 93,000 men are raped annually in the United States.

Other studies suggest that at least 20% of adult women, 15% of college women, and 12% of adolescent girls have experienced sexual abuse or assault during their lifetimes. The FBI estimates that a woman is raped every three minutes in the United States. Approximately 80% of the cases involve forcible rape, and the remainder include assaults or attempts to commit forcible rape. In the 1990s, significant declines in the frequency of rape or sexual assault were reported. A demographic shift resulting in fewer 18- to 25-year-olds (the age group accounting for most violent crime) may have contributed to this decreasing trend. A 2005 nationwide survey of high school students found that 8% reported having been forced to have sex (11% of females and 4% of males).

Rape is often accompanied by physical assault; 41.4% of women and 33.9% of men who were raped since age 18 years were physically assaulted during their most recent rape. The physical assault included slapping, hitting, kicking, biting, choking, hitting with an object, beating, and using a gun or other weapon. Other estimates of the magnitude of the problem are far greater than conveyed by these figures. A frequency of rape 7–15 times higher than rates reported by government agencies has been estimated by some researchers.

These discrepancies indicate that the methods used to determine the number of rapes and sexual assaults occurring in the United States today are inherently limited. Rape is one of the most underreported crimes. It has been estimated that only one in five rapes is reported to law enforcement agencies. Other reporting estimates have ranged as low as 1 in 10 or 1 in 20 rapes reported. A Department of Justice survey found that only half of victims of rape or attempted rape had reported the crime to police.

Victims often hesitate to report rape because of the negative consequences and social stigma associated with sexual assault. Victims may experience shame, guilt, fear of retaliation, and a reluctance to expose themselves to what can be insensitive medical or law enforcement investigations. Rapes perpetrated by a friend, date, or spouse may not be reported because the victim fears that law enforcement officials will not believe her or because she herself may question whether a "real" rape occurred. Underreporting of rapes makes very difficult the task of tracking how frequently sexual assaults actually occur.

Stalking is also highly prevalent. In 2005–2006, an estimated 14 of every 1,000 persons aged 18 years or more were victims of stalking in the United States. The Department of Justice reports that more than 1 million women and approximately 400,000 men are stalked each year in the United States. Approximately half of stalking victims experienced at least 1 unwanted contact per week, and 11%

reported being stalked for 5 years or longer. Most stalking victims are female (78%), and most perpetrators are male (87%). As of 2006, 8% of women and 2% of men in the United States had been stalked at some point in their lifetime. In 2004, 20% of university undergraduates had been stalked or harassed by a former dating partner.

More than 50% of stalkers had a prior relationship with the victim, also known as intimate stalking. Approximately half of stalking victims reported experiencing fear from not knowing what would happen next. In stalking incidents of women by a current or former husband or cohabiting partner, 81% of victims were physically assaulted and 31% also were sexually assaulted. Serious violence was associated with a history of sexual intimacy with the stalker, the stalker appearing previously at the victim's home, the absence of a criminal record, and a shorter duration of stalking.

According to the Central Intelligence Agency in 2005, an estimated 50,000 women and children are trafficked into the United States each year for sexual exploitation or forced labor. These individuals often are deceived into believing that they are migrating to the United States for job opportunities and end up becoming the victims of forced prostitution and recurrent rape/sexual assault.

Throughout the discussion that follows, terms are used for descriptive purposes that may imply that rape is only or even primarily a heterosexual problem. It should be noted that same-sex rape—like same-sex domestic violence—occurs and is captured (to the extent it is reported) in the statistics cited. Impediments to reporting various forms of same-sex violence, however, are likely to be even greater than those involving heterosexual acts of violence.

WHAT ARE THE CONSEQUENCES OF RAPE AND SEXUAL ASSAULT?

Immediate medical concerns after rape include injury and the need for legal documentation. Psychological trauma, risk of pregnancy, and the potential for contracting sexually transmitted diseases are also major health concerns. Psychological impacts are both acute and long term. Initial reactions to sexual assault include shock, guilt, numbness, withdrawal, and denial. The aftereffects of rape are persistent and long-lasting, and victims often react with chronic anxiety, feelings of vulnerability, loss of control, and self-blame long after the event. Nightmares and feelings of alienation and isolation are frequent. Between 17% and 19% of rape victims make suicide attempts. A 2006 Department of Justice survey found that 31.5% of women and 16.1% of men raped since age 18 years sustained a physical injury as a result of rape. More than one-third of injured female victims received medical treatment.

Victims of rape and sexual assault by strangers often fear that their assailant may return and harm them again. These initial reactions usually decrease two weeks after the rape or assault. The victim then may begin a period of denial during which the person outwardly appears to be adjusting. Frequently, however, for several months after the assault, these symptoms may return and become more intense. During this time, the victim may seek help for her problems and concerns, sometimes without divulging the rape or assault experience from which the problem originated.

The aftereffects of rape can include a sense of alienation, isolation, blaming oneself, fear that one has lost control, feelings of vulnerability, and problems in sexuality and general physical well-being. Rape victims may continue to have high levels of fear and anxiety for many years after the rape or assault. Other long-term problems include mistrust of people, phobias, depression, and hostility. The victim may experience strained relationships with family, friends, and intimate partners, and loss of support from these individuals. It is often assumed that women who are the victims of stranger rapes are more severely traumatized than individuals victimized by persons they know. However, women assaulted by family members, dates, or other intimates experience similar levels of distress. Rape results in 25,000–32,000 pregnancies each year. The anger and stress that victims of sexual assault experience may lead to eating disorders and depression. Victims often engage in negative health behaviors and are more likely to smoke, engage in high-risk sexual activity, and try to escape the trauma of the assault through abuse of alcohol and drugs (which further disrupt physical and psychological well-being). Victims may experience disabilities that prevent a return to work.

Rape can result in serious injury to women, including hemorrhage, vaginal tears, and sexually transmitted infections. Sexual assaults represented 10% of all assault-related injury visits to U.S. emergency departments by females in 2006. Women who are raped by a stranger sustain more non-genital injuries (60%) than those raped by someone they know (43%). The most common injuries, in addition to the rape itself, are bruises, black eyes, and cuts. Other medical consequences include gastrointestinal disorders, premenstrual syndrome, back pain, facial pain, headaches, and disturbed sleeping and eating patterns. Sixty percent of rape victims receive medical care, and 30% are hospitalized.

The syndrome of rape trauma that follows rape involves a progression of emotional responses. The acute phase lasts days or months and includes symptoms such as fear, humiliation, rage, disbelief, disturbed eating and sleeping patterns, and genitourinary symptoms. Rape victims may experience flashbacks replaying the attack over and over in their minds, loss of the ability to concentrate, acute anxiety attacks, and nightmares. Denial of the rape can occur, as well as a general emotional numbing. This is followed by a longer-term second phase during which the victim begins to rebuild her life. This period will vary according to the circumstances in the victim's life, such as economic status, prior mental health problems, and the presence or absence of support from family or friends. Many women continue to experience distress throughout the second phase.

Physicians and mental health care providers have recognized that the aftereffects of rape and sexual assault may include post-traumatic stress disorder. This involves severe psychological distress associated with intense, intrusive re-experiences of the trauma and avoidance of anything associated with it. Studies of adult women with a history of sexual assault indicate that one- to two-thirds experience post-traumatic distress disorder. However, few women are diagnosed and treated because a history is not obtained by many treating physicians.

WHO IS A RAPIST OR SEX OFFENDER?

A rapist or sex offender most often is not a stranger and can be the victim's relative, husband, boyfriend, date, or other acquaintance. In 2005, 73% of rape and sexual assault victims knew their offender. Of these, 38% were assaulted by friends or acquaintances and 28% were assaulted by intimate partners. In a nationally representative survey reported in 2007, intimate partners were the offenders in 30.4% of first rape female victims and in 15.9% of first rape male victims; family members were offenders in 23.7% of female rapes and in 17.7% of male rapes; and acquaintances perpetrated 20% of female rapes and 32.3% of male rapes. A 2008 Department of Justice survey found that non-strangers (intimate partners, relative, friend, or acquaintance) were the sexual offenders of 63% of female victims and all male victims.

For many years researchers have attempted to understand the behavior and motivation of rapists and sex offenders by studying their psychological makeup and attitudes, family background and situational setting, and hostilities toward women. Many of these studies have been conducted on incarcerated offenders, which creates a bias because most rapists are never convicted. Thus, no character or other profile of the typical rapist has been widely accepted. We do know that children are at the greatest risk from assaults by family members and other caretakers. Adolescents and young women are most at risk of rape by acquaintances and dates, and have the least risk from a stranger. Young and older women are more vulnerable to sexual assault from their husbands or ex-husbands than from acquaintances, other family members, or strangers combined. However, many men who commit rape are not identifiable by any particular personality, social, or demographic characteristic.

Although there is no definitive profile of a sex offender, researchers are in agreement about several characteristics. The first is that rape and sexual assault are acts driven by a desire for power and control. Rapists assert power through the use of physical force and threats. Most men who commit rape are not psychotic. Rather the rapist may be using violence and sexual assault to resolve conflicts in a pathological manner. Rapists and sex offenders often demonstrate hostility and misogynistic attitudes toward women, tend to have coercive sexual fantasies, a preference for impersonal sex, and impulsive and antisocial tendencies. They may have a childhood history of sexual and physical abuse or witnessed family violence as a child.

Sexual violence is made commonplace in our culture through mass media and pornography, and by behavior learned in violent and emotionally unsupportive families. It is believed that many rapists have had early life exposure to settings where sexual violence is common and accepted. Media and cultural norms may contribute through their implicit support of sexual violence, male superiority and sexual entitlement, and women's inferiority and sexual submissiveness.

Most rapists and sex offenders are the same race as their victims. In 70%–90% of instances, White victims are attacked by White offenders and Black victims are attacked by Black offenders. Black men uncommonly rape White women. A disproportionate number of arrested rapists are Black and from the poorest areas. However, studies have shown that poverty is a bigger factor than race in most crimes, and in the United States a higher proportion of Black men are poor. Up to one-half of convicted rapists were drinking alcohol at the time they raped. Drug use is another individual risk factor. For some, the desire to assault sexually is only present when they have been drinking. Rapists and sex offenders more frequently associate with sexually aggressive and delinquent peers.

Approximately two-thirds of rapists are between the ages of 16 and 24 years. Sex offenders are older than other violent offenders. Research has demonstrated that among college men, attitudes that support rape, rather than psychological characteristics, per se, determine the level of sexual aggression. A survey of high school students found that 56% of girls and 76% of boys believed that forced sex was acceptable under some circumstances. A majority of the boys and more than 40% of the girls said that forced sex was acceptable if the boy spent a lot of money on the girl or if they had been dating for more than six months. One-third of male college students admitted that, under certain circumstances, they would commit rape if they believed they would not be caught.

Of those arrested, the average sexual offender committed 117 sexual assaults before being caught. Perpetrators of sexual assault may become repeat offenders. Past sexual offenders are four times more likely to be arrested again for a sex crime than the general population. Within three years of release from prison in 1994, 5.3% of sex offenders were rearrested for a sex crime. The rearrest rate for convicted child predators is 52%. In one study, 46% of rapists who were released from prison were rearrested within three years of their release for another crime, 18.6% of them for another violent offense. Two-thirds of U.S. sex offenders at any time are not in prison, and many live in cars and other transient settings.

Sexually aggressive men consider their aggression normal, have conservative beliefs about female sexuality, and accept rape myths. These men hold the view that women are primarily responsible for preventing their rapes and maintain traditional beliefs about women's roles. Such attitudes illustrate how social and cultural norms and stereotypes can provide a context in which rapists rationalize and even justify their behavior.

WHO GETS RAPED OR SEXUALLY ASSAULTED?

Women of all ages, races, social classes, and educational backgrounds are vulnerable to rape. However, not all women are equally at risk of rape. Those at highest risk are young, single, Black women from poor urban communities. Their attackers are also young and Black. Black females are victimized by rape and attempted rape at a much higher and disproportionate rate to that of Whites. Because Whites are the majority in the United States, a larger number of White women are raped than all other races combined. A study in Philadelphia found that rape was 12 times more common in Blacks than in Whites, even though Blacks comprised only 10% of the population.

American Indian/Alaska Native women are also significantly more likely than women of other races to report they were raped. Hispanic women were significantly less likely to report they were raped at some time in their life. Among 8,000 women surveyed in 1995–1996, 17.9% of non-Hispanic Whites, 11.9% of Hispanic Whites, 18.8% of Blacks, 34.1% of American Indian/Alaska Natives, 6.8% of Asian/Pacific Islanders, and 24.4% of women of mixed race experienced an attempted or a completed rape at some time in their lives. Rape rates in the 2008 Crime Victimization Survey were higher for Blacks and individuals with origins in two or more races (1.9 per 1,000) than for Whites (0.6 per 1,000) or other races (0.9 per 1,000) and non-Hispanics (0.8 per 1,000).

In the 2008 Crime Victimization Survey, the age groups with the highest rates of rape were 16–19 years (2.2 per 1,000) and 20–24 years (2.1 per 1,000), followed by the age groups 12–15 years (1.6 per 1,000) and 35–49 years (0.8 per 1,000). In a nationally representative survey reported in 2007, it was found that 60.4% of females were first raped before age 18 years (of these, 25.5% were first raped before age 12 years and 34.9% were first raped at 12–17 years). Women were first raped by intimate partners (30.4%), family members (23.7%), and acquaintances (20%). Approximately 70% of male victims were first raped before age 18 years (41% before age 12 years and 28% at 12–17 years). Men were first raped by acquaintances (32.3%), family members (17.7%), friends (17.6%), and intimate partners (15.9%).

The majority of rape victims are aged 13–25 years. In 2005, people aged 16–19 years had the highest rate of sexual victimization of any age group (3.2 sexual assaults per 1,000). It is difficult to be certain what the actual high-risk age group is for rape, however, because so many instances of rape go unreported. Older victims may conceal incidents of rape more often than young adults and adolescents. However, there is a relationship between being raped as a minor before age 18 years and subsequent victimization as an adult. Those reporting juvenile rape were twice as likely to report being raped as an adult.

The Department of Justice has reported that rape victims are usually members of low-income families. Half of all victims typically have a reported family income of less than $20,000. Women who are separated and divorced or who never marry are more likely to be raped than those who are married. Females living in central parts of a city are twice as likely to be raped as residents of suburban or rural areas. Women with disabilities were more than four times more likely to have been sexually assaulted in the prior year (2005) than women without a disability. In 2005, 56% of women with physical disabilities reported abuse, of which 66% was sexual and 87% was physical. One study found that more than 10% of sexually assaulted adult males had cognitive disabilities.

Between one-fifth and one-fourth of college women reported experiencing an attempted or completed rape in college. Among high school students in 2005, 9.3% of Black students, 7.8% of Hispanic students, and 6.9% of White students reported that they were forced to have sexual intercourse at some time in their lives.

It often is assumed in society that women "ask for" rape or sexual assault by their clothing, behavior, and actions. Furthermore, it is a common belief that any woman can resist a rape if she really wants to and tries. Another problematic view is that rape victims, female or male, enjoyed being assaulted. Even some health and social service professionals, law enforcement officers, and victims themselves share these attitudes. In fact, there is little evidence in support of these views. However, these social and cultural beliefs facilitate rape and rapists. Myths abound that suggest rape victims are often sexually promiscuous. Other incorrect notions include the following: Rape victims are especially attractive women who invite rape through their behavior; women should enjoy rape; a woman who accompanies a man to his home is giving tacit consent to a sexual encounter; a woman who charges a man with rape is seeking revenge for something unrelated; and women provoke rape by wearing sexually suggestive clothes. There is no population-based evidence supporting these myths.

Does a victim's behavior put her at risk for rape and sexual assault? Studies to determine what distinguishes the behavior of a victim of rape from that of non-victims have been inconclusive. The myth that women invite rape causes some women to inappropriately accept partial responsibility for rape while at the same time rationalizing deviant male sexual aggression. Fortunately, over the past two decades many states have moved to enact legislation to protect victims from attacks on their sexual history or credibility so as to encourage them to come forward and press for the prosecution of assailants.

CAN MEN BE RAPED?

Yes. Men can be raped and sexually assaulted. Until the mid-1980s, little consideration was given to the issue of male rape and sexual assault was discussed exclusively in the context of female victims. In recent years, society has become more aware of male rape. There has been much documentation of the psychological trauma associated with the rape of female victims. Although less research has been conducted about male rape victims, the evidence suggests that males also commonly experience many of the reactions that females experience (as described earlier in this chapter).

Reports of men who have been raped by women are infrequent, but men can be and are raped by other men. Approximately 3% of American men—a total of 2.78 million men—have experienced a rape at some point in their lifetime. It is difficult to estimate how often male rape occurs, because rape is even less likely to be reported by males than by females. In 2003, it was estimated that one in every ten rape victims was male. In 1990 the Department of Justice reported approximately 10,000 completed rapes of males older than 12 years in the United States and perhaps another 10,000 rape attempts. During a 10-year period, 123,000 male rapes occurred. The National Crime Victimization Survey reported 39,340 rapes, attempted rapes, and sexual assaults on males aged 12 years or more in 1999. The National Violence Against Women Survey estimated in 2006 that approximately 93,000 men are raped annually in the United States.

Many male rapes occur in prison or juvenile detention facilities. However, male rape occurs frequently outside of this setting as well. Several studies have found that up to one-fifth of inmates in state prisons experience non-consensual sex. Human Rights Watch estimated in 2001 that 22% of male inmates in the United States have been raped at least once during their incarceration; this equates to approximately 420,000 prisoners each year. Although the rape/sexual assault of men may be more common than traditionally thought, the risk is much higher for women than for men.

The most common locations for male rape involving post-puberty victims are remote outdoors areas and in automobiles (the latter usually involves hitchhikers). Boys in their early and mid-teens are more likely to be victimized than older males (median victim age of 17 years). Gang rape is more common in male sexual assault than in female sexual assault. Also, multiple sexual acts are more likely to occur and weapons are more likely to be displayed and used. Physical injury—and more serious injury—is more likely to occur with male rape than female rape.

As a group, men do not perceive themselves to be potential victims of rape the way that women do and often believe that they could resist a sexual assault. A significant concern facing male rape victims is society's belief that men should be able to protect themselves, and therefore, it is their fault that they were raped. Male rape/sexual assault is one of the most underreported crimes, quite possibly because of these factors and also perhaps because of the victim's fear of being labeled a homosexual and of not being believed by authorities.

In fact, men who rape men are not necessarily homosexual. Male sexual assault has nothing to do with the sexual orientation of the attacker or the victim. One study of male rapists of men found that half described themselves as heterosexual and approximately 40% indicated that they had sex with both men and women. Of the victims, one-half stated that they were exclusively heterosexual. Straight, gay, and bisexual men all can be victims of sexual assault by other men. It is a violent crime that affects heterosexual men as much as gay men. Use of the phrase "homosexual rape" to designate male–male rape distorts the fact that the majority of rapists are not generally homosexual. Studies report that sexual offenders are relatively indiscriminate with respect to their choice of a victim; their victims included both males and females, as well as both adults and children. Their choice of a victim seemed determined more by accessibility than the sexual orientation, gender, or age of the victim.

The reactions of men and adolescents who are raped by men do not differ greatly from those of female rape victims, and include anger, guilt, depression, sexual dysfunctions, and suicidal feelings. Male victims of sexual assault are as likely to suffer post-traumatic stress syndrome as women who have been raped. Sexual dysfunctions, confusion about the victim's sense of masculinity and sexuality, and a desire to avoid intimate relationships may follow male rape. Gay men tend to believe that the assault occurred because they are gay, whereas, straight men often begin to question their sexual identity and are more disturbed by the sexual aspect of the assault than the violence, per se. Local rape crisis centers offer emergency/crisis services, counseling, and support services to male as well as female victims of rape. Victims should contact their local rape crisis center, no matter how long it has been since the rape or assault occurred. Counselors on staff either can provide support or help direct the victim to trained professionals who can. Most centers have counselors of either gender available, and if a preference exists this should be stated by the victim.

IN WHAT SITUATIONS DO RAPE AND SEXUAL ASSAULT OCCUR?

Rape occurs in virtually any setting. Many rapes are not spontaneous but are planned by the rapist. Most rapists (63%–73%) know their victims, and they may target a specific person and attempt to draw her into a situation in which the rape can be successfully completed with a minimum of risk to the rapist. Forty-three percent of rapes occur between 6:00 p.m. and midnight, 24% occur between midnight and 6:00 a.m., and the other 33% take place between 6:00 a.m. and 6:00 p.m. Rapes occur more commonly on weekends than on weekdays.

Women who live alone are more likely to be raped than those who live with others. More than one-third of rapes in 2005 took place in the victim's home, 20% occurred at or near a friend's home, and 20% occurred on the street. More than 50% of all rape/sexual assault incidents were reported by victims to have occurred within one mile of their home or at their home. Women who live in rented accommodations are more likely to be raped than those who own their own homes, particularly those living in dormitories, halfway and boarding houses, and apartments with four or more units.

Most rapes are committed by unarmed offenders, and 90% involve a lone assailant of the same race as the victim. Rape is twice as likely to occur at or near a woman's home if the victim knows her assailant than if the rapist is a stranger. Approximately half of rapes by strangers occur in open areas or public places, but one-fourth occur at or near the victim's home. In stranger rapes the act is planned in advance, but the victim is not targeted beforehand as part of the plan. The stranger rapist may stalk a victim or simply wait for an opportunity to present itself. Because it is so often planned, it is clear that rape is the specific goal of the rapist and is not a random act of violence.

When rape occurs spontaneously, alcohol or drugs may be contributing factors. Alcohol is frequently associated with rape. It decreases inhibitions and normal restraints on aggression. Some evidence indicates that the victim's consumption of alcohol also may increase her risk for rape. One-tenth to one-quarter of rape victims had been using alcohol when they were raped. Rape is more likely to occur in settings where men do not correctly interpret a woman's resistance, such as parties where sexual themes and conversation have been commonplace. A review of sexual assault cases presenting to an emergency department found that 12% of cases were identified as suspected drug-facilitated assaults.

According to the Department of Justice, between 10% and 20% of sexual offenders are armed with a weapon. Strangers are more often armed (29%) than assailants known to the victim (17%). Strangers are equally likely to use a handgun or a knife, but rapists known to the victim are more likely to use knives or other sharp objects. The 2008 National Crime Victimization Survey found that 19% of victims did not know if a weapon was used when they were sexually assaulted.

A 2007 study of women in a physically abusive intimate relationship found that 68% also reported having been sexually assaulted by the perpetrator. Approximately 80% of these sexually assaulted women reported more than one incident of forced sex. Women who contacted the police after the first rape were 59% less likely to be raped by the partner again compared with women who did not call the police. Women who applied for a protective order after the first rape were 70% less likely to be raped again. Two-thirds of the children in these homes had witnessed the abuse and later in life experienced more depression and behavioral problems than children of mothers who had not been sexually assaulted.

WHY DO MEN RAPE?

Men use anger and aggression to exert power and to terrorize their victims. Men do not, for the most part, rape because they are mentally ill. The rapist does not necessarily hate women. The rapist is generally hostile and aggressive, often after drinking alcohol. Research indicates that there are at least two types of rapists: a minority who are driven by a deep psychological disorder that is expressed through the rape, and the majority who are not very different in psychology from the average male—except for their propensity to act out hostility toward women by committing rape. Indeed, the rapist is typically compelled to rape repeatedly. The rapist has a strong need to control and degrade women. Unfortunately, because these qualities often are not easily recognizable in a man, it is difficult to identify a potential rapist before he commits rape.

There are several theories about why men rape. Psychoanalytic theory suggests that when a boy's sexual attraction to his mother is rejected, he may become angry and frustrated. Sexual and aggressive impulses become confused. Later, a desire to control and perhaps humiliate women is substituted for the rage he feels toward his mother. This perversion of the sexual act may be required for sexual satisfaction. The rapist may have a history of feelings of sexual inadequacy and absence of a strong male figure with which to identify to help balance the maternal influence and express aggression through acceptable means.

Two kinds of rapists emerge from the psychoanalytic theory: those who idealize women and those who believe that women invite sexual advances regardless of what they say and do to the contrary. The rapist who idealizes women invests them with great symbolic power, and consequently perceives himself as being diminished by women. As a result, when faced with rejection, the rapist's response is greatly exaggerated and characterized by aggression and violence. He directs his aggression to the object of his frustrations, a woman, and raping her is a method of re-establishing his own self-esteem. This rapist experiences little remorse and is likely to rape repeatedly. The other kind of rapist interprets anything a woman says or does as an expression of interest in having sex, of "asking for" a sexual advance. This rapist's act usually is driven by an impulse built on self-deception, and he may experience regret for the act.

It is unclear whether the primary motivation of rape is to express aggression or to obtain a distorted form of sexual gratification. Some rapes involve not only intercourse but also severe beatings or homicide. This kind of rape often is committed by a stranger. The violent rapist is believed to be displacing rage felt toward specific women, perhaps in the rapist's family, to any woman who shares some common physical characteristics. He may have difficulty with relationships in general and may otherwise be a violent individual. Another type of rapist seems motivated predominantly by the desire to engage in sex, and although he acts aggressively and forcefully, it is not with the intent to seriously injure the victim. Once the act of rape has been completed and the need for sex satisfied, this rapist does not usually inflict further violence on the victim. He does not usually behave in other antisocial ways. Some rapists combine aspects of the two types and rape both to fulfill sexual needs and aggressive tendencies, needing violence for sexual stimulation and gratification.

A sociobiological explanation of rape is that a man fails to learn the cultural rules that shape how sexual needs can be met acceptably. This may occur when the rules about how to appropriately have sexual relations with women are conveyed early in life in a painful or shameful manner. A young man whose sexual development has been adversely affected does not accept cultural norms and rules about sex and tries to fulfill his sexual needs using aggression. The degree of aberrancy will vary along a spectrum from individuals who rape once to those who resort regularly to rape to obtain sex. This rapist does not intend to injure his victim but intends to get sex, and he believes that coercion is a normal part of sex in male–female relationships. Feminism contends that our society's method of socializing children tends to reinforce these patterns and teaches young males that using force, or at least coercion, to obtain sex is masculine, expected, and appropriate.

CAN A MAN RAPE HIS WIFE?

Yes. This kind of sexual assault is known as marital rape. Any sexual act that does not involve mutual consent, in which the woman does not agree to participate in sex, is a form of sexual assault, and if penetration occurs, it is rape. These sexual acts can include intercourse; anal or oral sex; forced sexual behavior with other individuals; and other unwanted, painful, and humiliating sexual activities. It is an assault if one partner uses force, threats, or intimidation to get the other to submit to sexual acts. Marital rape is committed in relationships where no other form of physical abuse is occurring but is more commonly observed in relationships where other violence is ongoing.

There are at least three kinds of marital rape. Battering rape involves forced sex combined with battering and is characterized primarily by anger toward the victim. The sexual abuse is either part of the physical abuse or a result of the husband later asking his wife to prove she forgives him for the beating by having sex with him. In force-only rape, the husband uses only as much force as necessary to coerce his wife into sexual activity. This type of sexual assault seems to be primarily motivated by the need for power over the victim. In the husband's mind, he is merely asserting his right to have sex with his wife on demand. This is the most common type of marital rape. In obsessive rape, the husband's sexual interests include deviant or perverse acts, and he is willing (or has a preference) to use force to carry these activities out. This seems to be the least common form of marital rape.

One-third to one-half of women who are victims of physical assault by partners also are sexually assaulted. This may occur several times a month. Although battered women are more at risk for marital rape than their non-battered counterparts, some men will rape their wives and never beat them. Others will beat them, but not rape them.

Historically there has been no legal or social recognition of marital rape. In this regressive view, rape cannot occur in the state of marriage because of the commitment underlying the union of two persons in matrimony. Although all 50 U.S. states have laws against marital rape, 33 states consider marital rape a lesser crime than other types of rape, typically charging the attacker with spousal abuse or battery instead of rape. Convictions for marital rape are difficult to achieve unless the couple has been separated or divorced, or if other acts of violence accompanied the rape.

The frequency of marital rape has not been identified clearly because of a lack of reporting. Although little data are available on marital rape, an idea of the magnitude of the problem may be provided by looking at the extent of other forms of intimate violence. Studies now clearly show that American women are more likely to be assaulted, raped, or killed by a current or previous male partner than by all other types of assailants combined. A survey of intact couples in the mid-1980s found that one of every eight husbands had carried out one or more acts of physical aggression against their wives during the survey year. More than one-third of those assaults involved severe aggression, such as punching, kicking, choking, beating, or using a knife or gun. Studies show that marital rape is the most common type of rape; 10%–14% of all completed rapes are committed by husbands or ex-husbands, and in line with rape reporting statistics nationwide, this is likely an underestimation of the actual incidence of marital rape.

Because of underreporting, there is general agreement that the probable frequency of violence perpetrated by a partner involves approximately four million severely assaulted women per year in the United States. One-fifth to one-third of all women will be physically assaulted by a partner or ex-partner during their lifetime. In addition, victims of violence by intimates are much more likely to be assaulted again within six months of the first attack than those assaulted by non-intimates. One of the most common myths about marital rape is that it happens when the wife withholds sex from her husband. There is little evidence that a wife's withholding sex is the cause of or leads to marital rape. The cause of marital rape is not fundamentally different from the rape of other individuals, as discussed earlier.

Victims of marital rape have very little of the support that other rape victims can access. Many people around the victim may not believe it was rape at all. Victims of marital rape, perhaps more than victims of other types of rape, find themselves having to cope in isolation. Sexual assault as an expression of marital violence is very serious and can result in severe injuries and a devastating psychological impact. Victims of marital rape suffer much the same impacts and consequences as other rape victims, but their hopelessness can produce particularly severe reactions, such as deep depression and high suicide risk. Unfortunately, because this kind of violence is among the least likely to be reported or detected, the victims are among the least likely to receive medical, psychological, and support services. Victims of marital rape should seek services and assistance from local rape crisis centers, agencies that assist victims of domestic violence, and local police and law enforcement.

ARE ALCOHOL AND DRUGS ASSOCIATED WITH RAPE?

Yes. Alcohol and drugs are associated with the risk of rape and sexual assault. Studies indicate that many times individuals who perpetrate rape and sexual assault frequently have been consuming alcohol and that the victims also have had at least several drinks. Alcohol and other drugs are widely recognized as disinhibitors of the normal social and psychological constraints that we impose on our behavior.

Approximately one-half of rape/sexual assault victims in a Department of Justice survey believed that the assailant was under the influence of drugs or alcohol at the time of the assault. Some 55% of females and 75% of males admit to drinking or using drugs when acquaintance rape occurred. Ninety percent of all campus rapes occur when alcohol has been used by either the assailant or the victim. As many as 70% of college students admit to having engaged in sexual acts primarily as a result of being under the influence of alcohol when they would not have otherwise if they had been sober.

Studies of college men have indicated that consumption of alcohol and the states of diminished capacity that result are commonly used to rationalize or justify deviant behavior. Alcohol and drugs impair the ability of potential victims to remain sensitive to their surroundings and increased male sexual aggression. They also can compromise a woman's ability to effectively resist a sexual assault through escape or self-defense.

WHAT IS DATE RAPE?

Date rape is forced or coerced sexual intercourse involving harm or the threat of injury within a non-marital relationship. It is a type of rape that may not fit legal definitions of rape in some states. Date rape is also called acquaintance rape because 70% or more of victims know their attackers. A number of studies find that 20%–25% of college women experience a sexual assault during their time on campus. The Department of Justice reports that approximately 3% of college women experience a completed or attempted rape during a typical college year. For completed rapes, approximately 60% that took place on campus occurred in the victim's residence, 31% occurred in other living quarters on campus, and 10% occurred at a fraternity. Most off-campus victimizations, especially rapes, also occurred in residences. One study found that 42% of surveyed women college students reported some type of sexual assault or rape. Between 51% and 60% of college men report they would rape a woman if they were certain that they could get away with it. One of 12 college men surveyed had committed acts that met the legal definition of rape. Approximately 1 in 10 high school students has experienced some form of physical violence in a dating relationship. The frequency of rape does not vary much on the basis of whether the school was large or small, or located in an urban, metropolitan, or rural area.

Date rape occurs frequently in the victim's or perpetrator's home or car. It also occurs at parties on college campuses, where alcohol and drugs used by both victim and perpetrator can cause disinhibition of usual restraints on behavior. Drug-facilitated rape/sexual assault may occur when a perpetrator intentionally causes a weak and confused—or completely unconscious—state in a victim. Rohypnol (or "roofies"), gamma hydroxy butyrate (GHB; "liquid ecstasy"), and ketamine ("super K" or "ket kat") are drugs used to facilitate date rape. These drugs can be inconspicuously slipped into the drink of an intended victim, are highly potent and fast-acting (30–60 minutes), and are used against both men and women. Most date rape drugs are virtually undetectable because they are colorless, odorless, and usually tasteless. They can cause partial or complete loss of memory for a period of time during which an assault may have occurred, and can be fatally toxic. However, alcohol is the most widely used date rape drug and remains responsible for the majority of drug-facilitated sexual assaults. It is important to note that if you have had sex but cannot remember it or offering consent, you have been raped under the law, whether a date rape drug has been used or not.

As occurs with other forms of sexual assault, it is thought that date rape is much underreported. Victims of date rape often are confused and unsure if the sex was consensual or not for several reasons. First, the realization that a date rape has occurred often is delayed; awareness of an assault may not occur in real time. Date rapes may involve drugs or alcohol which create altered mental states that affect the extent of memory and clarity of recall. In addition to these factors, because date rape often involves an acquaintance and possible romantic interest, victims may not be sure if they consented or not.

Until recently, violence in dating relationships has not been considered a serious problem, and few services were established to care for date rape victims. Fortunately this is changing, and women in high schools and colleges can now often access services at their institutions if they have been date raped. Educational programs for young men on the nature and consequences of date rape are greatly needed and increasing across the country.

HOW CAN I PROTECT MYSELF FROM DRUG-FACILITATED RAPE?

There are ways to protect yourself from drug-facilitated rape. At parties, do not accept drinks from other people. If possible, bring your own drinks to parties. Open drink containers yourself and keep your drink with you at all times, even when you go to the restroom or make a call. If you realize you left your drink unattended, discard it. Do not share drinks or drink from punch bowls or other common, open containers (because they already may have been drugged). If someone offers to get you a drink from a bar or at a party, go with the person to order your drink and observe the drink being poured, and then carry it yourself. Do not drink anything that appears, tastes, or smells strange (GHB may taste salty). In very crowded parties or clubs, cover your drink with your hand to prevent easy access.

Remember that other women and not just men may be complicit in drug-facilitated rape. Have a designated non-drinking friend with you at parties to check up on you throughout the night to ensure that nothing happens. This simple measure of friends watching out for each other's safety now and again over the course of an evening can be very effective in preventing a drug-facilitated assault. If one of your friends or you feel drunk and have not consumed any alcohol, or if you feel like the effects of drinking alcohol are stronger than usual, get help right away. Call 911 immediately.

HOW CAN I TELL IF I HAVE BEEN DRUGGED AND RAPED?

It is difficult to tell. Most victims do not remember being drugged or sexually assaulted. You might not be aware of the attack until 8–12 hours after it occurred. The drugs are metabolized and leave the body rapidly. Once a victim gets help, there might be no proof that drugs were involved in the attack. Signs that you might have been drugged include the following: you feel drunk and have not consumed any alcohol, or you feel like the effects of drinking alcohol are stronger than usual; you wake up feeling very hungover and disoriented or have no memory of a period of time; you remember having a drink, but cannot recall anything after that; you find that your clothes are torn or not on right; you feel like you had sex, but you cannot remember it.

Signs that a sexual assault has taken place can include soreness or bruising in the genital or anal areas; bruising on the inner or outer thighs; bruising on the wrists and forearms; defensive bruising or scratching (that would occur during a struggle); used condoms near you or in nearby garbage containers; and traces of semen or vaginal fluids on your clothes or body.

WHAT SHOULD I DO IF I THINK I HAVE BEEN DRUGGED AND RAPED?

You should seek medical care right away. Call 911 or have a trusted friend take you to a hospital emergency department. Do not urinate, douche, bathe, brush your teeth, wash your hands, change clothes, or eat or drink before you go in order to preserve any evidence of the rape. Do not clean up where you think the assault might have occurred because there could be critical evidence left behind (e.g., in a glass or on bed sheets).

The hospital will use a "rape kit" to collect evidence and assess for sexually transmitted disease. At the hospital, ask to have a urine sample collected that can be used to test for date rape drugs. The drugs leave your system quickly (Rohypnol can be detected in the urine up to 72 hours, and GHB can be detected up to 12 hours). Do not urinate before going to the hospital.

Call the police from the hospital. Tell the police exactly what you remember. Be honest about all your activities. Remember, nothing you did—including drinking alcohol or doing drugs—can justify rape.

Seek counseling and treatment. Feelings of shame, guilt, fear, and shock are common after sexual assault. A counselor can help you work through these emotions and begin the healing process. Calling a crisis center or a hotline can immediately bring you much needed support and information.

WHAT CAN I DO TO PREVENT BEING RAPED OR SEXUALLY ASSAULTED?

Rather limited specific strategies to prevent rape and sexual assault have been identified, in part because the factors that influence individuals to rape are poorly understood. Many researchers and public health practitioners believe that the only way rape can be prevented is to eliminate the social conditions that perpetuate rape and to promote social action and community change. A first step would be to decrease the social acceptability of sexual aggression against women and change the attitudes and beliefs of men.

Generally, women should avoid men who do not treat women with respect and who demonstrate hostile or misogynistic attitudes toward women. Women should avoid situations with such men in which sexual tensions may be present. Men who exploit other people, whether they are men or women, should be avoided. Because such men tend to view people as objects in non-dating situations, they are likely to regard a woman as an object and use coercion with her to meet their sexual needs. The same logic applies to men who have little regard for laws and rules more broadly.

Programs that teach women how to defend themselves in threatening situations can be helpful in preventing rape and sexual assault. Police department records show that rapists try to intimidate women and incapacitate them. Self-defense courses are available that teach women fighting techniques through the simulation of rape situations. Courses use martial arts techniques to teach women to temporarily disable or knock out assailants. These powerful fighting techniques can help women deliver effective counterattacks against rape. Women who use self-protective measures are less likely to be victims of a completed rape. Many of the general strategies noted in Chapter 10 on stranger violence apply to rape and sexual assault prevention.

Women should know their neighborhoods and neighbors, identifying and avoiding potential danger areas that are not well-lighted or often traveled by others. If you encounter an individual in an area that appears suspicious, trust your instincts. Find a safe place and call the police. You are better off embarrassed than a victim of rape. Check the identification of repair and delivery men. Ask delivery men with a package for neighbors to leave it outside your door, and then wait a while before opening the door; if suspicious appearing, call their supervisor to check their authenticity. If a man wants to use your telephone to call for assistance, offer to make the call for him rather than letting him into your home. Keep the curtains of your home closed at night. Use initials on mailboxes and in the telephone directory, not your first name. Similarly, try to have a male friend or family member craft your answering machine message.

Other strategies include insisting that your apartment landlord keep all areas well-lighted and ensuring there are secure locks on all building doors. Avoid riding alone in elevators with an unknown man. Never jog alone in secluded areas. Carry the keys to your apartment and car in your hand so that you do not have to pause and fumble for them. Ask whoever is driving you home, including a taxi driver, to wait until you gain entry to your home before leaving. On the street, if you feel you are being followed, cross over to the other side, turn around, and walk in the opposite direction. If a car is following you, walk in the opposite direction and enter the closest open store or neighbor's home. If you are accosted on the street, make as much noise as you can (scream "fire" rather than "help") and throw an object (a shoe, your purse) through a nearby window to draw attention to yourself.

In your car, keep your doors locked at all times, including when you are inside, and check the back seat visually before getting in. Always try to park in well-lighted areas. If your car should break down, stay in it with doors locked, getting out only to raise the hood. Ask persons who offer to help to call the police or a garage on your behalf. Consider getting a cell phone if you travel extensively by car. If you should be followed by another car, do not go home, but directly to the nearest police station. Never give parking lot attendants or car repairmen your entire set of keys. House keys can quickly and easily be copied. Never place your name and address on a key chain; if your keys were lost, you would be vulnerable. Do not hitchhike, pick up hitchhikers, or accept rides from individuals whom you do not know well. In subways, wait near the change booth or near people. Do not walk off by yourself. If you are bothered on a bus, inform the driver and do not get off at any stop that does not have many people around.

Clearly, there are limits to what an individual can do to prevent herself or himself from being raped. As in other areas of violence prevention, one must balance restrictions on personal freedom and lifestyle against reducing the risk of sexual assault. Perhaps no greater preventive strategy exists than using common sense. Women, particularly when alone, should maintain sensitivity to male sexual aggression and attitudes that support rape in social interactions. Women should ensure that they are not isolated with such men and that they remain in public areas.

This is particularly true in social situations in which alcohol is being consumed. Do not drink a lot with a man whom you do not know very well; drinking lowers inhibitions and impairs your (and a potential assailant's) judgment. If you are with a man whom you do not know very well and who is getting drunk, be sure to have other trusted individuals around or exit the situation. Avoid settings where there is strong peer pressure from other men. Always carry enough money to get home by yourself so that you are not dependent on a date for transportation.

Women who have experienced a rape and who fear a recurrence of rape, or who have reason to fear rape in their home, should seek help from community service organizations. Most jurisdictions in the United States have a rape crisis/prevention service organization or a private or public agency that deals with domestic violence. The listings at the end of this chapter may be useful in locating one. In all cases of repeated rape or sexual assault, women should report their problem to local law enforcement and seek personal protection and prosecution of the rapist under the law.

WHAT SHOULD I DO WHEN I AM SEXUALLY ASSAULTED?

The best resistance you can use against an attacker is to stay calm, not panic, and think your way through a possible escape. It is critical to bear in mind that initially you are not trying to fight the assailant but attempting to divert the person long enough so that you can get away. Always look for a way to escape.

If an assailant has a weapon, use your common sense. Fighting could be more dangerous than the intended assault. Do not do anything that may upset the assailant. Try to convince the person to put away the weapon. Talk to your assailant, and show sympathy and understanding. This makes it more difficult for the attacker to see you as an object, not as an individual.

If the attacker is unarmed, you may be able to frighten, distract, or injure the person long enough to make your escape. Scream "FIRE" and "POLICE" or create a disturbance that will attract attention. Assert yourself and fight back if you can do so safely. Break away and run toward an area where there are people.

Be observant so that you will be able to remember and identify the assailant. Report the incident to the police as soon as possible.

WHAT SHOULD I DO AFTER I HAVE BEEN RAPED?

The first thing to do if you have been raped is to get to a safe place, call the police, and call a friend or relative to be with you. As a rape victim, you are entitled to medical and legal assistance. The local rape crisis center will likely have a service to transport you to the hospital and to the police, or your friend can do this if you wish. There is nothing to be gained from concealing a rape or sexual assault. Your instinct may be to shower and change clothes, but you should avoid doing so because your clothes and physical condition are critical evidence.

Over the weeks, months, and possibly years after a rape, you will need the assistance and services provided by health care and social service professionals and possibly the protective services of local law enforcement. Rape and sexual assault are crimes, and under no circumstances whatsoever should you keep an assault a secret or tolerate an assault because of fear of retaliation. Denial and psychological repression of a rape can cause far more severe and long-term consequences than acknowledging and treating the problem with the confidential assistance of a small group of professionals.

After a rape or sexual assault, you should seek medical care at an emergency department or rape crisis center to prevent pregnancy, to check for internal and external injuries, to obtain emotional support, and to collect medical evidence for legal prosecution of the rapist. These professionals will obtain a history of what has occurred and document it. A physical examination will be conducted to determine whether there is any injury requiring immediate treatment. Samples will be collected to ensure that a sexually transmitted disease, including HIV which causes AIDS, has not infected you. A social worker or other mental health professional will offer counseling and referral for emotional support services. Many hospitals will not routinely report a rape to police. You should.

You can feel comfortable in being completely candid with these professionals. They are bound by law and by the ethical code of their professions to protect your confidentiality and to strive to ensure your personal well-being. Trust them—these are compassionate, dedicated professionals who are committed to helping the victims of rape and sexual assault get through their crises.

For information on shelters and services in your community, look in the Yellow Pages under "Human Services Organizations" or "Social Service Organizations."

If you are unable to contact your local emergency department or rape crisis center for assistance, call your local police department or 911 and communicate that you have been sexually assaulted. The police department will send a patrol car to investigate and transport you to a center where services are provided. The police will ask you to give a description of the rapist. Later you may be asked to review photographs to see if you can identify the assailant, and if he is apprehended, you will be asked to make identification. This chapter provides the names and addresses of national and state organizations that can refer you to services in your community.

Talk to friends, family members, and counselors about your rape. Seek their support. Allow yourself to experience the array of emotions associated with rape, and recognize that it will take some time to recover and heal. Be prepared to encounter uncomfortable and sometimes insensitive reactions from parents, spouses, partners, and friends. Remember that they share in this crisis too. Bring them into the counseling and healing process with you so that you can support each other.

WHAT DO I DO IF I FEEL THE URGE TO RAPE?

If you experience the urge to rape, you should seek help. The urge to rape is believed to arise from personal conflicts and problems. These conflicts, the anger, and the urge to assault someone can be treated. Support and counseling services have been established to help men deal with sexual aggression, difficult relationships, personal conflicts, and the urge to sexually assault a person. To prevent yourself from acting on the urge to rape, it is imperative that you contact a local agency to help you. These exist in many communities. Your confidentiality will be respected throughout the process. This chapter lists the names and addresses of several national organizations that can refer you to local ones in your community for help. Seek them out immediately. Do not delay.

WHAT IS SEXUAL HARASSMENT AND HOW CAN I PREVENT IT?

Sexual harassment is any unwanted sexual behavior that may or may not involve physical contact but that embarrasses, humiliates, or intimidates an individual on the basis of his or her sex or sexual preferences. Sexual harassment can make an individual's work or school environment hostile and uncomfortable, and can contribute to poor performance. It can assume a number of forms, including sexist remarks and jokes, sexual propositions, obscene phone calls, casual sexually oriented comments, sexual graffiti, photographs and pinups, remarks with double (sexual) meaning, or gender-related criticisms. Other ways that harassment can occur involves pornographic visual displays or physical gestures. The victim as well as the harasser may be a woman or a man. The victim does not have to be of the opposite gender. Although sexual harassment usually consists of a male bothering a female, the reverse can occur. Women can sexually harass male employees, particularly women in advanced or senior managerial positions in which they supervise men.

A common characteristic of sexual harassment is that one person tries to exert power over another who is usually at a disadvantage and made to feel uncomfortable. But there is no typical person who sexually harasses others and few reliable ways in which to predict who will harass another. The harasser can be the victim's supervisor, an agent of the employer, a supervisor in another area, a co-worker, or a non-employee.

This form of sexual intimidation is frequently misunderstood. Some of the myths about sexual harassment are as follows: people appreciate sexual flattery, harassment is just another form of masculine behavior, sexual harassment is rare, and the victim somehow provoked the harassing behavior. None of these views are valid. It is also incorrect that sexual harassment must involve physical contact or touching; it may only involve comments, staring, or other inappropriate displays of sexual interest in another person.

Sexual harassment occurs not only in an office, school, or commercial setting but also in any situation in which a supervisor, colleague, or co-worker expresses unwanted sexual interest in a person (whether it be at home or on business trips). Contrary to popular belief, sexual harassment also may occur with occasional and fractional employees and consultants, and not necessarily full-time employees. The harasser can be a non-employee.

The Equal Employment Opportunity Commission (EEOC) of the federal government is charged with monitoring civil rights, equity, and discrimination in the U.S. workplace. It has noted characteristics that help define sexual harassment: The behavior is sexually oriented and unwanted, and can be physical, verbal, or visual in nature. In addition, the person harassing an individual can be any co-worker, whether a supervisor or not, or a non-employee, and the harassment does not have to involve an economic threat or injury to the victim. Furthermore, the victim does not have to be the person at whom the harassment is directed, but can include anyone exposed to and offended by the behavior.

Sexual harassment is thought to be very common, appearing in the workplace, in the classroom or at the school campus, on the street, in virtually any social setting. Approximately 15,000 sexual harassment complaints are made to the EEOC each year. In fiscal year 2008, the EEOC received 13,867 charges of sexual harassment. Sixteen percent of those charges were filed by males. The EEOC resolved 11,731 sexual harassment charges in 2008 and recovered $47.4 million in monetary benefits for charging parties and other aggrieved individuals (not including monetary benefits obtained through litigation).

Sexual harassment is suspected to be much underreported because victims fear losing their jobs, feel out of control in harassment situations, or encounter disbelief or indifference when they complain. Studies suggest anywhere between 40% and 70% of women and 10% and 20% of men have experienced sexual harassment in the workplace. Research indicates that the large majority of sexual harassment complaints have merit. Some victims of harassment feel displaced shame or guilt because they wonder if they could have done something to prevent the behavior. Others tolerate it because they do not know that harassment is against the law and that there are options available to them to counter this inappropriate behavior.

There are two forms of sexual harassment. The first is called "quid pro quo," a Latin phrase meaning "something in exchange for something else." Here a supervisor attempts to coerce an employee into a sexual relationship as payment for a promotion, raise, or other work-related benefit. This form of extortion may also be negatively directed, as in the case of a supervisor threatening to terminate or demote an employee if he or she were to refuse sexual advances.

The organization in which sexual harassment occurs can be held legally responsible both for harassment of an employee and for any discrimination that may result against other qualified employees when the victim is unfairly advanced. The other kind of sexual harassment creates an environment, through repetitive behavior, that is hostile or offensive and compromises or interferes with an employee's ability to perform his or her job. Employers also are liable for this form of sexual harassment if they are aware of its occurrence and make no effort to stop it.

It is important that individuals make accusations of sexual harassment only after deliberation and with certainty that harassment has actually occurred. Consideration should be given to what may appear to be sexual harassment but is not, at least in legal terms. Casual comments at work, if not explicitly sexual, or behavior outside of the workplace that does not involve co-workers is not sexual harassment. If the behavior does not affect the workplace (e.g., the office, school, or a commercial setting) or your work performance, it is not sexual harassment. Invitations to socialize do not constitute sexual harassment. If the organization at which an individual works allows employees to date each other, asking a person at work for a date is not sexual harassment.

An accusation of sexual harassment can affect both the harasser and the victim in subsequent jobs. Prevention and avoidance is therefore the best approach. It is best to discuss your concerns about sexually suggestive remarks or behavior with the person who is producing them. Let the person or a supervisor know that you find certain behaviors or remarks offensive. Some individuals just do not recognize normal boundaries of conversation or behavior. Although ignorance is no excuse, you can short-circuit a difficult situation by being forthright rather than waiting for it to become intolerable and confrontational.

Try to assess whether an organization that you are considering working for is one in which harassment may be likely. Any behavior that bothers you, whether immoral or offensive, should be a warning signal to you. Consult with other employees, particularly other women, about the working situation. They may advise you to avoid being alone with a particular person or confirm your experiences with a particular co-worker. Here it is important that you distinguish real concerns from the usual workplace gossip.

Having romantic relationships with people in your workplace invites situations where sexual harassment can occur, especially from someone whom you have dated. Avoiding such workplace relationships may help reduce the chance of being sexually harassed.

If you have tried one or more of these strategies and the harassment persists, be sure to keep all relevant correspondence or notes sent to you and keep records of conversations that were offensive. Keep a written record of the date, place, and nature of specific instances of harassment.

If you are confident that your complaint is legitimate, file it promptly, usually with the personnel or human resources department within your organization. Most organizations will have a formal policy and procedure to investigate and terminate sexual harassment. If your organization has no policy against harassment, consult with senior management. Document all communications about sexual harassment within your organization in writing. Contact the EEOC directly if the organization does not respond to your concerns. You can find an office of the EEOC in the telephone book under "Agencies of the U.S. Government."

WHERE CAN I GET MORE INFORMATION AND HELP?

For resources and information about rape and sexual assault, contact your local health department, local medical centers and hospitals, and other social service providers. These agencies can refer you to an organization that provides specific services for your needs. Rape and sexual assault shelters for women can be found in most U.S. cities. For information on shelters and services in your community, look in the yellow pages under "Human Services Organizations" or "Social Service Organizations."

Crisis intervention services provide immediate legal, economic, housing, and medical assistance to women who have been raped or assaulted. To find a rape crisis center near your home, visit http://centers.rainn.org/ on the internet or call the National Sexual Assault Hotline 24 hours a day at (800) 656-HOPE (4673). Also contact your local police department or call 911, especially if you have been the victim (or fear becoming the victim) of a rape or sexual assault.

Appendix 1 at the back of the book provides a state-by-state website listing of compensation and assistance programs for victims of violence and crime. You may find assistance by contacting one of your state programs. Appendix 2 is a bibliography for further reading on each of the violence topics discussed in this volume, organized chapter by chapter.

The following are national and state organizations and internet websites that offer information and services to victims, families, and professionals about rape and sexual assault.

NATIONAL ORGANIZATIONS

Battered Women's Justice Project
(800) 903-0111

Break the Cycle
(310) 286-3383

Centers for Disease Control and Prevention
National Center for Injury Prevention and Control
(800) CDC-INFO (232-4636)

EMERGE: Counseling and Education to Stop Male Violence
(617) 547-9879

Institute on Violence, Abuse, and Trauma
(858) 527-1860

Men Can Stop Rape
(202) 265-6530

National Center on Domestic and Sexual Violence
(512) 407-9020

National Center for Victims of Crime, National Crime Victim Helpline
(800) FYI-CALL; TYY (800) 211-7996

National Clearinghouse on Marital and Date Rape
(510) 524-1582

National Crime Prevention Council
(202) 466-6272

National Institute of Justice
National Criminal Justice Reference Service
(800) 851-3420

National Online Resource Center on Violence Against Women
(800) 537-2238; (800) 553-2508 TTT

National Organization for Victim Assistance
(800) TRY-NOVA (879-6682)

National Resource Center on Domestic Violence
(800) 537-2238 ext. 5; TTY (800) 553-2508

National Sexual Violence Resource Center
(877) 739-3895; TTY (717) 909-0715

Rape, Abuse, & Incest National Network (RAINN)
(800) 656-HOPE

SAFER: Students Active For Ending Rape
(347) 465-7233

Security on Campus
(888) 251-7959

Victims of Crime Resource Center
(800) VICTIMS (842-8467)

Women in Crisis, Inc.
(212) 242-4880

STATE SEXUAL ASSAULT COALITIONS, CRISIS CENTERS, AND HOTLINES

Alabama Coalition Against Rape
www.acar.org
(334) 264-0123

Alaska Network on Domestic and Sexual Violence
www.andvsa.org
(907) 586-3650

Arizona Sexual Assault Network
www.azsan.org
(480) 831-1986

Arkansas Coalition Against Sexual Assault
www.acasa.ws
(866) 632-2272

California Coalition Against Sexual Assault
www.calcasa.org
(916) 446-2520

Colorado Coalition Against Sexual Assault
www.ccasa.org
(877) 372-2272

Connecticut Sexual Assault Crisis Services, Inc.
www.connsacs.org
(888) 999-5545
(888) 568-8332

Delaware—CONTACTLifeline
www.contactlifeline.org
(302) 761-9100

District of Columbia Rape Crisis Center
www.dcrcc.org
(202) 328-1371

Florida Council Against Sexual Violence
www.fcasv.org
(888) 956-7273

Georgia Network to End Sexual Assault
www.gnesa.org
(866) 354-3672

Hawaii Coalition for the Prevention of Sexual Assault
(808) 733-9038

Idaho Coalition Against Sexual & Domestic Violence
www.idvsa.org
(888) 293-6118

Illinois Coalition Against Sexual Assault
www.icasa.org
(217) 753-4117

Indiana Coalition Against Sexual Assault
www.incasa.org
(800) 691-2272

Iowa Coalition Against Sexual Assault
www.iowacasa.org
(800) 284-7821

Kansas Coalition Against Sexual and Domestic Violence
www.kcsdv.org
(785) 232-9784

Kentucky Association of Sexual Assault Programs, Inc.
http://kyasap.brinkster.net
(866) 375-2727

Louisiana Foundation Against Sexual Assault
www.lafasa.org
(888) 995-7273

Maine Coalition Against Sexual Assault
www.mecasa.org
(800) 871-7741

Maryland Coalition Against Sexual Assault
www.mcasa.org
(410) 974-4507

Massachusetts Coalition Against Sexual Assault and Domestic Violence
www.janedoe.org
(617) 248-0922

Michigan Coalition Against Domestic and Sexual Violence
www.mcadsv.org
(517) 347-7000

Minnesota Coalition Against Sexual Assault
www.mncasa.org
(800) 964-8847

Mississippi Coalition Against Sexual Abuse
www.mscasa.org
(888) 987-9011

Missouri Coalition Against Sexual Assault
www.mssu.edu/missouri/mocasa/mocasa.htm
(573) 636-8776

Montana Coalition Against Domestic & Sexual Violence
www.mcadsv.com
(888) 404-7794

Nebraska Domestic Violence Sexual Assault Coalition
www.ndvsac.org
(402) 476-6256

Nevada Coalition Against Sexual Violence
www.ncasv.org
(702) 990-3460

New Hampshire Coalition Against Domestic and Sexual Violence
www.nhcadsv.org
(866) 644-3574

New Jersey Coalition Against Sexual Assault
www.njcasa.org
(800) 601-7200

New Mexico Clearinghouse on Sexual Abuse and Adult Services
www.nmcsap.org
(505) 883-8020

New York State Coalition Against Sexual Assault
www.nyscasa.org
(518) 482-4222

New York City Alliance Against Sexual Assault
www.nycagainstrape.org
(212) 229-0345 (English)
(212) 229-0345 x306 (Spanish)

North Carolina Coalition Against Sexual Assault
www.nccasa.net
(919) 871-1015

North Dakota Council on Abused Women's Services
www.ndcaws.org
(888) 255-6240

Ohio—Sexual Assault Response Network of Central Ohio
www.ohiohealth.com/body.cfm?id=980#prog
(614) 267-7020

Oklahoma Coalition Against Domestic Violence and Sexual Assault
www.ocadvsa.org
(405) 524-0700

Oregon Coalition Against Domestic and Sexual Violence
www.ocadsv.com
(503) 230-1951

Pennsylvania Coalition Against Rape
www.pcar.org
(888) 772-7227

Rhode Island—Day One, the Sexual Assault and Trauma Resource Center
www.dayoneri.org/index.htm
(800) 494-8100

South Carolina Coalition Against Domestic Violence and Sexual Assault
www.sccadvasa.org
(800) 260-9293

South Dakota Coalition Against Domestic Violence & Sexual Assault
www.sdcadvsa.org
(605) 945-0869

Tennessee Coalition Against Domestic and Sexual Violence
www.tcadsv.org
(800) 289-9018

Texas Association Against Sexual Assault
www.taasa.org
(512) 474-7190

Utah Coalition Against Sexual Assault
www.ucasa.org
(801) 746-0404

Vermont Network Against Domestic and Sexual Violence
www.vtnetwork.org
(802) 223-1302

Virginia Sexual and Domestic Violence Action Alliance
www.vadv.org
(800) 838-8238

Virgin Islands Domestic Violence and Sexual Assault Council Women's Coalition of
St. Croix
wcscstx@attglobal.net
(340) 773-9272

Washington Coalition of Sexual Assault Programs
www.wcsap.org
(800) 775-8013

West Virginia Foundation for Rape Information and Services
www.fris.org
(304) 366-9500

Wisconsin Coalition Against Sexual Assault
www.wcasa.org
(608) 257-1516

Wyoming Coalition Against Domestic Violence and Sexual Assault
www.wyomingdvsa.org/index1.htm
(800) 990-3877

USEFUL INTERNET WEBSITES

Acquaintance/Date Rape Resources: http://www.vachss.com/help_text/date_rape.html
Asian Task Force Against Domestic Violence: www.atask.org
Battered Women's Justice Project: www.bwjp.org
Break the Cycle: www.breakthecycle.org
Centers for Disease Control and Prevention: www.cdc.gov
Center for Sex Offender Management: www.csom.org
EMERGE—Counseling and Education to Stop Male Violence: www.emergedv.com
Family Violence Prevention Fund: www.fvpf.org
Feminist.com: www.feminist.com/antiviolence/facts.html
Feminist Majority Foundation: www.feminist.org/911/crisis.html
Institute on Domestic Violence in the African American Community:
    www.dvinstitute.org

Institute on Violence, Abuse, and Trauma: www.ivatcenters.org

Male Survivor: www.malesurvivor.org

MEDLINEplus: www.nlm.nih.gov/medlineplus/domesticviolence.html

Men Can Stop Rape: www.mencanstoprape.org

Men Stopping Rape: www.men-stopping-rape.org

National Alliance to End Sexual Violence: www.naesv.org

National Center for Victims of Crime: www.ncvc.org

National Coalition on Domestic Violence: www.ncadv.org

National Crime Prevention Council: www.ncpc.org

National Gay and Lesbian Task Force: www.thetaskforce.org

National Institute of Justice, National Criminal Justice Reference Service: www.ncjrs.gov

National Network to End Domestic Violence: www.nnedv.org

National Online Resource Center on Violence Against Women (VAWnet): www.vawnet.org

National Organization for Victim Assistance: www.trynova.org

National Sex Offender Registry: www.nsopr.gov

National Sex Offender Registry: www.familywatchdog.us

National Sexual Violence Resource Center: www.nsvrc.org

National Victim Assistance Academy: www.ojp.usdoj.gov/ovc/assist/vaa.htm

National Violence Against Women Prevention Research Center: http://www.musc.edu/vawprevention

National Women's Health Information Center: www.womenshealth.gov

Office for Victims of Crime: www.ovc.gov

Office on Violence Against Women: www.usdoj.gov/ovw

Rape, Abuse & Incest National Network: www.rainn.org

SAFER: Students Active For Ending Rape: www.safercampus.org

Stalking Resource Center: www.ncvc.org/src

Stalking Victim's Sanctuary: www.stalkingvictims.com

Stop Family Violence: www.stopfamilyviolence.org

STOP IT NOW!: www.stopitnow.org

Stop Our Silence: web.mit.edu/stop/www/home.htm

Survivors of Incest Anonymous: www.siawso.org

Violence Against Women Online Resources: www.vaw.umn.edu/sxasault.asp

Women's Justice Center: www.law.pace.edu/bwjc

Women in Crisis: www.wics.org

Women Organized Against Rape: www.woar.org

CHAPTER 8

Elder Abuse and Violence Against the Elderly

- What is elder abuse?
- How frequently are the elderly victimized by violence?
- How common is elder abuse?
- What is the difference between elder abuse and other forms of violence committed against the elderly?
- What are the signs of elder abuse?
- Can elder abuse cause serious injury or kill?
- Who abuses the elderly?
- Who is a typical victim of elder abuse?
- In what situations does elder abuse occur?
- Why does elder abuse occur?
- Are there laws against elder abuse?
- How can I reduce my risk of becoming a victim of elder abuse?
- How can elder abuse be prevented?
- What should I do if I know that an elder is being abused or if I am a victim of elder abuse?
- What can I do if I am abusing an elderly person?
- Where can I get more information and help?

WHAT IS ELDER ABUSE?

Elder abuse is any action that, either by commission or omission, harms an elderly person. Elder abuse and neglect are complex problems that have evaded clear definition. One of the more commonly accepted definitions of elder abuse, used by the World Health Organization, is "a single, or repeated act, or lack of appropriate action, occurring within any relationship where there is an expectation of trust which causes harm or distress to an older person." Abuse of the elderly involves neglect, physical injury by caregivers, psychological abuse, financial exploitation, and violation of human rights.

Yet experts vary greatly on what exactly constitutes elder abuse. Although child and spouse abuse have been clearly recognized for a number of years, elder abuse has received substantial attention only recently. It is unclear, for example, as to whether the definition of physical abuse should include the failure to provide medical care to an elderly person. Should it include lack of supervision or lack of personal care, or should it be restricted to include only the perpetration of physical injuries? Does elder abuse occur when the victim is 55 years and older, or 65 years and older? Widely differing viewpoints have been expressed on these and other issues.

It is possible, however, to identify several aspects of elder abuse. Physical abuse involves direct physical assault and use of force to threaten or physically injure an elder. This would include rough handling; threats with a weapon; objects being thrown at the elderly; and elderly persons being pushed, grabbed or shoved, hit with a fist, slapped, kicked, or otherwise intentionally struck. Force-feeding and improper use of restraints or medications also constitute physical abuse of the elderly.

Sexual abuse involves sexual contact that is forced, tricked, threatened, or coerced on an elder, including persons unable to grant consent.

Emotional or psychological abuse would include verbal attacks, rejection, social isolation, or threats that belittle or create fear, anguish, and anxiety. Emotional abuse occurs when an elderly person is humiliated or intimidated, or caused mental anguish and distress. It also may include denying an older person participation in decisions that affect his or her life or isolating the elder by not speaking to or comforting him or her.

Financial abuse or exploitation of elderly individuals, who may be easy targets, includes theft, fraud, and use of inappropriate influence to gain control over or unauthorized use of an elder's money or property by an advisor or caretaker. Elders may be coerced or manipulated to give away their money, rewrite their wills, relinquish control of their finances, assign durable power of attorney, or sign away ownership of their homes and property.

Neglect is a caregiver's failure or refusal to meet the needs of an elderly person, for example, withholding or failing to provide that person with the essentials of life, such as food, shelter, clothing, and the means for personal hygiene, medical care, and social stimulation. Neglect often overlaps with other kinds of elder abuse. Abandonment is the desertion of a frail or vulnerable elder by any individual with a duty of care.

Elder abuse can be intentional or unintentional. If unintentional, elder abuse usually results from ignorance or inexperience in a caregiver or a lack of desire to provide care. Some organizations recognize self-neglect and self-abuse among the elderly, which is neglectful or abusive behavior by an older person that threatens his or her own health and safety. It usually results from physical or mental impairment in an elderly person, particularly when he or she is socially isolated.

The problem of elder abuse is becoming better understood. Early publicity about elder abuse centered around elderly residents of nursing homes in which there were incidents of abuse by employees. However, because most of the care provided for elderly Americans occurs in the home, it is not surprising that the majority of elder abuse happens in the home setting. Some of the underlying causes of elder abuse include the vulnerability of older individuals; the high level of violence in society in general; and family stress, substance abuse, and poverty among both victims and abusers.

HOW FREQUENTLY ARE THE ELDERLY VICTIMIZED BY VIOLENCE?

People over the age of 65 years are generally the least likely of all age groups in America to be violently victimized. However, although the elderly are less frequently victimized, they are more likely to be seriously injured in any given episode of violence. In 2005, 85,000 people over the age of 65 years were victims of nonfatal crime, and 633 people in this age group were murdered.

Among the elderly, city dwellers are at higher risk for crime. As in other age groups in the United States, elderly men are more often victimized than elderly women. Elderly Black persons and the elderly who are separated or divorced are at higher risk for violent crime. Elderly persons who are renters experience a greater degree of all forms of personal crime, including assault and robbery. Elderly persons with lower incomes are more likely to be victims of violence.

Crimes against the elderly have declined over the past two decades, although the elderly seem to be targeted especially for crimes that are motivated by economic gain, for example, burglary and robbery. When an older person is killed violently, it is most often during the commission of another crime, such as robbery. Homicides among the elderly are as likely to be committed by a relative or an acquaintance as by a stranger, which contrasts with younger people who are killed more often by an acquaintance.

HOW COMMON IS ELDER ABUSE?

Comprehensive national data on elder abuse are not collected, and state statistics vary widely because there is no uniform reporting system. Estimates of the frequency of elder abuse derive from a number of well-designed studies that provide data on this question. The estimates range from 2% to 10% of the nation's elderly having been abused at some point in their lives. In 2004, between one and two million elders in the United States were estimated to have been injured, exploited, or otherwise mistreated by a caregiver. A study conducted in the Boston area found a rate of elder abuse that, if similar to the rate for the rest of the United States, would suggest that between 700,000 and 1.1 million elderly persons (or 3.2% of the aged population) have been abused. The Health Select Committee on Aging of the U.S. Congress estimated in the mid-1980s that 1–1.5 million elderly Americans were physically, financially, or emotionally abused each year (or 4% of the elderly population). Other estimates are as high as two million cases of elder abuse each year. A 2008 review of 49 studies suggested that 6% of older people had reported significant abuse in the prior month and one-fourth reported significant levels of psychological abuse.

If reported rates reflect actual levels of elder abuse, the problem appears to be increasing in magnitude. In 1994 a survey of states found 241,000 reports of elder abuse, neglect, and exploitation, up 106% from 117,000 reports in 1986. Another study estimated that in 1996 a total of 449,924 elderly persons (aged 60 years and over) experienced abuse or neglect in domestic settings. In 2000, states reported 472,813 reports of elder abuse.

In studies of abuse in residential institutions for the elderly, more than one-third of nurses and nursing aides reported witnessing physical abuse of an elderly resident during the prior year. The most common forms of physical abuse, which were observed by approximately one-fifth of staff members, included excessive use of restraints, pushing, shoving, slapping, and hitting. Psychological abuse was observed by more than 80% of the staff, including yelling, insulting, or swearing at a resident. Approximately one-quarter witnessed a patient being socially isolated.

As with other forms of interpersonal violence, abuse of the elderly is greatly underreported by victims. Studies have suggested that only 7%–25% of cases of elder abuse are reported to authorities. Estimates of reporting are as low as 1 report for every 8–14 cases. One study found that 72% of elder abuse victims did not complain of the abuse when they appeared for treatment in an emergency department. The reporting of financial exploitation may be as low as 1 in 25 cases. There is also a problem in accurately detecting abuse whose effects may mimic the decline in physical health that is a natural part of aging. Victims may be difficult to communicate with because they are often physically or mentally impaired.

Failure to report incidents of elder abuse by victims may result from shame or fear of reprisal or expulsion from the home by relatives resulting in institutionalization. As with other forms of domestic violence, there is also concern that reporting may invite outside involvement in the private affairs of the family. It is often painful for victims of elder abuse to admit that an individual who they love (and presumably loves them) would harm them. One study found that up to one-third of elders who had been abused denied that they had been abused.

Difficulties in estimating the frequency of elder abuse also are related to the fact that up to 80% of abuse episodes are recurrent rather than isolated. Furthermore, many of the signs and symptoms of elder abuse, such as broken bones, bruises, and poor nutrition, may result from accidental injuries or processes that are common in aging. For example, the elderly bruise more easily and are susceptible to frequent falls that often break bones. Bruising on the abdomen or extremities may be attributed to tight restraints. Despite their pivotal role, medical personnel are also not typically or adequately trained to evaluate elderly victims for sexual abuse. Reduced appetite and impaired ability to prepare meals, rather than neglect, may result in malnutrition. In addition, the elderly can suffer from poor memory and confusion that may sometimes be mistaken for the mental effects of abuse. An elderly person's memory or hearing is often a major barrier to the investigation of suspected abuse. Some researchers in the field of elder abuse and neglect believe that the developmental state of medical knowledge and forensic science around elder abuse is equal to that of child abuse and neglect 2–3 decades ago.

There are differing views about how common various kinds of elder abuse may be. Several studies have suggested that physical assault is the most common form of elder abuse, representing between one- and two-fifths of all abuse. However, other studies show that neglect of the needs of an elderly person is the most frequent kind of abuse. One national agency estimates that 45% of all elder abuse is neglect. Psychological abuse also appears to be common. In several studies, financial abuse was most common, followed by verbal abuse, physical abuse, and then neglect. Multiple forms of elder abuse may coexist. Of reports substantiated by adult protective services in 2004, 20% involved caregiver neglect, 15% involved emotional psychological or verbal abuse, 15% involved financial exploitation, 11% involved physical abuse, and 1% involved sexual abuse.

Whatever the frequency, there is general agreement among experts that elder abuse represents one of the most underrecognized social problems in America. Approximately 80% of the dependent elderly living in the United States currently are cared for at home by their families. While the elder segment of an aging U.S. population grows from 41 million persons today to more than 66 million by 2030, the problem of elder abuse is likely to expand in coming years.

WHAT IS THE DIFFERENCE BETWEEN ELDER ABUSE AND OTHER FORMS OF VIOLENCE COMMITTED AGAINST THE ELDERLY?

The primary difference between elder abuse and other forms of violence against the elderly is that elder abuse involves a perpetrator who is in a relationship or position of trust with the victim. Elder abuse is infrequently perpetrated by strangers, but other forms of violence against the elderly may be. Elder abuse is a major contributor to violence against elderly people in the United States. Elder abuse also tends to occur in institutions as well as the home, whereas, most other kinds of violence against the elderly occur in and around their homes and neighborhoods.

WHAT ARE THE SIGNS OF ELDER ABUSE?

The signs of physical elder abuse depend on the kind of assault made on the victim. Bruises, slap marks, and lacerations around the eyes, mouth, and other parts of the face may indicate abuse. Similar injuries on the body, particularly in the shape of common household items or in the shape of a hand, may be observed. Bald spots from hair-pulling, burns, tooth loss, and skin discoloration or rope burns from being tied up or restrained are all possible signs. Bilateral bruising to the arms or legs in particular may indicate that an elder has been shaken, grabbed, or restrained. Multicolored bruises indicate that the injuries were sustained over time. Dislocations and bone fractures may occur. Weight loss, poor nutritional status and dehydration, bad hygiene, bed sores, and a general appearance of physical neglect are other signs. There may be over- or undermedication.

Unexplained sexually transmitted diseases may suggest sexual abuse, as would bruises around the breasts, inner thighs, or genital area. Genital or anal pain or difficulty walking or sitting may indicate sexual abuse. Underclothing may be torn, stained, or bloody. Many of these signs require medical assessment to determine the likely origin.

Psychological and emotional disturbances, such as depression, confusion, fearfulness, agitation, and anxiety, may be evident. Withdrawal from normal activities and emotional numbness, unexplained change in alertness, regressive behavior, or other unusual behaviors may result from emotional abuse or neglect. These signs may be wrongly attributed to dementia in the victim. Inconsistent histories given by the elderly person and the caregiver suggest possible abuse. Unexplained injuries or a history of injury that is not consistent with the type or degree of injury observed may indicate abuse. Unexplained delays in seeking care, seeking care from different medical facilities to avoid detection, vague or bizarre explanations, or the denial of obvious injuries are indications of maltreatment.

Victims may exhibit self-destructive behavior and fear or cowering in the presence of a caregiver.

Histories of being "accident prone" or "doctor shopping" and missed medical appointments may indicate an attempt to conceal abuse. A caregiver who demonstrates stress or low tolerance in interacting with the elder is a sign of a potentially abusive relationship. Suspicion should increase when the elderly person is not allowed to speak for himself or herself in the presence of the caregiver and is reluctant to respond when questioned. Untreated bedsores and rashes, unmet needs for medical or dental care, outdated prescriptions, dehydration, unclean clothing or bedding, poor hygiene, and excessively long hair or nails may indicate neglect at home or indifference and incompetence within an institution. Absence of necessities (including food, heat, eyeglasses, hearing aids, walkers, and dentures), an inadequate living environment or housing in disrepair, and animal or insect infestations may suggest neglect at home.

Sudden changes in finances and accounts, altered wills and trusts, unusual and large bank withdrawals, checks written as loans or gifts, and missing property may suggest financial exploitation of an elderly person. Unpaid bills, eviction notices, or notices to discontinue utilities may indicate financial exploitation. New "close or best friends" should be regarded with caution.

Elder abusers are not always easily identified. Although there is no standard profile of an abuser, there are behavioral signs or indicators that a caregiver or other individual is abusing an elder. Abusers will minimize or appear indifferent to an elder's suffering or injuries. Caregiver apathy or hostility is an important sign. Attempting to control the elder's actions—whom they see and talk to, and where they go—is often a telltale sign of an abuser. Isolating the elder from family and friends is another. Endeavoring to create or maintain emotional or financial dependency on the caregiver can indicate ongoing abuse. Threatening to leave is a method of coercion often used by abusers. Caregiver abuse of alcohol and drugs, mental illness, or criminal history should raise concerns about elder victimization.

If some of these signs are evident, elderly persons should be asked a few questions that may expose the abuse. Inquire if they are afraid of someone at home or if anyone at home has ever hurt or threatened them, or if they have ever been touched without their consent. It may be easier to elicit a response by asking whether anyone has ever failed to help take care of them or made them do things that they did not want to do. Ask if they spend much time alone. In the instance of financial abuse, elderly persons should be asked whether they have signed any documents that they did not understand or if anyone has taken anything of theirs without asking or against their wishes. Parallel questions to the caregiver or other members of the family or domicile also may be revealing.

CAN ELDER ABUSE CAUSE SERIOUS INJURY OR KILL?

Yes. Just like other forms of domestic violence, elder abuse can seriously injure or even kill its victims. Although the evidence is not conclusive regarding the extent, elder abuse does result in injuries, hospitalizations, and deaths every year in the United States. Punching and other assaults can result in damage to internal organs, fractures of bones, and lacerations and wounds to the face. Hemorrhages can occur in the brain. Bruises, burns, and bites have been documented. Neglect can result in physical wasting and weight loss, dehydration, and bed sores. Women tend to sustain more serious abuse and to suffer greater physical and emotional harm from mistreatment than men.

Psychologically, the elder abuse victim can become depressed, withdrawn, fearful, and angry. Elder abuse, and particularly sexual abuse, may produce post-traumatic stress disorder in victims. Sexual assault may cause a variety of other physical and emotional problems (see Chapter 7 on rape). Victims also may exhibit regressive infantile behaviors and agitation, and can have very low self-esteem. Because of age, the natural resiliency of the body and ability to heal is diminished for elderly victims. The impact of abuse is greater on the elderly than on younger people. Fractured bones and other injuries do not heal well, and lowered immunity may result in a potentially life-threatening infection. Unlike the abused child or spouse, a relatively minor episode of abuse of an elderly person can cause deterioration that results in a serious medical condition. Because older victims usually have fewer support systems and reserves—physically, psychologically, and economically—the impact of abuse and neglect is magnified. Often a single incident of mistreatment can precipitate a downward spiral leading to loss of independence, serious complicating illness, and even death.

From 1976 to 2000, the number and rate of homicides for persons age 65 years or older declined and then stabilized through 2005. Approximately 5% of all U.S. homicides were of persons age 65 years or older. Data reported from the National Violent Death Reporting System between 2003 and 2007 characterized victims, perpetrators, and circumstances that precipitated homicides by a caregiver. Sixty-eight incidents were categorized as homicide: by neglect (17); due to intentional injury of the victim (21); or as homicide followed by suicide of the perpetrator (30). Elder homicide victims killed by a caregiver were most often widowed (42%), non-Hispanic (97%), White (88%), and female (63%), and were largely killed in their homes (92%) with a firearm (35%) or by intentional neglect (25%) by a husband (30%) or a son (22%). The largest group of victims was aged 80 years or older (49%), and 43% were aged 50–79 years. Many homicides by caregivers were precipitated by physical illness of the victim or caregiver, an opportunity for financial gain by the perpetrator, mental illness or substance use, or an impending crisis in the life of the caregiver not related to illness.

Financial abuse can be very damaging to elders. Crime victims aged 65 years or older lost $1.3 billion as the result of personal and property crimes in general in 2005. People over age 60 years comprised 9% of identity theft victims reporting the crime that year. Seven percent of internet fraud victims in 2006 were 60 years or older. The median loss per fraud complaint was $866 for people aged 60 years or older, an amount higher than for all other age groups. One-third of victims reporting telemarketing fraud in 2005 were aged 60 years or older.

WHO ABUSES THE ELDERLY?

The typical elder abuser in domestic settings is often a family member or relative who lives with the victim. Approximately two-thirds of abusers are family members of the victim, most often an adult child or the spouse. The majority of alleged perpetrators of elder abuse in 2004 were White, middle-class, and aged 30–50 years. Between 1992 and 1997, 75% of offenders were male and 50% were White. In 2004, more than half of alleged perpetrators of elder abuse were women. Of alleged perpetrators in 2004, 33% were adult children, 22% were other family members, 11% were spouses or intimate partners, and 16% had an unknown relationship to the victim.

The abuser commonly is under heightened stress, which may be financial, marital, or occupational in nature. The abuser, like the victim, may have experienced a recent deterioration in health or may be bereaving the loss of a loved one. Elder abusers frequently have histories of some form of mental illness, such as depression, or an intellectual disability. Family dysfunction is thought to be more common among abusers, and they are more likely to be unmarried and unemployed. Perpetrators of elder abuse tend to have long-standing personality traits increasing the risk of maltreatment, including hostility or bad temper, being hypercritical, and having a tendency to blame others for problems. Abusers typically lack interests and activities outside of the home.

Research has shown that substance and alcohol abuse is frequent among elder abusers, perhaps involved in one of every three cases. One study found that 44% of abusers self-identified as having alcohol or drug abuse problems. The abuser usually has cared for the victim for many years. Economic problems often are associated with elder abusers, as is a history of domestic violence or abuse. Financial abuse of the elderly most often is perpetrated by a distant relative or an acquaintance. One study in 1991 found that abuse was perpetrated by an adult child of the victim in 33% of cases, a spouse in 14% of cases, another relative in 13% of cases, and a friend or neighbor in 8% of cases. Abusers are often late middle-aged adults or seniors themselves. A 1996 study found that in approximately 90% of elder abuse and neglect incidents with a known perpetrator, it was a family member. Two-thirds of these perpetrators were the adult children or spouses of the victim.

Because an elderly individual is most likely to be abused by the person with whom he or she lives, it is not surprising to find abuse within a marriage. One study found that one-fourth of cases involve husbands abusing wives, or vice versa. In some situations such abuse is "domestic violence grown old," a situation in which the abusive behavior of a spouse or partner toward another continues into old age.

Perpetrators of sexual abuse include attendants, aides, custodial and other employees of care facilities, and family members (spouses as well). Elderly facility residents may also sexually assault a fellow resident. One study of perpetrators of sexual abuse of elders found that 23.2% had an incestuous familial relationship with the victim, 15.5% were a marital or common-law partner, 10.9% were an unrelated care provider, and 26.1% were strangers not known to the victim. Forty-seven percent of sexual offenders were aged 30–49 years. Almost all offenders were male.

Perpetrators of elder abuse in institutional settings are usually persons who have some legal or contractual obligation to provide the victim with care and protection. These include paid caretakers, staff, and professionals employed by an institution.

Perpetrators of financial elder abuse in one study were friends, neighbors, or acquaintances in 40% of instances; another one-third were sons or daughters; and one-fourth were other relatives. Those who are financially exploiting the elderly often have some sense of entitlement and feel justified in taking what they believe is "rightfully" theirs (e.g., relatives taking an advance on their inheritance). Many confidence games and scams are used, including promising lifelong care in exchange for money, property, or the changing of a will in favor of the caregiver. Some perpetrators may "groom" an older person (befriend or build a relationship with them) to establish a relationship of trust and then subtly coerce a transfer of assets from the victim.

Although it is clear that the elderly victim may be dependent on the abuser for care, there is evidence to suggest that some abusers are partially or totally dependent on the victim for housing and financial support. Researchers have referred to this as a "web of mutual dependency" between abuser and victim. Abusers were financially dependent on their victims in two-thirds of cases in one study. Elder abusers have usually cared for their victims for a long time, on average approximately ten years, but they often lack caregiving experience. They also may have been victims of abuse as a child. In some circumstances, it appears that the elderly individual and the caregiver are mutually abusive of each other.

WHO IS A TYPICAL VICTIM OF ELDER ABUSE?

Elder abuse victims come from every socioeconomic, racial, ethnic, and religious background. Individuals who become victims of elder abuse usually are physically or psychologically frail or impaired, which increases their dependence on other people. The elder abuse victim may not have close family ties, or if these relationships exist, they exist with family members who have some history of domestic violence. An abused elderly person is typically a White woman who lives with relatives. Approximately two-thirds of elder abuse victims in domestic situations are females, but some studies suggest that men are abused equally or more often. It is not clear whether the higher level of abuse found among females is due to a higher risk for victimization or to women's greater numbers in the senior population. Higher levels among men noted in some studies may be because elderly women are much more likely to live alone, which reduces their risk. Victims of elder abuse are often over 75 years old, and 40% are over 80 years old. Abuse increases with advancing age. The annual income of elder abuse victims is usually less than $10,000, and their presence in a household may create added financial strain.

In 1994, two-thirds of elder abuse victims were White, one-fifth were Black, and 10% were Hispanic. Between 1992 and 1997, divorced or separated elderly persons experienced more abuse than those who were married or widowed. In 2004, Blacks constituted 21% of elder abuse victims, despite representing only 8% of all Americans age 65 years or older.

Recent deterioration in the health or mental status of the victim seems to be a factor in abuse. Mental impairment is not uncommon and may increase dependence on the abuser. Elderly individuals who have behaviors that are difficult to manage, for example, who suffer bouts of aggression, wandering, or problems with incontinence, seem to be at higher risk. Alzheimer's disease and other forms of dementia are a major risk factor for abuse. One study found that 11.9% of dementia caregivers admitted having committed physical abuse; another study reported that 14% of caregivers committed physical abuse. These findings suggest that elder abuse among the demented elderly is particularly underreported. The disruptive behaviors that result from dementia are a strong cause of caregiver stress and thus may increase abuse risk. Alcohol or drug abuse may contribute to the dependency of an elderly person. Elder abuse victims often are isolated socially and lack social support networks, which reduce the chance that the abuse can be detected by people outside of the family. Elderly victims may be excessively loyal to their caregivers and refuse to report abuse.

Most data do not suggest that victims of physical abuse differ significantly from elders who are not abused. Others report that women are more commonly victimized by physical abuse. But when men are the perpetrators, the violence tends to be more severe. Physical abuse usually occurs between spouses. Verbal abuse is common between individuals who are married, and men and women are affected to a similar extent.

The majority of sexual abuse victims are women; however, older male victims have been reported in both home and institutional settings. Individuals with physical or cognitive disabilities are more likely to be sexually assaulted, and as occurs with other forms of abuse, persons who lack social support and are isolated are more frequently victimized.

Men and women about equally tend to be victims of financial elder abuse. The victim of financial abuse usually lacks consumer information, has decreased sensory abilities and a slower rate of assimilating information, and often is isolated socially. Such people tend to lack experience and self-confidence in financial and commercial matters. Often they live alone and suffer from poor health. The elderly are attractive targets because people over the age of 50 control more than 70% of the nation's wealth.

Victims of neglect are more often female and tend to have health conditions that limit their activities, easing the isolation that perpetrators of this form of abuse seek or need to impose.

IN WHAT SITUATIONS DOES ELDER ABUSE OCCUR?

There are three settings in which elder abuse usually occurs: domestically (in the home); institutionally (in nursing homes, hospitals, and long-term care facilities); and through self-neglect and self-abuse. Elder abuse may occur in a situation in which an elderly person's needs are exceeding, or will soon exceed, the ability of a caregiver to address them adequately. The caregiver experiences increasing frustration and stress as his or her ability to provide proper care diminishes.

A shared living situation is a major risk factor for physical abuse of elders, with older persons living alone at lowest risk. A shared residence increases the opportunities for contact, conflict, stress, and mistreatment. Elderly victims of physical abuse live with the abuser in the same home in 75% of instances. The usual setting for elder abuse is within families who have poor communication and dysfunctional emotional dynamics. Individual members of the family, or the family as a whole, may be facing serious external stresses, such as insufficient income or unemployment. Abuse tends to occur when the abuser is dependent on the victim for financial support or housing or when the victim, usually physically or psychologically impaired, is dependent on the family for care.

Although many studies have shown that abuse of the elderly tends to occur more frequently in White and middle-class families, it is not yet clear whether this is an actual trend or reflects the fact that more studies are conducted on this group. One study found that Blacks reported elder abuse disproportionately (21% of victims but only 8% of the population aged 65 years or older). Financially abused elders are more likely to live alone, where their isolation makes them more vulnerable to manipulation. Unlike other forms of abuse, financial exploitation can easily occur when the abuser and victim live apart.

In general, elder abuse tends to be a chronic or long-term victimization. One study found that over one-half of abused elderly people had been the victims of prior abuse. Other reports have found abuse to be recurrent in up to 70% of cases. Elder abuse does not typically end or resolve spontaneously. Elder abuse tends to increase in frequency and severity over time. The abuse usually escalates in much the same way as occurs in domestic battering, until a major change occurs in the care setting or the home. Change is not easily achieved, with 25%–75% of victims or families refusing to seek help for the abuse.

Elder abuse may occur more commonly in institutions where there is a shortage of beds, a surplus of patients, and low staff-to-patient ratios. In long-term-care settings, risk factors for elder abuse may include negligent hiring practices (failure to complete required background checks on aides and custodial workers), lack of administrative and supervisory oversight, and high staff turnover, inadequate staff training, or poorly paid staff. Risk factors reported from studies of elder abuse in institutional settings include staff burnout, younger staff, high level of conflict with residents, and physical aggression from residents.

WHY DOES ELDER ABUSE OCCUR?

A number of factors contribute to elder abuse, including psychological, social, medical, and economic influences. These influences affect an elderly person's interpersonal and family relationships. Four major areas have been identified as contributors to elder abuse: stress of the caretaker, impairment of a dependent elderly person, a cycle of violence perpetuated by succeeding generations of families, and personal problems of an abuser.

Caregivers of the elderly are challenged with a very demanding and stressful commitment. Especially when an elder is frail and physically disabled or mentally impaired, care providers may not be equipped materially or psychologically to manage the complex needs of the person. Stress, combined with inadequate coping skills, emotional problems, and other external stresses such as job loss, may produce a level of frustration in the caretaker that results in abuse. Financial difficulties and a lack of family and community support also may contribute to abusive behavior. Studies thus far have not found a direct relationship between elder abuse and functional impairment or poor health of the victim. There is at present little actual evidence that an older person's need for assistance or caregiver stress leads to greater risk of elder abuse.

Some experts believe that violent behavior is learned by younger generations from parents and transmitted in a cycle of violence. It can be observed that abusers more frequently come from families in whom violence was a normal and accepted pattern of behavior. In particular, it is generally accepted that victims of child abuse may grow up to become child abusers themselves and perpetuate a cycle of violence. Such individuals may carry a predisposition to violence with them throughout their lives. It is possible that neglected or abused children grow up to abuse their elders in a reciprocating fashion. However, while research is ongoing, there is at present no evidence that elder abuse is transmitted or modeled in an intergenerational manner.

Abusers may have mental health and emotional problems and may be abusing alcohol or drugs. Financial difficulties are common among abusers. Such factors may result in dependency on the elderly person, which evolves into resentment and anger that are ultimately expressed as abuse.

None of these explanations or factors fully explain elderly abuse, and other influences certainly exist across diverse settings.

ARE THERE LAWS AGAINST ELDER ABUSE?

There is currently no federal law protecting elders from abuse. However, all states have adopted laws specifically dealing with elder abuse, neglect, and financial exploitation. These laws vary from state to state. In some states, laws protect the elderly who are living alone or with family; in other states, laws also include persons living in nursing homes or long-term care facilities. States are increasingly defining criminal penalties for elder abuse, and several have begun ordering restitution of victims through monetary payment by the offender to the victim for harm done. Existing laws relating to homicide, battery, rape, assault, theft, fraud, and domestic violence apply to incidents of elder abuse. Some states specifically consider the victim's age when sentencing convicted offenders. Your state's laws can be learned from your state office on aging, attorney general's office, adult protective services agency, or local agency on aging (see the end of this chapter for state by state contact information).

HOW CAN I REDUCE MY RISK OF BECOMING A VICTIM OF ELDER ABUSE?

Every elderly person has a fundamental right to be safe and not to be harassed. Abuse is never the fault of elderly persons, and they are never responsible for the harm done to them. Nonetheless, there are a number of actions that can reduce your risk of becoming a victim of elder abuse. Remaining active and engaged in life, avoiding isolation, and cultivating a strong support network of family and friends will reduce your abuse risk. Be aggressive in taking care of your health problems, and endeavor to remain healthy because this lessens your vulnerability and dependency, situations where abuse occurs more often and risk is elevated.

Always refuse to allow anyone, including even close relatives, to add their name to your bank account without your clear consent. Never make important financial decisions under pressure, and avoid signing documents or transferring money or property to anyone without getting legal advice beforehand. Assert your right to be treated with respect and dignity, and be clear and vocal about what you will and will not tolerate. Set boundaries and insist that caregivers respect them. Above all, avoid denial. Ask for help if you need it, and do not delay.

HOW CAN ELDER ABUSE BE PREVENTED?

Prevention of elder abuse is made very difficult because it is a hidden, often invisible problem. Elder abuse remains hidden because of the traditional sanction of family privacy and because the elderly tend to be so isolated. For the reasons stated earlier, elderly victims and their families may deny that abuse is occurring, not only to the outside world but also to themselves. The best strategy for preventing elder abuse is to improve community support for the autonomy and independence of the elderly and to reduce the perception that the elderly are burdens. Independence is best fostered by providing adequate income, appropriate housing, health care, and social and transportation services. Services can be designed to help the elderly live independently or semi-independently, reducing forced cohabitation with family members and others who are unwilling or unable to care for them.

The problem of elder abuse was first noted in the United Kingdom in 1975 when episodes of "granny-bashing" were described. Later, the "battered parent" problem came to light in the United States. But ignorance of the problem remains high among professionals and the public alike. The first step in preventing elder abuse, therefore, is to increase public awareness and provide information about the problem to caregiving professionals and to the general public, including the elderly. Services available to the abused should be communicated to elders, and training for professional staff who work with the elderly should focus on prevention, detection, and provision of support in managing difficult elder behavior and reducing their frustration.

At the national level, the U.S. Administration on Aging is playing a leadership role in combating elder abuse by creating and supporting the National Center on Elder Abuse. It also provides funding to assist states and area agencies on aging in establishing and implementing elder abuse prevention activities. The U.S. Centers for Medicare and Medicaid Services has long worked to protect the residents of nursing homes and other long-term care facilities from elder abuse. The U.S. Department of Justice provides funding to support the operation of state and local victim assistance programs and services.

All 50 U.S. states have adopted some legislation on elder abuse, and state attorney general's offices and law enforcement agencies are working to detect and prosecute elder abuse crimes. However, laws vary considerably from state to state. Some states require mandatory reports of abuse, and in others reporting is purely voluntary. In some states only certain professional groups are required to report elder abuse, whereas, in others anyone who knows or suspects an instance of abuse has the legal obligation to report it. Currently, detection of much elder abuse rests with health care providers, such as doctors, because the abused elderly do not usually seek help unless they are seriously injured. If a physician is capable of detecting elder abuse through skilled diagnosis and screening, he or she can begin a process of legal, medical, and social support and intervention that can prevent further episodes of abuse. Unfortunately, compliance with the reporting requirement for elder abuse is poor in most states.

In many jurisdictions elder abuse prevention programs are available now. These programs usually target abusers and those at risk of becoming abusers. In group meetings, therapists educate participants about adult development and the process of aging. General programs for caregivers address problem-solving, emotional support, and mediation of family problems related to elder care. They offer advice on managing difficult situations and training in maintaining self-control. Because much elder abuse involves adult children who have problems with alcohol, mental illness, or difficulties in coping, appropriate programs for adult children who are living with their parents should be engaged.

Efforts are underway to teach elderly people how to pursue social and recreational activities, reduce their isolation, and develop family relations in ways that will protect them from abuse. Support groups for family caregivers with elderly members have emerged around the country. These groups emphasize that the difficulties encountered in caring for an aged person are universal. Support is offered in helping families recognize commonly experienced emotions of guilt, frustration, and anger that relate to providing care to an aged person, along with techniques for coping with and resolving problems.

Many communities have special projects that target families who have elderly members and assist them in meeting their practical and caretaking needs. Church-based programs of this kind can be found in communities across the country. In addition, work places are increasingly offering consultation about and referral services for elderly care to their employees. Local hospitals and medical centers also may have programs for the elderly.

Adult day care offers help in caring for an elderly person and in reducing the risk of elder abuse. Adult day care programs and services can be found in many U.S. cities. Adult day care helps the elderly maintain or improve their ability to stay in the community independently and offers relief to their caregivers. Adult day care may include social events, family assistance, provision of meals, transportation, health care, exercise, counseling and referral services, and various activities. Such programs usually are linked with other agencies and services in the community. The National Adult Day Services Association and the National Adult Protective Services Association can provide information about adult day care. Some county social service or health departments may run adult day care programs. National and state referral agencies are listed at the end of this chapter.

One of the complexities regarding intervention on behalf of elder abuse victims is finding an appropriate balance between protecting the elderly from harm and respecting their need and desire to make their own decisions. In serious instances of abuse, for example, a victim may have to be removed from an abusive setting until the conflict is resolved. This approach may not meet the needs or match the desires of the victim, however, especially if he or she is a property owner. Understandably, victims will resist being moved from homes that they own, even temporarily, to halt abuse. In such situations, the best strategy may be to involve a neutral person to help a victim directly and assist him or her in accessing available community resources. These individuals can act as advocates for abuse victims, educating them about their rights and options.

WHAT SHOULD I DO IF I KNOW THAT AN ELDER IS BEING ABUSED OR IF I AM A VICTIM OF ELDER ABUSE?

If you suspect that someone you know is a victim—or if you are a victim—of elder abuse, find someone to trust who is not involved in the abuse to talk to about the problem. Report any suspicions you have of elder abuse to the nearest authorities. If there are acute injuries needing immediate medical attention, visit your own doctor, a local clinic, or a hospital emergency department. Do not delay, because with advancing age even minor assaults can cause serious injury. Call the police or your local adult protective services agency immediately.

Adult Protective Services agencies take reports, investigate allegations, and assist elder abuse victims. All states have toll-free telephone hotlines for reporting elder abuse, which are provided at the end of this chapter. During the call you will be asked to provide the victim's name, address, and contact information, and details about why you are concerned. Note that you do not need to prove abuse to report it. You may be asked to provide contact information to reach you for follow-up questions, but you can remain anonymous if you prefer (state laws protect the confidentiality of individuals making reports). If abuse is confirmed, Adult Protective Services will work closely with other community organizations to ensure that the victim is safe and healthy.

If you are a resident of or concerned about a resident in a nursing home, long-term care facility, or assisted-living facility, you can contact your local Adult Protective Services agency and seek out your local long-term care ombudsman. For complaints of abuse occurring in long-term care institutions and nursing homes, reporting and investigation will be conducted by your state's long-term care ombudsperson. Each state has an ombudsperson responsible for stopping institutional elder abuse (these are listed at the end of this chapter or you can call the toll-free number for the Eldercare Locator provided). Some ombudsmen also will address abuse involving home care services. Many states have mandatory reporting laws for certain professionals, such as physicians and other health professionals. In instances of institutional abuse, the state health department or unit on aging also can be contacted.

Four kinds of services are available to elder abuse victims and abusers: treatment, protection, prevention, and support. These services will vary considerably from one area of the country to another. Physicians and health professionals are integrally involved in the treatment of elder abuse victims. Most major health care organizations will have a program to diagnose and treat elder abuse. Try to obtain counseling for the abuser. A therapist will provide follow-up on the victim, as well as counseling, and help ensure that the abuse stops. After being made public, and with therapy, elder abuse may stop.

If the abuse is a serious physical threat, the most important thing for you to do is to remove yourself or the victim immediately from the abusive setting. If necessary, get assistance in relocating. If you are unable to leave by yourself and fear being victimized, contact your local social services agency, health department, or hospital emergency department and inquire about services for the abused elderly. Many communities have area agencies on aging that can help with managing elder abuse. Adult Protective Services and the county department of social services may be designated to receive and investigate allegations of elder abuse and neglect.

Do not hide the fact that you are in an abusive situation. Let people know that you are at risk for physical injury or exploitation. It may be possible to assist you in relocating to another caregiving situation. If not, programs for adult day care and other community-based support for families and victims of elder abuse can be used to help reduce the stress within your family and your personal risk of abuse. Alternative care programs, training for caregivers, and respite and day-care services are available. It may be possible for you and your caregiver to participate in a support program that teaches both of you how to defuse difficult situations and reduce stress and the conflicts that contribute to abuse. Conjoint therapy, family counseling, or support groups may be helpful in cases of elder abuse inflicted by a spouse.

In any case, do not tolerate ongoing abuse. It will almost certainly not improve by itself, and if by chance it does, that may occur only long after you have been seriously injured. If abuse is violent and you fear injury, do not hesitate to contact the police by using the 911 emergency telephone number. Social service agencies and area agencies on aging in your community can provide transportation, meals, home health and nursing services, and homemaking assistance. Contact them by looking in the Yellow Pages of your telephone directory under "Senior Citizens." Other agencies may become involved in a case of elderly abuse, including the police, the prosecutor's office, and the courts.

Once reported, an investigation will ensue in which you and your family, neighbors, and friends may be interviewed. This investigation will determine whether you should remain in or be removed from the home. If you do not want to be placed in a residential or nursing home, be clear in expressing this. Support services will be made available, as well as measures to ensure that the abuse does not recur.

In cases of physical or sexual abuse, a physician will determine the type of abuse, assess its frequency and severity, and determine the danger to the victim. Other health and social service professionals, such as a social worker, visiting nurse, or geriatrician, may become involved in caring for the victim. The doctor will document any injuries, possibly taking photographs, x-rays, and laboratory specimens. He or she will assess the mental, emotional, and cognitive state of the victim and report the information to the appropriate authorities.

If the victim is competent (and can make decisions), the service team will provide information to the victim and outline available options, such as temporary relocation, home support, and services obtainable from local community agencies. Law enforcement and the prosecuting attorney may become involved if criminal charges are appropriate. If the victim is not competent to make decisions, it may be necessary to separate the victim and the perpetrator, perhaps by victim relocation. Advocacy services will be arranged for the victim, and possibly the victim may be placed under guardianship. Support services available include legal advocacy services, financial planning for the elderly, and foster care and group homes for elder abuse victims. Psychotherapy services, addiction counseling, and training in coping skills can be provided for both victims and abusers.

WHAT CAN I DO IF I AM ABUSING AN ELDERLY PERSON?

First, recognize that such behavior cannot be justified or rationalized. You may have become abusive as a result of stress. Perhaps you are frustrated with the difficulties involved in your caregiving role. You certainly have needs, and you are entitled to seek support for them. But, whatever stresses you face or however difficult it is to care for the older person in your environment, abuse is entirely unacceptable. You can seriously—perhaps fatally—injure the person in your care.

Although it is not easy to help yourself in a situation like this, you can learn to recognize the triggers that cause you to become angry, resentful, and abusive, and once learned, try to discipline yourself to physically leave whenever these triggers occur. As in most cases like yours, it will probably be necessary for you to seek outside help. Respite and alternative care are options to help ease your caregiving burden. Adult day care can dramatically change your situation and reduce the frustrations that you encounter as a caregiver. It is sometimes possible to modify work schedules to reduce conflicts between employment and caretaker obligations. Recognize the link of abuse to addiction problems. Alcohol or substance abuse places you at a high risk of being abusive. Reach out to support groups to manage your problem.

As described earlier, many services for both the abused elder victim and the abuser are available in your community. Your yellow and white pages directory will contain information about referral services for acquiring assistance in the home and services such as adult day care to relieve yourself and your family of some of the stress involved with taking care of an elderly person. Reducing your burden of stress will improve your coping abilities and decrease the impulse to be abusive. If you are reading this book, you have recognized that a potentially serious problem exists in your household. If this is so, do not hesitate to use these services and the referral contacts on the following pages.

WHERE CAN I GET MORE INFORMATION AND HELP?

For information about violence against the elderly and help for elder abuse, contact your local health department, local medical centers and hospitals, and other social service providers. These agencies can refer you to an organization that provides specific services for your needs. The white and Yellow Pages of the telephone directory for your community will include the numbers of local government and community organizations that provide assistance to the elderly and to elderly caregivers. For information on shelters or services in your community, look in the yellow pages under "Human Services Organizations" or "Social Service Organizations."

In addition, and particularly if you feel that you are at risk of imminent injury, contact your local police department or 911. You may also call the Eldercare Locator at (800) 677-1116.

Appendix 1 at the back of the book provides a state-by-state website listing of compensation and assistance programs for victims of violence and crime. You may find assistance by contacting one of your state programs. Appendix 2 is a bibliography for further reading on each of the violence topics discussed in this volume, organized chapter by chapter.

The following is a list of national organizations involved with preventing or treating elder abuse and violence, and a state-by-state listing of organizations for reporting home and community or institutional elder abuse. The final section provides websites that offer information and services to victims, families, and professionals about domestic and intimate violence.

NATIONAL ORGANIZATIONS

American Association for Retired Persons
(800) 687-2277; TYY (877) 434-7598

American Bar Association Commission on Law and Aging
(202) 662-8690

Center for Advocacy for the Rights and Interests of the Elderly (CARIE)
(800) 356-3606

Clearinghouse on Abuse and Neglect of the Elderly
(302) 831-3525

National Adult Day Services Association
(877) 745-1440

National Adult Protective Services Association
(217) 523-4431

National Association of State Units on Aging
(202) 898-2578

National Center on Elder Abuse
(302) 831-3525

National Center for Victims of Crime
(202) 467-8700

National Center for Victims of Crime, National Crime Victim Helpline
(800) FYI-CALL (394-2255); TYY (800) 211-7996

National Committee for the Prevention of Elder Abuse
(202) 682-4140

National Crime Prevention Council
(202) 466-6272

National Domestic Violence Hotline
(800) 799-7233; TYY (800) 787-3224

National Institute of Justice
National Criminal Justice Reference Service
(800) 851-3420

National Organization for Victim Assistance (NOVA)
(800) 879-6682

National Victims Resource Center (NVRC)
Department of Justice, Office for Victims of Crime
(202) 307-5950

ADULT PROTECTIVE SERVICES AGENCIES, ELDER ABUSE CRISIS CENTERS, AND HOTLINES

State	Report Elder Abuse That Is Domestic or in the Community	Report Elder Abuse in a Nursing Home or Long-Term Care Facility
Alabama	(800) 458-7214	(800) 458-7214
Alaska	(800) 478-9996 Outside of Alaska: (907) 269-3666	(800) 730-6393 Outside of Alaska: (907) 334-4483
Arizona	(877) 767-2385 TDD: (877) 815-8390	(877) 767-2385 TDD: (877) 815-8390
Arkansas	(800) 332-4443 (toll-free in Arkansas) Outside of Arkansas: (800) 482-8049	(800) 582-4887
California	(888) 436-3600 (toll-free in California)	(800) 231-4024
Colorado	(800) 773-1366	(800) 773-1366 or (800) 886-7689, Ext. 2800 (303) 692-2800
Connecticut	(888) 385-4225 or (860) 424-5241 After hours/emergency: 2-1-1 (in-state only)	(860) 424-5241
Delaware	(800) 223-9074	(800) 223-9074
District of Columbia	(202) 541-3950	(202) 434-2140

Florida	(800) 96-ABUSE or	(800) 96ABUSE or
	(800) 962-2873	(800) 962-2873
	TDD/TTY: (800) 453-5145	
Georgia	(888) 774-0152	(800) 878-6442
	(404) 657-5250	(404) 657-5728 (Metro-Atlanta)
	(Metro-Atlanta)	
Guam	(671) 475-0268	(671) 475-0268
	After hours: (671) 646-4455	After hours: (671) 646-4455
Hawaii	(808) 832-5115 (Oahu)	(808) 832-5115 (Oahu)
	(808) 243-5151 (Maui,	(808) 243-5151 (Maui,
	Molokai, and Lanai)	Molokai, and Lanai)
	(808) 241-3432 (Kauai)	(808) 241-3432 (Kauai)
	(808) 933-8820 (East Hawaii)	(808) 933-8820 (East Hawaii)
	(808) 327-6280 (West Hawaii)	(808) 327-6280 (West Hawaii)
Idaho	(877) 471-2777	(877) 471-2777
Illinois	(800) 252-8966 (toll-free in	(800) 252-4343 (toll-free in
	Illinois; voice and TTY)	Illinois)
	Outside of Illinois:	TTY: (800) 547-0466
	(217) 524-6911 or	Outside of Illinois:
	(800) 677-1116 (Eldercare	(217) 785-0321
	Locator)	
	After-hours hotline:	
	(800) 279-0400	
Indiana	(800) 992-6978 (toll-free in	(800) 992-6978 (toll-free in
	Indiana)	Indiana)
	Outside of Indiana:	Outside of Indiana:
	(800) 545-7763, Ext. 20135	(800) 545-7763, Ext. 20135
Iowa	(800) 362-2178	(877) 686-0027

Kansas	(800) 922-5330 (toll-free in Kansas) Outside of Kansas: (785) 296-0044	(800) 842-0078 (877) 662-8362 (toll-free in Kansas) Outside of Kansas: (785) 296-3017
Kentucky	Elder Abuse Hotline: (800) 752-6200 Spouse Abuse Hotline: (800) 544-2022	Elder Abuse Hotline: (800) 752-6200 Long-term Care Ombudsman: (800) 372-2991 TTY (for hearing impaired): (800) 627-4702 Attorney General's Patient Abuse Tip Line: (877) ABUSE TIP (228-7384)
Louisiana	(800) 259-4990 (toll-free in Louisiana) Outside of Louisiana: (225) 342-9722	(800) 259-4990 (toll-free in Louisiana) Outside of Louisiana: (225) 342-9722
Maine	(800) 624-8404 (toll-free in Maine) Outside of Maine: (207) 532-5047 or (207) 287-6083 (after hours) TTY: (800) 624-8404 TTY after hours (in-state): (800) 963-9490 TTY after hours (out-of-state): (207) 287-3492	(800) 383-2441 (toll-free in Maine) Local/out-of-state TTY: (207) 287-9312
Maryland	(800) 917-7383 (toll-free in Maryland) Outside of Maryland: (800) 677-1116 (Eldercare Locator)	(800) 917-7383 (toll-free in Maryland) (800) AGE-DIAL, Ext. 1091 (toll-free in Maryland) Outside of Maryland: (410) 767-1091

Massachusetts	(800) 922-2275 (toll-free in Massachusetts, voice/TTY) Outside of Massachusetts: (800) AGE-INFO (800) 243-4636 TDD/TTY: (800) 872-0166	(800) 462-5540 (800) AGE-INFO (800) 243-4636 Massachusetts Attorney General's Elder Hotline: (888) AG-ELDER (888) 243-5337 TTY: (617) 727-0434
Michigan	(800) 996-6228	(800) 882-6006
Minnesota	(800) 333-2433 TDD/TYY: (800) 627-3529	(800) 333-2433 TDD/TYY: (800) 627-3529
Mississippi	(800) 222-8000 (toll-free in Mississippi) Outside of Mississippi: (601) 359-4991	(800) 227-7308 (800) 222-8000 (toll-free in Mississippi) Outside of Mississippi: (601) 359-4991
Missouri	(800) 392-0210	(800) 392-0210
Montana	(800) 551-3191 (toll-free in Montana) Outside of Montana: (406) 444-4077	(800) 551-3191 (toll-free in Montana) Outside of Montana: (406) 444-4077
Nebraska	(800) 652-1999 (toll-free in Nebraska) Outside of Nebraska: (402) 595-1324	(800) 652-1999 (toll-free in Nebraska) Outside of Nebraska: (402) 595-1324
Nevada	(800) 992-5757	(800) 992-5757
New Hampshire	(800) 351-1888 or (603) 271-4680	(800) 442-5640 or (603) 271-4375

New Jersey	(800) 792-8820 (toll-free in New Jersey) Outside of New Jersey: (609) 943-3473	(800) 792-8820 (toll-free in New Jersey) Outside of New Jersey: (609) 943-3473
New Mexico	(800) 797-3260 or (505) 841-6100 (in Albuquerque)	(800) 797-3260 or (505) 841-6100 (in Albuquerque)
New York	(800) 342-3009 (toll-free in New York) press option 6	Nursing home complaints: (888) 201-4563 Adult care home complaints: (866) 893-6772
North Carolina	(800) 662-7030	(800) 662-7030
North Dakota	(800) 451-8693	(800) 451-8693
Ohio	(866) 635-3748 (toll-free in Ohio) Outside of Ohio: (800) 677-1116	(800) 342-0533 TDD: (614) 752-6490
Oklahoma	(800) 522-3511	(800) 522-3511
Oregon	(800) 232-3020 TTY/voice: (503) 945-5811	(800) 522-2602 or (503) 378-6533
Pennsylvania	(800) 490-8505	(800) 254-5164
Puerto Rico	(787) 725-9788 or (787) 721-8225	
Rhode Island	(401) 462-0550	(401) 785-3340
South Carolina	(803) 898-7318	(803) 898-2850
South Dakota	(605) 773-3656	(605) 773-3656

Tennessee	(888) APS-TENN (277-8366)	(888) APS-TENN (277-8366)
Texas	(800) 252-5400 (toll-free in Texas) Outside of Texas: (512) 834-3784	(800) 458-9858 (toll-free in Texas) Outside of Texas: (512) 834-3784
Utah	(800) 371-7897 (toll-free in Utah) Outside of Utah: (801) 264-7669	(800) 371-7897 (toll-free in Utah) Outside of Utah: (801) 264-7669
Vermont	(800) 564-1612 or (802) 241-2345	(800) 564-1612 or (800) 241-2345
Virginia	(888) 83-ADULT or (888) 832-3858 Richmond Area: (804) 371-0896	(888) 83-ADULT (3858) Richmond Area: (804) 371-0896
Washington	(866) EndHarm or (866) 363-4276	(800) 562-6078
West Virginia	(800) 352-6513	(800) 352-6513
Wisconsin	(608) 266-2536	(800) 815-0015 (toll-free in Wisconsin) Outside of Wisconsin: (608) 246-7013
Wyoming	(800) 457-3659 (toll-free in Wyoming) Outside of Wyoming: (307) 777-6137	(307) 777-6137 or (307) 777-7123

USEFUL INTERNET WEBSITES

American Bar Association Commission on Law and Aging: www.abanet.org./aging
Association for the Advancement of Retired Persons: www.aarp.org

Center for Advocacy for the Rights and Interests of the Elderly (CARIE):
   www.carie.org

Centers for Disease Control and Prevention: www.cdc.gov

Eldercare Locator: www.eldercare.gov

Family Violence Prevention Fund: www.fvpf.org

MEDLINEplus: www.nlm.nih.gov/medlineplus/domesticviolence.html

National Adult Day Services Association: www.nadsa.org/default.asp

National Adult Protective Services Association: www.apsnetwork.org

National Center for Victims of Crime: www.ncvc.org

National Center on Elder Abuse: www.ncea.aoa.gov

National Crime Prevention Council: www.ncpc.org

National Organization for Victim Assistance (NOVA): www.trynova.org

National Victim Assistance Academy: www.ojp.usdoj.gov/ovc/assist/vaa.htm

Office for Victims of Crime: www.ovc.gov

U.S. Administration on Aging: www.aoa.gov

CHAPTER 9

Murder and Homicide — Ever More Random

- What is homicide?
- What is murder?
- What is serial murder?
- What is manslaughter?
- How common is murder?
- Who is most likely to commit murder?
- Who is most likely to be a murder victim?
- In what situations is murder most likely to occur?
- How are murders committed?
- How much murder occurs in families?
- Who commits murder in families and who is killed?
- How can homicide be prevented?
- Where can I get more information and help?

WHAT IS HOMICIDE?

"Homicide" is the killing of one human being by another through an act or omission (a failure to act). Homicide occurs when a person knowingly, purposefully, recklessly, or negligently causes the death of another human being. The term "homicide" is itself neutral. "Homicide" simply describes the act; its use offers no judgment on the moral or legal nature of that act. Criminal homicide is murder, manslaughter, or negligent homicide.

Homicide is not necessarily a crime. It occurs in the crimes of murder and manslaughter, but there are instances in which homicide may be committed without criminal intent and without criminal consequences. For example, homicide may be the lawful execution of a judicial sentence, may occur in self-defense, or may be the only possible way to arrest an escaping felon.

Homicide is usually classified as justifiable, excusable, or felonious. Felonious homicide is the wrongful killing of a human being without justification. Certain willful killings are reported as justifiable. Justifiable homicide is defined as the killing of a felon by a peace officer in the line of duty or by a private citizen in self-defense or during the commission of a felony. There are two types of intentional homicide: murder and manslaughter.

WHAT IS MURDER?

"Murder" is the unlawful killing of a human being with "malice aforethought," or premeditation. "Premeditation" denotes that the homicide was planned with purpose. Criminal homicide is murder when the act is committed purposely, knowingly, or recklessly with indifference to the value of human life. Evidence of recklessness and indifference includes a homicide that occurs during the planning, commission, or flight after committing or attempting to commit a robbery, rape, arson, burglary, or kidnapping. This is felony murder.

Murder is the most serious of all acts of violence and all crimes. Many Americans believe that murder occurs more frequently today, and in a more vicious and senseless manner, than ever before in U.S. history. In fact, although murder rates today in the United States are high, they are not unprecedented, and indeed, rates of murder have declined over recent decades.

In most states, murder is divided into two categories for the purpose of imposing different penalties for different kinds of murder. Murder in the first degree is a homicide that is willful, deliberate, and premeditated. All other types of murder are murder in the second degree.

WHAT IS SERIAL MURDER?

"Serial murder" is a series or succession of murders where the victims are selected to be killed either on a random basis or because they share some characteristic. This characteristic can vary according to the inclination and psychopathology of the murderer.

WHAT IS MANSLAUGHTER?

"Manslaughter" is the unjustifiable, inexcusable, and intentional killing of a human being without any deliberation, premeditation, or malice aforethought.

Manslaughter is classified as voluntary or involuntary. A killing that would otherwise be murder, except that it was committed in response to adequate provocation, is voluntary manslaughter. The provocation is determined to be of a kind that would cause an ordinary and reasonable person to lose control and to act rashly and without reflection. The provocation also must have caused the person to kill the victim without there having passed enough time for the passions of a reasonable person to have cooled.

Criminal homicide is manslaughter when it is committed recklessly or under the influence of an extreme mental or emotional disturbance or stress for which there is a reasonable explanation or excuse. Voluntary manslaughter is a killing that occurs in the sudden heat of passion—for example, in a sudden quarrel—when two persons are fighting and one kills the other. It is the unlawful taking of another human life without malice, and in circumstances in which there is no premeditation or deliberate intention to kill.

Involuntary manslaughter is unintentional and occurs when a person kills another during the commission of an unlawful act that is not a felony or intended to harm another. It also occurs when a person is involved in a lawful act without appropriate caution or skill, acts negligently, and unexpectedly kills another. The distinguishing feature between voluntary and involuntary homicide is that the latter is characterized by the absence of intent to kill or commit an unlawful act that causes the death of another.

HOW COMMON IS MURDER?

In 2008 there were 16,272 murders in the United States. The murder rate in 2008 was 5.4 per 100,000 inhabitants. Although still disturbingly high, this represents a decline in homicide rates to levels last seen in the late 1960s. The murder rate in the United States increased from 5.1 murders per 100,000 residents in 1965 to 9.4 in 1973. The rate was fairly stable during the following years, usually ranging from 8 to 10 murders per 100,000 Americans. It peaked at 10.2 per 100,000 in 1980. The total number of murders in 1993 was 31% above that for 1984. By 1999, the rate of homicides nationally decreased to 6 per 100,000 inhabitants, a 3-decade low.

The dramatic decrease in the rate of murder is not broadly perceived by the public, whose fear remains high. This is perhaps partly explained by the fact that while the number of homicides decreased by one-third between 1990 and 1998, media coverage of homicides increased by 400% during the same period. From 1992 to 2000, the murder rate declined sharply. For the 5-year period between 2003 and 2007, the number of murder victims per year in the United States hovered between a low of 14,210 and a peak of 15,087, levels well below those experienced in the early 1970s.

Murder across the country has become more of a random event, with less murder occurring between individuals who are related or acquainted with each other and more murders occurring between strangers. As a result, the Federal Bureau of Investigation (FBI) states that "every American now has a realistic chance of murder victimization in view of the random nature the crime has assumed." The majority of Americans who are the victims of murder today are killed by strangers. This has created a profound sense of fear among the public. It seems today that the circumstances of murder in America are ever more irrational. Furthermore, as the number of homicides has fallen dramatically, so has the rate at which murders are solved—from 86% in 1968 to just 69% in 1998.

In past decades, murder usually occurred as a result of well-defined and predictable circumstances, for example, in the commission of felonies and in acts of passion or arguments among family members and acquaintances. In recent years, both murderers and their victims have been younger than ever before, greatly heightening public concern. Young people under age 24 years were largely responsible for the 16% increase in the total number of homicides occurring in America between 1975 and 1992. Between 1985 and 1992 there was a 25% increase in murders, and young people contributed to most of the increase.

During these years, the number of people who were murdered at age 50 years or older decreased by one-third. This is contrary to what was expected, because the elderly are the fastest growing segment of the American population, and it was thought that the number of murders occurring among the aged would increase accordingly. A study by the Centers for Disease Control and Prevention compared the homicide rate for children under age 15 years in the United States with the rates in several other industrialized nations. The number of homicides per 100,000 children in the United States was 5 times the number in the other nations combined (2.57 vs. 0.51). The rate of child homicides involving a firearm was 16 times greater in the United States than in the other countries combined (0.94 vs. 0.06). Homicides involving adult or juvenile gang violence increased approximately eight-fold from 1976 to 2005.

WHO IS MOST LIKELY TO COMMIT MURDER?

In the past 25 years, the relationship of a murderer to his or her victim has changed markedly. In the past, the majority of murders were committed by individuals who had a relationship or were acquainted with the victim. In 1965, for example, 5% of murder circumstances were unknown. By 1992, 28% were unknown. Murders by strangers and those with unknown relationship to the victim comprised 53% of all murders in the United States in 1992. In 1999, the relationship between the victim and the perpetrator was unknown in 30%. It is believed that increased trade in illegal narcotics may have driven the rise in the number of unknown murder circumstances and murderers who are strangers to the victim. In 2003, 33.6% of murder circumstances were unknown, and in 2005 the figure was 37.6%. In 2007, the circumstances of murder were unknown in 36.9% of the nation's murders. Of those known in 2007, 23.1% of the victims were murdered during the commission of felonies, mostly robbery- and narcotics-related, and 42.1% were killed during various arguments, including over money or property and romantic triangles. Another 9.5% were juvenile gang killings.

Seventy-seven percent of murderers in 1993 were aged 18–34 years according to the FBI. The average age of homicide offenders decreased from 33 years in 1965 to 27 years in 1999. These figures illustrate the increase in the number of young murderers in America. In 2008, 94.4% of victims were killed by adults aged 18 years or older.

In 2005, males were 10 times more likely to commit murder. From 1976 to 2007, most victims and perpetrators of homicide were male. In 2007, for murders where the offender's gender was known, 90.1% in 2007 were male, and 90% of murdered males and 91.1% of female victims were killed by male offenders. Where the relationship of the victim to the offender was known, 22.2% of victims in 2007 were killed by family members, 24.1% were murdered by strangers, and 53.7% were slain by acquaintances such as a neighbor, friend, or boyfriend. Among female victims, who are particularly at risk for intimate killings and sex-related homicides, 32.9% were murdered by their husbands or boyfriends in 2007. Male victims are more likely than females to be killed by acquaintances or friends.

Fifty-one percent of murderers in 1999 were Black, 46% were White, and the rest were individuals of other races. For the 20 years before 1999, Blacks were disproportionately represented among both homicide victims and offenders. The number of Whites arrested for murder increased by two-thirds between 1970 and 1992. This increase accounted for most of the increase in the total number of arrests for murder in the United States over this period. A large percentage of these White perpetrators who were arrested for murder were juveniles. By 1998, Blacks were seven times more likely than Whites to commit murder. Most murders are intraracial. From 1976 to 1999, 86% of White victims were killed by Whites and 94% of Black victims were killed by Blacks. In 2005, offending rates for Blacks were more than seven times those of Whites. In 2007, where race was known, 53.9% of murder offenders were Black, 44% were White, and 2% were other races. Between 1976 and 2005, Blacks were overrepresented in homicides involving drugs and were less often victims of sex-related and workplace homicides.

Homicide victimization rates for teenagers and young adults increased dramatically in the late 1980s, whereas rates for older groups declined. The rates at which homicide was committed followed a similar pattern, increasing markedly for teenagers and young adults in the late 1980s, as the number of older homicide offenders declined. Children killing children made up a relatively constant proportion of child murders between 1976 and 1994, accounting for approximately one-fifth of children who were murdered. Children under age 18 years were responsible for approximately 30% of murders of children in 1994. Between 1976 and 1999, juveniles were especially implicated as offenders in homicides involving multiple perpetrators and in the commission of felonies. In 2007, 126 (29.9%) of the 422 murders among children under age 18 years were committed by other children under 18 years.

WHO IS MOST LIKELY TO BE A MURDER VICTIM?

Murder cuts across all social, economic, age, and racial lines. Between 1976 and 2005, approximately one-third of murder victims and one-half of the offenders were under the age of 25 years. For both victims and offenders, the rate per 100,000 peaks in the age group 18–24 years. In 2007, 50.1% of victims were Black, 47.6% were White, and the remaining victims were of other races. In 2008, 88.7% of victims were 18 years or older.

Since the 1980s, a profound change has occurred in who is likely to be a victim of murder in the United States. Although three-fourths of all murder victims are killed after age 24 years, there has been a dramatic increase in younger victims, particularly in the number of murdered infants under 1 year old and children 10–14 years old. There have been relatively few victims in either of these age groups, but their numbers increased by 46% and 64%, respectively, between 1975 and 1992. Young persons aged 15–24 years are increasingly affected by murder. During the period 1975–1992, the number of murders of these young people increased by approximately 50% and was largely responsible for the 16% increase in U.S. murders between 1975 and 1992. From 1976 to 1999, the average age of homicide victims decreased from 35 to 31 years and has now leveled off. The number of homicides of children under age five years increased over the past two decades but declined recently. Young victims of homicide are more likely than older victims to know the offender.

From 1976 to 2000, the number and rate of homicides for persons age 65 years or older steadily declined and then stabilized through 2005. Approximately 5% of all homicides were of persons age 65 years or older. Older males were more likely than females of the same age to be homicide victims. Older homicide victims were more likely than younger victims to have been killed during a felony.

Women have only one-third the murder risk of men. From 1976 to 1999, 77% of murder victims and 90% of offenders were male. The victimization rate for males was three times that of females; the offending rate for males was eight times the female rate. In 2007, for murder victims for whom gender was known, 78.5% were male. From 1976 to 2005, both offender and victim were male in 65% of incidents, with a male offender and female victim in 23% of incidents, and a female offender and male victim in 9% of incidents. In 2005, males were four times more likely than females to be murdered.

Murder rates among minorities are higher than those for Whites at all ages, but this difference disappears as one moves from low- to high-income neighborhoods. From 1976 to 2005, Blacks were disproportionately represented as both homicide victims and offenders. The Black victimization rate in 2005 was six times higher than that of Whites. An intraracial trend in murder in the United States has been relatively constant for the past several decades. In 2007, 91.9% of Black victims were murdered by Black offenders, and 82.5% of White victims were killed by White offenders. Homicide remains the leading cause of death for young Black men.

IN WHAT SITUATIONS IS MURDER MOST LIKELY TO OCCUR?

We have noted the great change in the situations or circumstances in which murder occurs in the United States. Murder has become a more random event between individuals who are unknown to each other. The number of homicides in which the circumstances are unknown almost doubled from 1976 to 1999. In 2007, the circumstances of murder were unknown in 36.9% of the nation's murders. However, between 1976 and 2005, most homicides where the relationship between victim and offender was known involved people who knew each other. Only in 14% were they strangers. Of the known circumstances of murder in 2007, 23.1% of the victims were murdered during the commission of felonies, mostly robbery- and narcotics-related, and 42.1% were killed during various arguments (i.e., over money, property, or romantic triangles).

The most common situation for murder involves a single offender killing a single victim. Over the past 25 years, the number of murder victims killed as a result of romantic triangles and lovers' quarrels has decreased. Few homicides involve multiple offenders or multiple victims. In 2005, 20.3% of homicides involved multiple offenders and 4.4% involved multiple victims. Homicides committed by younger offenders are more likely to involve multiple offenders. In 2008, 48.9% of murders involved a single offender and a single victim, 11.7% involved a single victim and multiple offenders, and 5.2% involved a single offender and multiple victims (28.9% had unknown offender offenders). In 84.9%

of murders, both the victim and the offender were age 18 years or more (when both ages were known).

Over recent years, approximately 5% of murders have been associated with either juvenile gang or gangland killings, and 3% have been committed during fights in which offenders were under the influence of alcohol or drugs. Juvenile gang killings involve a perpetrator who is known to be associated with a juvenile gang. The murderer could be either an adult or an adolescent. From 1976 to 2005, the number of homicides involving adult or juvenile gang violence increased eight-fold. In 2007, 9.5% of murders were juvenile gang killings. Young murder victims are more likely than older victims to know the offender.

Juveniles were involved as victims of homicide more commonly in gang-related killings, family and sex-related homicides, and homicide by arson or poison. Older victims were involved more typically in felony-murder, workplace murder, and arson homicides. Where the relationship of the victim to the offender was known in 2007, 22.2% of victims were killed by family members, 24.1% were slain by strangers, and 53.7% were murdered by an acquaintance (e.g., neighbor, friend, boyfriend).

Among female victims in 2007, where the relationship was known, 32.9% were murdered by their husbands or boyfriends. Between 1976 and 2005, approximately 11% of murder victims were killed by an intimate, 54% were killed by a non-intimate, and the victim-offender relationship was undetermined in 35% (intimates are defined to include spouses, ex-spouses, boyfriends, and girlfriends). The number of men murdered by intimates declined 75% between 1976 and 2005. The number of women killed by intimates was stable for approximately two decades and after 1993 declined to its lowest level in 2004. Approximately one-third of female murder victims and 3% of male murder victims were killed by an intimate between 1976 and 2005. The proportion is increasing for female murder victims and decreasing for male murder victims.

Slightly more than half of workplace homicides are committed by a stranger, and 39% are committed by an acquaintance. Homicide is the fourth leading cause of fatal occupational injury. In 2006, 516 workplace homicides occurred in the United States, accounting for 9% of all workplace fatalities that year. Of these, 417 involved a firearm. Eighty percent of workplace homicides are committed by criminals unconnected to the workplace. The majority of victims of workplace violence are men, with the exception of rape or sexual assault, in which case women are victims 80% of the time. Homicide accounts for 40% of all workplace deaths among female workers.

Law enforcement reported 645 justifiable homicides in 2007. Of these, law enforcement officers justifiably killed 391 individuals and private citizens justifiably killed 254 individuals.

In terms of geographic location, although the United States has more than 3,000 counties, more than half of all murders each year are committed in only 75. These 75 counties are largely urban and the most populous ones in the country. In 1998 and 1999, homicide victimization rates of cities with a population of one million or more plummeted to the lowest level in two decades. Cities of one-quarter to a half-million had homicide rates equivalent to the largest cities. Small cities, suburbs, and rural areas had little change in homicide prevalence. In 2006 and 2007, there was a 2.2% decrease in murder in U.S. cities, most notably in those with more than 1 million people (a 9.7% decrease) and those with 250,000–499,999 people (a 4.3% decrease). Suburban areas also decreased by 0.3%. Smaller cities saw increases in murder of 1.3%–3.4% for populations of 25,000–249,999.

HOW ARE MURDERS COMMITTED?

Firearms have been used in approximately 70% of U.S. murders in recent years (65% in 1999). By 2008, 71.9% of homicides involved the use of firearms (when the type of weapon was known). More than half of these are handguns (51.2%). In 2008, where the weapon was known, cutting or stabbing weapons were used in 14.4% of murders and a blunt object, such as a club or hammer, was the weapon in 4.7%. Strangulation or asphyxiation was used in 1.3% of homicides. Hands, fists, feet, poison, narcotics, explosives, fire, drowning, and other uncommon weapons were used to kill the remaining 7.7% of victims.

Fifty-seven percent of homicides were by firearms in 1965. Gun-involved homicide incidents increased sharply in the late 1980s. Between 1985 and 1992, there was a 10% increase in murders that were committed using guns. By 1995, 7 of every 10 murders were committed with a firearm. For the five-year period between 2003 and 2007, the mix of firearms used to commit homicide (handguns, rifles, shotguns, other guns) remained relatively constant. Homicides involving all other weapons have declined slowly or fluctuated slightly from 1976 to 2005.

Guns are the leading weapon for murder in all victim age groups except for the very old (85 years or more) and children under the age of five years, in whom so-called personal weapons (e.g., hands, fists, and feet) are the primary method of killing. One-half of all child murders in 1994 were committed with a handgun, a sharp increase from the 1980s, when one-fourth of child murders were committed with a handgun. For the period 1976–1999, the percentage of homicide victims killed with a gun increased up to age 18 years and declined thereafter. Increases over the past 30 years are thought to reflect the fact that adolescents have greater access to guns and are more willing to use them. Between 1976 and 2005, gun homicides by persons aged 18–24 years declined after a peak in 1993 but have not returned to the lower levels seen before the mid-1980s. Gun homicides by adults 25 years and older declined through 1999 but have since increased. Homicides of teens and young adults are more likely to be committed with a gun than homicides of persons of other ages.

In 2007, firearms were involved in 51.8% of homicides among victims under age 18 years and 70.2% of those ages 18 years and over. Firearm use in homicide rose rapidly starting in victims aged 5–8 years (39.8%), continued increasing through adolescence (48% among victims aged 9–12 years and 77.2% among victims aged 13–16 years), and peaked at age 17–19 years (85.2% of victims). Thereafter it slowly declined (81.7% of victims aged 20–24 years, 80% of victims aged 25–29 years, and 76% among victims aged 30–34 years). In persons aged 45–74 years, firearms were involved in 44%–57% of homicides.

Firearms are used in the killing of 42% of all family murder victims, compared with 63% of victims killed outside the family. The number of male and female intimate victims killed with guns decreased between 1976 and 2005. More than two-thirds of spouse and ex-spouse victims were killed by guns; boyfriends were more likely to be killed by knives, and girlfriends were more likely to be killed by force. Gun involvement in homicide occurring during the commission of a felony increased from 55% in 1976 to 77% in 2005.

HOW MUCH MURDER OCCURS IN FAMILIES?

A Department of Justice survey of murder cases from 1976 to 1999 found that 15% of murder victims were killed by family members. During this period, among all murder victims, 7.1% were killed by spouses and 7.8% were killed by other family members. Another study found that in murders of children under the age of 12 years, the murderer was the victim's parent in 6 of 10 instances. A family member was involved in the murder of 27% of murder victims aged 60 years or older. One in 10 murder victims aged 60 years or older were killed by their child.

In 2007, 22.2% of murder victims were killed by a family member. Among female homicide victims, where the offender relationship is known, 32.9% were murdered by their husbands or boyfriends. Chapter 2 on child abuse discusses infanticide and child homicide within the family, and Chapter 6 provides information about murder committed between spouses and intimates.

WHO COMMITS MURDER IN FAMILIES AND WHO IS KILLED?

Spouses are most likely to kill each other. From 1976 to 2005, family homicides most often involved spouses or ex-spouses. These murders perpetrated by husbands or wives comprised most of the family murders reported in the United States over recent years. Approximately one-third of female murder victims and 3% of male murder victims were killed by an intimate between 1976 and 2005. Most intimate murders involve spouses (see Chapter 6). A husband or wife was the defendant or victim in 40% of all family murders. After spousal killing, children killed by their parents are the most frequent type of family homicide. A parent killed a child in 21% of family murders, and a child killed a parent in 12% of family murders. Among all murders within families, two-thirds of assailants were male. The mother was more frequently the murderer of a child in the family (55%). When a child killed a parent, sons were the assailant in 82% of cases. In spouse killings, husbands killed wives more frequently than wives killed husbands; 60% of spouse murderers were husbands.

Forty-five percent of victims of murder in families were female, compared with 18% of murder victims outside of families. In one-third of family murders, a female was the killer. When a mother murdered her own child, that child was more likely to be a son than a daughter. When fathers killed their own children, the child was equally likely to be a daughter or a son. When a son killed a parent, it was equally likely to be the mother or the father. However, when a daughter killed a parent, four-fifths of the time it was the father. Fathers are more likely than mothers to be killed by their children. Brothers are more likely than sisters to kill a sibling.

When a child under the age of 12 years is murdered, a family member is the most likely suspect. In children under the age of five years, a parent is the perpetrator in a majority of homicides. In 1994, more than 70% of murders of infants were carried out by a family member. In a majority of such cases, the child had been abused before being killed. For all murder victims under age 12 years, child abuse preceded death 57% of the time. When the child was murdered by a parent, child abuse had occurred before the murder in four-fifths of cases. From 1976 to 1999, the rate of infanticide increased steadily and now has stabilized. The younger the child, the greater the risk for infanticide. Of all children under age 5 years who were murdered from 1976 to 1999, 31% were killed by fathers, 30% were killed by mothers, and 23% were killed by male acquaintances. During 2000, although family members were most likely to murder a young child, a friend or acquaintance was most likely to murder an older child age 15–17 years. Death as a result of child abuse is discussed in greater depth in the chapter on physical and emotional abuse of children (Chapter 2).

HOW CAN HOMICIDE BE PREVENTED?

Homicide may be among the most difficult forms of violence to prevent, whether it be premeditated or driven by the heat of passion or lack of appropriate caution. Among families, child homicides would likely decrease if overall levels of and risk factors for child abuse were reduced. Because child abuse often precedes the killing of a child by a parent, efforts to treat known child abusers and better educate new parents can prevent fatal child abuse. Murder between spouses would similarly be reduced if we could improve education and treatment to prevent domestic and intimate violence.

Better consistency in the incarceration of perpetrators of domestic violence could decrease situations in which men batter their wives to death or kill them in a premeditated manner. This would also serve to decrease homicides that result from battered women who kill their abusive partners in self-defense.

Stranger assaults in which the victim is killed can be prevented in part by implementing the recommendations for improving personal, workplace, home, and car security made in Chapter 10 on stranger violence. Ultimately, however, deeper cultural and social changes may be required to substantially reduce homicide levels, including a rejection of violence in popular culture, increased social equity and economic opportunities, and expanded teaching of violence-reduction and conflict-resolution skills among current and future generations of Americans. A better public health prevention and treatment response to the epidemic of illegal drug use, combined with improved criminal measures, could reduce homicides. In addition, better policing, enforcement, and prosecution of criminals who use violence in their illegal activities may reduce the U.S. murder rate.

WHERE CAN I GET MORE INFORMATION AND HELP?

Many of the referral and information resources provided at the conclusion of preceding chapters can offer the reader assistance in instances where severe or evolving violence that may result in homicide is a concern. To obtain help when fatal child abuse is feared, refer to the national and state listings at the end of Chapter 2 on physical and emotional abuse of children. For assistance in preventing spouse and intimate partner murder, see the resources concluding Chapter 6 on spouse abuse and domestic violence. When murder of an elder is a risk, please see the resources listed at the conclusion of Chapter 8 on elder abuse.

However, concerns about an imminent murder, or one that has already occurred, should be communicated immediately by calling your local police department or 911.

Appendix 1 at the back of the book provides a state-by-state website listing of compensation and assistance programs for victims of violence and crime. You may find assistance by contacting one of your state programs. Appendix 2 is a bibliography for further reading on each of the violence topics discussed in this volume, organized chapter by chapter.

General information about homicide may be accessed as well from the following national resources by telephone or on the internet.

NATIONAL ORGANIZATIONS

Centers for Disease Control and Prevention
National Center for Injury Prevention and Control
(800) CDC-INFO (232-4636)

ChildHelp National Child Abuse Hotline
(800) 4-A-CHILD (24453); TDD (800) 2-A-CHILD (24453)

National Center for Victims of Crime, National Crime Victim Helpline
(800) FYI-CALL; TTY (800) 211-7996

National Center on Elder Abuse
(302) 831-3525

National Clearinghouse for Defense of Battered Women
(215) 351-0010

National Coalition Against Domestic Violence
(303) 839-1852; TTY (303) 839-8459

National Crime Prevention Council
(202) 466-6272

National Domestic Violence Hotline
(800) 799-SAFE (7233); TTY (800) 787-3224

National Institute of Justice
National Criminal Justice Reference Service
(800) 851-3420

National Organization for Victim Assistance
(800) 879-6682

National Resource Center on Domestic Violence
(800) 537-2238; (800) 553-2508 TTY

USEFUL INTERNET WEBSITES

Centers for Disease Control and Prevention: www.cdc.gov
National Center for Victims of Crime: www.ncvc.org
National Center on Elder Abuse: www.ncea.aoa.gov
National Coalition Against Domestic Violence: www.ncadv.org
National Crime Prevention Council: www.ncpc.org
National Institute of Justice, National Criminal Justice Referral Service:
  www.ncjrs.gov
National Network to End Domestic Violence: www.nnedv.org
National Organization of Parents of Murdered Children, Inc.: www.pomc.com
National Organization for Victim Assistance: www.trynova.org
National Resource Center on Domestic Violence: www.nrcdv.org
National Victim Assistance Academy: www.ojp.usdoj.gov/ovc/assist/vaa.htm
Office for Victims of Crime: www.ovc.gov

CHAPTER 10

Violence and Strangers

- What is stranger violence?
- How common is stranger violence?
- Does stranger violence cause serious injury to victims?
- What do we know about the strangers who commit violence?
- Who is a victim of stranger violence?
- In what situations does stranger violence occur?
- Are weapons commonly used in stranger violence?
- What are bias and hate crimes?
- How can I prevent myself from becoming a victim of stranger violence?
- Increasing your personal security
- Recommendations for security at your workplace
- Increasing security at your home
- Recommendations for security in your car
- Where can I get more information and help?

WHAT IS STRANGER VIOLENCE?

Violence committed by strangers differs in many respects from that committed by acquaintances. The term "stranger assailant" refers to perpetrators of violence who are unknown to the victim or known to their victims only by sight. Non-stranger violence is an act perpetrated by family members, intimates, friends, and acquaintances of the victim.

In considering the information that follows, it is important to bear in mind that violence between non-strangers, and particularly family members, is generally underreported. Individuals who have been victimized by relatives often are reluctant to discuss the violence, usually because of shame, embarrassment, fear of reprisal, or the presence of the offender. Violence occurring within the family also may not be perceived as violent in the way that acts of a similar nature outside the home may be. Attacks and injuries from a family member may be viewed as less serious than equivalent acts perpetrated by a stranger. These factors tend to exaggerate the importance of stranger violence relative to the greater violence epidemic.

HOW COMMON IS STRANGER VIOLENCE?

The Department of Justice reports that approximately one-third (36%) of all reported violent crimes were committed by strangers in 2008. The percentages of overall violence, robbery, and aggravated and simple assault committed by strangers are higher for male victims than for female victims. In 2008, strangers perpetrated 44% of violent crimes against men and 27% of violent crimes against women. Both men (49%) and women (70%) were more likely to be victimized by a friend, an acquaintance, or an intimate.

In 2008, 32% of all rapes and sexual assaults were committed by strangers, and entirely against female victims. This compares with 63% of sexual assaults that were committed by intimate partners, relatives, acquaintances, and friends, and 5% where the relationship was unknown. In 2005, approximately 7 in 10 female rape or sexual assault victims stated the offender was an intimate, a relative, a friend, or an acquaintance, and 26% were assaulted by a stranger.

Robbery was the crime most likely to be committed by a stranger in 2008. Strangers committed 61% of robberies against men and 45% of robberies against women. In 2005, 74% of males and 48% of females stated that they were robbed by a stranger, so the level of stranger robbery has declined somewhat over recent years. For aggravated assaults (involving a weapon) in 2008, 43% were committed by a stranger against males and 29% were committed against females.

Homicide is less likely to be committed by a stranger, with only 14% of homicides from 1976 to 2005 perpetrated by an individual unknown to the victim (43% of homicides in 2005 were of undetermined offender–victim relationship). In 33%–39% of homicides the offender is an acquaintance, and in another 12%–18% the offender is a relative.

The Department of Justice reports that more than 1 million women and approximately 400,000 men are stalked each year in the United States. As of 2006, 8% of women and 2% of men in the United States have been stalked at some point in their lifetime. In 27.6% of these incidents the stalker was a current or prior intimate, and in 10.6% the stalker was a stranger. The emergence of electronic aggression and cyber-stalking has increased the potential for stranger stalking. More than one-fourth of stalking victims report that some form of cyber-stalking was used (see Chapter 6 for more information on stalking and cyber-stalking).

DOES STRANGER VIOLENCE CAUSE SERIOUS INJURY TO VICTIMS?

Yes. However, violent crimes committed by strangers have tended to involve less injury than those committed by acquaintances or relatives. Although approximately 50% of all victimizations involving a relative and one-third of those involving an acquaintance in recent years resulted in injury, only 27% of victimizations by strangers injured the victim. Approximately four-fifths of injuries caused by strangers were minor, including bruises, black eyes, lacerations, and scratches. Approximately 1 in 100 injuries afflicted by a stranger was caused by a gun or knife. Fourteen percent of injuries resulting from stranger violence required some medical attention, and in only 1 case of every 25 was care sought at a hospital.

WHAT DO WE KNOW ABOUT THE STRANGERS WHO COMMIT VIOLENCE?

Men are most likely to be victimized by another man when confronted violently by a stranger. According to the Department of Justice, 97% of men are victimized by another man in an episode of stranger violence. A man will be the perpetrator of stranger violence approximately 80% of the time when the victim is a woman.

Stranger violence is largely intraracial, involving a perpetrator and a victim of the same races (although it is more interracial than violence between relatives or acquaintances). A White victim is likely to be attacked by a White stranger in 70% of instances and by a Black offender in 24% of instances. A Black victim is attacked by a Black offender in 77% of instances and by a White offender in 19% of instances.

In most violent crimes, the perpetrator is in the same age group as the victim. This is true as well for stranger violence. If the victim is 12–17 years old, the stranger offender will be a similar age 50% of the time. If the victim is 18–29 years old, the perpetrator will be the same age in approximately two-thirds of instances. If the victim is 30 years and older, the offender is the same age 43% of the time.

Violence committed by strangers involves multiple assailants more often than violent acts perpetrated by relatives or acquaintances. Approximately one-third of stranger violence involves more than a single assailant: 54% of robberies, 29% of assaults, and 16% of rapes involve more than 1 assailant.

WHO IS A VICTIM OF STRANGER VIOLENCE?

For most of 1980–2000, the Department of Justice reported that the victims of violent crimes perpetrated by strangers were mostly men. Approximately 70% of the victims of stranger violence were men. Seventy-seven percent of the victims of violent crimes perpetrated by relatives were women. Approximately one-third of all female victims of violent crimes described the offender as a stranger in 2000; 54% of male victims stated that the offender was a stranger. Approximately half of the men and women who were victims of stranger violence were never married. Eighty-four percent of stranger violence was inflicted on Whites and 14% was inflicted on Blacks, a racial breakdown similar to the statistics for non-stranger violence. Stranger homicides are more likely to cross racial lines than murders involving friends or acquaintances.

Violent crime generally affects younger people under the age of 30 years. This is also true for stranger violence, where the average victim age was 28 years in a Department of Justice study. The average age of victims of stranger violence was only a few years older than the age of victims of all violent crimes (which was 25 years). More than three-fourths of all victims of stranger violence were below the age of 35 years, and only 3% were age 65 years or more. In view of the increasing number and proportion of elderly people in the United States, they remain relatively unaffected by stranger violence. This may reflect the degree of social isolation in which many elderly individuals live.

IN WHAT SITUATIONS DOES STRANGER VIOLENCE OCCUR?

Of all U.S. victims of violent crime, 21% were involved in some form of leisure activity away from home at the time of their victimization, 28% were at home, and another 19% were at work or traveling to or from work when the crime occurred.

Violent crimes by strangers are most likely to occur in cities and urban settings, followed by the suburbs. Forty-three percent of crimes by strangers occur in a city, 39% occur in a suburban area, and 18% occur in rural areas. Victimizations by relatives and acquaintances are more likely to occur in the suburbs and rural areas. Forty-four percent of stranger violence occurs during the daytime. Approximately half of all violent crimes occur during the daytime between 6:00 a.m. and 6:00 p.m. The timing of violence does not vary much on the basis of whether the offender is a stranger, an acquaintance, or a relative.

Violence perpetrated by strangers occurs most often on the street. Two-fifths of violent acts occur on the street. Approximately 4% of stranger violence occurs inside the victim's home. This figure contrasts with 18% of violent acts that are committed in the home by acquaintances and 58% by relatives. Another 16% of incidents of stranger violence occur in commercial business or retail establishments, and 11% take place in a parking lot. Among women who experience crime at work, 40% are attacked by a stranger. The workplace is the scene of approximately one million violent crimes each year. Seven percent of all rapes and 16% of all assaults occur at work. Nine percent of violent acts by strangers occur near the victim's home, and 6% are in a school or on school property.

Fifty-six percent of workplace homicides over the past decade were committed by a stranger, 39% were committed by an acquaintance, and 1% were committed by an intimate. Homicide is the fourth leading cause of fatal occupational injury. In 2006, 516 workplace homicides occurred in the United States, accounting for 9% of all workplace fatalities that year. Of these, 417 involved a firearm. Eighty percent of workplace homicides are committed by criminals otherwise not connected with the workplace. Homicide accounts for 40% of all workplace deaths among female workers.

The majority of victims of workplace violence are men, with the exception of rape or sexual assault, in which case women are victimized 80% of the time. Female workers are at an elevated risk for nonfatal workplace violence. Women were the victims in approximately two-thirds of the injuries resulting from workplace assaults. Most of these assaults (70%) were directed at women employed in service occupations such as health care, and 20% occurred in retail locations such as restaurants and grocery stores.

ARE WEAPONS COMMONLY USED IN STRANGER VIOLENCE?

Yes. In general, a weapon is more likely to be used in crimes committed by strangers than by non-strangers. However, the majority of all violent crime victims (67%) do not face an armed offender. A Department of Justice study reported that a weapon was present in 36% of victimizations by strangers. These weapons included not only guns but also knives and various sharp objects, blunt objects (such as clubs), and other weapons. Approximately 10% of workplace violence involves offenders armed with handguns.

Homicides committed by strangers are more likely to involve guns than those committed by intimates or family members. However, crimes perpetrated by strangers are less likely to involve a physical attack than those committed by acquaintances and family members. Only 44% of victimizations by strangers involved an attack. In approximately one-fourth, the victims sustained an injury, most often of a minor nature. In only 1% was a gun or knife wound sustained.

WHAT ARE BIAS AND HATE CRIMES?

Bias and hate crimes involve the targeting of a victim on the basis of membership in a particular demographic, racial, or ethnic group, and can involve both crime against property and violent victimization. Individuals most frequently victimized by hate crime include Blacks, Jews, Hispanics, and gays and lesbians. Although not all hate and bias crimes are committed between strangers, these crimes often are perpetrated by strangers unknown to the victims.

In 2005, 7,163 hate crime incidents were reported to the Federal Bureau of Investigation (FBI), of which 5,190 were crimes committed against people (as opposed to businesses). Racial bias motivated 55% and religious beliefs motivated 17% of hate or bias crimes. Sexual orientation motivated 14% and ethnicity or nationality motivated 13% of hate or bias crimes. Of crimes targeting race, 68% were victims of anti-Black bias and 20% were motivated by anti-White bias; 5% targeted Asians/Pacific Islanders and 2% targeted American Indians/Alaska Natives. Of crimes based on ethnicity, anti-Hispanic incidents comprised 59% of 1,228 reported victims. Of the 1,405 victims of religious-bias offenses, 70% were Jewish and 11% were Islamic.

In 2006, there were 1,393 hate and bias incidents against lesbian, gay, bisexual, or transgender (LGBT) victims, of which approximately two-thirds were against gay males. In 2006, there were 11 homicides of LGBT individuals, 551 assaults or attempted assaults, and 63 sexual assaults. The majority (61%) of known offenders were White, and 20% were Black.

The homeless population is particularly vulnerable to hate and bias victimization. Between 1999 and 2006, 189 homeless people were murdered in the United States by people who were not homeless. During the same period, there were 425 non-lethal attacks against homeless individuals. Victims ranged in age from 4 months to 74 years, and a majority of the perpetrators were adolescents and young adults.

Hate groups have multiplied in the United States from 602 in 2000 to 926 in 2008, as reported by the Southern Poverty Law Center, which tracks extremist groups and works to limit their activities. Recent politically and racially motivated homicides by lone attackers have been committed against a Kansas physician who performed abortions, a military recruiting office, and a U.S. Holocaust Memorial Museum security guard. These three unconnected slayings occurred within two weeks of each other in 2009. One gunman was a fervent abortion opponent, one was a militant Muslim, and one was a White supremacist. In response, the FBI has launched the "Lone Wolf Initiative" to find those individuals who might plan and attempt a lone offender attack based on identity or political views. The program will intensify scrutiny of individuals at risk of committing acts of domestic terror, analyze records for suspicious purchases at fertilizer or chemical suppliers whose materials could be used in bombmaking, and check rolls of prisoners scheduled for release or recently released for past links to extremist groups.

HOW CAN I PREVENT MYSELF FROM BECOMING A VICTIM OF STRANGER VIOLENCE?

According to the Department of Justice, approximately three of every four victims of stranger violence try to protect themselves during an attack. In approximately one-third of these efforts, the victim tries to flee or otherwise evade the assailant, and in one-fourth of instances, the victim uses physical force against the assailant. In slightly less than one-fifth of instances, the victim will try to get help or to frighten, threaten, argue, or reason with the assailant. The most common form of self-defense—evasion—involves nonviolent resistance, including locking a door, hiding, and shielding oneself. There are little data to indicate how effective any of these measures are in preventing injuries during stranger violence.

Less than half of all stranger violence is actually reported to the police. Victims often do not report because they believe the incident is not important enough or that it is a private or personal matter. Unless violence is reported to authorities, little can be done to apprehend a perpetrator of stranger violence or to better patrol an area and prevent future episodes. It is critical that if you are victimized by a stranger, a report should be made to the local police.

Following are recommendations from police departments across the country and the National Center for Victims of Crime on protecting yourself from violent crime. Try and implement as many as you can and share them with family and friends.

INCREASING YOUR PERSONAL SECURITY

- Remain alert and attentive to your environment and the people around you. If you feel uneasy about your surroundings, even without a specific sense of why, leave.
- Act in a self-assured manner. Walk with confidence on busy streets and go directly to your destination. Make it difficult for anyone to take you by surprise. Avoid poorly lighted streets at night.
- If you are walking alone and you think someone is following you, turn around and look; a hostile gaze may prevent an attack. Walk toward people, lights, and traffic. If necessary, run and scream.
- If a car appears to be following you, turn and walk in the opposite direction, or walk to the other side of the street.

- If you must leave a shopping mall or other commercial establishment late at night, ask a security guard to escort you to your car.
- Carry your purse tucked close to your body or snugly under your arm. This will not deter the determined mugger, but may stop the easy snatch-and-run ones.
- Keep a minimum of cash in your purse or wallet. Carry only a few blank checks and a single credit card. Keep photocopies of identification and credit cards to make replacement easier.
- Do not place personal identification tags on your key ring so that your lost keys can used by a criminal.
- Ask taxi drivers to wait until you are safely inside your residence before they drive away.
- Use ATM machines during daylight hours, or those located inside supermarkets, convenience stores, or shopping malls. Attacks at ATM machines typically occur between 9 p.m. and midnight. Do not use an ATM if anyone is loitering around it.
- Teach your children to use the telephone for emergencies. Practice calling with them and have them memorize emergency numbers (such as 911). Instruct them to walk with friends, to refuse lifts from strangers, and to deny strangers access to your home. Teach them to go to a neighbor's house if they see a door open or a broken window when they come home, and teach them not to tell telephone callers that they are alone. Make sure they know how to use door and window locks.

RECOMMENDATIONS FOR SECURITY AT YOUR WORKPLACE

- When working late, try to coordinate schedules with another worker, and lock your office door if alone.
- Be cautious around isolated areas, those that are poorly lighted, or those that can be accessed by the public. These are the areas where an assault is most likely to occur.
- All office staff should be alert to strangers and suspicious individuals. Check the identification of repair service and other visiting personnel.
- Keep the telephone number for building security by your desk telephone.
- Be aware of your environment when coming in early or staying late at work. Avoid entries and exits where a stranger is loitering.
- Park in a secured area if possible. Ask a security guard to escort you to your vehicle if you are working late.
- If security is a particular concern at your workplace, have your name removed from reserved parking areas.

- Control the distribution of keys. If keys given to previous employees are not retrieved, change locks.

INCREASING SECURITY AT YOUR HOME

- Call your local police department's crime prevention unit for a free home safety check. They will provide you with specific tips to increase your home's security.
- Tape emergency numbers onto all telephones.
- Be aware of suspicious individuals around your home. Call neighbors to check on strange persons, and if they are unknown and remain in the area, call the police. Intruders often "case" or assess the vulnerabilities and access to homes before burglarizing them.
- Positively identify people before opening a door. Install a peephole (a wide-angle viewer) in all outside doors.
- When away from the residence for an evening, place lights and radio on a timer; these will create the illusion that someone is home. For extended absences, halt deliveries.
- Inform trusted neighbors of vacations or business trips. Ask that they pick up mail and newspapers. Alternatively, have your local post office hold your mail.
- Do not leave notes on your door when you are gone. These tell potential intruders that it is safe to break in.
- Do not hide your keys under the mat, over the door frame, or in flower pots and other obvious places. An experienced burglar may check these. Give a spare key to a trusted neighbor instead.
- If a stranger asks to use your telephone, offer to place the call for him or her yourself. Never let a stranger into your home, whatever the circumstances.
- Dogs are inexpensive and effective alarm systems as well as good friends, and they discourage intruders.
- Do not reveal your name in recorded messages on your telephone answering machine. Identify yourself by giving the residence phone number. Use plural "we" instead of "I" in your message, and do not say "I'm not home right now." If you are a woman living alone, consider asking a male relative or acquaintance to record your message for you. Never record that you are alone or that you will not be home until a certain time.
- If you arrive home and suspect someone is inside, do not enter. Leave and call 911 to report your suspicion.
- Any written or telephone threat you receive should be reported to the police.
- Install bright outside lighting, including an entry light at a height that makes removal difficult.

- Pull shades or curtains after dark. Easy visibility of the inside of your home can attract an intruder.
- Trim high shrubbery, particularly those around doors or windows. Tall vegetation provides cover for an intruder.
- Install locks on fence gates. Although installing locks is a passive measure that is easy to overcome, they may discourage an intruder enough to make him target another home.
- Entry doors should be composed of solid wood or metal of 1 3/4 inches thickness.
- Install dead bolts (with at least a one-inch throw) on outside doors. If you cannot account for all keys, change door locks and secure all spare keys. Always lock up, even for quick trips away.
- Keep doors and windows locked. It is surprising how many robberies occur because of unlocked doors or windows. Do not make it easy for intruders, who will take advantage of any unlocked entryway, however rarely you leave one unlocked.
- Place a dowel in sliding glass doors and all sliding windows.
- If you use an electric garage door device, do not leave the automatic door opener in your car. Doing so increases your vulnerability if it is stolen. Many electric garage door openers can be switched off or disabled when you will be away from home for an extended period.
- Keep your home fuse box locked. Keep a flashlight accessible.
- Install a loud exterior alarm bell that can be manually activated in more than one location.
- In considering a home alarm system, ensure that you contract with an established company, and check references before committing yourself to a security service.
- Prepare and brief household members on an evacuation plan. Practice it occasionally.
- Think carefully before buying a gun to protect yourself and your family. Firearms can be captured and used against you or the police. If you choose to buy or already own a gun, be sure to lock it up securely and learn how to use it safely.

RECOMMENDATIONS FOR SECURITY IN YOUR CAR

- When returning to your vehicle, have your key ready. Searching for keys in pockets or a purse gives an assailant essential time to assess and approach you.

- Pay attention to other cars and pedestrians around you, particularly at traffic lights and stop signs. If a suspicious person approaches your car, lean on the horn and drive away.
- If you are followed by another car, drive to a police or fire station, a hospital emergency department entrance, or any open business or gas station. Do not drive home.
- Park your car in well-lighted areas. If a parking lot requires that keys be surrendered, give only the ignition key to the attendant, and not your home keys.
- Try to keep a third of a tank of gas in your car at all times. Running out of gas in an unknown or unpopulated area can leave you vulnerable.
- Equip your gas tank with a locking cap. Then no one can remove fuel from your car in preparation for an assault or robbery.
- Always lock your car doors, even when inside and driving. Carjacking is increasingly common and may sometimes involve violent assaults.
- If your vehicle breaks down, pull over to the right as far as possible, raise the hood, and wait inside your vehicle for help. Do not get out of the car or unroll the window until the police have arrived.

WHERE CAN I GET MORE INFORMATION AND HELP?

If you have been victimized or fear being victimized by a stranger, for example, a suspicious individual who appears to be stalking you or your home, you should immediately contact your local police department or call 911 for help.

Appendix 1 at the back of the book provides a state-by-state website listing of compensation and assistance programs for victims of violence and crime. You may find assistance by contacting one of your state programs. Appendix 2 is a bibliography for further reading on each of the violence topics discussed in this volume, organized chapter by chapter.

Additional information and assistance may be obtained from the following organizations and agencies.

NATIONAL ORGANIZATIONS

Centers for Disease Control and Prevention
National Center for Injury Prevention and Control
(800) CDC-INFO (232-4636)

National Center for Missing and Exploited Children
(800) THE-LOST (843-5678); TDD (800) 826-7653

National Center for Victims of Crime, National Crime Victim Helpline
(800) FYI-CALL (394-2255); TTY (800) 211-7996

National Council on Crime and Delinquency
(510) 208-0500

National Crime Prevention Council
(202) 466-6272

National Institute of Justice
National Criminal Justice Reference Service
(800) 851-3420

National Organization for Victim Assistance
(800) TRY-NOVA (879-6682)

Rape, Abuse, & Incest National Network (RAINN)
(800) 656-HOPE

Security on Campus
(610) 768-9330 or (888) 251-7959

USEFUL INTERNET WEBSITES

Centers for Disease Control and Prevention: www.cdc.gov
National Center for Missing and Exploited Children: www.missingkids.com
National Center for Victims of Crime: www.ncvc.org
National Crime Prevention Council: www.ncpc.org
National Organization of Parents of Murdered Children, Inc.: www.pomc.com
National Organization for Victim Assistance: www.trynova.org
National Victim Assistance Academy: www.ojp.usdoj.gov/ovc/assist/vaa.htm
Office for Victims of Crime: www.ovc.gov
Security on Campus: www.securityoncampus.org
Stalking Resource Center: www.ncvc.org/src
Stalking Victim's Sanctuary: www.stalkingvictims.com
Workplace Violence Research Institute: www.workviolence.com

CHAPTER 11

Guns — Do They Increase or Defend Against Violence?

- How common are guns in America?
- How frequently are guns associated with violent acts?
- To what extent are guns involved in unintended injuries?
- Who is most likely to be victimized by gun violence and in what situations?
- Which guns are used for violence?
- Why are there so many guns in America?
- Are there nations more armed than America but less violent?
- What is the controversy about gun control and the infringement of a constitutional right?
- Do gun control policies and laws work?
- How can I protect my family from gunshot injuries?
- How can I be a more responsible and careful gun owner?
- Where can I get more information and help?

HOW COMMON ARE GUNS IN AMERICA?

With an estimated 283 million firearms in the United States as of 2004, firearm ownership is very common. Approximately one-third of all households own at least one firearm, and there is at least one firearm for every American adult. Approximately one in four adults owns at least one firearm. Firearm ownership is becoming increasingly concentrated, with a small number of adults owning a large proportion of the nation's firearms. The 2004 National Firearms Survey found that 38% of U.S. households and 26% of individuals reported owning at least 1 firearm. This corresponds to 42 million U.S. households with firearms and 57 million adult gun owners.

Sixty-four percent of gun owners—or 16% of American adults—reported owning at least 1 handgun in 2004. Long guns are the most common guns in the United States, representing 60% of the privately held gun stock, but handgun ownership is widespread (40% of the gun stock is handguns). Approximately half (48%) of all individual gun owners reported owning four or more firearms.

Men more often reported firearm ownership, with 45% stating that they personally owned at least 1 firearm, compared with 11% for women. The most common reason given for keeping a gun is personal protection against crime, followed by recreational and hunting interests. America is the only industrialized nation that does not effectively regulate private ownership of firearms. The U.S. civilian population is the most heavily armed in world history. Law-abiding U.S. citizens bought on average 3,177,256 guns every 3 months in 2008—enough to outfit the entire Chinese and Indian armies combined. Americans also bought 1,529,635,000 rounds of ammunition in just the month of December 2008 alone.

Firearm manufacturers in the United States sell more than two million handguns annually. There are almost as many firearms in the United States as people (approximately 307 million). Researchers have estimated ownership at approximately 25 guns per 100 people in countries such as Canada, New Zealand, Germany, France, and Sweden. The United States has an estimated 93 guns per 100 people.

From 1972–2006, the percentage of American households reporting having any guns in the home dropped approximately 20 percentage points, from a high of 54% in 1977 to 34.5% in 2006. From 1980 to 2006 the percentage of individual Americans who reported personally owning a gun dropped more than 9%, from a high of 30.7% in 1985 to a low of 21.6% in 2006. Throughout much of the 1990s a new firearm was purchased every 14 seconds in the United States. By 1999, there was a gun in 43% of U.S. households and a loaded gun in 1 of 10 households with children. Remarkably, in the United States between one and three million assault weapons are in private hands, weapons that have no conceivable recreational or hunting purpose and are used primarily for mass killing.

HOW FREQUENTLY ARE GUNS ASSOCIATED WITH VIOLENT ACTS?

The epidemiological data are consistent in indicating that a higher prevalence of firearms is associated with more firearm violence, homicide, gun-related assault, and injury in the United States. The ready availability of handguns makes it easy for misguided individuals to obtain a means of inflicting an injury with near certain lethality and escalating impulsive acts of interpersonal violence or suicidal thoughts into death. Firearm injury in the United States caused an average of 32,300 deaths annually between 1980 and 2006. It is the second leading cause of death from injury, exceeded only by motor vehicle crashes. The 2006 death rate from firearm injury was 10.2 per 100,000 population, with an estimated nonfatal injury rate of 23 per 100,000.

Firearm-related deaths peaked in 1993 at 40,000 and fell below 30,000 in 1999. Yet even at these lower levels, firearm injury has an enormous public health impact, accounting for 6.6% of premature death in this country (years of potential life lost before age 65 years). In 2004 alone, 29,569 Americans died by gunfire: 16,750 in firearm suicides, 11,935 in firearm homicides, 649 in unintentional shootings, and 235 in firearm deaths of unknown intent. The fatality rate of firearm violence is more than twice the U.S. Department of Health and Human Services' national goal for the year 2010. Many diseases that attract more public attention along with prevention and research funding cause far fewer deaths than do firearms.

In 2008, there were 343,550 firearm victims in the United States (including robberies), accounting for 7% of all violent incidents and a rate of 1.4 victims per 1,000 residents. Offenders used firearms in more than two-thirds of U.S. murders, 43.5% of robberies, and 21.4% of aggravated assaults. Firearms are involved in 52% of suicides. Compared with other industrialized countries, firearm death rates in the United States are disproportionately high. Within the 50 upper- and middle-income countries where data are available, an estimated 115,000 firearm deaths occur annually. Of these, the United States contributes approximately 30,000. Among industrialized nations, the U.S. firearm-related death rate is more than twice that of the next highest country and eight times the average rate of its economic counterparts (1.76). Compared with high-income Asian countries (Taiwan, Singapore, Hong Kong, and Japan), the firearm mortality rate in the United States is 70 times higher. The correlation between firearm availability and rates of homicide is consistent across high-income industrialized nations: Where there are more firearms, there are higher rates of homicide. The United States has among the highest rates of both firearm homicide and private gun ownership.

Between 1968 and 1991, the number of gun-related deaths in the United States increased sharply by 60% and then decreased to a low in 1999, when 562,870 victims of serious violent crimes (e.g., rape and sexual assault, robbery and aggravated assault) stated that they faced an offender with a firearm. Much of this crime was attributable to gun violence by juveniles and young adults. Nonfatal firearm-related crime has plummeted since 1993 before increasing in 2005. In 1993 there were 1,248,250 victims of firearm injuries (a rate of 5.9 victims per 1,000 residents), which constituted 11% of all violent incidents.

By 2000 the number of victims of firearms had dropped to 533,470 (a rate of 2.4 victims per 1,000 residents), involving 7% of all violent incidents. The percentage of all incidents of violent crime committed with firearms fluctuated between 6% and 9% during the 10-year period 1999–2008, but in 2008 it was almost identical to what it had been a decade earlier (7%). The rate of firearm violence among persons aged 12 years or more declined from 2.5 victimizations per 1,000 in 1999 to 1.4 per 1,000 in 2008.

An offender was armed with a gun, knife, or other object used as a weapon in an estimated 20% of all incidents of violent crime in 2008. Offenders used about equal percentages of firearms, knives, and other weapons to commit violent crimes overall. Robberies (40%) were the most likely crime to involve an armed offender, and firearms (24%) were the most common weapon used in robberies. Simple and aggravated assaults were the next most common crimes to involve use of a weapon (18%), with firearms used in 5% of incidents. A weapon rarely was used to commit rape or sexual assault.

America has the highest rate of gun-related homicide in the developed world. The Federal Bureau of Investigation estimated that 66% of the 16,137 murders committed in 2004 involved firearms. From 1960 to 1980 the population of the United States increased by 26%, and the homicide rate from firearms increased 160%. Fifty-seven percent of homicides were caused by firearms in 1965. Gun-involved homicide incidents increased sharply in the late 1980s. In 1990 in the state of Texas, deaths from firearms surpassed deaths from motor vehicles to become the leading cause of death from an injury. By 1995, seven of every ten murders were committed with a firearm. Gun involvement in homicide occurring during the commission of a felony increased from 55% in 1976 to 77% in 2005. In 2008, 71.9% of homicides involved the use of firearms (when the type of weapon was known). More than half of these were handguns (51.2%).

Guns are the leading weapon used to commit murder in all victim age groups except for children under the age of five years, for whom so-called personal weapons such as hands, fists, and feet are the primary method of killing, and among the very old (85 years or more). Homicides of adolescents and young adults are more likely to be committed with a gun than homicides of persons of other ages. Compared with homes without guns, the presence of guns in the home is associated with a two- to three-fold increase in homicide risk within the home. The risk increases to eight-fold when the offender is an intimate partner or relative of the victim.

Guns bought for protection are a threat to members of the family. Studies consistently show that in families with a history of domestic violence, a gun in the home increases the risk of a domestic homicide 12- to 20-fold. People who live in homes with a handgun are approximately three times as likely to commit a domestic homicide. The number of male and female intimate victims killed with guns fell between 1976 and 2005. Yet, more than two-thirds of spouse and ex-spouse victims were killed by guns. A study of risk factors for violent death among women in the home found that women living in homes with one or more guns were more than three times more likely to be killed in their homes. Women killed by a spouse, intimate acquaintance, or close relative were seven times more likely to live in homes with one or more guns. Family and intimate assaults with firearms are 12 times more likely than non-firearm assaults to result in death.

Guns in the home are involved with not only increased levels of homicide and suicide but also unintentional shootings among gun owners. Firearms now rank close to car crashes as a leading cause of trauma deaths in America. For every discharge of a gun in self-defense, there are 43 unintentional or unjustifiable fatal shootings. For every unintended fatal shooting there are 4–6 nonfatal injuries. Guns kept at home for protection against crime are 22–43 times more likely to kill a family member, a friend, or an acquaintance than to kill an intruder in self-defense. Guns intended to protect against crime in the home rarely are used in defense because there is usually insufficient warning and time to get the weapon.

Firearm injury disproportionately affects young people. Among the leading causes of death for those aged 15–24 years, homicide ranks second and suicide ranks third, and the majority of both are firearm-related. Every several hours in the United States, a child or teenager is killed by a gun in a homicide, suicide, or unintentional shooting. More than 10% of all deaths among American children and adolescents are caused by guns. Throughout the late 1980s and early 1990s, a teenager's chance of dying from a gunshot wound almost doubled, and the number of gunshot wounds to children 16 years old and younger increased 300%. Approximately one-fourth of all people arrested for weapons offenses are under 18 years old. Among homicide victims aged 10–24 years in 2007, 82% were killed with a firearm.

Gun shootings kill more teenage boys than any natural cause and are the leading cause of death for Black adolescents. For Blacks as a group, the statistics are staggering. The Department of Justice reports that over much of the 1990s, Black males were shot at 3–4 times the rate of Whites of comparable age and at eight times the rate of the general population. The rate of handgun crime against persons 16–19 years old is approximately 3 times the national average. Gun-related homicide among adolescent boys in the United States is 35 times higher than the combined total for 15 other industrialized countries. However, since the mid-90s, violent victimizations of young people, including those involving firearms, have fallen. Gun homicides by persons 18–24 years old peaked in 1993 but declined since then through 2005.

This level of child death and injury exists partly because 1 of every 20–25 students aged 10–19 years in American schools carries a handgun to school. More teens are carrying guns than ever before. One-fifth of male students in a study of inner-city high schools owned guns, and more than half said it would be easy to get one, often within an hour. In 2005, 19% of students in grades 9–12 reported they had carried a weapon anywhere, and 6% reported carrying a weapon on school property during the prior month. In a 2007 survey, 5.2% of youth in grades 9–12 reported that they had carried a gun on 1 or more days in the prior 30 days.

In 2005, 52% of all suicides involved the use of firearms and guns were consistently responsible for 50%–60% of suicide deaths. People who live in homes with a handgun are five times as likely to commit suicide. Children who completed suicide (and died) were more than twice as likely as suicide survivors to be from a home with a gun. The chance that an adolescent will complete suicide based on an impulse is increased five-fold in homes where there is a gun (death results in 92% of suicide attempts involving a gun).

Criminals use handguns as their primary weapons, and often a gun is used in a crime to coerce the victim into meeting the demands of the offender rather than to harm the victim, per se. In most instances a gun is not fired during the crime, but if it is, the risk of serious injury and death is much greater for the victim. Two-thirds of victims who are shot sustain injuries that require hospitalization.

Firearm death rates in the United States vary by state. The five states with the highest firearm death rates are Louisiana, Alaska, Nevada, Mississippi, and Alabama. The states with the lowest rates include Hawaii, Massachusetts, Rhode Island, Connecticut, and New York. For most states, firearm suicide rates exceed those of firearm homicide.

TO WHAT EXTENT ARE GUNS INVOLVED IN UNINTENDED INJURIES?

Guns contribute greatly to the occurrence of unintended injuries. Because firearms are found in one-third of all U.S. households, they are among the most common consumer products. A gun in the home is four times more likely to be used in an unintentional shooting than to be used in self-defense. Every year, approximately 640 people die from an unintentional shooting, and 15,700 people are wounded in an unintentional shooting but survive. Approximately 40% of these individuals require hospitalization. In 2006, firearm injuries were the third leading cause of injury deaths in the United States (17%), exceeded only by motor vehicle accidents and poisoning.

For children and teenagers aged 10–19 years, accidental firearm incidents are the third leading cause of death from unintended injury. Each year approximately 50 children ages 0–14 years are killed in an unintentional shooting, and an additional 802 are treated in an emergency department for an unintentional gunshot wound. The most common scenario occurs when a child unintentionally shoots a playmate or sibling with a loaded handgun that was found in the home. Preadolescent boys are most commonly the victims and the shooters in these incidents. The children most likely to be killed in this manner are boys living in non-metropolitan areas. Approximately 90% of children who are injured or killed in an unintentional shooting are shot in their own homes (50%) or in those of relatives or friends (40%). In a typical year, approximately 200 teenagers and young adults (aged 15–24 years) are shot and killed unintentionally, and an additional 7,500 are treated in an emergency department for an unintentional gunshot wound.

The mortality rate from accidental shootings is eight times higher in the four states with the most guns compared with the four states with the fewest guns. For children aged 5–14 years the mortality rate is 14 times higher in the states with high gun ownership than in the states with low gun ownership, and for children up to age 4 years the mortality rate is 17 times higher.

WHO IS MOST LIKELY TO BE VICTIMIZED BY GUN VIOLENCE AND IN WHAT SITUATIONS?

Gun violence crosses all socioeconomic and geographic boundaries, from inner cities, to remote rural areas, to high-income suburbs; in homes, public housing, schools, workplaces, recreational areas, and bars; and on the street. Gun violence victims are young and old, male and female, all races and ethnicities. Victim and offender are sometimes strangers, but often they are intimately related.

Guns are ideal weapons for the commission of violent crimes. Even when used by a physically weak or unskilled assailant, a gun presents a credible threat. Guns can be used to kill quickly, from a safe distance, and are an impersonal means for killing. Despite the pervasive nature of gun violence, several demographic groups are represented disproportionately among the victims of gun violence. Men, Blacks, city dwellers, and young individuals are most at risk for handgun violence and crime in the United States (just as they are to crime in general). Gun homicide victims are disproportionately young and predominantly male. Men are more than twice as likely as women to face a criminal carrying a handgun. Four of five victims of fatal and nonfatal gunshot wounds from crime are male.

Homicides of teens and young adults are more likely to be committed with a gun than homicides of persons of other ages. Between 1975 and 2005, approximately one-third of murder victims were under the age of 25 years. In 2007,

50.1% of victims were Black, 47.6% were White, and the remaining victims were of other races. Firearms were involved in 51.8% of homicides among victims under age 18 years and in 70.2% among victims aged 18 years and over. In 2007 firearm use in homicide increased rapidly starting in victims aged 5–8 years (39.8%), continued increasing through adolescence (48% among victims aged 9–12 years and 77.2% among victims aged 13–16 years), and peaked at age 17–19 years (85.2% of victims). Thereafter, it slowly declined (81.7% of victims aged 20–24 years, 80% of victims aged 25–29 years, 76% among victims aged 30–34 years). From ages 45–74 years, firearms were involved in 44%–57% of homicides. Between 1976 and 2005, gun homicides by persons aged 18–24 years declined after a peak in 1993 but have not returned to the lower levels seen before the mid-1980s. Gun homicides by adults 25 years and older declined through 1999 but have since increased.

Firearm homicide disproportionately affects Blacks. Approximately half of all gun homicide victims are Black, even though they represent less than 13% of the U.S. population. Black males between the ages of 15 and 24 years have the highest firearm homicide rate of any demographic group. Their firearm homicide rate of 103.4 deaths per 100,000 is 10 times higher than the rate for White males in the same age group (10.5 deaths per 100,000). From 1976 to 2005, Blacks were disproportionately represented as both homicide victims and offenders. The Black victimization rate in 2005 was six times higher than for Whites.

In 1997, 92% of homicides of young Black men occurred by firearms, compared with 68% of homicides by firearms in the general population. Handgun crimes comprise 25% of all violent crimes committed against Black men and 12% of those against Black women, compared with 9.1% and 6.6% against White men and women, respectively. Young Black men are victimized by offenders with handguns seven times more often than the rest of the population. Even though violent crime rates, including crimes committed with guns, have declined each year since 1993, guns remain the leading cause of death for young Black males. From 1976 to 2005, gun involvement in gang-related homicides increased, as it did in homicides that occurred during the commission of a felony (55%–77%).

When women are victimized by assailants with weapons, strangers are more likely to use a gun and intimate partners are more likely to be armed with knives or other sharp objects. Among female victims of intimate partner violence, 4% report having been threatened with a gun by an intimate partner, and 1% sustained firearm injuries in these assaults. In one study, 1 in 4 abused pregnant women aged 14–42 years reported that her batterer owned or had access to a gun.

Firearms are used in the killing of 42% of all family murder victims, compared with 63% of homicide victims killed outside the family. More than two-thirds of spouse and ex-spouse intimate victims were killed by guns between 1990 and 2005. From 1976 to 2002, a woman was 2.2 times more likely to be shot and killed by her male intimate than killed in any other way by a stranger. Handguns accounted for most of these deaths. Women killed by a spouse, intimate acquaintance, or close relative are 7 times more likely to live in homes with 1 or more guns and 14 times more likely to have a history of domestic violence compared with women killed by non-intimate acquaintances. One study of women physically abused by current or former intimate partners revealed a five-fold increased risk of a partner murdering a woman when the partner owned a firearm.

In one-half of instances where the location of assaults resulting in gunshot wounds was known, 23% occurred on a street or highway; 14% occurred in a home, apartment, or condominium; and 13% occurred in other areas (including schools and recreation areas). People who live in central cities experience twice as many crimes involving handguns per 1,000 residents compared with residents of the suburbs, and approximately 4 times as many as residents of nonmetropolitan areas. Most handgun crimes are committed by a lone offender who is of unknown relationship or a stranger to the victim one-half to three-fourths of the time. Four-tenths of violent crimes involving a handgun take place on the street, one-tenth occur in the victim's home, one-tenth occur near the victim's home, and one-fifth occur in a commercial establishment or business.

WHICH GUNS ARE USED FOR VIOLENCE?

All types of guns are associated with violence in the United States. Both handguns and long guns, such as rifles and shotguns, are involved in homicides, attempted murder, robbery, and unintentional injury. Because of the high prevalence of handguns in the United States, particularly in homes, and because they are so easily concealed, handguns contribute substantially to the epidemic of violence in America. Of all firearm-related crime, 86% involved handguns. In gunshot assaults where the firearm type is known, approximately 80% of nonfatal victims are shot with a handgun. In homicides, approximately 50% are killed with a handgun. For the five-year period between 2003 and 2007, the mix of firearms used to commit homicide (handguns, rifles, shotguns, other guns) remained fairly constant.

WHY ARE THERE SO MANY GUNS IN AMERICA?

The most prominent reason for the high prevalence of guns in the United States is that millions of Americans believe passionately that their liberty, their safety, or both are dependent on the widest availability of guns. The prevalence of firearms is often attributed to America's strong cultural sense of its frontier heritage. Throughout American history, from pre-revolutionary times through the American Revolution, the expansion westward, the Civil War, and well into the 20th century, guns have been essential tools of living. Whether used for hunting or self-defense, it is hard to imagine the historic development of the American nation without considering the role of firearms.

Some would argue that the evolution of violence into an integral element of American culture and life also would not have been possible without firearms. The gun tradition has been a rationale used as a basis by some to argue against any effort to regulate access to guns in modern times. Opponents of regulation deny or dismiss the massive increase in the number of guns in the United States and their contribution to current levels of violence. However, other countries, such as Canada, have a frontier tradition not too dissimilar from America's, but have only a fraction of U.S. rates of gun ownership, gun-related homicide, and firearm violence. Australia, another "frontier nation," has one-seventh the proportionate private handgun ownership as the United States. In fact, the historical ubiquity of guns in American life is in part myth. Until 1850, less than 10% of U.S. citizens possessed guns. Only 15% of violent deaths between 1800 and 1845 were caused by guns. The myth of gun ubiquity in America propagated the notion that gun possession gave citizens stature, made them more American, and were instruments of equality. ("God may have made men, but Samuel Colt made them equal.")

Fear of crime and criminals, and the need to defend oneself against them, are the most frequently articulated reasons of gun owners and advocates for their continued possession of firearms. But Americans' desire for gun ownership has also long been driven by a deep-rooted and historical fear of excessive government power and intrusion that dates from the era of the Founding Fathers. In part, the residua of a nation and a national culture born of revolution against tyranny, fear of government at all levels remains vibrant in American public life, discourse, and consciousness. The 9/11 attacks further fed public fears, this time from foreign invaders and imported or homegrown terrorists, and helped rationalize widespread gun ownership. Many gun owners fear that the government wants to (and will) "take away" their guns.

Among Americans, Whites are more likely than Blacks to own guns (despite the higher risk for firearm-related violence among Blacks). Men are more likely than women to own guns. An important predictor of gun ownership is whether an individual's parents owned a gun. One study found that adults whose parents owned a gun are twice as likely to own a gun than adults whose parents did not.

Ownership of a firearm seems to influence whether children will subsequently acquire a gun.

The United States is a prolific manufacturer (and exporter) of firearms. Guns are a major American industry and a highly profitable enterprise. Gun dealers, both commercial and "kitchen-table" dealers operating out of their homes, abound in the United States. America once had more gun dealers than gas stations (five states still do—Alaska, Idaho, Montana, Oregon, and Wyoming).

The number of federally licensed gun dealers in the United States has dropped dramatically as a result of licensing reforms implemented during the Clinton administration, combined with changes to the law made by the 1993 Brady Handgun Violence Prevention Act (the "Brady Law") and the 1994 Violent Crime Control and Law Enforcement Act. As a result of the new licensing requirements and increased scrutiny of applicants by the Bureau of Alcohol, Tobacco, Firearms and Explosives, the number of licensed federal firearm dealers in the United States has decreased 79%—from 245,628 in 1994 to 50,630 in 2007. California had the steepest decrease in the number of dealers, declining from 20,148 to 2,120, or by 89%. During the period of sharpest decline in the number of dealers, overall U.S. pistol production decreased approximately 60%, from 2.3 million to just under 1 million.

Another reason why there are so many guns in America is the longevity of firearms. When properly maintained, most guns have a life expectancy of many decades, and many firearms used to commit crimes in the United States are several decades old. It has been argued that if the United States was not to manufacture, import, or assemble any additional guns, enough firearms already have been distributed within the population to maintain current levels of violence for the next three decades.

And of course, there can be no avoiding Americans' passionate love affair with the power, persona, appearance, and even the sexuality of guns. From the dime-store novels of yesteryear to contemporary film, there is a global but also distinctly American cultural obsession with guns of all kinds. As Roger Rosenblatt has noted in *Time Magazine*, in recent movies "guns are displayed as art objects, people die in balletic slow motion, and right prevails if you own the most powerful handgun in the world."

ARE THERE NATIONS MORE ARMED THAN AMERICA BUT LESS VIOLENT?

Yes. There are nations where guns are more commonly owned than in America but with lower levels of civil and firearm-related violence (though rare because the level of gun ownership in the United States is so high). Israel and several South American countries are examples (societies that have faced recurrent internal or external armed conflicts). In Israel, approximately 15% of the adult Jewish population carry concealed handguns. Gun control advocates often point to Britain, Canada, Australia, and Japan as models where gun access is restricted and violent and firearm crime are a fraction of U.S. levels. They tend not to point to Switzerland, where guns are common in the home and crime is very low. The fact that such heavily armed countries exist with less violence occurring than in the United States often is cited by opponents of gun control to illustrate that "people kill people, not guns" and that the actual prevalence of guns and gun ownership are not related to levels of violence.

There can be no denying the fact that without people involved in acts of violence, guns could not cause injury and death. However, this argument is misleading and can be made for any tool or vehicle. For example, it is cars that kill pedestrians, not drunk drivers. Indeed, public health advocates are increasingly relating injury-prevention strategies to precisely this point—that guns, like automobiles, can be made safer without instituting bans or restrictions. Trigger locks to prevent children's gun injuries are likened to child-resistant medication bottles, and user handprint devices in handguns are seen as analogous to seatbelts in cars.

Nonetheless, the scientific evidence is overwhelming that guns are involved centrally in at least three deadly dimensions of the violence epidemic. First, as guns have become more prevalent, their lethality has transformed almost any violent intent or impulse into an act that does not just injure, but is fatal. This deadly quality of firearms, their lethality, has contributed greatly to the extreme nature of violence in America today. It has become cliché, but as evidenced from national data it is true that fights between kids on school playgrounds and among family members that used to result in bruises and lacerations now often result in handgun wounds and homicides.

Second, the evidence indicates that the greater availability and prevalence of guns are directly associated with the increasing number of violent acts in American society. With more guns available to any group and any individual, and with members of the public arming themselves in fear of crime and other perceived threats to their freedom or welfare, violence has become a more tolerated and accepted method of resolving differences. Guns are the easily acquired and deployed tools of violence. It is a remarkable irony that this has continued to occur over the past decade when overall violent crime and victimization in the United States have declined dramatically. Perhaps because of the continuous, on-demand feed of violent news from cable television and internet news ("if it bleeds it leads"), Americans are more fearful of violence (and seeking firearms to cope with their fear) during a time when they are actually safer than they have been in a generation.

Third, the sheer abundance of guns in America's households, workplaces, and schools has placed those who discover them innocently and in a state of ignorance, such as small children, at great risk of accidental injury and death from gunshot wounds. All of these factors contribute to the reality that the United States, compared with other nations, remains a global leader not only in firearm ownership but also in gun violence, injury, and death.

WHAT IS THE CONTROVERSY ABOUT GUN CONTROL AND THE INFRINGEMENT OF A CONSTITUTIONAL RIGHT?

The first federal legislation related to firearms was the Second Amendment, ratified in 1791. For 143 years of U.S. history, this was the only federal legislation regarding firearms. The next federal firearm legislation passed was the National Firearms Act of 1934, which established regulations for the sale of firearms and taxes on firearm sales, and required registration of some types of firearms such as machine guns. In the aftermath of the assassinations of Robert F. Kennedy and Martin Luther King Jr., the Gun Control Act of 1968 was enacted, which regulated gun commerce, restricted mail order sales, and allowed shipments only to licensed firearm dealers. The act prohibited felons, those under indictment, fugitives, illegal aliens, drug users, those dishonorably discharged from the military, and those in mental institutions from owning guns. The law also restricted importation of Saturday night specials and other types of guns, and limited the sale of automatic weapons and semiautomatic weapon conversion kits.

The Firearm Owners' Protection Act was passed in 1986, changing restrictions in the 1968 Act and allowing gun dealers licensed by the federal government, as well as individual unlicensed private sellers, to sell at gun shows, while continuing to require licensed gun dealers to perform background checks. The Brady Handgun Violence Prevention Act was passed in 1993 and imposed a waiting period before the purchase of a handgun in order for a background check to be completed. The Brady Act also established a national system to provide instant criminal background checks, with checks to be performed by firearms dealers. The Violent Crime Control and Law Enforcement Act, enacted in 1994, included the Federal Assault Weapons Ban and was a response to public concern over mass shootings. It prohibited the manufacture and importation of some semiautomatic firearms that exhibited military style features and magazines holding more than ten rounds. (In September 2004, the assault weapon ban expired under its sunset clause.)

The Domestic Violence Offender Gun Ban of 1996, also known as "the Lautenberg Amendment," prohibited anyone previously convicted of a misdemeanor crime of domestic violence from owning a firearm. It also banned shipment, transport, ownership, and use of guns or ammunition by individuals convicted of misdemeanor or felony domestic violence, and outlawed the sale or gift of a firearm or ammunition to such a person. In the immediate aftermath of Hurricane Katrina, police and National Guard units in New Orleans confiscated firearms from private citizens in an attempt to prevent violence. Congress passed the Disaster Recovery Personal Protection Act of 2006 in the form of an amendment to Department of Homeland Security Appropriations Act, 2007. Section 706 of the Act prohibits federal employees and those receiving federal funds from confiscating legally possessed firearms during a disaster.

Gun control proponents regard the data on the prevalence and national burden of firearm-induced homicides and injuries as evidence of a need to reduce the availability and presence of guns in the United States. Much of their focus has been on handguns and assault weapons, which, unlike rifles that are used for sport and hunting, have a single utility—killing people. The debate that has now raged for decades between advocates of gun control and unrestricted gun access has often been characterized by rhetoric and excess, equal parts policy and emotion. The legislative battles have been equally contentious. Advocates against gun control argue that decreasing the availability of guns will not reduce homicides or nonfatal assaults. The National Rifle Association (NRA), gun manufacturers, and merchants have argued that if guns are regulated, only criminals will be able to access them through illegal means such as theft or smuggling, leaving the law-abiding majority of the public unable to protect themselves.

This viewpoint is not supported by data. The majority of U.S. homicides are committed by otherwise law-abiding individuals who know the victim. It is a misconception that most killings are committed by habitual criminals for profit. Studies indicate that the opposite is true—most homicides are not associated with other felonies and are not committed for material gain. Yet 43% of robberies involve a gun, so the public would like to believe (and is led to believe by gun control opponents) that a firearm is an effective deterrent or prevention for robbery. Again, the evidence shows that guns purchased for self-defense are often used to kill and injure family members, intimates, and acquaintances—not strangers attempting to rob or assault a victim. Although it is unclear whether the public fully appreciates this reality, it seems that fear of stranger victimization (and hope that it can be preempted through the brandishing or skillful use of a firearm) continues to drive public passions about ease of gun access and ownership.

Another key argument of gun advocates is that any legislative action to control firearms, and particularly private ownership of guns, violates the constitutional right to keep and bear arms. The Second Amendment to the U.S. Constitution states that a well-regulated militia is necessary to the security of a free state, and "the right of the people to keep and bear arms cannot be infringed." When this amendment was enacted in the eighteenth century, it sought to ensure that a struggling young nation confronted by armed enemies would have the means to survive through ready access to defensive weapons. Citizens of the United States did not then enjoy our modern protections, including mobile police forces and modern communications. Sixty percent of Americans believe that private gun ownership and the ability of an individual to bear arms is a right protected by the Constitution. In June 2008 the Supreme Court ruled that such a right exists.

Public health and gun control advocates argue that the need addressed by the Second Amendment no longer exists and that a well-regulated militia as envisioned in the eighteenth century exists today in the National Guard. They regard the claimed need for guns for defensive purposes as illusory. Furthermore, gun control advocates note that another right entrenched in the Constitution is the assurance of domestic tranquility, meaning that an individual can be safe in his or her home and place of work, and on the streets without fear of intentional or unintentional injury from a heavily armed public. Health experts believe that Americans possess a basic right not to be killed by individuals who would use a gun with deadly intent and view the prevalence of firearms in our society as having compromised this right.

Much controversy has surrounded studies suggesting that guns are used far more often to defend people than in the commission of crimes. Several researchers have suggested that Americans use a gun in self-defense 2.5 million times a year. This figure has been regarded by other experts as a large overestimate based on flawed methodology. Each side has deployed their experts to carry forward the debate.

The continuing polarization in gun control policy and debate among advocates on either side of the issue overlooks a key reality: A large number of Americans still occupy the uncommitted center. These individuals, whose views can sway policy in one direction or the other, can be persuaded under varying circumstances that gun ownership should be protected, or that guns should also be more strictly controlled and regulated. Engagement of this uncommitted center in the gun control debate will be critical to shaping policies that maximize public safety while minimizing constrictions placed on legitimate access to guns by recreational enthusiasts and hunters.

DO GUN CONTROL POLICIES AND LAWS WORK?

There are more than 20,000 laws in the United States that deal with the sale, distribution, and use of firearms, many without any convincing evidence of effectiveness. The Supreme Court of the United States ruled on June 26, 2008, that the Second Amendment to the Constitution confers the right to keep and bear arms and that a District of Columbia law effectively prohibiting the possession of handguns by most citizens is unconstitutional. Most public health practitioners recognize that effective legal regulation of firearms by itself is too crude a vehicle for reducing firearm injuries. Indeed, when the Supreme Court ruled that the Second Amendment of the Constitution protects an individual right to bear arms in 2008, Justice Stephen G. Breyer, dissenting in the 5-to-4 decision, surveyed a substantial body of empirical research on whether gun control laws do any good, and wrote: "The upshot is a set of studies and counter-studies that, at most, could leave a judge uncertain about the proper policy conclusion."

There is evidence that denying guns to people who might use them in self-defense, often merely by brandishing them, tends to increase crime rates. There is also evidence that the possibility of confronting a victim with a gun deters some criminals from engaging in crimes. Between 1987 and 1990, McDowall found that guns were used in defense during a crime incident 64,615 times annually. This equates to 2 of every 1,000 incidents (0.2%) occurring in this time frame. For violent crimes (assault, robbery, and rape), guns were used 0.83% of the time in self-defense.

The findings of the McDowall study contrast with the findings of a 1993 study (and others) by Kleck, who found that as many as 2.45 million crimes are thwarted each year in the United States, and in most cases, the potential victim never fires a shot. The results of the Kleck studies have been cited many times in scholarly and popular media to illustrate the extent to which firearms are used constructively for self-protection. A study of gun use in the 1990s by Hemenway at the Harvard Injury Control Research Center found that criminal use of guns is far more common than self-defense use of guns. Research and statistics have consistently shown that guns intensify crime situations and increase the likelihood of a more violent or lethal outcome.

A study in the *New England Journal of Medicine* reported that the adoption of a gun-licensing law in the District of Columbia coincided with an abrupt 25% decline in homicide by firearms and a 23% decline of suicide by firearms. No similar declines were observed for homicides or suicides in which guns were not used, and no decline was seen in adjacent metropolitan areas where restrictive licensing did not apply (e.g., in Maryland and Virginia). These data suggest that restriction of access to handguns in the District of Columbia prevented an average of 47 violent deaths each year after the law was implemented. But this study has been criticized for using an inappropriate comparator in the upscale suburbs rather than another similar metropolitan area, such as Baltimore, and for using insufficient follow-up time to observe impact.

A brief defending the Washington, D.C., law filed by the American Public Health Association and other groups stated there were other collateral positive effects, including reductions in accidents, that gun control opponents tended to overlook or underestimate. More generally, the brief said, "banning handguns in Washington, D.C., appears to have reduced suicide and homicide rates." It cited the *New England Journal of Medicine* study and statistics showing that the District of Columbia has a very low suicide rate.

The international experience is also complex. According to a 2007 study considered by the Court, European nations with more guns had lower murder rates. The 7 nations with the most guns per capita had 1.2 murders annually for every 100,000 people. The rate in the 9 nations with the fewest guns was 4.4 per 100,000. At the Supreme Court, Justice Breyer was skeptical about what these comparisons proved and was unclear about "which is the cause and which the effect? The proposition that strict gun laws cause crime is harder to accept than the proposition that strict gun laws in part grow out of the fact that a nation already has a higher crime rate." Justice Breyer concluded that the mixed quality of the evidence on the efficacy of gun control, along with its varying interpretations, means that lawmakers should be allowed to assess it for themselves to set reasonable gun control policies. Justice Antonin Scalia, on the other hand, said the Constitution had effectively ended the discussion, writing for the majority: "gun violence is a serious problem . . . [but] the enshrinement of constitutional rights necessarily takes certain policy choices off the table."

Public health leaders have argued that the right to own or operate a firearm involves certain responsibilities and that the owners and operators of firearms should meet specific criteria. These criteria include being of a certain minimum age, being in healthy physical and mental condition, and demonstrating knowledge of and skill in the proper use of firearms. Many public health leaders view a system of gun registration and licensing for gun owners and users as essential. Pressure also is mounting on firearm manufacturers to make safer, smarter guns, for example, incorporating trigger locks into gun design or a fingerprint verification device into the grip of a handgun to identify the owner and prevent unauthorized users. Limiting multiple simultaneous handgun purchases—allowing one gun to be taken home at the sale and the others after a waiting period—is another strategy.

Advocates of a legislative approach to firearms control do not believe that enacting a law will provide a comprehensive solution to this complex problem.

Even an effective gun control law would not prevent shooting incidents, but it may reduce their number. Gun control laws do not have to prohibit gun ownership and access, but merely regulate it. One recent nationwide survey of Americans found that 84% favor the regulation of newly purchased handguns. The public supports limiting the sale of guns to people believed to be potentially dangerous, to people with criminal histories, and to minors under age 18 years. Four-fifths of Americans oppose repealing the ban on semiautomatic assault rifles. But only 40%–50% of the public supports banning civil possession of handguns.

Despite significant differences, gun owners and non-owners agree on many proposed firearm regulatory initiatives: on law enforcement agencies interrupting the flow of guns into communities and the hands of criminals; on toughening the application process to become a licensed gun dealer and tracing gun migration to criminals to reduce the availability of crime guns; and on stronger sentencing of criminals caught with a weapon while committing a crime (e.g., at least five years of mandatory time to be served in a distant federal prison without possibility of parole). Differences in opinion persist on proposed handgun bans. More than half of non-owners generally support handgun bans, whereas, only one-fourth of gun owners do, and both groups reject a total ban on civilian ownership of guns. In sum, it seems that the American public wants to preserve legitimate firearm use while gun crime is curtailed.

For many years, members of the U.S. Congress have been influenced by the NRA, which has endeavored to ensure the defeat of any elected official who votes for a federal gun control law. Nonetheless, the Brady Bill, which mandates a waiting period for firearm purchases during which a background check of the purchaser is conducted, passed Congress and became law during the first Clinton administration. Background checks are now required on felons, fugitives from justice, people addicted to unlawful controlled substances, court-ordered potentially dangerous mentally ill people, people in the country illegally, dishonorably discharged soldiers, people who have renounced U.S. citizenship, domestic violence abusers subject to a protective order, and domestic violence abusers convicted of a misdemeanor crime of domestic violence.

According to the Department of Justice, from inception of the Brady Act on March 1, 1994 through 2008, more than 97 million applications for firearms transfers or permits were subject to background checks. Brady background checks have contributed to a decline in lethal assaults by blocking 1.78 million attempts by high-risk people to buy a gun from a licensed gun dealer through the end of 2008. Applications from individuals with felony convictions accounted for almost half of the total number of blocked attempts to purchase a firearm, or an estimated

842,000 blocked gun purchase applications submitted by convicted felons. On average that is 169 thwarted attempts to purchase a gun by a felon in the United States every day. A domestic violence misdemeanor conviction or restraining order was the second most common reason for denial in 2008.

There is evidence that denial of handgun purchases to persons with a felony conviction may lower their rate of subsequent criminal activity and is an effective violence prevention strategy. A majority of Americans support the Brady Act; however, regulating firearms is not a comprehensive response to the role of guns in violence. Only 60%–70% of firearms sales in the United States are transacted through federally licensed firearm dealers, with the remainder taking place in the "secondary market." Most sales to youths and convicted felons take place in the "secondary market," in which previously owned firearms are transferred by unlicensed individuals. Indeed, those who proposed the Brady law viewed it as only the first step in an evolving legislative process. Further legislation is required to reduce the number of handguns used for malicious and criminal purposes without interfering with legitimate gun sports and recreational activities. Without the support of U.S. voters, however, elected officials will not risk a conflict with and retribution from the NRA, which has, in its pro-gun zeal, opposed virtually every form of gun control, including restrictions on machine guns, "cop-killer" bullets, and plastic guns.

HOW CAN I PROTECT MY FAMILY FROM GUNSHOT INJURIES?

The best method for protecting your family from unintentional gun injuries and death is to not keep a gun in the home. Approximately 1.2 million latchkey children can access a gun at home when they get home from school. One study found that among homes with children and firearms, 43% had at least 1 unlocked firearm, and 9% kept firearms unlocked and loaded. A total of 1.4 million homes, with 2.6 million children, stored firearms in a manner accessible to children. Because even the best-behaved children are naturally curious and always exploring, sooner or later they will encounter the gun and then their risk increases dramatically.

Adolescents are attracted to guns as symbols of power, masculinity, and adulthood. If a teenager knows there is a gun in the house, it is almost certain that he or she will find and investigate it. The risk that domestic disputes will erupt into serious violence, injury, or homicide and the risk of suicides in the home are greatly reduced if a gun is not kept at home. Parents should take steps to reduce the threat to their children from guns, much as they strive to reduce risk from other household dangers, such as prescription drugs, alcohol, poisons, or swimming pools. Adolescents who are aggressive, easily angered, and impulsive, or who have a history of violence should not be allowed to participate in gun shooting sports.

Children should be taught that if they find a gun in the home or elsewhere, they should not touch it and should immediately leave the area and report the finding to an adult. These reactions will not be natural to any child, who may want to investigate and play with a gun. Children should be helped to understand what they should do if they find a gun because they so often play in unsupervised settings where an accidental discharge resulting in injury or death can occur easily. Parents who own guns should empty firearms and lock up the ammunition, and ask their children's friends' parents to do the same. Guns should be locked away so they are not accessible to children, and trigger locks should be used to prevent their use if accessed.

Explaining to children the difference between guns as portrayed in "pretend" entertainment media, such as television, movies, and videogames, and the actual impact of guns in real life is essential. Children should understand that actors on television and other media use play guns that do not really hurt people, and that, after the show, a person who has been shot gets up unharmed. Most small children do not comprehend this reality. Parents should explain the impact of real life guns and violence to their children early and repeatedly. With parental guidance and explanation, a child can be helped to understand the difference between toy and real guns as well, and why it is critical never to confuse the two.

HOW CAN I BE A MORE RESPONSIBLE AND CAREFUL GUN OWNER?

Gun owners can use several methods to ensure that their firearms do not accidentally injure family members and acquaintances. The Centers for Disease Control and Prevention has consistently reported that nonfatal firearm injuries occur most commonly during routine gun-related activities, such as gun cleaning; loading/unloading; hunting; target shooting; and showing, handling, or carrying a gun. Safe gun-handling rules are well-defined and easily understood, and must always be followed. These rules include always keeping the gun pointed in a safe direction, away from you and others, and preferably toward the ground or upward. Fingers should be kept away from a gun's trigger at all times when handling a weapon. Gun owners should discipline themselves to overcome the natural tendency to grasp a gun as if about to shoot it. A gun should always be kept unloaded until the moment of use. Ammunition should be stored safely away.

Death and injuries among children and teenagers from the accidental discharge of guns can be reduced by limiting their access to loaded weapons. One report estimated that there are 3.3 million children living in American households with firearms that are always or sometimes stored loaded and unlocked. Adolescents tend to believe they are invincible. Combined with a curiosity about guns, they are at high risk for gun-related injuries. Most unintended gun deaths occur in a home and involve inappropriately stored weapons; therefore, safe and effective gun storage is essential.

Guns should be locked away at all times except when in use. Weapons should be kept separate from ammunition. Ammunition should be locked up as well. Firearms also can be modified to make them less lethal. Childproof safety devices, such as trigger locks, are available and can prevent young people from discharging a gun. Loading indicators alone, manufactured as a part of guns, could eliminate an estimated 23% of unintended gun deaths. These suggestions may sound obvious, but surveys indicate that more than half of gun owners keep guns unlocked, loaded, and ready to use. In some states, such as California and Florida, laws have been passed to make adults legally responsible for the inappropriate storage of guns.

It is important as a parent to teach your children about gun safety, even if no one in your family owns a gun. With one-third of American households possessing a gun, it is likely that someone you or your child knows has a gun. Your child could encounter a gun at a neighbor's house or when playing with friends. There is no minimum or appropriate age at which to begin talking with your children about gun safety. The NRA suggests that when a child starts acting out "gun play" or asking about guns, the time to discuss gun safety with them has arrived. Answering questions about guns honestly and openly can reduce the mystery surrounding them and perhaps decrease a child's curiosity. This can, in turn, help to prevent an accidental gun injury.

WHERE CAN I GET MORE INFORMATION AND HELP?

If you fear becoming the victim of gun-related violence, contact your local police department or call 911.

Appendix 1 at the back of this book provides a state-by-state website listing of compensation and assistance programs for victims of violence and crime. You may find assistance by contacting one of your state programs. Appendix 2 is a bibliography for further reading on each of the violence topics discussed in this volume, organized chapter by chapter.

The following national organizations and internet websites may be accessed for additional information, resources, and referrals on gun-related issues and firearm injury prevention.

NATIONAL ORGANIZATIONS

American Bar Association
(312) 488-5000 or (202) 662-1000

Brady Center to Prevent Handgun Violence
(202) 289-7319

Centers for Disease Control and Prevention
National Center for Injury Prevention and Control
(800) CDC-INFO (232-4636)

Children's Defense Fund
Violence Prevention Network
(800) 233-1200

Coalition to Stop Gun Violence/Educational Fund to End Handgun Violence
(202) 408-0061

National Center for Juvenile Justice
(412) 227-6950

National Center for Victims of Crime
(800) FYI-CALL (394-2255)

National Council on Crime and Delinquency
(510) 208-0500

National Crime Prevention Council
(202) 466-6272

National Institute of Justice Clearinghouse
National Criminal Justice Reference Service
(800) 851-3420

National Organization for Victim Assistance
(800) 879-6682

Office of National Drug Control Policy, Drug Policy Information Clearinghouse
(800) 666-3332

USEFUL INTERNET WEBSITES

American Bar Association's Coordinating Committee on Gun Violence:
   www.abanet.org/gunviol
Brady Campaign to Prevent Gun Violence: www.bradycampaign.org
Brady Center to Prevent Handgun Violence: www.bradycenter.org
Bureau of Alcohol, Tobacco, Firearms and Explosives (ATF): www.atf.gov
Centers for Disease Control and Prevention: www.cdc.gov
Children's Defense Fund: www.childrensdefense.org
Coalition to Stop Gun Violence/Educational Fund to Stop Gun Violence:
   www.csgv.org
Common Sense About Kids and Guns: www.kidsandguns.org
Community Policing Consortium: www.communitypolicing.org
Firearms Law Center: www.firearmslawcenter.org/content/home.asp
Johns Hopkins University Center for Gun Policy and Research:
   www.jhsph.edu/gunpolicy
Legal Community Against Violence: www.lcav.org
Million Mom March: www.millionmommarch.org
National Center for Health Statistics: www.cdc.gov/nchs/fastats/homicide.htm
National Center for Victims of Crime: www.ncvc.org
National Victim Assistance Academy: www.ojp.usdoj.gov/ovc/assist/vaa.htm
Office of National Drug Control Policy: www.whitehousedrugpolicy.gov
Office for Victims of Crime: www.ovc.gov
U.S. Department of Justice, Bureau of Justice Statistics:
   www.ojp.usdoj.gov/bjs/homicide/homtrnd.htm
Violence Policy Center: www.vpc.org

Violence to Oneself — Suicide

- What are suicides, suicide attempts, and suicide survivors?
- How common is suicide?
- Who commits suicide?
- How is suicide committed?
- What causes or precipitates suicide?
- What are the warning signs for suicide?
- Can suicide be prevented?
- What do I do if I think someone I know may be suicidal?
- What do I do if I feel suicidal?
- How do I cope with the loss of a loved one to suicide?
- Where can I get more information and help?

WHAT ARE SUICIDES, SUICIDE ATTEMPTS, AND SUICIDE SURVIVORS?

Suicide is self-inflicted death. Suicidal behavior spans a continuum from thinking about taking one's own life (or suicide ideation), to making plans for a suicide attempt, to dying by one's own hands. Suicide ideation involves thoughts of harming or killing oneself. A suicide attempt is a nonfatal, self-inflicted act with intent to kill oneself but that did not succeed. In a completed suicide, the effort to kill oneself is successful. Suicide survivors are family members and friends of a loved one who died by suicide.

HOW COMMON IS SUICIDE?

Suicide in the United States is common. However, the rate of suicide, adjusted for the age of the victim, is similar to the rates of other nations. In 2005, there were 32,637 suicides, which accounted for 1.3% of all deaths in the United States, ranking it as the 11th leading cause of death. In the United States, 11 of every 100,000 people kill themselves each year. An American commits suicide every 16 minutes. If we consider the number of people who kill themselves and the years by which their lives are reduced, approximately one million years of life are lost annually because of suicide in America. More people die by suicide than by homicide in the United States.

It is difficult to count the exact number of suicides that occur each year because some fraction of deaths from other causes, such as car crashes, drowning, and accidental drug overdoses, are listed as such, but in reality are suicides. In 2006, 162,359 people were hospitalized for self-inflicted injury. In 2008, more than 395,000 people with self-inflicted injuries were treated in U.S. emergency departments. Underreporting or undercounting of suicide may occur in 25%–50% of instances, and so the actual number of suicides in America could be as high as 48,000.

Overall suicide rates in the United States have been largely stable over time. Since 1990, rates have ranged between 10.7 and 12.4 per 100,000. Each year there are approximately 10 suicides for every 100,000 young people. During the 1990s, the suicide rate among U.S. children under age 15 years was twice the rate for all of the other industrialized nations combined (0.55 vs. 0.27 per 100,000). For suicides involving firearms, the U.S. suicide rate was 11 times higher than for the other nations combined (0.32 vs. 0.03 per 100,000). In 2005, suicide was the third leading cause of death among 15- to 24-year-olds. Only accidents and homicides kill more young people each year. Each day, 12 young people commit suicide; every 2 hours and 11 minutes a person under age 25 years takes his or her own life. The number of young people committing suicide has doubled since the 1950s, remaining stable at higher levels from the late 1970s to the mid-1990s, and decreasing 28.5% since 1994. Much of this increase occurred among White males. Surveys of adolescents often find that as much as 30% have contemplated suicide at some time. Elderly people (above age 65 years) also have disproportionally high rates of suicide, making up 13% of the general population but committing 19% of suicides. The elderly have rates of suicide approximately 50% higher than those of the rest of the population.

For every completed suicide in the United States, it is believed that there are 8–25 suicide attempts. This means that 256,000–816,000 suicide attempts are made each year in the United States, and translates into 1 suicide attempt every 39 seconds. An estimated 5–7 million living Americans have tried to kill themselves at some time. For each suicide attempt by a male, there are 2–3 attempts by a female.

A "suicide survivor" describes the family members and friends who have been affected by the suicide death of a loved one. For every completed suicide there are an estimated six survivors, including family members and friends, and so each suicide intimately affects at least six other people. As of 2009, it is estimated that at least 5.3 million Americans are suicide survivors of suicides completed since 1980. Surviving family members are also at higher risk for suicide and emotional problems themselves.

WHO COMMITS SUICIDE?

Suicide affects all ethnic, racial, economic, social, and age groups. Suicide in America occurs most commonly among White adolescents and the elderly. Males take their own lives at approximately 4 times the rate of females and represent 79.4% of all U.S. suicides. Suicide is the 8th leading cause of death for males and the 17th leading cause of death for females. Whites commit suicide more than twice as often as Blacks and other races, with rates of 12.3 and 5.1 per 100,000 in 2005, respectively. Together, White males and White females accounted for 90% of all suicides. Men over 75 years old and women aged 40–59 years have the highest rates of suicide.

There has been an epidemic of suicides among young people. Over the past 60 years, the suicide rate has quadrupled for males 15–24 years old and doubled for females of the same age. Whereas suicides were responsible for 1.3% of all deaths in the United States in 2005, they accounted for 12.3% of all deaths among those aged 15–24 years. Suicide rates for children between the ages of 10 and 14 years increased 50% between 1981 and 2005. Suicide is the second leading cause of death among those aged 25–34 years and the third leading cause of death among those aged 15–24 years.

It is estimated that more than 1,000 suicides occur on college campuses each year. In 2007, 14.5% of U.S. high school students reported they had seriously considered attempting suicide during the previous 12 months, and 6.9% reported making at least 1 suicide attempt in the 12 months before the survey. Approximately one-third of these attempts required medical attention. Young people used to comprise approximately 5% of all suicides, but by 1980 they comprised 20% of the total. By 1998, suicide killed more American teenagers and young adults than did cancer, heart disease, AIDS, birth defects, pneumonia, influenza, stroke, and chronic lung disease combined.

In 2005, rates of completed suicides were higher in Whites than in Blacks (12.3 vs. 5.1 per 100,000, respectively). The suicide rate among Black females was the lowest of all racial/gender groups. Certain minority age-specific ethnic and racial groups have elevated suicide rates. For example, suicide rates among American Indian and Alaska Native adolescents and young adults aged 15–34 years are

2.2 times higher than the national average for this age group. Hispanic female adolescents have double the rate of suicide attempts as Whites of the same age.

The elderly are among those at highest risk for suicide and are 50% more likely than young people to kill themselves. More than 5,000 people aged 65 years or more commit suicide during an average year in the United States. The elderly comprised 12.4% of the population in 2004 and accounted for 16.6% of all suicides. The rate of suicide for the elderly aged 65 years and older was 14.7 per 100,000 in 2005. Over the past 20 years, an increase in the elderly suicide rate occurred for the first time since the late 1930s. Elderly White men, particularly those who have been recently widowed, are most at risk, with an annual rate of approximately 33 suicides per 100,000. The rate of male suicides in late life was 5.2 times that of females. Older people attempt suicide less often than do other age groups, but they complete it more often. They use lethal weapons, such as guns, more frequently. Many of the elderly who commit suicide are unemployed and live alone, often in poor urban areas. They may be abusing alcohol, which increases their suicide risk.

Suicide attempts are 8–20 times as frequent as completed suicides. Many more people try to kill themselves than actually succeed. Risk of attempted (nonfatal) suicide is greatest among women and the young. Females are 2–3 times more likely than males to attempt suicide, but males are more likely to complete it. This pattern holds across all racial groups. It is not clear whether the lower rates of completion among women result from their choosing less effective means of suicide or from less real desire to die. For every completed suicide by youth, it is estimated that 100–200 attempts are made. In those aged more than 65 years, it is estimated that there is 1 suicide for every 4 attempts.

There is considerable variation in the rate of suicide across different regions of the United States, with the lowest rates in the northeast and the highest rates in the western part of the country. Rates of suicide are the highest in the intermountain states, where eight of the top ten state suicide rates are found. Suicide rates are highest among the divorced, separated, and widowed, and lowest among individuals who are married. Rates typically decrease in times of war and increase in times of economic distress. The frequency of suicide peaks during the spring and rises again in the fall.

HOW IS SUICIDE COMMITTED?

In 2005, 52% of all suicides involved the use of firearms. Firearms were used more often by males than by females (58% vs. 33%). The most common method of suicide for all females was poisoning (39%). Approximately 80% of all firearm suicides are committed by White men. People living in a household where a gun is kept are five times more likely to die by suicide as those who live in gun-free homes. Since 1970, the percentage of suicides committed by adolescents and young adults using a gun increased by 10% (to 58%). Firearms were the most common method used (72%) for completing suicide among the elderly, with men using firearms 11.5 times more often than women of this age. Suicide attempts with guns often are immediately lethal and allow no opportunity for reconsideration or resuscitation.

After shooting and poisoning, suffocation and hanging are the next most common methods of suicide (22%). Poisoning is also the most frequent method by which women attempt to commit suicide but fail. Less frequently, people kill themselves by drowning (1.1%), jumping from high elevations, or cutting or piercing part of the body with a knife or other sharp implement to cause massive bleeding (1.8%).

WHAT CAUSES OR PRECIPITATES SUICIDE?

Suicide is a complication of some psychiatric problem in a majority of individuals. More than 90% of all completed suicides occur in individuals who have suffered from a diagnosable psychiatric or mental illness or a substance abuse disorder. These include depression, personality disorders, schizophrenia, and alcohol or other drug abuse or dependency. The risk of suicide is increased by greater than 50% in individuals who are depressed. Suicide should be regarded as the major life-threatening complication of depression. Depression is present in two-thirds of all people who commit suicide (if alcoholics who are depressed are included, the figure is 77%). Approximately 16% of people will suffer from clinical depression at some point in their lives, and 20%–30% of these individuals will attempt suicide, half of them succeeding. A family history of suicide or psychiatric illness may be a factor in creating a disrupted family life, and this increases the risk of mental health problems in all family members and their risk of suicide. Depression is a leading cause of suicide among the elderly, in whom it may be undiagnosed or untreated.

Family breakdown increases the risk of suicide among family members; the highest rates of suicide are found among individuals who are divorced or separated. Domestic violence, including physical, emotional, and sexual abuse, also can promote suicide. Socially isolated and lonely individuals are generally at higher risk for suicide. There is increasing evidence that an individual's biology may predispose him or her toward suicide. Studies of neurochemicals in the brain, such as serotonin, have suggested that these are associated with suicide. It is not clear yet whether their effect is causative. The single most powerful predictor of a future suicide is a history of a suicide attempt.

An individual may commit suicide as a result of a severely stressful recent life event. A great personal loss, rejection, death of a spouse or other loved individual, or the loss of a job or retirement can precipitate suicide. Serious chronic or deadly diseases, such as cancer or AIDS, can cause a person to commit suicide. Diseases causing a slow, protracted death and severe pain may bring a person to the point of suicide. However, it is clear that certain individuals who kill themselves are not under stress and view their willful termination of life as a conscious expression of free will. For some, suicide symbolizes individual freedom and control over their lives.

Among young people, the increasing level of suicide has changed our thinking about the origins of this problem. Suicide usually has been considered a problem in mental health. Prevention would, therefore, involve detecting and treating symptoms such as depression. However, among the young, individuals who are at risk for suicide often are not depressed, but rather an attempt is precipitated by a significant stress. Such stress might include getting into trouble, having difficulties in school or dating relationships, or having an argument with one's parents. Because many young people experience these stresses during adolescence and do not attempt suicide, there is likely to be some other predisposing characteristic of the individual's personality or an associated mental illness. The mass shootings in U.S. schools perpetrated by students over recent years, in which the assailants clearly recognized the suicidal nature of violent acts, raise troubling new questions and concerns about adolescent suicide risk.

Another feature of suicide among the young is what is known as suicide clustering. Suicide "clusters" are suicides involving three or more individuals closely spaced geographically or in time. It is thought that these suicide clusters represent imitation of one or more suicides by other young people. Exposure to suicidal behavior in a family member, a friend, or an acquaintance, and the power of suggestion, may lead to similar behavior in a vulnerable person. Some researchers believe that exposure to suicide through the media also can have such an impact.

The idea that suicide is contagious is controversial and not well-documented. However, there appears to be a correlation between suicides that are grouped by locale or time. Accordingly, some researchers believe that news of suicides should not be widely publicized, particularly in schools. This is important because adolescents who were involved in cluster suicides knew about each other but often did not know one another personally. Newspaper accounts of the deaths of teens have been found among the personal affects of young people who committed suicide later. It appears that media accounts of a teenager's suicide that sensationalize or romanticize the death may provoke other adolescents to act in a self-destructive way.

Alcohol and drugs may facilitate the commission of suicide. They reduce inhibitions and impair the judgment of individuals who may be considering suicide. The risk of suicide in alcoholics is 50%–70% higher than in the general population. Alcohol has often been consumed before a suicide attempt. Drinking also may contribute to other factors that increase the risk of suicide, such as depression and other mental health problems. Toxicology testing of those committing suicide in 13 states in 2004 showed that 33.3% tested positive for alcohol, 16.4% tested positive for opiates, 9.4% tested positive for cocaine, 7.7% tested positive for marijuana, and 3.9% tested positive for amphetamines. Researchers believe that alcohol or drug intoxication is especially deadly if combined with a history of psychiatric illness and easy access to a method for committing suicide, such as a gun.

The availability and acceptability of different methods of suicide affect an individual's choice of a method and may influence suicide risk. Growth in the number of guns in the United States over the past 30 years has increased their availability and acceptance within the culture. People who are considering suicide most often do not go out and buy a gun to kill themselves. They find guns in their homes and other environments. Guns greatly increase the chances that a suicide attempt will be fatal.

WHAT ARE THE WARNING SIGNS FOR SUICIDE?

Three-quarters of all suicide victims gave some warning signs or cues of their intent to a family member or friend. Between 20% and 50% of suicide victims had attempted suicide previously. Not all suicide attempts are intended to result in death, but they are always expressions of great distress that should be addressed rapidly and aggressively. Talking about suicide, discussing or searching for methods of committing suicide, and wanting to end one's life are all examples of "suicidal ideation" and are important warning signs. People who exhibit this behavior often will subsequently try to end their lives. It is a myth that people who talk about suicide do not actually do it; in fact, they do. They may act as if they are saying goodbye forever or going away. Extraordinary focus on or discussion about death and dying could be suicidal ideation. Dramatic personality changes, such as a quiet and shy person becoming very outgoing and sensationalistic, could indicate a potential for suicide.

Increased alcohol or drug use is often a suicide warning sign. Expressing a sense of lack of purpose in life; feeling trapped, guilty, anxious, and agitated; being unable to sleep or sleeping all the time; feeling hopelessness and withdrawing from friends, family, and society; experiencing uncontrolled anger or rage; engaging in recklessness and risk-taking behavior; and experiencing dramatic mood changes could singly or in combination indicate an elevated risk for suicide.

If someone you know is going through a very stressful period, having difficult relationships, or failing to meet important personal goals, keep an eye out for signs of crisis. Listen for statements that describe feelings of depression and helplessness. These individuals often will express great loneliness and hopelessness. They will be very pessimistic and will have feelings of guilt and self-reproach. Persons who are suffering with painful or terminal diseases should be closely monitored for suicide warning signs. Bereaving spouses are also at increased risk for suicide. Watch persons who are putting their affairs in order, giving away cherished possessions, paying off debts, or changing a will. This may indicate planning for suicide. A decreased interest in work or hobbies is an important sign, particularly in people who are generally career-oriented or otherwise active. A sudden and intense lift in spirits may not mean that the depression has lifted but that the person is feeling relief at knowing that their problems will soon end (through suicide).

Although the majority of people with depression will never attempt suicide, most suicide victims experience depression before attempting suicide. Depression should be a concern if a number of the following behaviors persist for more than two weeks: sadness, crying, apathy, depressed mood, and feelings of worthlessness. There may be a change in appetite; loss of weight and disturbed sleep; slowed speech, thinking process, and movement; loss of interest in and pleasure derived from usual activities; decreased sex drive; and diminished concern about personal appearance. Fatigue and loss of energy are common, and the person may have difficulty remembering, making decisions, or concentrating. Depression that is characterized by agitation or anxiety or by alcohol and drug abuse should be especially concerning.

CAN SUICIDE BE PREVENTED?

Yes. Suicide can be prevented. Many suicides are preventable, and most suicidal people want desperately to live. However, they are unable to see alternatives to their problems. Although some suicides occur without any recognizable warning signs, most do not. Most suicidal people give definite warning signs of their suicidal intentions, but those who have close contact with them are often not aware of the significance of such warnings or do not know what to do.

The depression, substance abuse, changes in affect and behavior, and emotional crises that often precede suicide can be recognized and treated.

Identifying individuals at increased risk of suicide and treating them clinically are perhaps the most important and promising prevention strategies for suicide. Both psychotherapy and drug therapy (e.g., antidepressants) are available and may work effectively for a person who wants to end his or her life.

The treatment of depression is effective 60%–80% of the time. (However, antidepressant therapy in depressed children and adolescents can actually increase the risk of suicidal thinking and behavior, and thus, their clinical use must be balanced against heightened suicidality in these age groups.) Programs to train health care workers and teachers in schools to recognize individuals at risk for suicide have been found to be helpful in making sure people receive appropriate care and treatment. However, not all individuals commit suicide because of an underlying mental illness, major life stress, or unlivable situation.

A number of strategies are widely used to prevent suicide, though few of these have been evaluated for their actual impact. One of the best ways to prevent suicide is to reduce the availability of methods to commit suicide. Because it is sometimes carried out on impulse, reducing the availability of the means for suicide can decrease its frequency. In particular, reducing the easy availability of guns and pharmaceuticals may be of value. Eliminating access to guns in the home, even if these are locked away and unloaded, can make suicide harder to complete, particularly among adolescents. People often feel ambivalent about committing suicide, and if the means for it are not readily available, the impulse may pass.

The U.S. Department of Health and Human Services has articulated 11 goals within a national strategy for suicide prevention. These are summarized as follows:

- Goal 1: Promote awareness that suicide is a public health problem that is preventable
- Goal 2: Develop broad-based support for suicide prevention
- Goal 3: Develop and implement strategies to reduce the stigma associated with being a consumer of mental health, substance abuse, and suicide prevention services
- Goal 4: Develop and implement suicide prevention programs
- Goal 5: Promote efforts to reduce access to lethal means and methods of self-harm
- Goal 6: Implement training for recognition of at-risk behavior and delivery of effective treatment
- Goal 7: Develop and promote effective clinical and professional practices
- Goal 8: Improve access to and community linkages with mental health and substance abuse services

- Goal 9: Improve reporting and portrayals of suicidal behavior, mental illness, and substance abuse in the entertainment and news media
- Goal 10: Promote and support research on suicide and suicide prevention
- Goal 11: Improve and expand surveillance systems

Most communities have suicide prevention hotlines; however, the effectiveness of these has not been clearly shown. Because some individuals who are about to attempt suicide are ambivalent about dying, if given an opportunity to reach out for help and support, people may do so. Help is readily available by just picking up the phone and calling a local suicide emergency hotline. The number to call in your locality can be found in the telephone directory or on the internet, by asking the information operator servicing your phone, or by contacting the agencies listed at the end of this book.

In addition to suicide hotlines, many communities have suicide prevention or crisis intervention centers. These organizations combine a number of services that can be used by people who are suicidal, including telephone hotlines and counseling. Suicide prevention centers help to reduce the loneliness that an individual is experiencing and can provide a means of entry into the mental health care system. A suicide hotline or crisis center, however, should not be a substitute for obtaining mental health care from a professional with specific expertise in this problem.

Various kinds of health care providers offer suicide prevention and treatment services. Universities, high schools, and religious organizations also may provide assistance. Early identification and treatment of depression in elderly persons are important to preventing suicide among this at-risk group. Early recognition of and response to major stresses and conflicts among adolescents and the young may help to decrease their rates of suicide.

WHAT DO I DO IF I THINK SOMEONE I KNOW MAY BE SUICIDAL?

If you know someone who you think may be suicidal, you should respond to the signs that he or she is at risk. Do not be afraid to get involved. The social taboo against suicide often leads people to avoid doing things to help another that they would readily do if the person were physically sick or near death. All suicide threats and attempts should be taken very seriously. Listen attentively to the person. Try not to act shocked. It is imperative that you remain actively engaged with that individual and help them to obtain appropriate services and support. Be sure to get professional help; do not try to solve the problem by yourself, and do not act as the person's only counsel and support. Available data suggest that the best way to prevent an individual from taking his or her own life is to obtain psychiatric care. Some people may require hospitalization with continual observation and monitoring for a time. Appropriate treatment of alcohol or drug abuse is essential.

You may have to accompany the suicidal person to a psychiatric facility, hospital emergency department, or doctor's office. The person may be unwilling to seek help, which is often a reflection of being hopeless, having given up on life, and believing that he or she cannot be helped. But he or she can, and if he or she is not willing or able to seek help on his or her own and with your assistance, you should get help independently. This is not disloyalty, but a sign of true friendship and love. Remember that his or her judgment is impaired in the current state of mind, and that he or she can be restored to a normal and healthy life. Before you leave the person, make sure that he or she has received professional help from qualified mental health professionals or that the risk of suicide has dissipated.

If you are aware of someone in your environment who may be suicidal and is expressing suicidal thoughts, you can help this person contact any of the resources in your community or listed at the end of this chapter. Do not be afraid to ask a person if he or she is thinking about suicide. Ask whether a method has been selected. This will not encourage suicide but will convey that someone genuinely cares and is willing to listen and help. Contrary to popular belief, talking to someone about suicide does not "put ideas into their head." If an elderly person is depressed or a younger person is in a stressful situation that may precipitate a suicide, you can engage local resources and services in your community to help that person.

Do not be judgmental. Never dare suicidal persons to complete the act as a way to test their seriousness. It is not wise to argue in an effort to convince them not to commit suicide, or that their situation in life is actually satisfactory or fortunate, or that they will hurt their family if they kill themselves. People considering suicide need to feel more worthy and less guilty. Do not lecture about the value of living, and avoid being glib. Instead communicate that you care about the person and are very concerned. Ensure the person that he or she is not alone, and that the desire to commit suicide will pass. Explain that depression can be treated effectively and that other life problems can be solved. The message that you want to convey is that a suicide crisis is temporary, the pain can be survived and will pass, and help is available. Above all, be sure that your suicidal family member or friend gets attention from a mental health professional.

Stay with a suicidal person until help is available. Never leave a person at risk alone, even briefly. Remove drugs, sharp objects, and other items that can be used to inflict injury on oneself. If the person already has a weapon or other means of suicide at hand, call 911 emergency services for assistance. If the person talks about using a firearm that he or she owns for suicide, call the police so they may remove the firearm. Even after treatment has begun, it is important for you to stay involved with your family member or friend. He or she will need support during treatment. After the person has received help and is no longer imminently suicidal, help the person make appointments with a medical doctor and a therapist. If you live with the individual and medication is involved in his or her treatment plan, help ensure that he or she takes it regularly, and watch for side effects that need to be communicated to the doctor. If you do not live with the person, follow up with him or her on a regular basis to make sure that he or she is doing okay.

There are instances of individuals who, for the purposes of drama or getting attention, will talk about committing suicide with little actual intent or risk of attempting the act. However, the fact remains that many individuals who actually commit violence against themselves give clear indication beforehand, either in their behavior or by verbally expressing their desire to end their lives. It is better to be misled and falsely alarmed by someone not likely to actually commit suicide than to dismiss an individual as a craver of attention who attempts it or succeeds.

WHAT DO I DO IF I FEEL SUICIDAL?

Many people consider suicide at some time in their lives. This is not that unusual, unless the feelings and thoughts about ending life persist. You should not feel guilty or ashamed for considering suicide. If you feel suicidal, or are considering ending your life for some reason, you should seek help first by confiding in someone you trust. There are many people and service agencies that can help you through this difficult time. You can be helped back to a healthier perspective and state of mind. If you call the National Suicide Prevention Lifeline at (800) 273-TALK (8255), you will be routed to someone to speak with on a suicide telephone hotline in your community. Also you can call the National Hopeline Network at (800) SUICIDE (784-2433). The Deaf Suicide Hotline number is (800) 799-4TTY (4889).

You may be depressed, and this treatable problem can impel you to suicide. Your family represents a first line of support, as do your friends and colleagues. However, if you are unable to ask these people for help or for some reason you are uncomfortable in asking them for help, then it is very easy for you to reach out by yourself and obtain confidential professional services. In your community there is likely to be a suicide telephone hotline or crisis intervention center. If not, a hospital, a religious organization such as a church, or another community agency can assist in connecting you with appropriate service providers. You can find out how to reach any of these from your local telephone directory or by calling the information operator. The local police department or 911 also can be called for information about the suicide prevention center and services in your community.

There is help available to you, and that assistance can make a difference to your outlook and life. If you are reading this book, then obviously you are ambivalent enough about taking your life to at least consider getting help. Don't stop there. Call your local suicide hotline and talk with someone in your community who can help. Some friendly help and professional support in this difficult period will help you to overcome this challenge, improve your outlook over the long term, and live.

HOW DO I COPE WITH THE LOSS OF A LOVED ONE TO SUICIDE?

The 32,000 Americans who complete suicide each year leave behind many spouses, children, friends, and other loved ones who must grieve and work through their bereavement. These so-called suicide survivors may suffer from complex and serious emotional states and reactions. Depression is quite common, with fatigue, withdrawal, inability to concentrate, disturbed sleeping and eating patterns, and a general disinterest in life. Anger may occur and can be directed at family members or oneself, or possibly the loved one who died. Guilt about not preventing the suicide can be significant, along with an agonizing and persistent desire to understand why the loved one killed himself or herself. It seems that some feelings of guilt are unavoidable for most suicide survivors, but try not to allow guilt to dominate your experience. No one is to blame for most suicides. Shame also is experienced by some, and the stigma of suicide may be hard to avoid in social situations.

Over time these emotions decrease in intensity and become less intrusive. It is important to recognize these reactions in yourself and others. Just knowing that you are not alone in experiencing these feelings helps. Some of these feelings and states of mind are adaptive and can help you to overcome the sense of loss and the pain associated with losing a loved one through suicide. Emotional numbness helps to screen out pain and allows it to be managed in a gradual manner.

The American Suicide Foundation recommends a number of strategies for coping with the loss of a loved one through suicide. Keep close to other people during this period. Don't let yourself become isolated. Talk to loved ones about the suicide and seek their help. Help them to overcome the awkwardness and helplessness that they may feel. Share your feelings of loss and pain. Recognize the different ways in which others grieve, some of which may be very different from your own. Do not fail to realize that children will experience many of the same emotions and confusion as adults regarding the loss, and with similar intensity. Do not obsess about trying to understand the reasons for the suicide, and do not let this activity consume you. Slowly allow yourself to enjoy life again, and don't think that enjoying life is somehow disloyal or a betrayal of the lost person.

Support groups exist for suicide survivors. They can provide relief and an environment for communicating feelings and learning ways to strengthen oneself while moving forward and beyond the suicide. Groups also help overcome some of the isolation that survivors experience. Individual counseling with a mental health professional or a member of the clergy is another resource available to suicide survivors.

WHERE CAN I GET MORE INFORMATION AND HELP?

In searching for information and local resources on suicide prevention and treatment of mental health problems such as depression, you may contact a number of community service organizations, including your personal or family physician, local health department, local medical centers and hospitals, and other social service providers. For information on suicide prevention services in your community, look in the Yellow Pages under "Human Services Organizations" or "Social Service Organizations."

Talk to your spouse, another family member, a close friend, or a clergyman as well. If you are feeling suicidal, call your local police department or 911 and ask that they put you through immediately to a suicide crisis center or hotline.

To find a suicide crisis center near you, visit http://suicidehotlines.com/ on the internet or contact the National Suicide Hotline at (800) SUICIDE (784-2433) or (800) 273-TALK (8255).

Appendix 2 at the back of the book is a bibliography for further reading on each of the violence topics discussed in this volume, organized chapter by chapter.

The following are national organizations and useful internet websites that can refer you to specific services in your local community.

NATIONAL ORGANIZATIONS

American Association of Suicidology
(202) 237-2280

American Foundation for Suicide Prevention
(888) 333-2377

American Psychiatric Association
(888) 35-PSYCH (77924)

American Psychological Association
(800) 374-2721; TYY (202) 336-6123

Anxiety Disorders Association of America
(240) 485-1001

Centers for Disease Control and Prevention
National Center for Injury Prevention and Control
(800) CDC-INFO (232-4636)

Depression and Bipolar Support Alliance
(800) 826-3632

LGBT Youth Suicide Hotline
(866) 4-U-TREVOR (88-7386)

National Alliance on Mental Illness
(703) 524-7600

National Center for Victims of Crime
(800) FYI-CALL

National Clearinghouse for Alcohol and Drug Information
(877) SAMHSA-7; Spanish (877) 767-8432;
TDD (800) 487-4889

National Crime Prevention Council
(202) 466-6272

National Hopeline Network
(800) SUICIDE (784-2433)

National Institute of Justice
National Criminal Justice Reference Service
(800) 851-3420

National Mental Health Association
703-684-7722

National Organization for Victim Assistance
(800) 879-6682

National Suicide Prevention Lifeline
(800) 273-TALK (8255)

USEFUL INTERNET WEBSITES

American Association of Suicidology: www.suicidology.org
American Foundation for Suicide Prevention: www.afsp.org
American Psychiatric Association: www.psych.org
American Psychological Association: www.apa.org
Befrienders: www.befrienders.org
Boys Town: www.boystown.org
Centers for Disease Control and Prevention: www.cdc.gov/safeusa/suicide.htm
Crystal Palace: http://www.crystal.palace.net/~llama/selfinjury
Depression and Bipolar Support Alliance: www.dbsalliance.org
Mental Health America: www.nmha.org
National Alliance on Mental Illness: www.nami.org
National Center for Health Statistics: www.cdc.gov/nchs/fastats/suicide.htm
National Institute of Health National Library of Medicine:
    www.nlm.nih.gov/medlineplus/suicide.html
National Institute of Justice, National Criminal Justice Reference Service:
    www.ncjrs.gov
National Institute of Mental Health: www.nimh.nih.gov
National Organization for Victim Assistance: www.trynova.org
Save: www.save.org
Screening for Mental Health, Inc.: www.mentalhealthscreening.org
Suicide.org: www.suicide.org
Suicide and Suicide Prevention: http://www.psycom.net/
    depression.central.suicide.html
Suicide Hotlines by State: http://www.suicide.org/suicide-hotlines.html
Suicide Hotlines by State: http://suicidehotlines.com
Yahoo Suicide Resource: http://dir.yahoo.com/Society_and_Culture/
    death_and_dying/suicide

CHAPTER 13

Epilogue — Social Change and the Future of Violence Prevention

The dramatic increase in American violence since World War II is as difficult to understand as it is to control. Even as levels of some violence and associated deaths have declined, many forms of violence in the United States, especially within families and among intimates and acquaintances, remain intolerably and barbarically high. Although the U.S. criminal justice system is an important component of societal efforts to combat violence, the application of even the most robust crime control measures alone will not be sufficient to combat this epidemic of violence. The incidence of injuries and deaths from violence continues to be a major human and health care burden to our society despite ever greater resources devoted to crime control.

The criminal justice system has been built to respond only after the fact or the occurrence of violence. For the system to engage and respond, an incident must be reported to the police. Subsequently, an arrest may be made and the accused convicted and punished. The Department of Justice reports that the chance of resolving a violent incident through arrest is good. As sentencing of convicted criminals has become harsher, the chance of going to prison and the length of time served have both increased. These factors have nearly tripled the amount of prison time served for any violent crime in the United States.

The criminal justice system relies on arrests and incarcerations to deter, incapacitate, and rehabilitate convicted offenders. The expanded use of imprisonment by the criminal justice system is thought by law enforcement authorities to have reduced violent crime levels. By incapacitating and isolating more criminals, perhaps 10%–15% of violent crimes may have been prevented. Additional violence is prevented through deterrence, which discourages individuals from committing violent crimes because they know that they will be punished, and punished severely. It is difficult to estimate the impact of deterrence on violent crime.

Effective as this approach has been, violence is a social problem that extends well beyond the purview and reach of the law enforcement and criminal justice systems. We have seen that most violent injuries do not stem from criminal activities such as robbery, but from violent arguments, assaults, and abusive relationships among people who know each other. Because much violence occurs between intimates and within families, it is often not reported as crimes to law enforcement agencies. Most experts agree that what we are able to detect is probably just the tip of the iceberg. The problem demands that other strategies be developed and deployed. The criminal justice system has succeeded in keeping the epidemic of violence in a relative steady state and has contributed to a meaningful decline in reported levels of violence. However, to get beyond a "running in place" status quo, like the plumber who plugs one leaky pipe to find another breaching in a failing water system, violence control must also include treatment and a rigorous, far-reaching national strategy of violence prevention.

A DIVERSE LIFE CYCLE OF STRATEGIES FOR VIOLENCE PREVENTION

The National Academy of Sciences Panel on the Understanding and Control of Violent Behavior identified a series of promising strategies for the prevention of violence. These focus on several major areas, including child development, neurological and genetic processes, social and community-level interventions, and situational approaches. This approach to violence prevention demonstrates the kind of multidisciplinary, cross-sector, and full life-cycle strategies that are required to create and sustain a deep and long-term impact on the epidemic.

Programs and materials could be developed to teach parents to be nonviolent role models and how to provide children with consistent discipline that does not promote aggression and violence. Limiting children's exposure to violence in the media and in entertainment also is recommended. Efforts to reduce drug and alcohol abuse by mothers during pregnancy would reduce birth defects and possibly rates of violence against children with disabilities. Regular home visits by a public health nurse or other visitor following the birth of a child could provide health information and teach new parents, particularly those at elevated risk for abusing a child, good parenting skills. While baby care is provided, the visit offers an opportunity to detect early signs of child abuse and take appropriate action. Evidence supports the notion that preventing child abuse today will reduce adult criminal violence tomorrow.

Preschool enrichment programs, such as Head Start and tutoring early in a child's school life, can help to reduce school failure, which is a predisposing factor for later violence. Successful educational reform in the United States may be one of the pivotal keys to future success in violence prevention. Social and communication skills training programs for children as well as their parents would be of value. These should focus on nonviolent ways to express anger and resolve conflicts. Programs to prevent and stop bullying in schools are imperative. Intensive alcohol and drug abuse treatment and counseling programs for adolescents are needed.

At the social and community level, housing policies could help reduce the concentration of low-income families in certain geographic areas, although as discussed in Chapter 1, the outcomes of such initiatives have not always been as anticipated. Programs are needed to strengthen community organizations and families in a manner that promotes positive social values. Along with these efforts, investment is required to revitalize the economies of high-risk neighborhoods and communities and to create opportunities for individuals to advance themselves in positive, nonviolent activities. Improved community policing and more consistent punishment of criminals must remain important emphases.

Individuals at risk of abusing their children in the United States are frequently overwhelmed by stressful events and multiple crises in their lives. These groups fall outside the usual response system that has been established to prevent and treat child abuse. Ultimately, the primary solution for the broad spectrum of child abuse is social and economic change that reduces disenfranchisement and extends full societal membership to all parents and children. Treatment must be provided for abusers who were abused as children, even as individuals are held accountable for their acts of violence and abuse. Our society's failure to reduce alcohol and drug abuse raises the question of whether we can respond effectively to the more complex challenges of child abuse or domestic violence. If we are unable to meaningfully combat these other more discrete, in some ways more treatable problems, we should not delude ourselves that the problems of violence in American homes and families will be easily or quickly resolved.

Situational strategies may focus on preventing the minority of aggressive children from developing into violent young adults. Better cooperation between police and the proprietors of local businesses can help to identify and then eliminate high-risk "hot spots" where high levels of violence in the community occur. Most violent situations involve three elements that can be addressed through improved planning and policy: alcohol, illegal drugs, and firearms. Measures to prevent underage drinking along with alcoholism prevention programs, better law enforcement, and higher taxes on alcohol would decrease alcohol's contribution to violence. Similar strategies for reducing illegal drug use, including better treatment and prevention programs and coordination of prison drug treatment programs with follow-up after release, would decrease the role of drugs in promoting violent situations. Improved enforcement of laws that regulate the use of guns and decrease firearm access by young people (including sales to minors) is integral to violence prevention.

PUBLIC HEALTH PREVENTION VERSUS CRIMINAL JUSTICE RESPONSE: A COMPLEMENTARY DICHOTOMY

Prevention as a strategy to control violence cannot replace the criminal justice system response. These approaches are not competitive but complementary in nature and impact. There is a need to conduct long-term studies of the factors in our communities and families that cause a fraction of children to become violent adults. We need to better understand what makes these children different from those who grow up to lead healthy, nonviolent lives. The epidemic of violence in America is a deeply rooted problem. In severity and pervasiveness it marks the United States as an especially violent country among other industrialized nations.

It is not, however, unprecedented in U.S. history. Nor is it intractable. Many programs have had demonstrable effectiveness in reducing violence in specific community settings and individuals. The National Crime Prevention Council has published a resource guide for municipal agencies and community groups entitled "350 Tested Strategies to Prevent Crime." This valuable contribution includes 41 descriptions of programs around the nation that have met with success in reducing violence. Table 13.1 lists these strategies.

Many experts believe that non-domestic violence has increased substantially in American life because of failed national drug policies. It has been the policy of the federal government to control substance abuse through criminal law. However, by itself this policy has failed to slow drug abuse, and some believe it may have contributed to violence. The illicit income potential of drugs is so great that traffickers and street dealers will go to any lengths, no matter how violent, to maintain these profits. The lack of treatment and maintenance programs leads addicts to commit crimes to support their habits. Many experts believe that substance abuse should be treated as a public health, not a criminal problem, a view that is consistent with the position of the American Medical Association and the American Public Health Association that addiction is a disease. This perspective represents a basic shift in social policy, one that could substantially reduce violent crime.

Instead of spending billions of dollars annually trying to arrest and incarcerate America's large addict population—a policy that keeps prisons overcrowded (and violent offenders subject to early release)—many believe the United States should transfer a portion of these funds to the public health system for use by health,

TABLE 13.1 TESTED STRATEGIES TO PREVENT VIOLENT CRIME

Comprehensive Curricula
Train Professionals To Recognize Child Victims
Public Dialogue and Community Mediation
Information Networks on Gang Activity
Multi-agency Gang Interdiction Teams
Combine Corrections With Treatment
Target Serious Habitual Offenders
Restitution by Juvenile Offenders
Boot Camps
Teach Juveniles the Consequences of Violence
Address Violence as a Public Health Problem
In-School Probation
Diversion from Incarceration
Prevent Bullying
Assist Child Victims
Regulations and Ordinances on Gun Licensing
Promote Nonviolent Images of Youth
Involve Youth in Violence Prevention
Educate University Students About Crime Prevention
Train School-Age Youth to Mediate Conflicts
Support for Victims
Counsel Children Who Witness Violence
Family Therapy to Address Conflict and Delinquency
Gun Court
Court Programs to Assist Victims of Domestic Violence
Treatment for Male Batterers
Teach Teens to Prevent Dating Violence
Community Crisis Response Teams
Teach Entrepreneur and Job Skills to Youth
Corporate Support for Antiviolence Projects
Use State Laws and Ordinances to Combat Gangs
Teach Children About Gun Safety
After-School Programs for Latchkey Children
Hold Parents Accountable for Their Children's Behavior
Train Emergency Room Staff to Prevent Violence
Incentives for Positive Behavior
Performance as Therapy and Education
Teach Male University Students to Prevent Acquaintance Rape
Use School Organization and Policy to Address Violence
Gang Prevention Through Community Intervention With High-Risk Youth
Gun Interdictions

Adapted From "350 Tested Strategies To Prevent Crime." National Crime Prevention Council, 1700 K Street, NW, Second Floor, Washington, D.C. 20006-3817 mental health, and substance abuse professionals to expand the availability and impact of drug treatment, prevention, and education. Political leaders increasingly are recognizing the need to more effectively prevent and treat substance abuse as a fundamental element of local and national efforts to reduce violence.

Prevention strategies and programs for violence should be evaluated rigorously. The evidence thus far is not conclusive enough to suggest that the country should become committed exclusively to any particular set of strategies. Violence policies should be diverse and communities should invest in a variety of approaches rather than focusing resources on the implementation of only a few untested or incompletely evaluated ones. Because of the diverse nature of violence as evidenced in this book, no single prevention strategy could effectively have an impact across the broad spectrum of violent behavior.

To better understand and prevent violence, public health practitioners have proposed an approach similar to that applied successfully in the control of infectious diseases. Public health interventions can serve to change public attitudes and promote healthy behaviors. Easy access to lethal weapons is a major contributor to the high incidence of homicides, and just as public health strategies have reduced deaths from car crashes without banning cars, deaths from firearm injuries can be reduced without a ban of all guns. However, eliminating children's access to loaded guns is an absolute imperative.

Experts within the criminal justice system rightly point out that prevention is no panacea for violence in America, noting that the focus on abuse of women and children within public health often excludes other forms of violence that are very common. Violence also frequently occurs among adult and young men in robberies and brawls, in bullying adolescents, and in the conduct of crime. The criminal justice system addresses the fact that the majority of people killed or injured as a result of violence each year in the United States are adult males, not children or women. The criminal justice and public health approaches to violence emphasize different aspects of the violence epidemic, and neither alone is fully adequate.

In the criminal justice system, emphasis is placed on responding to violence once it has occurred. Prevention is based on estimates of future problems and typically requires attention and effort in more settings than does a responsive approach focused on specific situations, problems, and individuals. Policymakers note that prevention would be more realizable if there were a finite number of defined places or situations in which violence occurs, limiting the required resources and effort. Thus, the public and policymakers are often more receptive to a responsive strategy than to prevention, which addresses a remote and seemingly distant risk of future violence. In the past, our approach to violence could be compared with a janitor who, rather than fix the leaky pipes from which water flows, grabs as many mops and buckets as he can to feverishly soak up a never-ending flood. Balancing public health prevention with criminal justice response immediacy may enable us to fix the spouting leaks while continuing to ensure we are not engulfed by the waters raging at the moment.

Criminal justice experts argue that the system has, in fact, long been involved in preventing as well as responding to violence. A primary justification for arresting and prosecuting individuals for committing acts of violence is to prevent them from engaging in future violence through a combination of deterrence, incapacitation, and rehabilitation. Deterrence threatens potential violent offenders with imprisonment. Incapacitation isolates individuals in prison, and thus, reduces their ability to act violently within communities or homes. Rehabilitation endeavors to develop individuals' skills and evolve their beliefs in a manner that will reduce the likelihood they will be violent in the future. Although it is true that these tools are applied only after the fact when a violent crime has already been committed, the reality is that if society were able to effectively limit individuals who commit violence to a single crime over their lifetime, a large part of the epidemic would be prevented (because much violence is perpetrated by repeat offenders).

Many public health prevention strategies to reduce violence are most effective when combined with criminal justice efforts. In eliminating specific risk factors, such as young people accessing and carrying guns, the educational and other strategies of public health are complementary to law enforcement activities. Strategies for reducing violence should be viewed as a continuum of prevention through response and must include educational, civil, and criminal approaches.

The concept of a guilty individual being held accountable for violent crimes is fundamental to criminal justice. The criminal justice process is intended to determine whether an individual deserves punishment. It does not seek to identify, as do public health and prevention, what would be effective in controlling future violence. Criminal justice seeks to produce morally appropriate, as well as effective responses to violence. Public health does not focus on judgments about moral accountability or the motivation or values of violent perpetrators but instead on risk factors and causes that result in violence. The emphasis of public health is on science and technique rather than morality and passion. The question remains unanswered: Can we control the violence epidemic combining science and technique with morality and passion?

To prevent violent deaths, injuries, and disability, we must learn how to weaken and break the varied chains of events that lead to acts of violence. Predisposing events and conditions are identifiable and often predictable. But much remains to be learned, and there is a need for intensified study of the factors that contribute to violence. Often we have no understanding of why an individual behaves violently or of the background factors that encourage one individual to be violent and another not. This process of discovery, research, and communication has begun, but its future course and success will be a test of our fortitude in sticking with the task.

ENGAGEMENT AND LEADERSHIP AT ALL LEVELS, ACROSS ALL SECTORS

The United States is long overdue for a sustained public and civil dialogue on the epidemic of violence that is a social and physical malignancy, destroying not only our bodies but also the nation's soul. Periodic, transient public outrage about the violence epidemic often erupts briefly after events such as the child sex abuse scandal in the Catholic Church, the mass shootings at Columbine High and Virginia Tech, the abductions/serial sexual assaults of Jaycee Dugard or Elizabeth Smart, the Oklahoma City bombing, the bullying induced suicide of Phoebe Prince, or the cases of O.J. Simpson, Susan Smith, and Casey Anthony. In the absence of strong political and policy leadership, this moral repugnance and outrage achieves nothing. The names may change over time, but the stories are recurrent. America's political leaders have a duty to facilitate a candid examination of the violence problem and to coordinate a national strategy bridging the contributions of the criminal justice and public health systems, of community and religious leaders, educators, media executives, medical and social service professionals, and gun control advocates and opponents.

Most law enforcement officers agree that more police and prisons alone is an insufficient tactic. America's public effort to decrease violence must penetrate every home, school, and community and not focus predominantly on the radical fringe or the celebrated case, however more discrete and manageable a problem the latter may seem. It also must be implemented from the grassroots up by average people in average communities, with the assistance of—but not dependent on—professional resources, be they politicians and policymakers, police officers, doctors, or public health experts.

The violence crisis warrants crisis measures in response. Violence education and prevention activities must become as common and routine in American life as violence itself. Violence must be addressed by families in the home directly and consistently, with strong support from local religious and community organizations. The greatest potential for controlling the epidemic lies in parental responsibility and influence, as models and teachers of what is right and wrong. With so much focus on single-parent families and family breakdown, "mainstream" and intact families have abdicated parental responsibilities in the prevention of violence.

Conflict resolution should become an integral, continuous component of the curriculums of elementary and high schools, as well as colleges. The same is true of teaching young men to understand and manage the emotional/psychological dynamics and responsibilities of gender relationships so as not to treat women as objects or violently. From the beginning of gender differentiation through maturation and beyond, American males must be helped to understand what constitutes sexual and gender violence and how to avoid it. We need, perhaps most importantly, to shed ourselves of the cultural notion that equates masculinity with violence, and violence with courage, nobility, and a means of resolving problems. The perpetrators of many of the media-celebrated acts of violence noted earlier probably viewed their actions as "manly" and even courageous.

Without compromising artistic value or freedom of expression, it is possible to reduce the graphic violence content of the information and entertainment media. Violence prevention at the community level, in the form of recreational activities to divert the young from violent preoccupations, is working. But such activities and ideas should evolve from within the community rather than be imposed from without. All new parents in the United States, irrespective of income or socioeconomic class, should be offered education about child abuse prevention before they take their baby home from the hospital, much as they are about the importance and method of breastfeeding. This should be reinforced at every school and pediatric visit, and in high-risk instances, with home visits. We should greatly improve our methods of surveillance, detection, and intervention on behalf of sexually abused children both within and outside the home setting. Training in violence detection and prevention counseling for teachers, physicians, and other health and social service professionals is much needed.

Education and guidance about preventing spouse abuse should be offered to couples obtaining marriage licenses, seeking marital counseling, or engaging in divorce proceedings. We need much greater public outreach to women in abusive relationships. The law should be used to make it clear to abusers of children and women that violence, however they rationalize it, will not be tolerated, and if abusers persist in their behavior and fail to seek treatment, they will lose their freedom. Providing substance abusers with adequate treatment would help to reduce a major contributor to violence in America. These diverse efforts must not be socially stigmatized if we are to make progress in controlling violence. Much as occurred slowly over time with cancer, tuberculosis, alcoholism, and other health scourges, the violence epidemic must be de-sensationalized and become an integral part of our daily social discourse.

A large body of scientific evidence now clearly illustrates that firearms, while not wholly responsible for violence, contribute to both its frequency and lethality and increase the risk for violence. Guns, and particularly handguns (which have no other use but to commit justifiable or criminal homicide), provide tacit social approval and a context for our national culture of violence. Yet, guns alone are not the source of this epidemic. The U.S. homicide rate has fallen over the past decade as gun ownership has remained relatively stable, and clearly much American violence, including rape, child abuse, spouse abuse, and elderly abuse, comprises mostly gun-less inhumanities. Whatever the complexities and inconsistencies of the various positions on gun control, it is inconceivable—and socially unacceptable— that the polarized camps in this critical debate refuse to engage in meaningful and productive dialogue. The quality of life and safety of Americans must not be compromised by shouting voices on the far ends of an ideological spectrum. As a society we must not tolerate an environment in which voices of moderation and balance are drowned out by zealots on either side of the issue.

We have seen that violence in America is a problem with diverse causes upon which many social, economic, family, and psychological influences act. Violence is not simply a problem of incompletely effective law enforcement or an overwhelmed judicial system. These systems are critical to any effort to control violence; they are necessary but not sufficient. Violence is also not a problem that can be considered solely as a public health issue and approached in isolation from its origins in social, racial, and gender inequities, from failures of the educational system, or without recognizing the responsibility of families to resolve conflicts and raise children nonviolently. As occurs with most human behaviors, violence is a complex phenomenon that defies easy, convenient explanations and resists simple solutions. No single strategy can but modestly reduce violence on its own, and engagement of any and all strategies must be fully owned by those affected—that is, by us all.

VIOLENCE AS AN AMERICAN "DIS-EASE"

This book began with note taken of the great public reaction to the darkness and drama of the tragedies in the Catholic Church, at Columbine High School and Virginia Tech, of the media-sensationalized abductions, sexual assaults, and murders of so many children, and of the terror generated in Oklahoma City. From these we gain insight into the magnitude and depth of our violence problem. Such events generate a national mobilization of attention and sympathy along with an outpouring of resources and kindness. Our collective response demonstrates compellingly that given effective leadership and public will, a path out of this epidemic exists. Over time we are learning how far we must yet journey to end racial and gender inequities not only to ensure justice but also to prevent violence. In various school mass murders, we see how unimaginably early in life our individual and collective pathology of violence begins. In the Catholic Church scandals, we witness how even the most trusted of institutions and relationships can be undermined by pedophilia. If these horrors can inspire our political leadership to struggle against our national obsession with violence, and if they can motivate public support for political courage to experiment with change, then those who died and suffered will not have done so in vain.

It is clear that violence is truly a "dis-ease" tearing at the very core of American life and that it will continue to challenge our very concept of civility. But America can beat this deadly epidemic and greatly reduce the level of violence in our society. We can change ourselves, our families, our communities, and our social and cultural institutions. We have no other choice if we want our children—and their children—to live peaceful, full, and enriching lives.

APPENDIX 1

State Crime Victim Compensation and Assistance Programs

State Crime Victim Compensation Programs:

Alabama	www.acvcc.state.al.us
Alaska	www.state.ak.us/admin/vccb
Arizona	www.acjc.state.az.us/victim/victcomp.asp
Arkansas	www.acic.org/justice
California	www.vcgcb.ca.gov
Colorado	http://dcj.state.co.us/ovp/comp_english.htm
Connecticut	www.jud.ct.gov/crimevictim
Delaware	http://courts.delaware.gov/vccb
District of Columbia	www.dccourts.gov/dccourts/superior/cvcp.jsp
Florida	www.myfloridalegal.com/victims
Georgia	http://cjcc.ga.gov/victimDetails.aspx?id=62
Hawaii	www.hawaii.gov/cvcc
Idaho	http://www.crimevictimcomp.idaho.gov
Illinois	www.illinoisattorneygeneral.gov/victims/cvc.html
Indiana	www.in.gov/sba/files/Victim_Assistance.pdf
Iowa	www.state.ia.us/government/ag/helping_victims/index.html
Kansas	www.ksag.org/content/page/id/117
Kentucky	www.cvcb.ky.gov
Louisiana	http://www.cole.state.la.us/programs/cvr.asp
Maine	http://www.maine.gov/ag/crime/victims_compensation/index.shtml
Maryland	www.dpscs.state.md.us/victimservs/vs_cicb.shtml
Massachusetts	www.ago.state.ma.us/sp.cfm?pageid=1657
Michigan	www.michigan.gov/mdch/0,1607,71322940_3184,00.html
Minnesota	www.ojp.state.mn.us/MCCVS/FinancialHelp
Mississippi	http://www.ago.state.ms.us/index.php/sections/victims/victim_compensation
Missouri	http://www.dps.mo.gov/CVC/index.htm

Montana	www.doj.state.mt.us/victims/default.asp
Nebraska	www.ncc.state.ne.us/services_programs/crime_victim_reparations.htm
Nevada	http://dadmin.state.nv.us/Victims_FAQs.htm
New Hampshire	http://doj.nh.gov/victim/compensation.html
New Jersey	www.state.nj.us/victims
New Mexico	www.state.nm.us/cvrc
New York	www.cvb.state.ny.us
North Carolina	www.nccrimecontrol.org/vjs
North Dakota	http://www.ndcrimevictims.org
Ohio	http://www.ohioattorneygeneral.gov/Services/Victims
Oklahoma	www.ok.gov/dac/Victims_Services/Victims_Comp_Claim_Status_&_Payment_Lookup/index.html
Oregon	www.doj.state.or.us/crimev/comp.shtml#compensation
Pennsylvania	http://www.attorneygeneral.gov
Rhode Island	www.treasury.ri.gov/crimevictim
South Carolina	www.govoepp.state.sc.us/sova
South Dakota	http://www.sdvictims.com/gov/elderlyservices/services/cvc
Tennessee	http://treasury.tn.gov/injury/index.html
Texas	http://www.oag.state.tx.us/criminal/criminal.shtml#cvs
Utah	www.crimevictim.utah.gov
Vermont	http://www.ccvs.state.vt.us/joomla/index.php?option=com_content&task=view&id=15&Itemid=38
Virginia	www.cicf.state.va.us
Washington	www.lni.wa.gov/ClaimsInsurance/CrimeVictims/default.asp
West Virginia	www.legis.state.wv.us/Joint/victims/main.cfm
Wisconsin	www.doj.state.wi.us/cvs
Wyoming	http://vssi.state.wy.us/vcomp.htm

State Victim Assistance Agencies:

Alabama	www.ago.state.al.us/victim.cfm
Alaska	www.dps.state.ak.us/cdvsa
Arizona	www.azvictims.com
Arkansas	www.arkansas.gov/dfa/igs/igs_voca.html
California	http://ag.ca.gov/victimservices

Colorado	http://dcj.state.co.us/ovp/VOCA.html
Connecticut	www.jud.ct.gov/crimevictim
Delaware	www.state.de.us/cjc/victim.shtml
District of Columbia	http://ovs.dmpsj.dc.gov/ovs/site/default.asp
Florida	http://myfloridalegal.com/victims
Georgia	http://cjcc.ga.gov/grantDetails.aspx?id=234
Hawaii	http://hawaii.gov/ag/cpja/main/gp
Idaho	http://www.crimevictimcomp.idaho.gov
Illinois	www.icjia.org/public/index.cfm?metaSection=Grants& metaPage=ICJIAGrants
Indiana	www.in.gov/attorneygeneral/2340.htm
Iowa	www.state.ia.us/government/ag/helping_victims/services/ grant_program.html
Kansas	www.ksag.org/content/page/id/58
Kentucky	http://ag.ky.gov/victims
Louisiana	www.lcle.state.la.us/programs/cva.asp
Maine	www.maine.gov/dhhs/index.shtml
Maryland	www.dhr.state.md.us/victim
Massachusetts	www.mass.gov/mova
Michigan	www.michigan.gov/mdch/0,1607,71322940_3184,00.html
Minnesota	www.ojp.state.mn.us/grants/crime_victim_grants/index.htm
Mississippi	www.dps.state.ms.us/dps/dps.nsf/divpages/ ps2ojp?OpenDocument
Missouri	http://www.dps.mo.gov/CVSU/Main/CVSUhome.htm
Montana	http://doj.mt.gov/victims/default.asp
Nebraska	www.ncc.state.ne.us
Nevada	www.dhhs.nv.gov
New Hampshire	www.doj.nh.gov/victim/compensation.html
New Jersey	www.nj.gov/lps/dcj/victimwitness/index.html
New Mexico	www.state.nm.us/cvrc/voca.html
New York	http://www.cvb.state.ny.us/HelpforCrimeVictims/ HelpforCrimeVictims.aspx
North Carolina	www.nccrimecontrol.org/vjs
North Dakota	http://www.ndcrimevictims.org
Ohio	http://www.ohioattorneygeneral.gov/Services/Victims/ Victims-Compensation-Application
Oklahoma	www.ok.gov/dac/Victims_Services/index.html

Oregon	www.doj.state.or.us/crimev/vawa.shtml
Pennsylvania	http://www.pccd.state.pa.us/portal/server.pt/community/victims_of_crime/5255
Rhode Island	www.rijustice.state.ri.us/voca
South Carolina	www.scdps.org/ojp/voca/voca_grant.html
South Dakota	http://www.sdvictims.com
Tennessee	http://www.ojp.usdoj.gov/ovc/help/map/tn.htm
Texas	www.governor.state.tx.us/divisions/cjd
Utah	www.crimevictim.utah.gov
Vermont	www.ccvs.state.vt.us
Virginia	www.dcjs.virginia.gov/victims
Washington	www.lni.wa.gov/ClaimsIns/CrimeVictims/default.asp
West Virginia	www.wvdcjs.com/justiceprograms/victimsofcrime.html
Wisconsin	www.doj.state.wi.us/cvs/voca/voca_program.asp
Wyoming	http://vssi.state.wy.us

Victims' Rights Organizations:

Alaska Office of Victims' Rights	www.officeofvictimsrights.legis.state.ak.us
Arizona Voice for Crime Victims	www.voiceforvictims.org
Colorado Organization for Victim Assistance	www.coloradocrimevictims.org
Connecticut: Office of the Victim Advocate	www.ova.state.ct.us
Florida Network of Victim Witness Services	www.fnvws.org
Iowa Organization for Victim Assistance	www.iowaiova.com
Kentucky: The Mary Byron Project	www.marybyronfoundation.org
Maryland Crime Victims' Resource Center	www.mdcrimevictims.org
Maryland Crime Victims' Rights Compliance Initiative	http://www.goccp.maryland.gov/victim/victim-service-board.php
The Crime Victim Foundation	www.crimevictimfoundation.org
Michigan Victim Alliance	www.mivictims.org
Minnesota Center for Victim Services	www.ojp.state.mn.us/MCCVS/CVJU/complaint.htm
Minnesota: Crime Victim Justice Unit	www.ojp.state.mn.us/MCCVS/CVJU/about.htm

Missouri Victim Assistance Network	http://mova.missouri.org
New Mexico Crime Victims Association	www.candothat.com/nmcva
North Carolina Victim Assistance Network	www.nc-van.org
Ohio Victim Witness Association	www.ovwa.org
Oregon Crime Victims' Assistance Network	www.oregonvictims.com/cvanonly.htm
Crime Victims United of Oregon	www.crimevictimsunited.org
South Carolina: Crime Victims' Ombudsman	www.govoepp.state.sc.us/cvo
South Carolina Victim Assistance Network	www.scvan.org
Texans for Equal Justice	www.texansforequaljustice.org
Texas Victim Services Association	http://www.txvsa.org
Utah Council on Victims of Crime	www.crimevictim.utah.gov/UCVC/about_UCVC.html
Washington Coalition of Crime Victim Advocates	www.wccva.org
Wisconsin Crime Victims Council	www.doj.state.wi.us/cvs/Boards_&_Advisory_groups/Wisconsin_Crime_Victims_Council.asp
Wisconsin: Crime Victim Rights Board	www.doj.state.wi.us/cvs/CVRB.asp
Wisconsin Victim Resource Center (complaint mediation)	www.doj.state.wi.us/cvs/victims_rights/Victim_Resource_Center.asp
Wyoming Crime Victims Coalition	www.wycrimevictims.org

APPENDIX 2
References and Suggestions for Further Reading

A bibliography is presented that may be used to explore in greater depth many of the issues covered in the various chapters of the book. Most of the content of this volume has been drawn from these resources. Included are articles drawn from the professional and scientific literature (mostly journals), reports of government agencies, books written for people who work with victims and perpetrators of violence, and books and articles in the popular press for the general public. The commercially published books may be found in bookstores, online, and in public libraries. The more professionally oriented books, reports, and articles from scientific journals can be found in university libraries, on the websites listed at the end of a particular chapter, or through databases accessed on the Internet, such as the PubMed database of biomedical publications (found at www.ncbi.nlm.nih.gov/pubmed/).

CHAPTER 1: DETERMINANTS OF VIOLENCE—IS AMERICA MORE VIOLENT THAN OTHER SOCIETIES?

American Medical Association. *Violence: A Compendium from JAMA, American Medical News, and the Specialty Journals of the American Medical Association.* Chicago, IL: American Medical Association, 1989.

Bureau of Justice Statistics. *Crime and the Nation's Households.* Washington, DC: U.S. Department of Justice, Bureau of Justice Statistics, 1993. NCJ 143288.

Bureau of Justice Statistics. *Criminal Victimization in the United States: 1973–90.* Washington, DC: U.S. Department of Justice, Bureau of Justice Statistics, 1994. NCJ 139564.

Catalano, S.M. *Criminal Victimization, 2005.* Washington, DC: U.S. Department of Justice, Bureau of Justice Statistics, 2005. NCJ 214644.

DeFrances, C.J., and S.K. Smith. *Crime and Neighborhoods.* Washington, DC: U.S. Department of Justice, Bureau of Justice Statistics, 1994. NJC 147005.

Federal Bureau of Investigation. *Crime in the United States, 1993.* Washington, DC: Federal Bureau of Investigation, U.S. Department of Justice, 1994.

Gelman, D. The violence in our heads. *Newsweek,* August 2, 1993, 48.

Levitt, S.D., and S.J. Dubner. *Freakonomics: A Rogue Economist Explores the Hidden Side of Everything.* London, UK: Penguin Books, 2006.

Lorenz, K. *On Aggression.* New York, NY: Harcourt, Brace and World, 1963.

Martin, S. Physical and sexual assault of women with disabilities. *Violence Against Women* (2006):12:823.

May, R. *Power and Innocence: A Search for the Sources of Violence.* New York, NY: W.W. Norton, 1972.

National Committee for Injury Prevention and Control. *Injury Prevention: Meeting the Challenge.* New York, NY: Oxford University Press, 1989.

Rand, M. *Criminal Victimization, 2008.* Washington, DC: Bureau of Justice Statistics, U.S. Department of Justice, Office of Justice Programs, 2009. NCJ 22777.

Reiss, A.J., J.A. Roth, eds., and the Panel on the Understanding and Control of Violence Behavior of the National Research Council. *Understanding and Preventing Violence.* Volumes 1–4. Washington, DC: National Academy Press, 1993.

Rosenberg, M.L, and M.A. Fenley. *Violence in America: A Public Health Approach.* New York: Oxford University Press, 1991.

Rosin, H. American murder mystery. *The Atlantic,* July/August 2008, 40–54.

Roth, J.A. *Understanding and Preventing Violence.* Washington, DC: National Institute of Justice, U.S. Department of Justice, 1994. NCJ 145645.

Rothenberg, M.B. Effect of television violence on children and youth. *Journal of the American Medical Association* (1975):234:1043–6.

Smolowe, J. Danger in the safety zone. *Time,* August 23, 1993, 29–32.

Somers, A.R. Violence, television, and the health of American youth. *New England Journal of Medicine* (1976):294:811–17.

Teaster, P., T. Dugar, M. Mendiondo, et al. *The 2004 Survey of State Adult Protective Services: Abuse of Adults 60 Years of Age and Older.* Washington, DC: National Center on Elder Abuse, 2006.

Teplin, L. Crime victimization in adults with severe mental illness: Comparison with the National Crime Victimization Survey. *Archives of General Psychiatry* (2005):62:911–21.

United Nations. *World Report on Violence Against Children.* Geneva, Switzerland: United Nations, 2006.

U.S. Department of Health and Human Services, Children's Bureau. *Child Maltreatment, 2004.* Washington, DC: U.S. Department of Health and Human Services, 2005.

U.S. Department of Health and Human Services, Children's Bureau. *Murder, 2005.* Washington, DC: U.S. Department of Health and Human Services, 2006.

U.S. Department of Justice, Federal Bureau of Investigation. *Hate Crime Statistics, 2005.* Washington, DC: U.S. Department of Justice, 2006.

U.S. Department of Justice, Office of Justice Programs, Bureau of Justice Statistics. *Crime in the United States, 2005: Expanded Homicide Data.* Washington, DC: U.S. Department of Justice, 2006.

—*Criminal Victimization and Perceptions of Community Safety in 12 Cities, 1998.* Washington, DC: U.S. Department of Justice, 1999. NCJ 173940.

—*Criminal Victimization in the United States, 2000.* Washington, DC: U.S. Department of Justice, 2000. NCJ 188290.

—*Criminal Victimization 2000: Changes 1999–2000 with Trends 1993–2000.* Washington, DC: U.S. Department of Justice, 2001. NCJ 187007.

—*Injuries from Violent Crime, 1992–98.* Washington, DC: U.S. Department of Justice, 2001. NCJ 168633.

—*Intimate Partner Violence in the U.S. 1993–2004.* Washington, DC: U.S. Department of Justice, 2006.

—*Juvenile Offenders and Victims: 1999 National Report.* Washington, DC: U.S. Department of Justice, 1999. NCJ 178257.

—*National Crime Victimization Survey 2000.* Washington, DC: U.S. Department of Justice, 2000.

—*An Update on the Cycle of Violence.* Washington, DC: U.S. Department of Justice, 2001. NCJ 184894.

—*Urban, Suburban, and Rural Victimization, 1993–98.* Washington, DC: U.S. Department of Justice, 2000. NCJ 182031.

—*Violence Against Women.* Washington, DC: U.S. Department of Justice, 1994. NCJ 145325.

—*Violent Crime.* Washington, DC: U.S. Department of Justice, 1994. NCJ 147486.

—*Violent Victimization and Race, 1993–98.* Washington, DC: U.S. Department of Justice, 2001. NCJ 176354.

Widom, C.S. Does violence beget violence? A critical examination of the literature. *Psychological Bulletin* (1989):106:3–28.

—The cycle of violence. *Science* (1989):244:160–6.

World Health Organization. *Preventing Child Maltreatment: A Guide to Taking Action and Generating Evidence.* Geneva, Switzerland: World Health Organization, 2006.

—*Violence Prevention: The Evidence.* Geneva, Switzerland: World Health Organization, 2009.

——*World Report on Violence and Health.* Geneva, Switzerland: World Health Organization, 2002.

Zawitz, M.W., P.A. Klaus, R. Bachman, et al. *Highlights from 20 Years of Surveying Crime Victims: The National Crime Victimization Survey, 1973–92.* Washington, DC: U.S. Department of Justice, Bureau of Justice Statistics, 1993. NCJ 144525.

CHAPTER 2: PHYSICAL AND EMOTIONAL ABUSE OF CHILDREN

American Medical Association. *Violence: A Compendium from JAMA, American Medical News, and the Specialty Journals of the American Medical Association.* Chicago, IL: American Medical Association, 1989.

Chaffin, M., and B. Friedrich. Evidence-based treatments in child abuse and neglect. *Children and Youth Services Review* (2004):26:1097–113.

Check, W.A. *Child Abuse.* New York, NY: Chelsea House Publishers, 1989.

Colman, R., and C. Widom. Childhood abuse and neglect and adult intimate relationships: A prospective study. *Child Abuse and Neglect* (2004):28(11):1133–51.

Coohey, C. Battered mothers who physically abuse their children. *Journal of Interpersonal Violence* (2004):19:943–52.

Dallam, S.J. The long-term medical consequences of childhood maltreatment. In: Franey, K., R. Geffner, and C. Falconer, eds., *The Cost of Child Maltreatment: Who Pays? We All Do.* San Diego, CA: Family Violence & Sexual Assault Institute, 2001, 53–69.

Daro, D. *Confronting Child Abuse.* New York, NY: Free Press, 1988.

De Bellis, M.D., and F.W. Putnam. The psychobiology of child maltreatment. *Child and Adolescent Psychiatry Clinics of North America* (1994):3:663–78.

Duncan, A., J.C. Thoman, and C. Miller. Significance of family risk factors in development of childhood animal cruelty in adolescent boys with conduct problems. *Journal of Family Violence* (2005):20:235–9.

Durfee, M.J., G.A. Gellert, and D. Tilton-Durfee. Origins and clinical relevance of interagency child death review teams. *Journal of the American Medical Association* (1992):267:3172–5.

Felitti, V., R. Anda, D. Nordenberg, et al. Relationship of childhood abuse and household dysfunction to many of the leading causes of death in adults. *American Journal of Preventive Medicine* (1998):14(4):245–58.

Fergusson, D.M., J.M. Boden, and L.J. Horwood. Exposure to childhood sexual and physical abuse and adjustment in early adulthood. *Child Abuse & Neglect* (2008):32:607–19.

Finkelhor, D. *Childhood Victimization: Violence, Crime, and Abuse in the Lives of Young People.* New York, NY: Oxford University Press, 2008.

Finkelhor, D., R. Ormrod, H. Turner, and S. Hamby. The victimization of children and youth: A comprehensive national survey. *Child Maltreatment* (2005):10:5–25.

Finkelhor, D., H. Turner, R. Ormrod, S. Hamby, and K. Kracke. *Children's Exposure to Violence: A Comprehensive National Survey.* Washington, DC: Juvenile Justice Bulletin, Office of Justice Programs, U.S. Department of Justice, October 2009. NCJ 227744.

Fromm, S. *Annual Cost of Child Maltreatment, Prevent Child Abuse America.* Washington, DC: Prevent Child Abuse America, 2001.

Gil, D.G. *Violence Against Children: Physical Abuse in the United States.* Cambridge, MA: Harvard University Press, 1970.

Gil, E. *Treatment of Adult Survivors of Childhood Abuse.* Walnut Creek, CA: Launch Press, 1988.

Gilbert, R., C.S. Widom, K.D. Browne, D.M. Fergusson, E. Webb, and S. Janson. Burden and consequences of child maltreatment in high-income countries. *The Lancet* (2009):373:68–81.

Green, A.H. Child sexual abuse: Immediate and long-term effects and intervention. *Journal of the American Academy of Child and Adolescent Psychiatry* (1993):32:890–902.

Hakins, P. *Children at Risk*. Bethesda, MD: Adler and Adler, 1986.

Heins, M. The battered child revisited. *Journal of the American Medical Association* (1984):251:3295–300.

Helfer, R.E. *Childhood Comes First: A Crash Course in Childhood for Adults*. Lansing, MI: Helfer Publications, 1984.

Helfer, R.E., and R.S. Kempe, eds. *The Battered Child*. Chicago, IL: University of Chicago Press, 1988.

Kaufman, J., and E. Zigler. Do abused children become abusive parents? *American Journal of Orthopsychiatry* (1987):57:186–92.

Kempe, C.H. Approaches to preventing child abuse. *American Journal of Diseases of Children* (1976):130:941–7.

Kempe, R.S., and C.H. Kempe. *Child Abuse*. Cambridge, MA: Harvard University Press, 1978.

Kempe, C.H., F.N. Silverman, B.F. Steele, W. Droegemueller, and H.K. Silver. The battered-child syndrome. *Journal of the American Medical Association* (1962):181:17–24.

Langsford, J.E., S. Miller-Johnson, L.J. Berlin, K.A. Dodge, J.E. Bates, and G.S. Pettit. Early physical abuse and later violent delinquency: A prospective longitudinal study. *Child Maltreatment* (2007):12:233–45.

Leeb, R.T., L. Paulozzi, C. Melanson, T. Simon, and I. Arias. *Child Maltreatment Surveillance: Uniform Definitions for Public Health and Recommended Data Elements, Version 1.0*. Atlanta, GA: Centers for Disease Control and Prevention, National Center for Injury Prevention and Control, 2007.

APPENDIX 2

Ludwig, S., and A.E. Kornberg, eds. *Child Abuse: A Medical Reference*. New York, NY: Churchill Livingston, 1992.

National Center for Child Death Review. *Child Death Review Findings: A Road Map for MCH Injury and Violence Prevention; Part I*. Washington, DC: National Center for Child Death Review, 2007.

National Committee for Injury Prevention and Control. *Injury Prevention: Meeting the Challenge*. New York, NY: Oxford University Press, 1989.

National Research Council, Panel on Research on Child Abuse and Neglect. *Understanding Child Abuse and Neglect*. Washington, DC: National Academy Press, 1993.

National Scientific Council on the Developing Child. *Excessive Stress Disrupts the Architecture of the Developing Brain*. Working Paper No. 3, 2005. Available at: http://developingchild.harvard.edu/initiatives/council. Accessed February 16, 2010.

Newberger, E.H., ed. *Child Abuse*. Boston, MA: Little Brown, 1982.

Pelcovitz, D., S. Kaplan, B. Goldenberg, et al. Post-traumatic stress disorder in physically abused adolescents. *Journal of the American Academy of Child and Adolescent Psychiatry* (1994):22:305–12.

Salzinger, S., R.S. Feldman, M. Hammer, and M. Rosario. The effects of physical abuse on children's social relationships. *School Psychology Review* (1987):16:156–68.

Seligmann, J., S.J. Springen, D. Witherspoon, and L. Lazarovici. Emotional child abuse: Discipline's fine line. *Newsweek,* October 3, 1988, 91–92.

Smith, P., M. Bohnstedt, E. Lennon, and K. Grove. *Long-Term Correlates of Child Victimization: Consequences of Intervention and Non-Intervention*. Washington, DC: National Center on Child Abuse and Neglect, 1985.

Spinetta, J.J., and D. Rigler. The child abusing parent: a psychological review. *Psychological Bulletin* (1972):77:296–304.

U.S. Department of Health and Human Services, Administration for Children and Families, Administration on Children, Youth and Families, Children's Bureau. *Child Maltreatment 1998—Reports From the States to the National Child Abuse and Neglect Data System*. Washington, DC: U.S. Government Printing Office, 2000.

——*Child Maltreatment 2007*. Washington, DC: U.S. Government Printing Office, 2009.

——*Emerging Practices in the Prevention of Child Abuse and Neglect*. Washington, DC: U.S. Government Printing Office, 2003.

——*Understanding the Effects of Maltreatment on Early Brain Development*. Washington, DC: U.S. Government Printing Office, 2001.

U.S. Department of Justice, Office of Justice Programs, Bureau of Justice Statistics. *Children as Victims*. Washington, DC: U.S. Department of Justice, 2000. NCJ 180753.

——*The National Center on Child Fatality Review*. Washington, DC: U.S. Department of Justice, 2000. FS-200112.

U.S. Department of Justice. Office of Justice Programs, Office of Juvenile Justice and Delinquency Prevention. *Child Abuse Reported to the Police*. Washington, DC: U.S. Department of Justice, May 2001. NCJ 187238.

Wald, M., and P.H. Leiderman. *Protecting Abused and Neglected Children*. Palo Alto, CA: Stanford University Press, 1988.

Widom, C., N. Marmorstein, and H. White. Childhood victimization and illicit drug use in middle adulthood. *Psychology of Addictive Behaviors* (2006):20: 394–403.

Wissow, L.S. Child abuse and neglect. *New England Journal of Medicine* (1995):332:1425–31.

APPENDIX 2

CHAPTER 3: SEXUAL ABUSE OF CHILDREN

Abel, G., and N. Harlow. *Stop Child Molestation Book*. Bloomington, IN: XLibris, 2001.

Adams, C., and J. Fay. *No More Secrets*. San Luis Obispo, CA: Impact Publishers, 1981.

American Medical Association. *Diagnostic and Treatment Guidelines on Child Sexual Abuse*. Chicago, IL: American Medical Association, 1992.

Bachmann, G. Childhood sexual abuse and the consequences in adult women. *Obstetrics and Gynecology* (1988):April:631–42.

Bagley, C.R., and R.J. Thomlison, eds. *Child Sexual Abuse. Critical Perspectives on Prevention, Intervention, and Treatment*. Middletown, OH: Wall and Emerson, Inc., 1991.

Basile, K.C., J. Chen, M.C. Lynberg, and L.E. Saltzman. Prevalence and characteristics of sexual violence victimization. *Violence and Victims* (2007):22: 437–48.

Bassett, K. *My Very Own Special Body Book*. Redding, CA: Hawthorne Press, 1981.

Beitchman, J.H., K.J. Zucker, J.E. Hood, G.A. daCosta, D. Akman, and E. Cassavia. A review of the long term effects of child sexual abuse. *Child Abuse & Neglect* (1992):16:101–18.

Berliner, L., and J.F. Wheeler. Treating the effects of sexual abuse on children. *Journal of Interpersonal Violence* (1987):2:415–34.

Boatman, E.E., L. Borkan, and D.H. Schetky. Treatment of child victims of incest. *American Journal of Family Therapy* (1981):9:42–51.

Browne, A., and D. Finkelhor. Impact of child sexual abuse: A review of the research. *Psychological Bulletin* (1986):99:66–77.

Burgess, A. *The Sexual Assault of Children and Adolescents*. Lexington, MA: Lexington Books, DC Heath and Company, 1982.

Centers for Disease Control and Prevention. Physical dating violence among high school students—United States, 2003. *Morbidity and Mortality Weekly Report* (2006):55:532–5.

Centers for Disease Control and Prevention. Youth Risk Behavior Surveillance—United States. 2005. Surveillance Summaries, 2006. *Morbidity and Mortality Weekly Report* (2006):55:SS-5.

Crewdson, J. *By Silence Betrayed: Sexual Abuse of Children in America*. Boston, MA: Little, Brown and Co., 1988.

Daugherty, L.B. *Why Me? Help for Victims of Child Sexual Abuse*. Racine, WI: Mother Courage Press, 1984.

Dayee, F.S. *Private Zone*. Edmonds, WA: The Charles Franklin Press, 1982.

Dube, S.R., R.F. Anda, C.L. Whitfield, et al. Long-term consequences of childhood sexual abuse by gender of victim. *American Journal of Preventive Medicine* (2005):28:430–8.

Dubowitz, H. *Child Maltreatment in the U.S.: Etiology, Impact, and Prevention*. Washington, DC: Office of Technology Assessment, U.S. Congress, 1987.

Dubowitz, H., M. Black, D. Harrington, and A. Verschoore. A follow-up study of behavior problems associated with child sexual abuse. *Child Abuse & Neglect* (1993):17:743–54.

Elliott, M., K. Browne, and J. Kilcoyne. Child sexual abuse prevention: What offenders tell us. *Child Abuse & Neglect* (1995):5:579–94.

Faller, K.C., and the U.S. Department of Health and Human Services, National Center on Child Abuse and Neglect. *Child Sexual Abuse: Intervention and Treatment Issues*. Washington, DC: Department of Health and Human Services, 1993.

APPENDIX 2

Fay, J.J. *He Told Me Not To Tell*. Renton, WA: King County Rape Relief, 1979.

Fay, J.J., and B.J. Flerehinger. *Top Secret*. Renton, WA: King County Rape Relief, 1982.

Fergusson, D.M., J.M. Boden, and L.J. Horwood. Exposure to childhood sexual and physical abuse and adjustment in early adulthood. *Child Abuse & Neglect* (2008):32:607–19.

Fergusson, D., L. Horwood, and M. Lynskey. Childhood sexual abuse, adolescent sexual behavior, and sexual revictimization. *Child Abuse & Neglect* (1997):21: 789–803.

Finkelhor, D. *Childhood Victimization: Violence, Crime, and Abuse in the Lives of Young People*. New York, NY: Oxford University Press, 2008.

——The international epidemiology of child sexual abuse. *Child Abuse & Neglect* (1994):18:409–17.

——Sexually Victimized Children. New York, NY: The Free Press, 1979.

——*A Sourcebook on Child Sexual Abuse*. Beverly Hills, CA: Sage Publications, Inc., 1986.

——The trauma of child sexual abuse: Two models. *Journal of Interpersonal Violence* (1987):2:348–66.

Finkelhor, D., and J. Dziuba-Leatherman. Children as victims of violence: A national survey. *Pediatrics* (1994):94:413–20.

Finkelhor, D., H. Hammer, and A. Sedlak. *Sexually Assaulted Children: National Estimates and Characteristics*. Washington, DC: U.S. Department of Justice, Office of Justice Programs, Office of Juvenile Justice and Delinquency Prevention, 2008.

Finkelhor, D., G. Hotaling, I.A. Lewis, and C. Smith. Sexual abuse in a national survey of adult men and women: Prevalence, characteristics, and risk factors. *Child Abuse & Neglect* (1990):14:19–28.

Finkelhor, D., H. Turner, R. Ormrod, S. Hamby, and K. Kracke. *Children's Exposure to Violence: A Comprehensive National Survey.* Juvenile Justice Bulletin. Washington, DC: Office of Justice Programs, U.S. Department of Justice, October 2009. NCJ 227744.

Finkelhor, D., L.M. Williams, and N. Burns. *Nursery Crimes: Sexual Abuse in Day Care.* Newbury Park, CA: Sage Publications, Inc., 1988.

Forward, S., and C. Buck. *Betrayal of Innocence: Incest and Its Devastation.* New York, NY: Penguin Books, 1979.

Friedrich, W.N. *Psychotherapy of Sexually Abused Children and Their Families.* New York, NY: Norton, 1990.

Gellert, G.A., M.J. Durfee, C.D. Berkowitz, K.V. Higgins, and V.C. Tubiolo. Situational and sociodemographic characteristics of children infected with HIV from pediatric sexual abuse. *Pediatrics* (1993):91:39–44.

Goldman, R.L., and R.M. Gargiulo, eds. *Children at Risk. An Interdisciplinary Approach to Child Abuse and Neglect.* Austin, TX: Pro-ed, Inc., 1990.

Goodman, G.S., S. Ghetti, J.A. Quas, et al. A prospective study of memory for child sexual abuse: New findings relevant to the repressed-memory controversy. *Psychological Science* (2003):14:113–18.

Goodman-Brown, T.B., R.S. Edelstein, G.S. Goodman, D.P.H. Jones, and D.S. Gordon. Why children tell: A model of children's disclosure of sexual abuse. *Child Abuse & Neglect* (2003):27:525–40.

Groth, A.N., and H.J. Birnbaum. *Men Who Rape.* New York, NY: Plenum Press, 1979.

Herman, J. *Father-Daughter Incest.* Cambridge, MA: Harvard University Press, 1981.

Hotaling, G.T., and D. Finkelhor. *The Sexual Exploitation of Missing Children: A Research Review.* Washington, DC: Office of Juvenile Justice and Delinquency Prevention, U.S. Department of Justice, 1988. NCJ 114273.

James, B., and M. Nasjleti. *Treating Sexually Abused Children and Their Families.* Palo Alto, CA: Consulting Psychologists Press, Inc., 1983.

Justice, B., and R. Justice. *The Broken Taboo: Sex in the Family.* New York, NY: Human Science Press, 1979.

Kempe, C.H. Sexual abuse, another hidden pediatric problem: The 1977 C. Anderson Aldrich lecture. *Pediatrics* (1978):62:382–9.

Kendler, K., C. Bulik, J. Silberg, J. Hettema, J. Myers, and C. Prescott. Childhood sexual abuse and adult psychiatric and substance use disorders in women: An epidemiological and Cotwin Control Analysis. *Archives of General Psychiatry* (2000):57:953–9.

Koop, C.E. *The Surgeon General's Letter on Child Sexual Abuse.* Washington, DC: U.S. Department of Health and Human Services, 1988.

Langan, P.A., and C. Wolf Harlow. *Child Rape Victims, 1992.* Washington, DC: U.S. Department of Justice, Bureau of Justice Statistics, 1994. NJC 147001.

Lisak, D. The psychological impact of sexual abuse: Content analysis interviews with male survivors. *Journal of Traumatic Stress* (1994):7:525–48.

Mandell, J.G., L. Damon, P.C. Castaldo, et al. *Group Treatment for Sexually Abused Children.* New York: Guilford Press, 1989.

Martin, S. Physical and sexual assault of women with disabilities. *Violence Against Women* (2006):12:823.

McLeer, S.V., E. Deblinger, M.C. Atkins, et al. Post-traumatic stress disorder in sexually abused children. *Journal of the American Academy of Child and Adolescent Psychiatry* (1988):27:650–4.

McLeer, S.V., E. Deblinger, D. Henry, and H. Orvaschel. Sexually abused children at high risk for post-traumatic stress disorder. *Journal of the American Academy of Child and Adolescent Psychiatry* (1992):31:875–9.

National Center for Missing and Exploited Children. *CyberTipline: Annual Report Totals*. Alexandria, VA: National Center for Missing and Exploited Children, 2006.

Nelson, M., and K. Clark, eds. *The Educator's Guide to Preventing Child Sexual Abuse*. Santa Cruz, CA: Network, 1986.

Noll, J.G., P.K. Trickett, and F.W. Putnam. A prospective investigation of the impact of childhood sexual abuse on the development of sexuality. *Journal of Consulting and Clinical Psychology* (2003):71:575–86.

O'Donohue, W., and J.H. Geer, eds. *The Sexual Abuse of Children: Theory and Research*. Vol. 1; *The Sexual Abuse of Children: Clinical Issues*. Vol. 2. Hillsdale, NJ: Lawrence Erlbaum Associates, Inc., 1992.

Putnam, F. Ten-year research update review: Child sexual abuse. *Journal of the American Academy of Child and Adolescent Psychiatry* (2003):42:269–78.

Rush, F. *The Best Kept Secret: Sexual Abuse of Children*. New York, NY: McGraw-Hill, 1980.

Salter, A.C. *Treating Child Sex Offenders and Victims: A Practical Guide*. Newbury Park, CA: Sage Publications, Inc., 1988.

Sgroi, S.M. *A Handbook of Clinical Intervention in Child Sexual Abuse*. Lexington, MA: Lexington Books, 1982.

Sgroi, S.M., ed. *Vulnerable Populations. Evaluation and Treatment of Sexually Abused Children and Adult Survivors*. Vol. 1; *Vulnerable Populations. Sexual Abuse Treatment for Children, Adult Survivors, Offenders, and Persons with Mental Retardation*. Vol. 2. Lexington, MA: Lexington Books, 1988.

Silverman, J.G., A. Raj, L. Mucci, and J. Hathaway. Dating violence against adolescent girls and associated substance use, unhealthy weight control, sexual risk behavior, pregnancy, and suicidality. *Journal of the American Medical Association* (2001):286:572–9.

Snyder, H.N. *Sexual Assault of Young Children as Reported to Law Enforcement: Victim, Incident, and Offender Characteristics.* Washington, DC: U.S. Department of Justice, Office of Justice Programs, July 2000. NCJ 182990.

Summit, R.C. The child sexual abuse accommodation syndrome. *Child Abuse & Neglect* (1983):7:177–92.

Sweet, P.E. *Something Happened to Me.* Racine, WI: Mother Courage Press, 1981.

Tschirhart Sanford, L. *Come Tell Me Right Away.* Fayetteville, NY: Ed U Press, Inc., 1982.

——*The Silent Children.* New York, NY: McGraw-Hill Book Company, 1980.

U.S. Department of Health and Human Services, Administration on Children Youth & Families. *Child Maltreatment 1998—Reports From the States to the National Child Abuse and Neglect Data System.* Washington, DC: U.S. Department of Health and Human Services, 2000.

——*Child Maltreatment 2007.* Washington, DC: U.S. Department of Health and Human Services, 2009.

——*Children as Victims.* Washington, DC: U.S. Department of Health and Human Services, 2000. NCJ 180753.

——*Sexual Assault of Young Children as Reported to Law Enforcement: Victim, Incident, and Offender Characteristics.* Washington, DC: U.S. Department of Health and Human Services, 2000. NCJ 182990.

U.S. Department of Justice, Office of Justice Programs, Bureau of Justice Statistics. *The Decline in Child Sexual Abuse Cases.* Washington, DC: U.S. Department of Justice, 2000. NCJ 184741.

U.S. Department of Justice, Office of Justice Programs, Office of Juvenile Justice and Delinquency Prevention. *Child Abuse Reported to the Police.* Washington, DC: U.S. Department of Justice, May 2001. NCJ 187238.

U.S. House of Representatives, Select Committee on Children, Youth, and Families. *Abused Children in America: Victims of Official Neglect*. Washington, DC: U.S. Government Printing Office, 1987.

Vale Allen, C. *Daddy's Girl*. New York, NY: Berkley Books, 1982.

Walker, L.E., ed. *Handbook on Sexual Abuse of Children. Assessment and Treatment Issues*. New York, NY: Springer Publishing Company, 1988.

Weinberg, S.K. *Incest Behavior*. Secaucus, NY: Citadel Press, 1955.

Williams, J. *Red Flag Green Flag. Rape and Abuse Crisis Center of Fargo*. Fargo, ND: Moorhead, 1980.

Wolak, J., J. Mitchel, and D. Finkelhor. *Online Victimization of Youth: Five Years Later*. Alexandria, VA: National Center for Missing and Exploited Children, 2006.

Wolitzky-Taylor, K.B., K.J. Ruggiero, C.K. Danielson, et al. Prevalence and correlates of dating violence in a national sample of adolescents. *Journal of the American Academy of Child and Adolescent Psychiatry* (2008):47:755–62.

Wooden, K. *Child Lures. What Every Parent and Child Should Know About Preventing Sexual Abuse and Abduction*. Arlington, TX: Summit Publishing Group, 1995.

CHAPTER 4: YOUTH AND SCHOOL VIOLENCE

ACCESS ERIC. School Safety: A Collaborative Effort (Special Issue). *The ERIC Review*. (7)1. Rockville, MD: U.S. Department of Education, Office of Educational Research and Improvement, 2000.

Allen-Hagen, B., M. Sickmund, and H.N. Snyder. *Juveniles and Violence: Juvenile Offending and Victimization*. Fact Sheet #19. Washington, DC: Office of Juvenile Justice and Delinquency Prevention, U.S. Department of Justice, 1994. NCJ FS09419.

APPENDIX 2

American Medical Association. *Violence: A Compendium from JAMA, American Medical News, and the Specialty Journals of the American Medical Association.* Chicago, IL: American Medical Association, 1989.

American Psychological Association and American Academy of Pediatrics. *Raising Children to Resist Violence: What You Can Do.* Elk Grove Village, IL: American Academy of Pediatrics and American Psychological Association, 1995.

American Psychological Association, Commission on Violence and Youth. *Violence & Youth. Psychology's Response.* Washington, DC: American Psychological Association, Public Interest Directorate, 1993.

Ascher, C. *Gaining Control of Violence in the Schools: A View from the Field.* New York, NY: ERIC Clearinghouse on Urban Education, September, 1994.

Bastian, L.D., and B.M. Taylor. *School Crime: A National Crime Survey Report.* Washington, DC: U.S. Department of Justice, Bureau of Justice Statistics, 1991. NCJ 131645.

Centers for Disease Control and Prevention, National Center for Injury Prevention Control. *The Prevention of Youth Violence: A Framework for Community Action.* Atlanta, GA: Centers for Disease Control and Prevention, 1993.

——School-associated student homicides—United States, 1992–2006. *Morbidity and Mortality Weekly Report* (2008):57(02):33–6.

——Youth risk behavior surveillance—United States, 2005. *Morbidity and Mortality Weekly Report* (2006):a-55(SS-5):1–108.

——Youth risk behavior surveillance—United States, 2007. *Morbidity and Mortality Weekly Report* (2008):57(SS-4):1–131.

Children's Safety Network Economics & Data Analysis Resource Center. *State Costs of Violence Perpetrated by Youth.* Available at: www.edarc.org/pubs/tables/youth-viol.htm. Accessed February 16, 2010.

Department of Health and Human Services. *Youth Violence: A Report of the Surgeon General, 2001*. Available at: http://www.surgeongeneral.gov/library/youthviolence/youvioreport.html. Accessed March 26, 2010.

Dwyer, K., and D. Osher. *Safeguarding Our Children: An Action Guide.* Washington, DC: U.S. Department of Education, U.S. Department of Justice, and American Institutes for Research, 2000.

Ellickson, P.L., and K.A. McGuigan. Early predictors of adolescent violence. *American Journal of Public Health* (2000):90:566–72.

Ellickson, P., H. Saner, and K.A. McGuigan. Profiles of violent youth: Substance use and other concurrent problems. *American Journal of Public Health* (1997):87: 985–91.

Finkelhor, D., H. Turner, R. Ormrod, S. Hamby, and K. Kracke. *Children's Exposure to Violence: A Comprehensive National Survey.* Washington, DC: Juvenile Justice Bulletin, Office of Justice Programs, U.S. Department of Justice, October 2009. NCJ 227744.

Garbarino, J., N. Dubrow, K. Kostelny, and C. Pardo. *Children in Danger: Coping with the Consequences of Community Violence.* San Francisco, CA: Jossey-Bass, 1992.

Hamilton Fish Institute. *Effective Violence Prevention Programs.* Washington, DC: Hamilton Fish Institute, 2000.

Henkoff, R. Kids are killing, dying, bleeding. *Fortune,* August 1992, 62–9.

Howell, J.C. *Youth Gangs: An Overview.* Washington, DC: Office of Juvenile Justice and Delinquency Prevention, U.S. Department of Justice, 1998.

Howell, J.C. *Guide for Implementing the Comprehensive Strategy for Serious, Violent, and Chronic Juvenile Offenders.* Washington, DC: Office of Juvenile Justice and Delinquency Prevention, U.S. Department of Justice, 1995. NCJ 153681.

Kashani, J.H., A.E. Daniel, A.C. Dandoy, and W.R. Holcomb. Family violence: Impact on children. *Journal of the American Academy of Child and Adolescent Psychiatry* (1992):31:181–9.

Kaufman, P., X. Chen, S. Choy, et al. *Indicators of School Crime and Safety, 2000.* Washington, DC: National Center for Education Statistics, 2001. NCES 2001-017.

Kracke, K., and H. Hahn. The nature and extent of childhood exposure to violence: What we know, why we don't know more, and why it matters. *Journal of Emotional Abuse* (2008):8(1/2):29–49.

Lipsey, M.W., and J.H. Derzon. Predictors of violent and serious delinquency in adolescence and early adulthood: A synthesis of longitudinal research. In: Loeber, R., and D.P. Farrington, eds., *Serious and Violent Juvenile Offenders: Risk Factors and Successful Intervention.* Thousand, Oaks, CA: Sage Publications, 1998, 86–105.

McAlister Groves, B., B. Zuckerman, S. Marans, and D.J. Cohen. Silent victims: Children who witness violence. *Journal of the American Medical Association* (1993):269:262–3.

McGill, D.E. *Big Brothers Big Sisters of America.* Boulder, CO: Center for the Study and Prevention of Violence, University of Colorado at Boulder, Institute of Behavioral Science, 1997.

Mercy, J., A. Butchart, D. Farrington, and M. Cerda. Youth violence. In: Krug, E., L.L. Dahlberg, J.A. Mercy, et al., eds., *The World Report on Violence and Health.* Geneva, Switzerland: World Health Organization, 2002, 23–56.

National Center for Education Statistics. *Indicators of School Crime and Safety: 2007.* Washington, DC: Institute of Education Sciences, U.S. Department of Education and Bureau of Justice Statistics, U.S. Department of Justice, Office of Justice Programs, 2007. NCES 2008-021/NCJ 219553.

Newman, G. *Bomb Threats in Schools.* Washington, DC: Office of Community Oriented Policing Services, 2005.

Office of Juvenile Justice and Delinquency Prevention. *Creating Safe and Drug-Free Schools: An Action Guide. Report.* Washington, DC: U.S. Department of Justice, Office of Justice Programs, Office of Juvenile Justice and Delinquency Prevention, 1996.

Pollack, I., and C. Sundermann. *Creating Safe Schools: A Comprehensive Approach.* Washington, DC: Juvenile Justice, Office of Juvenile Justice and Delinquency Prevention, June 2001. NCJ 188160.

Prothrow-Stith, D. *Deadly Consequences: How Violence Is Destroying Our Teenage Population and a Plan to Begin Solving the Problem.* New York, NY: Harper Perennial, 1991.

Pynoos, R.S., and K. Nader. Children's exposure to violence and traumatic death. *Psychiatric Annals* (1990):20:334–44.

Resnick, M.D., M. Ireland, and I. Borowsky. Youth violence and perpetration: What protects? What predicts? Findings from the National Longitudinal Study of Adolescent Health. *Journal of Adolescent Health* (2004):35:424.

Schwartz, W. *Preventing Violence by Elementary School Children.* New York, NY: ERIC Clearinghouse on Urban Education, November, 1999.

Sheppard, D., H. Grant, W. Rowe, and N. Jacobs. *Fighting Juvenile Gun Violence.* Washington, DC: U.S. Department of Justice, Office of Justice Programs, Office of Juvenile Justice and Delinquency Prevention, Juvenile Justice Bulletin, September 2000. NCJ 182678.

Small, M., and K.D. Tetrick. *School Violence: An Overview. Juvenile Justice.* Washington, DC: Office of Juvenile Justice and Delinquency Prevention, June, 2001.

Snyder, H.N., and M. Sickmund. *Juvenile Offenders and Victims: A National Report.* Washington, DC: Office of Juvenile Justice and Delinquency Prevention, U.S. Department of Justice, 1995. NCJ 153569.

Somers, A.R. Violence, television, and the health of American youth. *New England Journal of Medicine* (1976):294:811–17.

APPENDIX 2

Spergel, I., D. Curry, R. Chance, et al. *Gang Suppression and Intervention: Problem and Response.* Washington, DC: Office of Juvenile Justice and Delinquency Prevention, U.S. Department of Justice, 1994. NCJ 149629.

Thornton, T.N., C.A. Craft, L.L. Dahlberg, B.S. Lynch, and K. Baer. *Best Practices of Youth Violence Prevention: A Sourcebook for Community Action (Rev.).* Atlanta, GA: Centers for Disease Control and Prevention, National Center for Injury Prevention and Control, 2002.

U.S. Department of Education and U.S. Department of Justice. *2000 Annual Report on School Safety.* Washington, DC: U.S. Department of Education and U.S. Department of Justice, 2000. NCJ 193163.

U.S. Department of Education. *Summary, Campus Crime and Security Statistics 2002–2004: Criminal Offenses.* Washington, DC: U.S. Department of Education, 2006.

U.S. Department of Justice, Bureau of Justice Statistics. *National Crime Victimization Survey (NCVS).* Washington, DC: U.S. Department of Justice, 2005. NCJ 209911.

U.S. Department of Justice, Office of Justice Programs, Office of Juvenile Justice and Delinquency Prevention. *Characteristics of Crimes Against Juveniles.* Washington, DC: U.S. Department of Justice, 2001. NCJ 179034.

—*The Growth of Youth Gang Problems in the United States: 1970–98, Part 1.* Washington, DC: U.S. Department of Justice, 2001. NCJ 181868.

—*Highlights of the 1999 National Youth Gang Survey.* OJDP Fact Sheet. Washington, DC: U.S. Department of Justice, November, 2000. FS-200020.

—*Indicators of School Crime and Safety, 2001.* Washington, DC: U.S. Department of Justice, 2001. NCJ 190075.

—*Juvenile Offenders and Victims: 1999 National Report.* Washington, DC: U.S. Department of Justice, 1999. NCJ 178257.

—*Violence After School, 1999 National Report Series, Juvenile Justice Bulletin.*

Washington, DC: U.S. Department of Justice, November, 1999. NCJ 178257.

Whitaker, C.J., and L.D. Bastian. *Teenage Victims: A National Crime Survey Report*. Washington, DC: U.S. Department of Justice, Bureau of Justice Statistics, 1991. NCJ 128129.

Wolitzky-Taylor, K.B., K.J. Ruggiero, C.K. Danielson, et al. Prevalence and correlates of dating violence in a national sample of adolescents. *Journal of the American Academy of Child and Adolescent Psychiatry* (2008):47:755–62.

CHAPTER 5: BULLYING—NOT JUST KIDS' STUFF

Agatston, P., R. Kowalski, and S. Limber. Students' perspectives on cyber bullying. *Journal of Adolescent Health* (2007):41(6 Suppl 1):S59–S60.

Boulton, M.J., and P.K. Smith. Bully/victim problems in middle school children: Stability, self-perceived competence, peer perceptions and peer acceptance. *British Journal of Development Psychology* (1994):12:315–29.

California Association of School Psychologists. *The Good, the Bad, and the Bully* Resource Paper. April 1997, 1–8.

Dawkins, J. Bullying in schools: Doctors' responsibilities. *British Medical Journal* (1995):310:274–5.

Ericson, N. *Addressing the Problem of Juvenile Bullying*. Washington, DC: U.S. Department of Justice, June 2001. FS-200127.

Estroff Marano, H. Big. Bad. Bully. *Psychology Today* (1995):Sept/Oct:51–82.

Fein, R.A., B. Vossekuil, W. Pollack, R. Borum, M. Reddy, and W. Modzeleski. *Threat Assessment in Schools: A Guide to Managing Threatening Situations and Creating Safe School Climates*. Washington, DC: U.S. Department of Education and U.S. Secret Service, May 2002.

Finkelhor, D., H. Turner, R. Ormrod, S. Hamby, and K. Kracke. *Children's Exposure to Violence: A Comprehensive National Survey*. Washington, DC:

APPENDIX 2

Juvenile Justice Bulletin, Office of Justice Programs, U.S. Department of Justice, October 2009. NCJ 227744.

Foltz-Gray, D. The bully trap. *Teaching Tolerance,* Fall 1996, 19–23.

Franklin, D. Charm school for bullies. *Hippocrates,* May/June 1989, 75–7.

Fried, S., and P. Fried. *Bullies & Victims: Helping Your Child Through the Schoolyard Battlefield.* New York, NY: M. Evans and Company, Inc., 1996.

Garrity, C., K. Jens, W. Porter, N. Sager, and C. Short-Camilli. *Bully-Proofing Your School: A Comprehensive Approach for Elementary Schools.* Longmont, CO: Sopris West, 1994.

Greenbaum, S., B. Turner, and R.D. Stephens. *Set Straight on Bullies.* Malibu, CA: Pepperdine University Press, 1989.

Hazler, R.J. Bullying breeds violence: You can stop it! *Learning,* February 1994, 38–40.

Hertz, M.F., and C. David-Ferdon. *Electronic Media and Youth Violence: A CDC Issue Brief for Educators and Caregivers.* Atlanta, GA: Centers for Disease Control, 2008.

Hodges, E.V., and D.G. Perry. Victims of peer abuse: An overview. *Reclaiming Children and Youth* (1996):Spring:23–8.

Hoover, J.H., and R. Oliver. *The Bullying Prevention Handbook: A Guide for Principals, Teachers, and Counselors.* Bloomington, IN: National Educational Service, 1996.

Howell, J.C. *Youth Gangs: An Overview.* Washington, DC: Office of Juvenile Justice and Delinquency Prevention, U.S. Department of Justice, 1998.

Kaufman, P., X. Chen, S. Choy, et al. *Indicators of School Crime and Safety: 2000.* Washington, DC: National Center for Education Statistics, 2001. NCES 2001-017.

Kerbs, J.J., and J.M. Jolley. The joy of violence: What about violence is fun in middle-school? *American Journal of Criminal Justice* (2007):32:No.1–2.

Kowalski, R.M., and S.P. Limber. Electronic bullying among middle school students. *Journal of Adolescent Health* (2007):41(6 Suppl 1):S22–S30.

Limber, S.P. Bullying among school children. *School Safety,* Fall 1996, 8–9, 30.

Marr, N., and T. Field. *Bullycide: Death at Playtime—An Exposé of Child Suicide Caused by Bullying.* Oxfordshire, UK: Success Unlimited, 2001.

McCoy, E. Bully-proof your child. *Reader's Digest,* November 1992, 199–204.

Mercy, J., A. Butchart, D. Farrington, and M. Cerda. Youth violence. In: Krug, E., L.L. Dahlberg, J.A. Mercy, et al., eds., *The World Report on Violence and Health.* Geneva, Switzerland: World Health Organization, 2002, 23–56.

Nansel, T.R., M. Overpeck, R.S. Pilla, et al. Bullying behaviors among U.S. youth: Prevalence and association with psychosocial adjustment. *Journal of the American Medical Association* (2001):285(16):2094–100.

National Center for Education Statistics. *Indicators of School Crime and Safety: 2007.* Washington, DC: Institute of Education Sciences, U.S. Department of Education and Bureau of Justice Statistics, U.S. Department of Justice, Office of Justice Programs, 2008. NCJ 219553.

National Conference of State Legislatures. *School Bullying.* Washington, DC: National Conference of State Legislatures, 2007.

Olweus, D. Bullying at school: Basic facts and effects of a school-based intervention program. *Journal of Child Psychology and Psychiatry* (1993):35:1171–90.

—*Bullying at School: What We Know and What We Can Do.* Cambridge, MA: Blackwell, 1993.

—Bully/victim problems at school: Facts and effective intervention. *Reclaiming Children and Youth* (1996):Spring:15–22.

APPENDIX 2

—*Olweus' Core Program Against Bullying and Antisocial Behavior: A Teacher Handbook*. Bergen, Norway: Research Center for Health Promotion, 2001.

—Victimization by peers: Antecedents and long-term outcomes. In: Rubin, K.H., and J.B. Asendorf, eds., *Social Withdrawal, Inhibition and Shyness in Childhood*. Hillsdale, NJ: Lawrence Erlbaum Associates, 1993, 315–341.

Olweus, D., and S. Limber. *Blueprints for Violence Prevention: Bullying Prevention Program (Book Nine)*. Boulder, CO: University of Colorado at Boulder, Institute of Behavioral Science, Center for the Study and Prevention of Violence, 1999.

Rao, V. Bullying in schools. *British Medical Journal* (1995):310:1065–6.

Rigby, K. What children tell us about bullying in schools. *Children Australia* (1997):22(2):28–34.

Roland, E., and E. Munthe, eds. *Bullying: An International Perspective*. London, UK: David Fulton Publisher, 1989.

Ross, D.M. *Childhood Bullying and Teasing: What School Personnel, Other Professionals, and Parents Can Do*. Alexandria, VA: American Counseling Association, 1996.

Ross, P.N. *Arresting Violence: A Resource Guide for Schools and Their Communities*. Toronto, Canada: Public School Teachers' Federation, Toronto, 1998.

Sato, K., I. Ito, S. Morita, and K. Akaboshi. Neuroses and psychosomatic syndromes of bullied children. *Japanese Journal of Child and Adolescent Psychiatry* (1987):28: 110–15.

Saunders, C.S. Taming your child's bully. *Good Housekeeping,* November 1995, 206.

Sharp, S., and P.K. Smith. *Tackling Bullying in Your School: A Practical Handbook for Teachers*. London, UK: Routledge, 1994.

Smith, P.K., and S. Sharp. *School Bullying: Insights and Perspectives*. London, UK: Routledge, 1994.

Spergel, I., D. Curry, R. Chance, et al. *Gang Suppression and Intervention: Problem and Response*. Washington, DC: Office of Juvenile Justice and Delinquency Prevention, U.S. Department of Justice, 1994. NCJ 149629.

Tattum, D., and G. Herbert. *Countering Bullying: Initiatives by Schools and Local Authorities*. Stoke-on-Trent, UK: Trentham Books, 1993.

Tattum, D., and D.A. Lane, eds. *Bullying in Schools*. Stoke-on-Trent, UK: Trentham Books, 1989.

U.S. Department of Education. *Preventing Bullying: A Manual for Schools and Communities*. Washington, DC: U.S. Department of Education, 1998.

U.S. Department of Justice, Bureau of Justice Statistics. *National Crime Victimization Survey (NCVS)*. Washington, DC: U.S. Department of Justice, 2005. NCJ 209911.

Webster-Doyle, T., and A. Russ. *Why Is Everybody Always Picking on Me: A Special Curriculum for Young People to Help Them Cope with Bullying*. Middlebury, VT: Atrium Society Publications, 1994.

Weinhold, B.K., ed. *Spreading Kindness: A Program Guide for Reducing Youth and Peer Violence in the Schools*. Colorado Springs, CO: The Kindness Campaign, University of Colorado, 1994.

Whitney, I., and P.K. Smith. A survey of the nature and extent of bullying junior/middle and secondary schools. *Educational Research* (1993):35:3–25.

Williams, K.D., J.P. Forgás, and W. von Hippel, eds. *The Social Outcast: Ostracism, Social Exclusion, Rejection, & Bullying*. New York, NY: Psychology Press, 2005.

Williams, K.R., and N.G. Guerra. Prevalence and predictors of Internet bullying. *Journal of Adolescent Health* (2007):41(6 Suppl 1):S14–S21.

APPENDIX 2

CHAPTER 6: SPOUSE ABUSE, DOMESTIC VIOLENCE, AND INTIMATE PARTNER VIOLENCE

Ackerman, R.J., and S.E. Pickering. *Abused No More, Recovery for Women from Abusive or Co-Dependent Relationships*. Blue Ridge Summit, PA: Human Services Institute/TAB Books, 1989.

Allstate Foundation National Poll on Domestic Violence, 2006. Tracking Survey conducted for The Advertising Council and the Family Violence Prevention Fund. Los Angeles, CA: Lieberman Research Inc., 2006.

American Medical Association. *Diagnostic and Treatment Guidelines on Domestic Violence*. Chicago, IL: American Medical Association, 1992 AA22, 92–406 20M.

American Medical Association. *Violence: A Compendium from JAMA, American Medical News, and the Specialty Journals of the American Medical Association*. Chicago, IL: American Medical Association, 1989.

Arriaga, X.B., and V.A. Foshee. Adolescent dating violence. Do adolescents follow in their friends' or their parents' footsteps? *Journal of Interpersonal Violence* (2004):19:162–84.

Barnett, O.W., and A.D. LaViolette. *It Could Happen to Anyone: Why Battered Women Stay*. Newbury Park, CA: Sage Publications, 1993.

Benedict, H. *Recovery: How to Survive Sexual Assault for Women, Men, Teenagers, Their Friends and Families*. Garden City, NY: Doubleday, 1986.

Benson, M., and G. Fox. *When Violence Hits Home: How Economics and Neighborhood Play a Role*. Washington, DC: National Institute of Justice, 2004.

Berry, D.B. *The Domestic Violence Sourcebook*. Los Angeles, CA: Lowell House, 1995.

Blinder, M. *Lovers, Killers, Husbands and Wives*. New York, NY: St. Martin's Press, 1985.

Block, C.R. How can practitioners help an abused woman lower her risk of death? *NIJ Journal* (2003):250:4–7.

Bowker, L.H. *Ending the Violence: A Guidebook Based on the Experience of 1000 Battered Wives*. Holmes Beach, FL: Learning Publications, Inc., 1986.

Brinegar, J. *Breaking Free from Domestic Violence*. Minneapolis, MI: CompCare Publishers, 1992.

Browne, A. *When Battered Women Kill*. New York, NY: Collier MacMillan, 1987.

Bureau of Justice Statistics. *Violence Between Intimates*. Washington, DC: U.S. Department of Justice, Bureau of Justice Statistics, 1994. NCJ 149259.

Catalano, S.M. *Criminal Victimization, 2005*. Washington, DC: U.S. Department of Justice, Bureau of Justice Statistics, 2005. NCJ 214644.

Centers for Disease Control and Prevention. National Center for Injury Prevention and Control. *Costs of Intimate Partner Violence Against Women in the United States*. Atlanta, GA: Centers for Disease Control, 2003.

——Physical dating violence among high school students—United States, 2003. *Morbidity and Mortality Weekly Report* (2006):55:532–5.

Day, R., ed. *Plain Talk about Wife Abuse*. Washington, DC: National Institute of Mental Health, Division of Scientific and Public Information, Department of Health and Human Services, 1983.

Davis, D. *Something Is Wrong at My House: A Book about Parents' Fighting*. Seattle, WA: Parenting Press, 1984.

Deschner, J.P. *The Hitting Habit: Anger Control for Battering Couples*. New York, NY: Free Press, 1984.

Edleson, J.L., and R.M. Tolman. *Intervention for Men Who Batter: An Ecological Approach*. Newbury Park, CA: Sage Publications, 1992.

Feiring, C., and W.C. Furman. When love is just a four-letter word: Victimization and romantic relationships in adolescence. *Child Maltreatment* (2000):5:293–8.

Felson, R., and M. Outlaw. The control motive and marital violence. *Violence and Victims* (2007):22:387–407.

Ferrato, D., and A. Jones. *Living with the Enemy.* New York, NY: Aperture Foundation, Inc., 1991.

Fleming, J.B. *Stopping Wife Abuse.* New York, NY: Anchor Books Doubleday, 1979.

Forward, S., and J. Torres. *Men Who Hate Women and the Women Who Love Them.* New York, NY: Bantam, 1986.

Gelles, R.J. *Family Violence.* Newbury Park, CA: Sage Publications, 1987.

Gelles, R.J., R. Lackner, and G.D. Wolfner. Men who batter: The risk markers. *Violence Update* (1994):4:1.

Gelles, R.J., and C.C. Pedrick. *Intimate Violence in Families.* Newbury Park, CA: Sage Publications, 1990.

Gondolph, E.W. *Men Who Batter: An Integrated Approach for Stopping Wife Abuse.* Holmes Beach, FL: Learning Publications, 1985.

Goodwin, S.N., D. Chandler, and J. Meisel. *Violence Against Women: The Role of Welfare Reform. Final Report to the National Institute of Justice.* Washington, DC: US Department of Justice, 2003. NCJ 205791.

Halpern, C.T., S.G. Oslak, M.L. Young, S.L. Martin, and L.L. Kupper. Partner violence among adolescents in opposite-sex romantic relationships: Findings from the National Longitudinal Study of Adolescent Health. *American Journal of Public Health* (2001):91:1679–85.

Hennekens, C. *Healing Your Life: Recovery from Domestic Violence.* New York, NY: Pro Writing Services and Press, 1991.

Hertz, M.F., and C. David-Ferdon. *Electronic Media and Youth Violence: A CDC Issue Brief for Educators and Caregivers.* Atlanta, GA: Centers for Disease Control, 2008.

Jaffe, P., M. Sudermann, D. Reitzel, and S. Killip. An evaluation of a secondary school primary prevention program on violence in intimate relationships. *Violence and Victims* (1992):7:129–46.

Jaffee, P.G., D.A. Wolfe, and S. Kaye Wilson. *Children of Battered Women.* Newbury, CA: Sage Publications, 1990.

James, D., and F. Farnham. Stalking and serious violence. *Journal of the American Academy of Psychiatry and the Law* (2003):31:432–9.

Jones, A. *Next Time, She'll Be Dead: Battering and How to Stop It.* Boston, MA: Beacon Press, 1994.

Jones, A., and S. Schechter. *When Love Goes Wrong: What to Do When You Can't Do Anything Right.* New York, NY: HarperCollins, 1993.

Kellerman, A.L., and J.A. Mercy. Men, women, and murder: Gender-specific differences in rates of fatal violence and victimization. *Journal of Trauma* (1992):33:1–5.

Kilgore, N. *Sourcebook for Working with Battered Women.* Chicago, IL: Volcano Press, 1992.

Kurz, D. Interventions with battered women in health care settings. *Violence and Victims* (1990):4:243–56.

Langan, P.A., and C.A. Innes. *Preventing Domestic Violence Against Women.* Washington, DC: Bureau of Justice Statistics, U.S. Department of Justice, 1986. NCJ 172837.

Langly, R., and R.C. Levy. *Wife Beating: The Silent Crisis.* New York, NY: E.P. Dutton, 1977.

Martin, D. *Battered Wives.* New York, NY: Pocket Books, 1983.

Max, W., D.P. Rice, E. Finkelstein, R.A. Bardwell, and S. Leadbetter. The economic toll of intimate partner violence against women in the United States. *Violence and Victims* (2004):19(3):259–72.

Meisel, J., D. Chandler, and D.M. Rienzi. Domestic violence prevalence and effects on employment in two California TANF populations. *Violence Against Women* (2003):9:1191–212.

National Coalition Against Domestic Violence. *National Directory of Domestic Violence Programs, 1994.* Denver, CO: National Coalition Against Domestic Violence, 1994.

National Committee for Injury Prevention and Control. *Injury Prevention: Meeting the Challenge.* New York, NY: Oxford University Press, 1989.

NiCarthy, G. *Getting Free: A Handbook for Women in Abusive Relationships.* Seattle, WA: The Seal Press, 1982.

NiCarthy, G. *Getting Free: You Can End the Abuse and Take Back Your Life.* Seattle, WA: The Seal Press, 1986.

NiCarthy, G., and S. Davidson. *You Can Be Free: An Easy-to-Read Handbook for Abused Women.* Seattle, WA: The Seal Press, 1989.

Paymar, M. *Violent No More: Helping Men End Domestic Abuse.* New York, NY: Hunter House, 1992.

Rennison, C. *Intimate Partner Violence.* Washington, DC: U.S. Department of Justice, Office of Justice Programs, 2003. NCJ 197838.

Rosenfeld, B. Violence risk factors in stalking and obsessional harassment. *Criminal Justice and Behavior* (2004):31:1.

Roy, M. *The Abusive Partner.* New York, NY: Van Nostrand Reinhold, 1982.

Russell, D.E. *Rape in Marriage.* New York, NY: MacMillan, 1982.

Schecter, S. *Women and Male Violence.* Boston, MA: South End Press, 1983.

Silvern, L., and L. Kaersvang. The traumatized children of violent marriages. *Child Welfare* (1989):56:142–6.

Snell, J.E., R.J. Rosenwald, and A. Robey. The wifebeater's wife: A study of family interaction. *Archives of General Psychiatry* (1964):11: 107–13.

Sonkin, D.J., and M. Durphy. *Learning to Live Without Violence*. San Francisco, CA: Family Violence Project, 1981.

Sorenson, S., and C. Taylor. Female aggression toward male intimate partners: An examination of social norms in a community-based sample. *Psychology of Women Quarterly* (2005):29:78–96.

Statman, J.B. *The Battered Woman's Survival Guide: Breaking the Cycle*. Dallas, TX: Taylor Publishing Company, 1990.

Steinmetz, S., and M. Straus, eds. *Violence in the Family*. New York, NY: Dodd & Mead, 1977.

Straus, M., and R. Gelles. *Physical Violence in American Families*. New Brunswick, NJ: Transaction Publishers, 1990.

Straus, M., R. Gelles, and S. Steinmetz. *Behind Closed Doors: Violence in the American Family*. Newbury Park, CA: Sage Publications, 1988.

Tjaden, P., and N. Thoennes. *Stalking in America: Findings from the National Violence Against Women Survey*. Washington, DC: U.S. Department of Justice, National Institute of Justice, 2000. NCJ 181867.

U.S. Department of Justice, Federal Bureau of Investigation. *Crime in the United States, 2005: Expanded Homicide Data*. Washington, DC: U.S. Department of Justice, 2006.

U.S. Department of Justice, Office of Justice Programs, Bureau of Justice Statistics. *Intimate Partner Violence and Age of Victim, 1993–99*. Washington, DC: U.S. Department of Justice, 2000. NCJ 187635.

——*Intimate Partner Violence in the U.S. 1993–2004*. Washington, DC: U.S. Department of Justice, 2006. NCJ 178247.

——Rennison, C.M., and S. Welchans. *Intimate Partner Violence*. Washington, DC: U.S. Department of Justice, 2000. NCJ 178247.

——Tjaden, P., and N. Thoennes. *Extent, Nature, and Consequences of Intimate Partner Violence. Findings from the National Violence Against Women Survey.* Washington, DC: U.S. Department of Justice, 2000. NCJ 181867.

U.S. Department of Justice, Office of Justice Programs, Bureau of Justice Statistics. *Full Report of the Prevalence, Incidence, and Consequences of Violence Against Women: Findings from the National Violence Against Women Survey.* Washington, DC: U.S. Department of Justice, 2000. NCJ 183781.

——*Violence Against Women*. Washington, DC: U.S. Department of Justice, 1994. NCJ 145325.

——*Violence by Intimates: Analysis of Data on Crimes by Current or Former Spouses, Boyfriends, and Girlfriends*. Washington, DC: U.S. Department of Justice, 1998. NCJ 167237.

Walker, L. *The Battered Woman*. New York, NY: Harper & Row, 1982.

——*The Battered Woman Syndrome*. New York, NY: Springer Publications, 1984.

CHAPTER 7: RAPE AND SEXUAL ASSAULT OF ADULTS

Abbey, A., and P. McAuslan. A longitudinal examination of male college students' perpetration of sexual assault. *Journal of Consulting and Clinical Psychology* (2004):72(5):747–56.

Abel, G.G., J.V. Becker, and L.J. Skinner. *Behavioral Approaches to Treatment of the Violent Sex Offender*. Washington, DC: Department of Health and Human Services, 1985.

Acierno, R., H. Resnick, D.G. Kilpatrick, B. Saunders, and C.L. Best. Risk factors for rape, physical assault, and post-traumatic stress disorder in women: Examination of differential multivariate relationships. *Journal of Anxiety Disorders* (1999):13:541–63.

American Medical Association. *Strategies for the Treatment and Prevention of Sexual Assault.* Chicago, IL: American Medical Association, 1995.

American Medical Association. *Violence: Compendium from JAMA, American Medical News, and the Specialty Journals of the American Medical Association.* Chicago, IL: American Medical Association, 1989.

Basile, K.C., J. Chen, M.C. Lynberg, and L.E. Saltzman. Prevalence and characteristics of sexual violence victimization. *Violence and Victims* (2007):22(4):437–48.

Basile, K.C., and L.E. Saltzman. *Sexual Violence Surveillance: Uniform Definitions and Recommended Data Element Version 1.0.* Atlanta, GA: Centers for Disease Control and Prevention, National Center for Injury Prevention and Control, 2002.

Becker, J., L.J. Skinner, G.G. Abel, and E.C. Treacy. Incidence and types of sexual dysfunctions in rape and incest victims. *Journal of Sex and Marital Therapy* (1982):8: 65–74.

Botash, A.S., R. Braen, and V.J. Gilchrist. Acute care for sexual assault victims. *Patient Care* (1994):Aug 15:112–37.

Brownmiller, S. *Against Our Will: Men, Women and Rape.* New York, NY: Simon and Schuster, 1975.

Catalano, S.M. *Criminal Victimization, 2005.* Washington, DC: Department of Justice, Bureau of Justice Statistics, 2005. NCJ 214644.

Centers for Disease Control and Prevention, Youth Risk Behavior Surveillance—United States, 2005. Surveillance Summaries, 2006. *Morbidity and Mortality Weekly Report* (2006):55:SS-5.

Centers for Disease Control and Prevention. *Web-based Injury Statistics Query and Reporting System, 2007 [online].* National Center for Injury Prevention and Control. Available at: http://www.cdc.gov/injury/wisqars/index.html. Accessed February 16, 2010.

APPENDIX 2

Champion, H.L., K.L. Foley, R.H. DuRant, R. Hensberry, D. Altman, and M. Wolfson. Adolescent sexual victimization, use of alcohol and other substances, and other health risk behaviors. *Journal of Adolescent Health* (2004):35(4):321–8.

Clements, P.T., P.M. Speck, P.A. Crane, and M.J. Faulkner. Issues and dynamics of sexually assaulted adolescents and their families. *International Journal of Mental Health Nursing* (2004):13(4):267–74.

Donaldson, D. Rape of males. In: Dynes, W., ed., *Encyclopedia of Homosexuality.* New York, NY: Garland Publications, 1990.

Estrich, S. *Real Rape.* Cambridge, MA: Harvard University Press, 1987.

Evans, M.C. The Missouri Supreme Court confronts the sixth amendment in its interpretation of the rape victim shield statute. *Missouri Law Review* (1987):52:925.

Fairstein, L.A. *Sexual Violence: Our War Against Rape.* New York, NY: William Morrow & Co., 1993.

Fisher, B.S., F.T. Cullen, and M.G. Turner. *The Sexual Victimization of College Women.* Washington, DC: U.S. Department of Justice National Institute of Justice, 2000. NCJ 182369.

Goode, S. Where a boyfriend becomes no friend. *Insight,* April 20, 1987, 58–9.

Groth, A.N. *Men Who Rape: The Psychology of the Offender.* New York, NY: Plenum Press, 1979.

Groth, A.N., and A.W. Burgess. Male rape: Offenders and victims. *American Journal of Psychiatry* (1980):137:806–10.

Hampton, H.L. Care of the woman who has been raped. *New England Journal of Medicine* (1995):332:234–7.

Holmes, M.M., H.S. Resnick, D.G. Kilpatrick, and C.L. Best. Rape-related pregnancy: Estimates and descriptive characteristics from a national sample of women. *American Journal of Obstetrics and Gynecology* (1996):175:320–4.

Howard, D.E., and M.Q. Wang. Risk profiles of adolescent girls who were victims of dating violence. *Adolescence* (2003):38(149):1–14.

Illinois Coalition Against Sexual Assault. *Acquaintance Rape. Sexual Violence: Facts and Statistics.* Springfield, IL: Illinois Coalition against Sexual Assault, 1994.

Kanin, E.J. Date rape: Unofficial criminals and victims. *Victimology* (1984):9:95–108.

Kilpatrick, D.E, P.A. Resnick, and L.J. Veronen. Effects of a rape experience: A longitudinal study. *Journal of Social Issues* (1981):37:105–22.

Koss, M.P., C.A. Gidcyz, and N. Wisniewski. The scope of rape: Incidence and prevalence of sexual aggression and victimization in a national sample of higher education students. *Journal of Consulting and Clinical Psychology* (1987):42: 162–70.

Lang, A.J., C.S. Rodgers, C. Laffaye, L.E. Satz, T.R. Dresselhaus, and M.B. Stein. Sexual trauma, posttraumatic stress disorder, and health behavior. *Behavioral Medicine* (2003):28(4):150–8.

Langan, P.A. *Recidivism of Sex Offenders Released from Prison in 1994.* Washington, DC: U.S. Department of Justice, National Institute of Justice, 2003. NCJ 198281.

Lipscomb, G.H., D. Muram, P.M. Speck, and B.M. Mercer. Male victims of sexual assault. *Journal of the American Medical Association* (1992):267:3064–6.

Loh, C., C.A. Gidycz, T.R. Lobo, and Luthra R. A prospective analysis of sexual assault perpetration: Risk factors related to perpetrator characteristics. *Journal of Interpersonal Violence* (2005):20(10):1325–48.

McCombie, S.L., ed. *The Rape Crisis Intervention Handbook.* New York, NY: Plenum Press, 1980.

McGregor, M.J. An exploratory analysis of suspected drug facilitated sexual assault seen in a hospital emergency department. *Women and Health* (2003):37:75.

McMullen, R.J. *Male Rape: Breaking the Silence on the Last Taboo.* London, UK: GMP Publishers Ltd., 1990.

Mezey, G., and M. King. The effects of sexual assault on men: A survey of 22 victims. *Psychological Medicine* (1989):19:205–9.

Muehlenhard, C. Date rape and sexual aggression in dating situations: Incidence and risk factors. *Journal of Counseling Psychology* (1987):34:186–96.

Nadelson, C., M. Notman, H. Zackson, et al. A follow-up study of rape victims. *American Journal of Psychiatry* (1982):139:1266–70.

National Committee for Injury Prevention and Control. *Injury Prevention: Meeting the Challenge.* New York, NY: Oxford University Press, 1989.

Parrott, A., and L. Bechofer, eds. *Acquaintance Rape: The Hidden Crime.* New York, NY: John Wiley and Sons, Inc., 1991.

Rand, M. *Criminal Victimization, 2008.* Washington, DC: Bureau of Justice Statistics, U.S. Department of Justice, Office of Justice Programs, 2009. NCJ 22777.

Rapaport, K., and B.R. Burkhardt. Personality and attitudinal characteristics of sexually coercive college males. *Journal of Abnormal Psychology* (1984):93:216–21.

Rickert, V.I., C.M. Wiemann, R.D. Vaughan, and J.W. White. Rates and risk factors for sexual violence among an ethnically diverse sample of adolescents. *Archives of Pediatrics and Adolescent Medicine* (2004):158(12):1132–9.

Russell, D.E.H. The prevalence and incidence of forcible rape of females. *Victimology* (1982):7:81–93.

Taylor, L.R., and N. Gaskin-Laniyan. Sexual assault in abusive relationships. *National Institute of Justice Journal* (2007):256:12–14.

Tjaden, P., and N. Thoennes. *Extent, Nature, and Consequences of Rape Victimization: Findings from the National Violence Against Women Survey.* Washington, DC: U.S. Department of Justice, 2006. NCJ 210346

U.S. Department of Justice, Office of Justice Programs, Bureau of Justice Statistics. *Intimate Partner Violence.* Washington, DC: U.S. Department of Justice, 2000. NCJ 178247.

——*Sexual Offenses and Offenders: An Analysis of Data on Rape and Sexual Assault.* Washington, DC: U.S. Department of Justice, 1997. NCJ 163392.

——*Sexual Victimization of College Women.* Washington, DC: U.S. Department of Justice, 2001. NCJ 182369.

——*Violence by Intimates: Analysis of Data on Crimes by Current or Former Spouses, Boyfriends, and Girlfriends.* Washington, DC: U.S. Department of Justice, 1998. NCJ 167237.

White, J.W., and P.H. Smith. Sexual assault perpetration and re-perpetration: From adolescence to young adulthood. *Criminal Justice and Behavior* (2004):31(2):182–202.

Wolitzky-Taylor, K.B., K.J. Ruggiero, C.K. Danielson, et al. Prevalence and correlates of dating violence in a national sample of adolescents. *Journal of the American Academy of Child and Adolescent Psychiatry* (2008):47:755–62.

CHAPTER 8: ELDER ABUSE AND VIOLENCE AGAINST THE ELDERLY

Age Concern, British Association of Social Workers, British Geriatrics Society, et al. *Abuse of Elderly People: Guidelines for Action.* London, UK: Age Concern England, 1993.

Aravanis, S.C., R.D. Adelman, R. Breckman, et al. *Diagnostic and Treatment Guidelines on Elder Abuse and Neglect.* Chicago, IL: American Medical Association, 1993.

Bachman, R. *Bureau of Justice Statistics Special Report: Elderly Victims.* Washington, DC: U.S. Department of Justice, 1992.

Baumhover, L.A., and S.C. Beall, eds. *Abuse, Neglect, and Exploitation of Older Persons: Strategies for Assessment and Intervention.* Baltimore, MD: Health Professions Press, 1996.

Bleiszner, R., and J.M. Alley. Family care-giving for the elderly: An overview of resources. *Family Relations, Journal of Applied Family and Child Studies* (1990):39:1.

Block, M.R., and J.D. Sinnot, eds. *The Battered Elder Syndrome: An Exploratory Study, Center on Aging.* College Park, MD: University of Maryland, 1979.

Botwinick, J. *Aging and Behavior.* 3rd ed. New York, NY: Springer Publishing Co., 1984.

Bourland, M.D. Elder abuse. *Postgraduate Medicine* (1990):87:139–44.

Boydston, L.S., and J.A. McNairn. Elder abuse by adult caretakers: An exploratory study. In: *Physical and Financial Abuse of the Elderly* [pub no 97-2971]. Washington, DC: U.S. House of Representatives Select Committee on Aging, 1981.

Brillon, Y. *Victimization and Fear of Crime among the Elderly.* Toronto, Canada: Butterworth Publishing, 1987.

Bureau of Justice Statistics. *Elderly Crime Victims: National Crime Victimization Survey.* Washington, DC: U.S. Department of Justice, Office of Justice Programs, Bureau of Justice Statistics, 1994.

Burgess, A. *Elderly Victims of Sexual Abuse and Their Offenders.* Washington, DC: U.S. Department of Justice, 2006.

Burgess, A., and N. Hanrahan. *Identifying Forensic Markers in Elder Sexual Abuse.* Washington, DC: National Institute of Justice, 2006.

Burston, G.R. Letter: Granny battering. *British Medical Journal* (1975):3(5983):592.

Byers, B., and Hendricks, J.E. *Adult Protective Services: Research and Practice.* Springfield, IL: C.C. Thomas, 1993.

Cammer Paris, B.E., D.E. Meier, T. Goldstein, M. Weiss, and E.D. Fein. Elder abuse and neglect: How to recognize warning signs and intervene. *Geriatrics* (1995):50: 47–51.

Clark, C.B. Geriatric abuse: Out of the closet. *Journal of the Tennessee Medical Association* (1984):77:470–1.

Cooper, C., A. Selwood, and G. Livingston. The prevalence of elder abuse and neglect: A systematic review. *Age and Aging* (2008):37:151–60.

Dyer, C.B., M.T. Connolly, and P. McFeeley. The clinical and medical forensics of elder abuse and neglect. In: Bonnie, R.J., and R.B. Wallace, eds., *Elder Mistreatment: Abuse, Neglect, and Exploitation in an Aging America.* Washington, DC: National Academies Press, 2003, 344–360.

FHP Foundation. *Silent Suffering: Elder Abuse in America: Elder Abuse in Rural and Urban Settings: Report on Focus Group Activities and Recommendations for the 1995 White House Conference on Aging.* Long Beach, CA: FHP Foundation, 1995.

Fulmer, T., and J. Ashley. Neglect: What part of abuse? *Journal of Long-Term Care* (1986):5:18–24.

Fulmer, T., and G. Paveza. Neglect in the elderly patient. *Nursing Clinics of North America* (1998):33(3):457–67.

Galbraith, M., ed. *Elder Abuse: Perspective on an Emerging Crisis.* Kansas City, KS: Mid-American Congress on Aging, 1986.

Gardner, K., and V.J. Halamandaris. *Elder Abuse: An Examination of a Hidden Problem. A Report with Additional Views by the Select Committee on Aging.* Washington, DC: U.S. House of Representatives Select Committee on Aging, 1981.

Greenfeld, L. *Sex Offenses and Offenders: An Analysis of Data on Rape and Sexual Assault.* Washington, DC: Bureau of Justice Statistics, Office of Justice Programs, U.S. Department of Justice, 1997. NCJ 163392.

Gwyther, L., and D. Gold. *Prevention of Elder Abuse and Neglect: Coping with Family Conflict.* Durham, NC: Duke University Medical Center, 1987.

Homer, A.C., and C. Gilleard. Abuse of elderly people by their caregivers. *British Medical Journal* (1990):301:1359–62.

Hydle, I. Violence against the elderly in Western Europe: Treatment and preventive measures in the health and social services fields. *Journal of Elder Abuse and Neglect* (1989):1:75–85.

Johnson, I.M., and R.T. Sigler. Forced sexual intercourse among intimates. *Journal of Family Violence* (2000):15:95–108.

Klaus, P. *Crimes against Persons Age 65 and Older, 1993–2002*. Washington, DC: U.S. Department of Justice, Bureau of Justice Statistics, 2005. NCJ 206154.

Kosberg, J.I., ed. *Abuse and Maltreatment of the Elderly: Causes and Interventions*. Boston, MA: John Wright, 1983.

Kosberg, J.I. Preventing elder abuse: Identification of high risk factors prior to placement decisions. *Gerontologist* (1988):28:43–50.

Lachs, M.S., and K. Pillemer. Abuse and neglect of elderly persons. *New England Journal of Medicine* (1995):332:437–43.

Lachs, M.S., and K. Pillemer. Elder abuse. *The Lancet* (2004):364:1192–263.

McGhee, J. The vulnerability of elderly consumers. *International Journal of Aging and Human Development* (1983):17:223–46.

National Advisory Council on Aging, Consumer Fraud and Seniors. National Advisory Council on Aging. Minister of Supply and Services Canada, Cat. No. H71-2/3-1-1991, Ottawa, Canada, 1991.

National Center on Elder Abuse. *A Response to the Abuse of Vulnerable Adults: The 2000 Survey of State Adult Protective Services*. Washington, DC: National Center on Elder Abuse, 2003.

National Committee for Injury Prevention and Control. *Injury Prevention: Meeting the Challenge*. New York, NY: Oxford University Press, 1989.

National Institute of Justice. *Triad: Reducing Crime against the Elderly: An Implementation Handbook.* Washington, DC: U.S. Dept. of Justice, National Institute of Justice, 1993. NCJ 146205.

National Research Council Panel to Review Risk and Prevalence of Elder Abuse and Neglect. *Elder Mistreatment: Abuse, Neglect and Exploitation in an Aging America.* Washington, DC: National Research Council Panel, 2003.

Nerenberg, L. *Forgotten Victims of Elder Financial Crime and Abuse: A Report and Recommendations.* Washington, DC: Goldman Institute on Aging and the National Center on Aging, 1999.

——*Improving the Police Response to Domestic Elder Abuse: Instructor Training Manual and Participant Training Manual.* Washington, DC: Police Executive Research Forum, 1993.

Parrot, A. *Acquaintance Rape and Sexual Assault: A Prevention Manual.* Holmes Beach, FL: Learning Publications Inc., 1991.

Periodic health examination, 1994 update: 4. Secondary prevention of elder abuse and treatment. Canadian Task Force on the Periodic Health Examination. *Canadian Medical Association Journal* (1994):151:1413–35.

Pillemer, K. The dangers of dependency: New findings on domestic violence against the elderly. *Social Problems* (1985):22:146–58.

Pillemer, K., and D. Finkelhor. Causes of elder abuse: Caregiver stress versus problem relatives. *American Journal of Orthopsychiatry* (1989):59:179–87.

——The prevalence of elder abuse: A random sample survey. *The Gerontologist* (1988):28:51-7.

Pillemer, K., and J.J. Suitor. Violence and violent feelings: What causes them among family caregivers? *Journal of Gerontology* (1992):47:S165–72.

Podnieks, E., and K. Pillemer. *Survey on Abuse of the Elderly in Canada.* Toronto, Canada: Ryerson Polytechnical Institute, 1989.

Quinn, M., and S. Tomita. *Elder Abuse and Neglect: Causes, Diagnosis, and Intervention Strategies.* New York, NY: Springer Publishing, 1986.

Ramsey-Klawsnik, H. Elder sexual abuse: Research findings and clinical issues. Introduction. *Journal of Elder Abuse & Neglect* (2008):20(4):301–5.

Rathbone, M., E. Goodstein, and R.K. Goodstein. Elder abuse: Clinical considerations. *Psychiatric Annals* (1985):15:331–3.

Schlesinger, B., and R. Schlesinger, eds. *Abuse of the Elderly: Issues and Annotated Bibliography.* Toronto, Canada: University of Toronto Press, Toronto, 1988.

Steinmetz, S.K. Battered parents. *Society* (1978):July–August:54–5.

——*Duty Bound: Elder Abuse and Family Care.* Newbury Park, CA: Sage Publications, 1988.

Subcommittee on Health and Long-Term Care, Select Committee on Aging of the U.S. House of Representatives. *Elder Abuse: A Decade of Shame and Inaction.* Washington, DC: U.S. Government Printing Office, 1990.

Taler, G., and E.F. Ansello. Elder abuse. *American Family Physician* (1985):32: 107–14.

Tatara, T. *An Analysis of State Laws Addressing Elder Abuse, Neglect, and Exploitation: A Final Report.* Washington, DC: National Center on Elder Abuse, 1995.

——*Elder Abuse: Questions and Answers.* Washington, DC: National Center on Elder Abuse, 1994.

——*Summaries of the Statistical Data on Elder Abuse in Domestic Settings for FY90 and FY91: A Final Report.* Washington, DC: National Aging Resource Center on Elder Abuse, 1993.

Teaster, P. *The 2004 Survey of State Adult Protective Services: Abuse of Adults 60 Years of Age and Older.* Washington, DC: National Center on Elder Abuse, 2006.

U.S. Department of Health and Human Services, Administration on Aging. *The National Elder Abuse Incidence Study.* Washington, DC: U.S. Department of Health and Human Services, 2001.

U.S. Department of Justice, Office of Justice Programs, Bureau of Justice Statistics. *Crimes against Persons Age 65 or Older, 1992–97.* Washington, DC: U.S. Department of Justice, 2000. NCJ 176352.

—*Homicide Trends in the U.S.* Washington, DC: U.S. Department of Justice, 2006.

Vinton, L. *Abused Elders or Older Battered Women?* Report on the AARP Forum, October 29–30, 1992. Washington, DC: AARP Women's Initiative, 1993.

Wigdor, B.T., and the National Advisory Council on Aging. *Elder Abuse: Major Issues from a National Perspective.* Ottawa, Canada: National Advisory Council on Aging. Minister of Supply and Services Canada, Cat. No. H71-2/3-2-1991, 1991.

Wolf, R.S. Elder abuse: Ten years later. *Journal of the American Geriatrics Society* (1988):36:758–62.

Wolf, S., and K. Pillemer. *Helping Elderly Victims: The Reality of Elder Abuse.* New York, NY: Columbia University Press, 1989.

CHAPTER 9: MURDER AND HOMICIDE—EVER MORE RANDOM

Dawson, J.M., and P.A. Langan. *Murder in Families.* Washington, DC: Bureau of Justice Statistics, U.S. Department of Justice, 1994. NCJ 143498.

Homicide Studies: An Interdisciplinary & International Journal. Sage Publications, 1997 to present.

National Committee for Injury Prevention and Control. *Injury Prevention: Meeting the Challenge.* New York, NY: Oxford University Press, 1989.

National Crime Prevention Council. *Crime and Crime Prevention Statistics.* Washington, DC: National Crime Prevention Council, 1991.

APPENDIX 2

National Victim Center. *Assault at a Glance*. National Victim Center Infolink volume 1, no. 3. Arlington, VA: National Victim Center, 1992.

Rand, M. *Criminal Victimization, 2008*. Washington, DC: Bureau of Justice Statistics, U.S. Department of Justice, Office of Justice Programs, 2009. NCJ 22777.

Roth, J.A. *Understanding and Preventing Violence*. Washington, DC: National Institute of Justice, U.S. Department of Justice, 1994.

U.S. Department of Health and Human Services, Administration for Children and Families, Administration on Children, Youth and Families, Children's Bureau. *Child Maltreatment 1998—Reports From the States to the National Child Abuse and Neglect Data System*. Washington, DC: U.S. Government Printing Office, 2000.

U.S. Department of Health and Human Services. *Preventing Homicide in the Workplace*. DHHS (NIOSH) Publication No. 93-109. Atlanta, GA: National Institute for Occupational Safety and Health, May 1995.

U.S. Department of Justice, Federal Bureau of Investigation, *Crime in the United States, 1993*. Washington, DC: U.S. Department of Justice, 1994.

——*Crime in the United States, 2005: Murder*. Washington, DC: U.S. Department of Justice, 2006.

——*Criminal Justice Information Services Division, 2007 Crime in the United States*. Washington, DC: U.S. Department of Justice, 2008.

U.S. Department of Justice, Office of Justice Programs, Bureau of Justice Statistics. *Homicide Trends in the United States*. Washington, DC: U.S. Department of Justice, 1999. NCJ 173956.

——*Homicide Trends in the U.S.* Washington, DC: U.S. Department of Justice, 2006.

——*The National Center on Child Fatality Review*. Washington, DC: U.S. Department of Justice, 2001. FS 200112.

U.S. Department of Justice. Office of Justice Programs, National Institute of Justice, *A Study of Homicide in Eight U.S. Cities*. Washington, DC: U.S. Department of Justice, November 1997.

CHAPTER 10: VIOLENCE AND STRANGERS

Bureau of Labor Statistics. *Four Most Frequent Work-Related Fatal Events, 1992–2006*. Washington, DC: U.S. Department of Labor, Bureau of Labor Statistics, 2007.

Duhart, D. *Violence in the Workplace, 1993–99*. Washington, DC: Bureau of Justice Statistics, U.S. Department of Justice, Office of Justice Programs, 2001.

Federal Bureau of Investigation. *Hate Crime Statistics, 2005*. Washington, DC: U.S. Department of Justice, 2006.

National Committee for Injury Prevention and Control. *Injury Prevention: Meeting the Challenge*. New York, NY: Oxford University Press, 1989.

National Crime Prevention Council. *The Art of Street Smarts: Knowing How to Protect Yourself and Your Friends Makes Good Sense*. Washington, DC: National Crime Prevention Council, 1990.

Occupational Safety and Health Administration. *Safety and Health Topics: Workplace Violence*. Washington, DC: U.S. Department of Labor, 2007.

Patton, C. *Anti-Lesbian, Gay, Bisexual, and Transgender Violence in 2006*. New York, NY: National Coalition of Anti-Violence Programs, 2007.

Rand, M. *Criminal Victimization, 2008*. Washington, DC: Bureau of Justice Statistics, U.S. Department of Justice, Office of Justice Programs, 2009. NCJ 22777.

Timrots, A.D., and M.R. Rand. *Violent Crime by Strangers and Nonstrangers*. Washington, DC: Bureau of Justice Statistics, U.S. Department of Justice, 1987.

U.S. Department of Justice, Federal Bureau of Investigation. *Crime in the United States, 1993.* Washington, DC: U.S. Department of Justice, 1994.

U.S. Department of Justice, Office of Justice Programs, Bureau of Justice Statistics. *Crimes Against Persons Age 65 or Older, 1992–97.* Washington, DC: U.S. Department of Justice, 2000. NCJ 176352.

——*Criminal Victimization in United States.* Washington, DC: U.S. Department of Justice, 2000.

——*Criminal Victimization 2000: Changes 1999–2000 with Trends 1993–2000.* Washington, DC: U.S. Department of Justice, 2001. NCJ 187007.

——*Homicide Trends in the United States.* Washington, DC: U.S. Department of Justice, 1999. NCJ 173956.

——*Injuries From Violent Crime, 1992–98.* Washington, DC: U.S. Department of Justice, 2001. NCJ 168633.

——*National Crime Victimization Survey 2000.* Washington, DC: U.S. Department of Justice, 2001.

——*Urban, Suburban, and Rural Victimization, 1993–98.* Washington, DC: U.S. Department of Justice, 2000. NCJ 182031.

CHAPTER 11: GUNS—DO THEY INCREASE OR DEFEND AGAINST VIOLENCE?

Abdullah, C.H., and N.P. Gannon. *Straight Talk about Risks (STAR): A Pre-K—Grade 12 Curriculum for Preventing Gun Violence.* Washington, DC: Center to Prevent Handgun Violence, 1992.

Alexander, G.R., R.M. Massey, T. Gibbs, and J.M. Altekruse. Firearm-related fatalities: An epidemiologic assessment of violent death. *American Journal of Public Health* (1985):75:165–8.

American Medical Association Council on Scientific Affairs. Firearm injuries and deaths: A critical public health issue. *Public Health Reports* (1989):104: 111–20.

Bailey, J.E., A.L. Kellermann, G.W. Somes, J.G. Banton, F.P. Rivara, and N.P. Rushforth. Risk factors for violent death of women in the home. *Archives of Internal Medicine* (1997):157:777–82.

Baker, S.P. Without guns, do people kill people? *American Journal of Public Health* (1985):75:587–8.

Boyd, J.H., and E.K. Moscicki. Firearms and youth suicide. *American Journal of Public Health* (1986):76:1240–2.

Butterfield, G.E. *Weapons in Schools.* Malibu, CA: National School Safety Center, 1990.

Callahan, C.M., and F.P. Rivara. Urban high school youth and handguns: A school-based survey. *Journal of the American Medical Association* (1992): 267:3038–42.

Campbell, J.C., D.W. Webster, J. Koziol-McLain, et al. Risk factors for femicide within physically abusive intimate relationships: Results from a multi-site case control study. *American Journal of Public Health* (2003):93:1089–97.

Centers for Disease Control. *Youth Suicide in the United States, 1979-1980.* Atlanta, GA: Centers for Disease Control, 1986.

Center to Prevent Handgun Violence. *A Generation Under the Gun: A Statistical Analysis on Youth Firearm Murder in America.* Washington, DC: Center to Prevent Handgun Violence, 1990.

——*Handgun Safety Guidelines.* Washington, DC: Center to Prevent Handgun Violence, 1987.

Dwortzan, M. Locked and against gun injuries. *Harvard Public Health Review,* Fall, 2000, 8–10.

Fingerhut, L.A. *Firearm Mortality Among Children and Youth*. Advance Data From Vital and Health Statistics of the National Center for Health Statistics. Washington, DC: U.S. Department of Health and Human Services, 1993.

Fingerhut, L.A., D.D. Ingramm, and J.J. Feldman. Firearm and nonfirearm homicide among person 15 through 19 years of age: Differences by level of urbanization, United States, 1979 through 1989. *Journal of the American Medical Association* (1992):267:3048–53.

Hemenway, D., D. Azrael, and M. Miller. Gun use in the United States: Results from two national surveys. *Injury Prevention* (2000):6:263–7.

Hemenway, D., and M. Miller. Firearm availability and homicide rates across 26 high-income countries. *Journal of Trauma* (2000):49:985–8.

Hepburn, L., M. Miller, D. Azrael, and D. Hemenway. The US gun stock: Results from the 2004 national firearms survey. *Injury Prevention* (2007):13: 15–19.

Ikeda, R.M., R. Gorwitz, S.P. James, K.E. Powell, and J.A. Mercy. *Fatal Firearm Injuries in the United States 1962–1994*. Atlanta, GA: Centers for Disease Control and Prevention, National Center for Injury Prevention and Control, Violence Surveillance Summary Series, No. 3, 1997.

Kellermann, A.L., R.K. Lee, J.A. Mercy, and J. Banton. The epidemiologic basis for the prevention of firearm injuries. *Annual Review of Public Health* (1991):12: 17–40.

Kellermann, A.L., F.P. Rivara, and N.B. Rushforth, et al. Gun ownership as a risk factor for homicide in the home. *New England Journal of Medicine* (1993):329:1084–91.

Kellermann, A.L., F.P. Rivara, G. Somes, et al. Suicide in the home in relation to gun ownership. *New England Journal of Medicine* (1992):327:467–72.

Kleck, G. Measures of gun ownership levels of macro-level crime and violence research. *Journal of Research in Crime and Delinquency* (2004):41:3–36.

Krug, E.G., K.E. Powell, and L.L. Dahlberg. Firearm-related deaths in the United States and 35 other high- and upper middle-income countries. *International Journal of Epidemiology* (1998):27:214–21.

McDowall, D., and B. Wiersema. The incidence of defensive firearm use by U.S. crime victims, 1987 through 1990. *American Journal of Public Health* (1994):84:1982–4.

Murray, J.M. *50 Things You Can Do about Guns.* San Francisco, CA: Robert Reed Publisher, 1994.

National Committee for Injury Prevention and Control. *Injury Prevention: Meeting the Challenge.* New York, NY: Oxford University Press, 1989.

National Rifle Association of America. *A Parent's Guide to Gun Safety.* Fairfax, VA: National Rifle Association of America, 1992.

Ordog, G.J., J. Wasserberg, I. Schataz, et al. Gunshot wounds in children under 10 years of age: A new epidemic. *American Journal of Diseases of Children* (1988):142:618–22.

Patterson, P.J., and L.R. Smith. Firearms in the home and child safety. *American Journal of Diseases of Children* (1987):141:221–3.

Rand, M.R. *Handgun Crime Victims.* Washington, DC: Bureau of Justice Statistics, U.S. Department of Justice, 1990.

Rand, M., M. DeBerry, P. Klaus, and B. Taylor. *The Use of Weapons in Committing Crimes. Bureau of Justice Statistics.* Washington, DC: U.S. Department of Justice, 1986.

Richmond, T., R. Cheney, and C.W. Schwab. Global burden of non-conflict related firearm mortality. *Injury Prevention* (2005):11:348–52.

Rosenblatt, R. Get rid of the damned things. *Time* (1999):154(6):38.

Saltzman, L.E., J.A. Mercy, P.W. O'Carroll, et al. Weapon involvement and injury outcomes in family and intimate assaults. *Journal of the American Medical Association* (1992):267:3043–7.

Schuster, MA., T.M. Franke, A.M. Bastian, et al. Firearm storage patterns in U.S. homes with children. *American Journal of Public Health* (2000):90: 588–94.

Sheley, J.F., and J.D. Wright. *Gun Acquisition and Possession in Selected Juvenile Samples*. Washington, DC: National Institute of Justice, U.S. Department of Justice, 1993.

Sloan, J.H., A.L. Kellermann, D.T. Reay, et al. Handgun regulations, crime, assaults, and homicide. *New England Journal of Medicine* (1988):319: 256–62.

Smith, D., and B. Lautman. *A Generation Under the Gun: A Statistical Analysis of Youth Firearm Murder in America*. Washington, DC: Center to Prevent Handgun Violence, 1990.

Smith, D., B. Lautman, and V. Scherzer. *Caught in the Crossfire: A Report on Gun Violence in Our Nation's Schools*. Washington, DC: Center to Prevent Handgun Violence, 1990.

——*The Killing Seasons: A Study of When Unintentional Shootings among Children Occur*. Washington, DC: Center to Prevent Handgun Violence, 1989.

Teret, S.P., and G.J. Wintemute. Policies to prevent firearm injuries. *Health Affairs* (1993):Winter:96–108.

U.S. Centers for Disease Control and Prevention, WISQARS database.

U.S. Department of Justice. *Federal Bureau of Investigation, Criminal Justice Information Services Division, 2007 Crime in the United States*. Washington, DC: U.S. Department of Justice, 2008.

U.S. Department of Justice. Office of Justice Programs, Bureau of Justice Statistics. *Background Checks for Firearm Transfers, 1999*. Washington, DC: U.S. Department of Justice, 2000. NCJ 180882.

——*Federal Firearm Offenders, 1992–1998*. Washington, DC: U.S. Department of Justice, 2000. NCJ 180795.

——*Firearms and Crimes of Violence: Selected Findings from National Statistical Series*. Washington, DC: U.S. Department of Justice, 1994.

——*Firearm Injury and Death from Crime, 1993–97*. Washington, DC: U.S. Department of Justice, 2000. NCJ 182993.

——*Firearm Use by Offenders*. Washington, DC: U.S. Department of Justice, 2001. NCJ 189369.

——*Guns and Crime*. Washington, DC: U.S. Department of Justice, 1994.

——*Homicide Trends in the U.S.* Washington, DC: U.S. Department of Justice, 2006.

——*Presale Handgun Checks, the Brady Interim Period, 1994–98*. Washington, DC: U.S. Department of Justice, 1999. NCJ 175034.

——*Survey of State Procedures Related to Firearm Sales, Midyear 1999*. Washington, DC: U.S. Department of Justice, 2000. NCJ 179022.

Wintemute, G.J., C.A. Parham, J.J. Beaumont, M. Wright, and C.M. Drake. Mortality among recent purchasers of handguns. *New England Journal of Medicine* (1999):341:1583–9.

Wintemute, G.J., M.A. Wright, and C.M. Drake. Increased risk of intimate partner homicide among California women who purchased handguns. *Annals of Emergency Medicine* (2003):41:281–3.

Wright, J.D., P.H. Rossi, K. Daly, and E. Weber-Burdin. *Weapons, Crime, and Violence in America: A Literature Review and Research Agenda*. Washington, DC: Government Printing Office, 1983.

Zawitz, M.W., and K.J. Strom. *Firearm Injury and Death from Crime, 1993–97*. Washington, DC: Bureau of Justice Statistics, Selected Findings, 2000. NCJ 182993.

APPENDIX 2

CHAPTER 12: VIOLENCE TO ONESELF—SUICIDE

Andrews, J.A., and P.M. Lewinsohn. Suicidal attempts among older adolescents: Prevalence and co-occurrence with psychiatric disorders. *Journal of the American Academy of Child and Adolescent Psychiatry* (1992):31:655–62.

Asarnow, J.R. Pediatric emergency department suicidal patients: Two-site evaluation of suicide ideators, single attempters, and repeat attempters. *Journal of the American Academy of Child and Adolescent Psychiatry* (2008): 47:958.

Berman, A.L., and D.A. Jobes. Suicide prevention in adolescents (age 12-18). *Suicide & Life-Threatening Behavior* (1995):25:143–54.

Bolton, J.M. Anxiety disorders and risk for suicide attempts: Findings from the Baltimore epidemiologic catchment area follow-up study. *Depression and Anxiety* (2008):25:481.

Brent, D.A., M.M. Kerr, C. Goldstein, J. Bozigar, M. Wartella, and M.J. Allan. An outbreak of suicide and suicidal behavior in a high school. *Journal of the American Academy of Child and Adolescent Psychiatry* (1989):28:918–24.

Brent, D.A., J.A. Perper, and C.J. Allman. Alcohol, firearms, and suicide among youth. *Journal of the American Medical Association* (1987):257:3369–72.

Brent, D.A., J.A. Perper, C.J. Allman, et al. The presence and accessibility of firearms in the homes of adolescent suicides: A case-control study. *Journal of the American Medical Association* (1991):266:2989–95.

Burns, C.D. Treatment compliance in adolescents after attempted suicide: A 2-year follow-up study. *Journal of the American Academy of Child and Adolescent Psychiatry* (2008):47:948.

Casiano, H. Mental disorder and threats made by noninstitutionalized people with weapons in the National Comorbidity Survey Replication. *The Journal of Nervous and Mental Disease* (2008):196:462.

Centers for Disease Control and Prevention. *Morbidity and Mortality Weekly Report* (2004):53(SS-2).

——*Morbidity and Mortality Weekly Report* (2004):53(4).

——Suicide trends among youths and young adults aged 10-24 years—United States, 1990–2004. *Morbidity and Mortality Weekly Report* (2008):56:905–8.

——Web-based Injury Statistics Query and Reporting System (WISQARS) [http://webappa.cdc.gov/sasweb/ncipc/mortrate.html]. Atlanta, GA: National Center for Injury Prevention and Control, Centers for Disease Control and Prevention, 2008.

——Youth risk behavior surveillance—United States, 1999. CDC Surveillance Summaries, June 9, 2000. *Morbidity and Mortality Weekly Report* (2000):49(SS-5):10.

——Youth risk behavior surveillance—United States, 2007. CDC Surveillance Summaries, June 6. *Morbidity and Mortality Weekly Report* (2008):57(SS-4):1–131.

——*Youth Suicide Prevention Program: A Resource Guide.* Atlanta, GA: U.S. Department of Health and Human Services, Public Health Service, CDC, 1992.

Coleman, L. *Suicide Clusters.* Boston, MA: Faber and Faber, 1987.

Ellis, T., and C.F. Newman. *Choosing to Live: How to Defeat Suicide through Cognitive Therapy.* Oakland, CA: New Harbinger Publications, 1996.

Garland, A.F., D. Shaffer, and B. Whittle. A national survey of school-based suicide prevention programs. *Journal of the American Academy of Child and Adolescent Psychiatry* (1989):28:931–4.

Garlow, S.J. Depression, desperation, and suicidal ideation in college students: Results from the American Foundation for Suicide Prevention College Screening Project at Emory University. *Depression and Anxiety* (2008):25:482.

Gould, M.S., and D. Shaffer. The impact of suicide in television movies. *New England Journal of Medicine* (1986):315:690–4.

Grossman, D.C. Risk and prevention of youth suicide. *Pediatric Annals* (1992):21: 448–54.

Haw, C. Life problems and deliberate self-harm: Associations with gender, age, suicidal intent and psychiatric and personality disorder. *Journal of Affective Disorders* (2008):109:139.

Hawton, K., and J. Catalan. *Attempted Suicide: A Practical Guide to Its Nature and Management.* New York, NY: Oxford University Press, 1982.

Hayes, L.M. Suicide prevention in juvenile facilities. *Juvenile Justice* (2000):7(1):24–32.

Herba, C.M. Victimization and suicide ideation in the TRAILS study: Specific vulnerabilities of victims. *Journal of Child Psychology and Psychiatry* (2008): 49:867.

Hilt, L.M. Longitudinal study of nonsuicidal self-injury among young adolescents—rates, correlates, and preliminary test of an interpersonal model. *Journal of Early Adolescence* (2008):28:455.

Jacobson, C.M. Psychiatric impairment among adolescents engaging in different types of deliberate self-harm. *Journal of Clinical Child and Adolescent Psychology* (2008):37:363.

Karch, D., A. Crosby, and T. Simon. Toxicology testing and results for suicide victims—13 states, 2004. *Morbidity and Mortality Weekly Report* (2006):55: 1245–8.

Kellerman, A.L., F.P. Rivara, G. Somes, et al. Suicide in the home in relation to gun ownership. *New England Journal of Medicine* (1992):327:467–72.

Klomek, A.B. Childhood bullying as a risk for later depression and suicidal ideation among Finnish males. *Journal of Affective Disorders* (2008):109:47.

Krug, E.G., L.L. Dahlberg, J.A. Mercy, et al., eds. *World Report on Violence and Health* [serial online]. May 2004. Available at: www.who.int/violence_injury_ prevention/violence/world_report/wrvh1/en. Accessed February 16, 2010.

APPENDIX 2

Lilley, R. Hospital care and repetition following self-harm: Multicenter comparison of self-poisoning and self-injury. *British Journal of Psychiatry* (2008):192:440.

Lipschitz, A. Suicide prevention in young adults (age 18-30). *Suicide & Life-Threatening Behavior* (1995):25:155–70.

Lloyd-Richardson, E.E. Adolescent non-suicidal self-injury: Who is doing it and why? *Journal of Developmental and Behavioral Pediatrics* (2008):29:216.

Madge, N. Deliberate self-harm within an international community sample of young people: Comparative findings from the Child & Adolescent Self-harm in Europe (CASE) Study. *Journal of Child Psychology and Psychiatry* (2008):49:667.

Mangnall, J. A literature review of deliberate self-harm. *Perspectives in Psychiatric Care* (2008):44:175.

Maris, R.W. Suicide prevention in adults (age 30-65). *Suicide & Life-Threatening Behavior* (1995):25:171–9.

McCaig, L.F., and E.N. Nawar. National hospital ambulatory medical care survey: 2004 emergency department summary. Advance data from vital and health statistics. Report no. 372. Hyattsville, MD: National Center for Health Statistics, 2006.

McIntosh, J.L. Suicide prevention in the elderly (age 65-99). *Suicide & Life-Threatening Behavior* (1995):25:180–92.

Miller, M. *Suicide After Sixty: The Final Alternative.* New York, NY: Springer, 1979.

Motto, J.A. Suicide and suggestibility: The role of the press. *American Journal of Psychiatry* (1967):124:252–6.

National Committee for Injury Prevention and Control. *Injury Prevention: Meeting the Challenge.* New York, NY: Oxford University Press, 1989.

Nrugham, L. Predictors of suicidal acts across adolescence: Influences of familial, peer, and individual factors. *Journal of Affective Disorders* (2008):109:35.

APPENDIX 2   417

O'Carroll, P.W., L.B. Potter, and J.A. Mercy. Programs for the prevention of suicide among adolescents and young adults. *Morbidity and Mortality Weekly Reports* (1994):43(RR-6):1–7.

Ohmann, S. Self-injurious behavior in adolescent girls. *Psychopathology* (2008):41:614.

Petronis, K.R., J.F. Samuels, E.K. Moscicki, and J.C. Anthony. An epidemiologic investigation of potential risk factors for suicide attempts. *Social Psychiatry and Psychiatric Epidemiology* (1990):25:193–9.

Phillips, D.P., and D.T. Paight. The impact of televised movies about suicide. *New England Journal of Medicine* (1987):317:809–11.

Prevention Division of the American Association of Suicidology. *Guidelines for School Based Suicide Prevention Programs*. Washington, DC: Prevention Division of the American Association of Suicidology, 1999.

Reiss, N.S. Suicidality in nursing home residents: Part I. Prevalence, risk factors, methods, assessment, and management. *Professional Psychology, Research and Practice* (2008):39:264.

Reiss, N.S. Suicidality in nursing home residents: Part II. Special issues. *Professional Psychology, Research and Practice* (2008):39:271.

Rosenberg, M.L., J.A. Mercy, and L.B. Potter. Firearms and suicide. [Editorial]. *New England Journal of Medicine* (1999):341(21):1609–11.

Rosenberg, M.L., J.C. Smith, L.E. Davidson, and J.M. Conn. The emergence of youth suicide: An epidemiological analysis and public health perspective. *Annual Review of Public Health* (1987):8:417–40.

Schneider, B. How do personality disorders modify suicide risk? *Journal of Personality Disorders* (2008):22:233.

Shaffer, D., A. Garland, M. Gould, et al. Preventing teenage suicide: A critical review. *Journal of the American Academy of Child and Adolescent Psychiatry* (1988):27:675–87.

Silverman, M.M., and R.W. Maris, eds. *Suicide Prevention: Toward the Year 2000.* New York, NY: Guilford Press, 1995.

Suicide Prevention Resource Center. *Promoting Mental Health and Preventing Suicide in College and University Settings.* Newton, MA: Education Development Center, Inc., 2004.

U.S. Public Health Service. *The Surgeon General's Call to Action to Prevent Suicide.* Washington, DC: U.S. Public Health Service, 1999.

Velting, D.M., and M.S. Gould. Suicide contagion. In: Maris, R.W., and M.M. Silverman, eds., *Review of Suicidology.* New York, NY: Guilford Press, 1997, 96–137.

CHAPTER 13: EPILOGUE—SOCIAL CHANGE AND THE FUTURE OF VIOLENCE PREVENTION

Catalano, S.M. *Criminal Victimization, 2005.* Washington, DC: U.S. Department of Justice, Bureau of Justice Statistics, 2005.

Hawkins, D.F. Inequality, culture, and interpersonal violence. *Health Affairs* (1993): Winter:80–95.

May, R. *Power and Innocence: A Search for the Sources of Violence.* New York, NY: W.W. Norton, 1972.

Mercy, J.A., M.L. Rosenberg, K.E. Powell, C.V. Broome, and W.L. Roper. Public health policy for preventing violence. *Health Affairs* (1993):Winter:30–3.

Moore, M.H. Violence prevention: Criminal justice or public health? *Health Affairs* (1993):Winter:34–45.

National Committee for Injury Prevention and Control. *Injury Prevention: Meeting the Challenge.* New York, NY: Oxford University Press, 1989.

National Crime Prevention Council. *350 Tested Strategies to Prevent Crime: A Resource for Municipal Agencies and Community Groups.* Washington, DC: National Crime Prevention Council, 1995.

Rand, M. *Criminal Victimization, 2008*. Washington, DC: Bureau of Justice Statistics, U.S. Department of Justice, Office of Justice Programs, 2009. NCJ 227777.

Rosenberg, M.L, and M.A. Fenley. *Violence in America: A Public Health Approach*. New York, NY: Oxford University Press, 1991.

Rosin, H. American murder mystery. *The Atlantic,* July/August 2008, 40–54.

Shalala, D.E. Addressing the crisis of violence. *Health Affairs* (1993):Winter:30–3.

U.S. Department of Health and Human Services, Children's Bureau. *Child Maltreatment, 2004*. Washington, DC: U.S. Department of Health and Human Services, 2005.

U.S. Department of Justice, Office of Justice Programs, Bureau of Justice Statistics. *Alcohol and Crime: An Analysis of National Data on the Prevalence of Alcohol Involvement in Crime*. Washington, DC: U.S. Department of Justice, 1998. NCJ 168632.

——*Criminal Victimization and Perceptions of Community Safety in 12 Cities*. Washington, DC: U.S. Department of Justice, 1999. NCJ 173940.

——*Prior Abuse Reported by Inmates and Probationers*. Washington, DC: U.S. Department of Justice, 1999. NCJ 172879.

——*An Update on the Cycle of Violence*. Washington, DC: U.S. Department of Justice, 2001. NCJ 184894.

——*Violent Victimization and Race, 1993–98*. Washington, DC: U.S. Department of Justice, 2001. NCJ 176354.

INDEX

About the Author

George Gellert, a physician, specializes in epidemiology and public health. He received his medical degree from McGill University and graduate training in public health, preventive medicine, and public policy from Yale, UCLA, and Harvard, respectively. Dr. Gellert has worked in public health within the United States and internationally in developing countries. His research, which has focused on child sexual abuse, fatal child abuse, and mass violence inflicted upon vulnerable populations around the world, has been published in medical and public health journals. He lives in Portland, OR.